Exodus 18

Exodus 18

Its Literary Unity and Its Key Transitional Role in the Exodus Narrative

Noppawat Kumpeeroskul

WIPF & STOCK · Eugene, Oregon

EXODUS 18
Its Literary Unity and Its Key Transitional Role in the Exodus Narrative

Copyright © 2024 Noppawat Kumpeeroskul. All rights reserved. Except for brief quotations in critical publications or reviews, no part of this book may be reproduced in any manner without prior written permission from the publisher. Write: Permissions, Wipf and Stock Publishers, 199 W. 8th Ave., Suite 3, Eugene, OR 97401.

Wipf & Stock
An Imprint of Wipf and Stock Publishers
199 W. 8th Ave., Suite 3
Eugene, OR 97401

www.wipfandstock.com

PAPERBACK ISBN: 979-8-3852-1847-9
HARDCOVER ISBN: 979-8-3852-1848-6
EBOOK ISBN: 979-8-3852-1849-3

VERSION NUMBER 07/01/24

To my parents, Supongse and Pornipa;
and to my siblings, Suwipa†, Narudom, and Suchada.

ζητεῖτε δὲ πρῶτον τὴν βασιλείαν [τοῦ θεοῦ] καὶ τὴν δικαιοσύνην αὐτοῦ, καὶ ταῦτα πάντα προστεθήσεται ὑμῖν.

"But seek first the kingdom of God and his righteousness, and all these things will be provided to you."

Matthew 6:33

הַרְפּוּ וּדְעוּ כִּי־אָנֹכִי אֱלֹהִים אָרוּם בַּגּוֹיִם אָרוּם בָּאָרֶץ׃

"Be still and know that I am God! I will be exalted among the nations; I will be exalted in the earth."

Psalm 46:11 [Eng 10]

Contents

Acknowledgments | xi
Abbreviations | xiii
Abstract | xix

Chapter 1
Introduction | 1
    The Introduction and Summary of the Account of Exodus 18   1
    The Thesis   5
    The Current Status of the Question   5
        The Problem in the Account of Exodus 18   6
        The Divisions of the Book of Exodus   9
        Scholars in Favor of Exodus 15 as the Main Transition in the Book of Exodus   12
        The Role of Exodus 18 as the Main Transition in the Book of Exodus   14
        The Relationships of Exodus 18 in the Book of Exodus   17
            The Relationship of Exodus 18 with the Midianite Accounts (Exod 2–4)   17
            The Relationship of Exodus 18 with the Preceding Chapters (Exod 1–17)   18
            The Relationship of Exodus 18 with the Preceding Scene (Exod 17:8–16)   19

    The Relationship of Exodus 18 with the Following Scene
    (Exod 19–20) 20

    The Relationship of Exodus 18 with the Following Chapters
    (Exod 19–40) 20

The Book in the Context of Current Scholarship 21

The Methodological Procedure to Be Employed 26

Chapter 2
An Original Translation and Textual Notes on Exodus 18 | 29

An Original Translation on Exodus 18 29

Textual Notes on Exodus 18 31

    Exodus 18:1 31
    Exodus 18:2 33
    Exodus 18:3 34
    Exodus 18:4 36
    Exodus 18:5 38
    Exodus 18:6 39
    Exodus 18:7 39
    Exodus 18:8 41
    Exodus 18:9 44
    Exodus 18:10 45
    Exodus 18:11 46
    Exodus 18:12 49
    Exodus 18:13 52
    Exodus 18:14 53
    Exodus 18:15 55
    Exodus 18:16 56
    Exodus 18:17 58
    Exodus 18:18 59
    Exodus 18:19 59
    Exodus 18:20 62
    Exodus 18:21 63
    Exodus 18:22 66

Exodus 18:23   68
Exodus 18:24   69
Exodus 18:25   70
Exodus 18:26   71
Exodus 18:27   71

Chapter 3
Narrative Analysis of Exodus 18 | 73
   The Structure of Exodus 18   73
   Other Narrative Elements of Exodus 18   80
      The Narrator   81
      The Characters   84
      The Plot   87
      Time and Space   89
         Time   89
         Space   91
      Style   92
         Three Verbs for the Salvation of Yahweh   94
         One Verb for Arrival, Entry, and Bringing of Cases   95
         Two Verbs for the Activity of Mediating the Knowledge of Yahweh   95
         Two Verbs for Denoting the Knowledge of Yahweh   96
         Frequent Repetition of the Noun דָּבָר   97
      Inclusio   98
      Repeated Clauses   99
      Repeated Sentences   100

Chapter 4
The Figure of Jethro in Exodus 18 and in the Exodus Narrative | 103
   The Names and Titles of Jethro in the Exodus Narrative   104
   The Narrative Roles of Jethro in Exodus 18   107
   The Rhetorical Uses of Jethro in the Exodus Narrative as a Whole   115

Chapter 5

The Retrospective Function of Exodus 18 | 123

    The Jethro Accounts   124

    Yahweh Saving the Israelites from External Threats through His Mighty Acts of Deliverance   129

    The Presence of Yahweh in Various Places   135

    The Knowledge of Yahweh by Yahweh's Self-revelation through His Mighty Acts of Deliverance   141

    Moses as the Judge, Acting as "God" to Pharaoh and the Egyptians   146

    The Israelites as the Egyptian Slaves   153

Chapter 6

The Prospective Function of Exodus 18 | 157

    The Salvation of Yahweh from an Internal Threat through Yahweh's Gracious Forgiveness   157

    The Presence of Yahweh in Specific Places in the Midst of the Israelites   165

    The Knowledge of Yahweh by Yahweh's Self-revelation through His Statutes and Laws, Covenant, and Merciful Forgiveness   172

    Moses as the Judge to the Israelites   183

    The Israelites as the Chosen Servant of Yahweh   187

Chapter 7

Conclusion | 192

Bibliography | 197

Acknowledgments

IN THE COMPLETION OF my dissertation, I am indebted to many people who have equipped me, encouraged me, and supported me while I read, thought, and wrote.

First, thanks be to God for leading and guiding me to study here at Concordia Seminary in St. Louis, Missouri, through his faithful and gracious provision, especially through his strength and wisdom.

I would like to thank my Concordia Seminary professors, especially Dr. David L. Adams, Dr. Thomas J. Egger, Dr. Jeffrey J. Kloha, Dr. Paul R. Raabe, Dr. Timothy E. Saleska, Dr. Bruce G. Schuchard, Dr. Mark A. Seifrid, Dr. James W. Voelz, Dr. David R. Maxwell, and Dr. Robert L. Rosin, for their insightful knowledge and support of my PhD study, and also for teaching me to read and to love God's words.

I would like to express my sincere gratitude to my dissertation advisor or *Doktorvater*, Dr. Thomas J. Egger, for the continuous support of my dissertation and related research, and also for his patience, motivation, and immense knowledge. Even though he plays a new and busy role as the eleventh president of Concordia Seminary, his guidance helped me in all the time of research and writing of my dissertation. I could not have imagined having a better advisor for my dissertation. Besides my *Doktorvater*, I would like to thank my dissertation readers—Dr. David L. Adams, Dr. Jeffrey A. Gibbs, Dr. Bruce G. Schuchard, and Dr. Timothy P. Dost—for their insightful comments and encouragement, but also for the hard questions which incented me to widen my dissertation from various perspectives. My sincere thanks also goes to my dissertation helpers, including Dr. Bruce G. Schuchard, Dr. Kevin L. Armbrust, and Seminarian Devin K. Murphy, for helping me with their insightful comments and support of my dissertation. Lastly, I would like to thank the Concordia Seminary Graduate School, especially Dr. Bruce G. Schuchard, Dr. Gerhard H. Bode, Dr. Joel C. Elowsky, Dr. David R. Maxwell, Dr. Beth J. Hoeltke, and Dr. Ruth E. H. McDonnell, for helping me get through my PhD study with their great assistance.

I would like to offer my special thanks to my financial support from Concordia Seminary, St. Paul Thai Lutheran Church in Chicago, Illinois, and my great-grandfather's scholarship fund in Thailand, for granting me their ongoing generous support throughout my study here. Besides my financial support, I would like to extend my special thanks to my host family, Dr. Robert A. Kolb and his wife, Mrs. Pauline J. Kolb, for showing me their warm welcome and generosity throughout my study here. My special thanks, lastly, goes to my parents, siblings, and friends for supporting me by their ongoing encouragement and prayers.

Finally, I am deeply grateful to God for working in my life, preparing me for his ministry for his people, and leading me to walk humbly and faithfully in his righteous path through his beloved son, Jesus Christ. Indeed, without God, I am nothing, so I give thanks, sing praises, and give glory to God who "is greater than all gods" (Exod 18:11a).

Abbreviations

AB	Anchor Bible
ABD	*The Anchor Bible Dictionary*. Edited by David Noel Freedman. 6 vols. New York: Doubleday, 1992
ABRL	Anchor Bible Reference Library
ACCSOT	Ancient Christian Commentary on Scripture: Old Testament
AGSJU	Arbeiten zur Geschichte des Späteren Judentums und des Urchristentums
ApOTC	Apollos Old Testament Commentary
ASBT	Acadia Studies in Bible and Theology
ATSAT	Arbeiten zu Text und Sprache im Alten Testament
AUSTR	American University Studies, Series 7: Theology and Religion
AYBRL	Anchor Yale Bible Reference Library
BBC	Blackwell Bible Commentaries
BBHG	*Basics of Biblical Hebrew Grammar*. Gary D. Pratico and Miles V. Van Pelt. 3rd ed. Grand Rapids: Zondervan, 2019
BBR	*Bulletin for Biblical Research*
BCBC	Believers Church Bible Commentary
BDB	Brown, Francis, S. R. Driver, and Charles A. Briggs. *The Brown-Driver-Briggs Hebrew and English Lexicon: With an Appendix Containing the Biblical Aramaic*. Boston, MA: Houghton, Mifflin and Company, 1906. Repr., Peabody, MA: Hendrickson, 2005

BH	Bible in History
Bib	*Biblica*
BibInt	Biblical Interpretation Series
BibSem	The Biblical Seminar
BiStC	Bible Study Commentary
BLC	Bible in Literature Courses
BLS	Bible and Literature Series
BSC	Bible Student's Commentary
BST	Bible Speaks Today
BTCB	Brazos Theological Commentary on the Bible
CBC	Cambridge Bible Commentary
CBET	Contributions to Biblical Exegesis and Theology
CBQ	*Catholic Biblical Quarterly*
CC	*Cross Currents*
CPNIVC	College Press NIV Commentary
CRC	Chi Rho Commentary
CTJ	*Calvin Theological Journal*
CV	*Communio Viatorum*
Davidson	Davidson, A. B. *Hebrew Syntax*. 3rd ed. Edinburgh: T&T Clark, 1901
DCH	*The Dictionary of Classical Hebrew*. Edited by David J. A. Clines. 8 vols. Sheffield: Sheffield Academic, 1993–2001; Sheffield: Sheffield Phoenix, 2007–2011
DOTP	*Dictionary of the Old Testament: Pentateuch*. Edited by T. Desmond Alexander and David W. Baker. Downers Grove, IL: InterVarsity, 2003
DSB	Daily Study Bible
EBS	Encountering Biblical Studies
ECC	Eerdmans Critical Commentary
EEC	Evangelical Exegetical Commentary
Even	Even-Shoshan, Abraham, ed. *A New Concordance of the Bible: Thesaurus of the Language of the Bible Hebrew and Aramaic Roots, Words, Proper Names, Phrases, and Synonyms*. Jerusalem: Kiryat Sefer, 1990

FAT	Forschungen zum Alten Testament
FM	*Faith and Mission*
FOTL	Forms of the Old Testament Literature
FRC	The Family, Religion, and Culture
GBHS	*A Guide to Biblical Hebrew Syntax*. Bill T. Arnold and John H. Choi. 2nd ed. Cambridge: Cambridge University Press, 2018
GBS	Guides to Biblical Scholarship
Gibson	Gibson, J. C. L. *Davidson's Introductory Hebrew Grammar-Syntax*. 4th ed. Edinburgh: T&T Clark, 1994
GKC	*Gesenius' Hebrew Grammar*. Edited by E. Kautzsch. Translated by A. E. Cowley. 2nd ed. Oxford: Clarendon, 1910
GorBibSt	Gorgias Biblical Studies
HALOT	*The Hebrew and Aramaic Lexicon of the Old Testament*. Ludwig Koehler and Walter Baumgartner. Translated and edited by M. E. J. Richardson. 2 vols. Leiden: Brill, 2001
HCOT	Historical Commentary on the Old Testament
HOTE	Handbooks for Old Testament Exegesis
IBHS	*An Introduction to Biblical Hebrew Syntax*. Bruce K. Waltke and M. O'Connor. Winona Lake, IN: Eisenbrauns, 1990
IBT	Interpreting Biblical Texts
IECOT	International Exegetical Commentary on the Old Testament
ILBS	Indiana Literary Biblical Series
Int	*Interpretation*
ITC	International Theological Commentary
JBL	*Journal of Biblical Literature*
JBQ	*Jewish Bible Quarterly*
Joüon	Joüon, Paul, S.J. *A Grammar of Biblical Hebrew*. Translated and revised by T. Muraoka. 2 vols. SubBi 14/1–14/2. Rome: Pontifical Biblical Institute, 1991
JPSTC	JPS Torah Commentary
JSOT	*Journal for the Study of the Old Testament*
JSOTSup	Journal for the Study of the Old Testament Supplement Series

KEL	Kregel Exegetical Library
LHBOTS	The Library of Hebrew Bible/Old Testament Studies
MBI	Methods in Biblical Interpretation
ML	Meridian Library
MRCS	Melton Research Center Series
MT	Masoretic Text
MTL	Marshalls Theological Library
NAC	New American Commentary
NBf	*New Blackfrairs*
NCB	New Century Bible
NCBC	New Cambridge Bible Commentary
NIBCOT	New International Biblical Commentary on the Old Testament
NIDOTTE	*The New International Dictionary of Old Testament Theology and Exegesis.* Edited by Willem A. VanGemeren. 5 vols. Grand Rapids: Zondervan, 1997
NIVAC	NIV Application Commentary
NSBT	New Studies in Biblical Theology
OBS	Oxford Bible Series
OT	Old Testament
OTG	Old Testament Guides
OTL	Old Testament Library
OTM	Old Testament Message
OTSS	Old Testament Survey Series
OTWS	*Old Testament Word Studies.* William Wilson. Grand Rapids: Kregel, 1978
PB	People's Bible
PBM	Paternoster Biblical Monographs
PRJ	*Puritan Reformed Journal*
RBS	Resources for Biblical Study
SBEC	Studies in the Bible and Early Christianity
SBLDS	Society of Biblical Literature Dissertation Series

SBLMS	Society of Biblical Literature Monograph Series
SBTS	Sources for Biblical and Theological Study
SCMBC	SCM Book Club
SEPT	Septuagint Commentary Series
SHBC	Smyth & Helwys Bible Commentary
SRB	Studies in Rewritten Bible
SSN	Studia Semitica Neerlandica
StBibLit	Studies in Biblical Literature
SubBi	Subsidia Biblica
TBC	Torch Bible Commentaries
TCT	Textual Criticism and the Translator
TDOT	*Theological Dictionary of the Old Testament*. Edited by G. Johannes Botterweck, Helmer Ringgren, and Heinz-Josef Fabry. Translated by John T. Willis, Geoffrey W. Bromiley, David E. Green, and Douglas W. Stott. 15 vols. Grand Rapids: Eerdmans, 1974–2006
TLOT	*Theological Lexicon of the Old Testament*. Ernst Jenni and Claus Westermann. Translated by Mark E. Biddle. 3 vols. Peabody, MA: Hendrickson, 1997
TOTC	Tyndale Old Testament Commentaries
TWOT	*Theological Wordbook of the Old Testament*. Edited by R. Laird Harris, Gleason L. Archer, Jr., and Bruce K. Waltke. 2 vols. Chicago: Moody, 1980
TynBul	*Tyndale Bulletin*
UBSHS	UBS Handbook Series
VOT	*The Vocabulary of the Old Testament*. Francis I. Andersen and A. Dean Forbes. Rome: Pontifical Biblical Institute, 1989
VT	*Vetus Testamentum*
WBC	Word Biblical Commentary
Williams	Williams, Ronald J. *Williams' Hebrew Syntax*. Rev. and exp. by John C. Beckman. 3rd ed. Toronto: University of Toronto Press, 2007

Abstract

Kumpeeroskul, Noppawat. "Exodus 18: Its Literary Unity and Its Key Transitional Role in the Exodus Narrative." PhD diss., Concordia Seminary, 2022. 249 pp.

THIS DISSERTATION ARGUES THAT Exod 18:1–27 functions literarily and theologically as the key transitional midpoint in the Exodus narrative. As such, the chapter's function is both retrospective (recalling key features of chapters 1–17) and prospective (anticipating key features of chapters 19–40) at the midpoint of the book. The characterization of the chapter's most prominent figure, Jethro, the priest of Midian, the father-in-law of Moses, offers the first strong indication of the chapter's retrospective and prospective interest as Jethro and Jethro's daughter, the wife of Moses, and the sons of Moses reappear in the narrative of the book in this chapter only (cf. the early prominence and only other appearance of the same characters in Exod 2:16–22; 3:1; 4:18–20, 24–26). On the first day, Jethro comes from Midian to the mountain of God where Moses is encamping. Moses recalls the events of the recent past as he tells Jethro how, through Moses, Yahweh delivered Israel from the hand of Pharaoh and the Egyptians, so that Yahweh might dwell with his people, and his people might dwell with him. Jethro comes to "know that Yahweh is greater than all gods." Jethro confesses and worships Yahweh by taking a burnt offering and sacrifices to Yahweh and eating bread with Aaron and all the elders of Israel in the presence of Yahweh. On the second day, the father-in-law of Moses offers Moses good counsel regarding the future responsibility which Moses will have as the mediator of the word and will of Yahweh to Israel. Moses heeds Jethro. Through Moses, Israel will be called upon to heed Yahweh. And Jethro returns to Midian. Thus,

ABSTRACT

Exod 18 draws to a close a first narrative movement in the first half of the book in which Yahweh is seen and known through his mighty acts of deliverance. Through Moses, Yahweh delivers. Exodus 18 also signals a shift in the second half of the book to a self-revelation of Yahweh which will feature Israel's need to heed the word and will of Yahweh as mediated through Moses. Through Moses, Yahweh will govern. Through Moses, Yahweh will dwell with his people, acting in extraordinary terms to preserve them from the threat which they will be to themselves for the sake of his equally extraordinary purposes for them and through them. A close literary and theological reading of the book shows that Exod 18 (rather than other options which have been proposed) is the book's key transitional midpoint and recommends to the reader of the book a way of reading the book in keeping with these themes.

— Chapter 1 —
Introduction

The Introduction and Summary of the Account of Exodus 18

In Exod 18:1–27, Jethro or Reuel, the priest of Midian, the father-in-law of Moses (Exod 18:1; cf. 2:18; 4:18) makes another appearance in the Exodus narrative. Because he heard all that Yahweh had done for Moses and Israel, Jethro comes with Moses' wife, Zipporah, and two sons, Gershom and Eliezer (Exod 18:2–4; cf. 2:21–22; 4:20, 25) to meet Moses at the mountain of God, Mount Horeb or Sinai. After meeting each other, Moses recounts to Jethro all that Yahweh had done to Pharaoh and the Egyptians because of Israel and all the hardship which had come upon Israel on the way. Jethro rejoices in all the good that Yahweh had done for Israel, and then he praises Yahweh and acknowledges that Yahweh, who had delivered Israel out of the hand of Pharaoh and the Egyptians and from all the hardship that had come upon Israel on the way, is greater than all gods. Jethro worships Yahweh by taking a burnt offering and sacrifices to Yahweh and eating bread with Aaron and all the elders of Israel (and, presumably, Moses) in the presence of Yahweh (Exod 18:1–12).

On the next day, Moses sits to judge Israel from morning until evening. Because he saw all that Moses was doing by himself for Israel, Jethro asks Moses about all the deeds, and Moses then answers Jethro with his three responsibilities—a mediator, a judge, and an instructor. Jethro then advises Moses concerning his responsibilities as the mediator between Yahweh and Israel by being as Israel in the presence of Yahweh to inquire of Yahweh, as the instructor for Israel by making known and teaching Yahweh's statutes and laws, and as the judge by judging Israel's cases and setting lesser chiefs (or judges) over Israel. Moses obeys and does all that Jethro had said. Finally, Moses sends away Jethro, and Jethro goes to his own country (Exod 18:13–27).

This event consisting of two main parts (Exod 18:1–12 and 13–27)[1] comes at a critical juncture in the narrative: *after* Yahweh has brought Israel out through the great redemptive events, which occur in the land of Egypt, at the Red Sea, and on the wilderness journey to Mount Sinai, and *before* Yahweh will lead and guide Israel as the people of Yahweh through Yahweh's statutes and laws. As a formative character in the Exodus narrative, Jethro's reappearance along with Moses' wife and son(s) serves to highlight and cap off Yahweh's salvific activity (Exod 18:1–12) while also preparing Moses as Yahweh's agent for Mount Sinai and beyond (Exod 18:13–27). These factors suggest that this event, Exod 18 as a whole,[2] functions as the bridge[3] and the key transitional midpoint of the

---

1. Noth, *Exodus*, 145–46. See also Fretheim, *Exodus*, 195; Zweck, *Freed to Follow*, 159; Houtman, *Exodus*, 2:396; Alexander, *Exodus*, 345.

2. Many commentators approach Exod 18 as a whole, a unified account, with literary work and features (see Childs, *Exodus*, 321; Coats, *Exodus 1–18*, 147; Carpenter, "Exodus 18," 94–98), with theological work and themes (see Fretheim, *Exodus*, 195), and, specifically, with Abraham's family reunion theme, related to the book of Genesis (see Durham, *Exodus*, 240, 241, 248). Furthermore, as considering literary work of Exod 18, whereas vv. 1–12 are mostly from the E source and partly from the J source, vv. 13–27 are completely from the E source as a whole (see Hyatt, *Exodus*, 186). Nevertheless, because Exod 18 is mostly from the E source and partly from the J source, Noth, *Exodus*, 146, notes, "The chapter [Exod 18] is not a complete literary unity." Interestingly, Alexander, *Exodus*, 354, notes, "All importantly, gospel precedes law within this chapter [Exod 18] and within Exodus as a whole. Although the divine deliverance of the Israelites from Egypt was not due to their being inherently more righteous than others, the outworking of their redemption should result in their becoming more righteous than other people."

3. Sarna, *Exploring Exodus*, 128, emphasizes, "the two parts" (vv. 1–12 and 13–27) of Exod 18 "form a most appropriate bridge between the foregoing and the following sections." See also Meyers, *Exodus*, 136; Bailey, *Exodus*, 196–97; Carpenter, *Exodus*, 1:602; Alexander, *Exodus*, 345. Furthermore, by observing the "two narratives" (vv. 1–12 and 13–27) of Exod 18, Propp, *Exodus*, 1:634, concludes, "Thus Exodus 18 is a narrational pivot, looking both backward and forward." Whereas Exod 18 functions as "a bridge," it shows "a pause," which does not interrupt the whole Exodus narrative (see Murphy, *Exodus*, 120; Carpenter, "Exodus 18," 92), to consider and know Moses' faith (see Finegan, *Let My People Go*, 101), to look backward to Yahweh's redemptive events with joy (see Childs, *Exodus*, 327; Burns, *Exodus, Leviticus, Numbers*, 137; Zweck, *Freed to Follow*, 161; Brueggemann, "Exodus," 1:824), to prepare for Yahweh's great revelatory event at Mount Sinai (see Sarna, *Exploring Exodus*, 126, 128), and to rest in שָׁלוֹם between two storms at the Red Sea and at Mount Sinai (see Carpenter, *Exodus*, 1:602,

Exodus narrative[4] in two ways: (1) the redemptive conclusion of Yahweh in Egypt, at the Red Sea, and in the wilderness as narrated throughout Exod 1–17 and (2) the instructive anticipation of Yahweh at Mount Sinai as narrated throughout Exod 19–40.[5]

Commentators have long noted many passages which are thought to play transitional roles in the Exodus narrative, for example, Exod 1:1–7; 2:23–25; 3:1–4:31; 12:1–13:16; 15:1–21 (or 15:1b–18); 15:22–18:27; 18:1–27 (or 18:13–27); 19:1–6; 24:12–18; and 40:34–38.[6] However, many significant scholars, including Childs, Propp, Dozeman, Shreckhise, and Russell, have argued that the main transitional narrative in the book of Exodus is Exod 15:1–21 (or 15:1b–18), the Song of the Sea.[7] Throughout this Song, Moses and Israel sing praises to Yahweh who delivered Israel from Pharaoh and the Egyptians at the Red Sea (Exod 15:1–12, 19–21)

624; Carpenter, "Exodus 18," 92–93, 106, 108; Ber, "Moses and Jethro," 150, 152).

4. By observing Childs and Cassuto's claims concerning the role of Exod 18, Carpenter, "Exodus 18," 91, acknowledges, "In fact, it seems to me that Exodus 18 is perhaps the major transitional chapter in the book of Exodus, summarizing the past events (Exod. 1–17) and preparing for the coming revelation at Sinai (Exod. 19–40)." See also Carpenter, "Exodus 18," 107; Meyers, *Exodus*, 136; Bailey, *Exodus*, 199; Bruckner, *Exodus*, 163; Carpenter, *Exodus*, 1:602, 603; Alexander, *Exodus*, 345. Furthermore, Egger, "Visiting Iniquity," 464, considers the transitional function of Exod 15:22–18:27 by concluding, "Thus, Exodus can be seen as a two-part narrative, with the closing of the first movement (15:22–18:27) serving also an intermediate and transitional function as they anticipate major themes to be developed in the second movement [Exod 19–40]."

5. Carpenter, "Exodus 18," 91. See also Carpenter, "Exodus 18," 93; Wendland, *Exodus*, 121; Brueggemann, "Exodus," 1:829; Houtman, *Exodus*, 2:395, 401; Larsson, *Bound for Freedom*, 123; Carpenter, *Exodus*, 1:603; Egger, "Visiting Iniquity," 464.

6. Coats, "A Structural Transition in Exodus," 129–42; Fretheim, *Exodus*, 7; Propp, *Exodus*, 1:37–38; Utzschneider and Oswald, *Exodus 1–15*, 22, 23, 24; Longman and Dillard, *Introduction to the Old Testament*, 70; Ska, *Introduction to Reading the Pentateuch*, 29; McEntire, *Struggling with God*, 87–88. For Exod 1:1–7, realized as a transition between the end of the book of Genesis and the beginning of the book of Exodus, see Wendland, *Exodus*, 1; Rendtorff, *Old Testament*, 139; Ska, *Introduction to Reading the Pentateuch*, 17. For Exod 15:1–21, approached as the key transition between the first part of the Exodus narrative (Exod 1:1–15:21) and the second part of the Exodus narrative (Exod 15:22–40:38), see Cole, *Exodus*, 11; Keil and Delitzsch, *Pentateuch*, 1:417; Gispen, *Exodus*, 7; Osborn and Hatton, *Exodus*, 2–3; Propp, *Exodus*, 1:38. For Exod 18:1–27, considered as the key transition between the first part of the Exodus narrative (Exod 1:1–17:16) and the second part of the Exodus narrative (Exod 19:1–40:38), see Carpenter, "Exodus 18," 91, 107; Carpenter, *Exodus*, 1:21–22; Alexander, *Exodus*, 10. For Exod 40:34–38, recognized as a transition between the end of the book of Exodus and the beginning of the book of Leviticus, see Keil and Delitzsch, *Pentateuch*, 1:417–18; Ska, *Introduction to Reading the Pentateuch*, 17.

7. Childs, *Exodus*, 252; Propp, *Exodus*, 1:38; Dozeman, *Exodus*, 332–33; Shreckhise, "I Will Sing," 244–45; Russell, *Song of the Sea*, 149.

and who is going to lead and guide Israel to Yahweh's holy abode and sanctuary, the mountain of Yahweh's inheritance, so that Yahweh will reign over Israel forever and ever (Exod 15:13–18).[8]

However, this book will consider and propose Exod 18:1–27, rather than Exod 15:1–21 and other options which have been proposed, as the key transitional midpoint in the book of Exodus. Exodus 18 operates as a better retrospective midpoint by capping with the reappearance of Jethro, the father-in-law of Moses, along with the wife and son(s) of Moses (Exod 18:1–4) and also by employing two summarizing clauses: "all which God had done for Moses and for Israel, his people"[9] (Exod 18:1; cf. 18:8, 9) and "all the hardship which had come upon them [Israel] on the way" (Exod 18:8). These clauses encompass the salvation of Yahweh for Israel in the land of Egypt, at the Red Sea, and on the wilderness journey to Mount Sinai (Exod 1–17). Moreover, Exod 18 functions better prospectively as it prepares Moses for his impending roles in the imminent and great revelatory events at Mount Sinai, where Yahweh will dwell with his people, Israel, where Yahweh will appear and speak to Moses alone with Yahweh's statutes and laws, covenant, and merciful forgiveness, and

---

8. Watts, "The Song of the Sea," 378, notes, "Beginning with the victory at the sea, relating victories during the journey and in Canaan, and climaxing with the occupation of Jerusalem and the establishment of the temple." Watts considers Exod 15:1b–18 as a hymn of praise for Yahweh as "the exalted and victorious King" who establishes the victory over Pharaoh and the Egyptians at the Red Sea and who will reign over Israel in the future throughout the wilderness journey, at Mount Sinai, in the land of Canaan, and in Jerusalem (see Watts, "The Song of the Sea," 378). See also Coats, "The Song of the Sea," 12–13; Crenshaw, *Old Testament Story and Faith*, 67–68; Mann, *Book of the Torah*, 79; Wells, "Exodus," 54; Chen, *Eschatological Sanctuary*, 1. Nevertheless, Dozeman, *Exodus*, 46, notes, "The hymns in chap. 15 look back over the battlefield and answer the question raised up in chap. 1: Yahweh is indeed a warrior God, possessing power over Pharaoh and over all the forces of nature [Exod 1:1–14:31]. . . . The hymns in Exodus 15 also provide a change in focus from the exodus to the unfulfilled promise of land. Yahweh's power over Pharaoh leads to the confident conclusion that God will lead the Israelite people in a march through the wilderness, with images of conquest pointing to the fulfillment of the promise of land (15:13–18). The utopian vision of life in a land ruled by God introduces the theme of divine presence with Israel. Although never realized, the theme of divine presence in the promised land is central to the second half of Exodus [Exod 15:22–40:38]. Instead of the promised land, the wilderness becomes the setting for exploring a variety of ways in which Yahweh dwells with Israel as they journey toward Canaan."

9. All translations are by the author.

where the responsibilities of Moses as the mediator,[10] the instructor,[11] and the judge[12] will be prominent (Exod 19–40).[13]

The Thesis

Exodus 18:1–27 functions literarily and theologically as the key transitional midpoint in the Exodus narrative.

The Current Status of the Question

The current status of the question will present what other scholars, especially Exodus specialists have argued and worked on in Exod 18:1–27. Its contents will be expressed under five topics: (1) "The Problem in the Account of Exodus 18" will briefly look at a problem of chronology in Exod 18. (2) "The Divisions of the Book of Exodus" will explore how a number of Exodus scholars have organized the text. (3) "Scholars in Favor of Exodus 15 as the Main Transition in the Book of Exodus" will survey scholarship defending a major alternative to this book's position. (4) "The Role of Exodus 18 as the Main Transition in the Book of Exodus" will examine how other Exodus scholars have maintained a similar stance to this book. And (5) "The Relationships of Exodus 18 in the Book of Exodus" will review what the connections between Exod 18 and the Exodus narrative are.

---

10. Various Exodus scholars acknowledge Moses alone as the mediator between Yahweh and his people, Israel (see Childs, *Exodus*, 321, 324, 330; Propp, Exodus, 1:632; Dozeman, *Exodus*, 408–9; Hamilton, *Exodus*, 288; Thompson, *Origin Tradition*, 150).

11. Several Exodus commentators consider Moses alone as the instructor (or the teacher or the preacher) for Israel with Yahweh's statutes and laws (see Childs, *Exodus*, 330; Fretheim, *Exodus*, 199; Larsson, *Bound for Freedom*, 124; Bruckner, *Exodus*, 167; Thompson, *Origin Tradition*, 150).

12. Many Exodus scholars approach Moses alone as the (highest) judge (or the magistrate or the arbitrator or the adjudicator) over Israel (see Hyatt, *Exodus*, 193; Childs, *Exodus*, 324, 330; Houtman, *Exodus*, 2:395, 401, 414, 415, 420; Stuart, *Exodus*, 415, 416, 418, 419; Carpenter, *Exodus*, 1:616–17, 625; Carpenter, "Exodus 18," 100–101).

13. Whereas Houtman explains that Moses' roles as the mediator between Yahweh and his people, Israel, and the lawgiver will possess the narratives of Exod 19–40 (see Houtman, *Exodus*, 2:401), Thompson describes that Moses' roles as the instructor for Israel and the mediator between Yahweh and Israel, are certified (see Thompson, *Origin Tradition*, 150).

The Problem in the Account of Exodus 18

Even though some scholars[14] see Exod 18:1–27 as improperly placed in the Exodus narrative due to its apparent non-chronological sequence,[15] other scholars, including Cassuto, Childs, Sarna, Durham, Propp, Enns, Stuart, Dozeman, and Carpenter, argue that Exod 18:1–27 has been intentionally and deliberately located in its present location[16] because of its thematic and theological functions rather than its chronological function.[17]

According to Abraham ibn Ezra, at least five issues in the account of Exod 18 demonstrate its improper place because of non-chronological sequence: (1) Moses (and, presumably, the Israelites) are already encamped at "the mountain of God," that is, Mount Horeb or Sinai (Exod 18:5) while Exod 19 reported the arrival of the Israelites at Mount Sinai, "On the third new moon, after the sons of Israel had gone out of the land of Egypt, on that day, they came into the wilderness of Sinai. Then

---

14. Propp refers to Rabbi Eleazar of Modiim, Rashi, Abraham ibn Ezra, and Rashbam (see Propp, *Exodus*, 1:627–28). See also Cassuto, *Exodus*, 211; Childs, *Exodus*, 321–22; Sarna, *Exodus*, 97; Jacob, *Exodus*, 494; Alexander, *Exodus*, 346. Furthermore, Childs refers to John Lightfoot (see Childs, *Exodus*, 321–22). See also Kaiser, "Exodus," 2:411. Propp also refers to A. H. McNeile, D. A. Glatt, and J. Van Seters (see Propp, *Exodus*, 1:627–28).

15. Sarna notes the improper chronological order of Exod 18:1–27 in the Exodus narrative (see Sarna, *Exploring Exodus*, 127–28). See also Davies, *Exodus*, 147; Hyatt, *Exodus*, 188; Sarna, *Exodus*, 97–98; Propp, *Exodus*, 1:627–28; Bailey, *Exodus*, 31–32, 196, 198. Sailhamer argues that vv. 1–26 are not out of place, but only v. 27 is out of place which is located after Num 10:29 (see Sailhamer, *Pentateuch as Narrative*, 281).

16. Regarding the non-chronological place of Exod 18, some commentators agree that the account of Exod 18 has been placed in its recent place in the book of Exodus with logic/purpose/intention/deliberation (see Durham, *Exodus*, 246; Enns, *Exodus*, 367; Stuart, *Exodus*, 402; Robinson, "Acknowledging One's Dependence," 140; Reiss, "Jethro the Convert," 90).

17. Childs, *Exodus*, 322; Davis, *Moses and Gods of Egypt*, 199; Kaiser, "Exodus," 2:411; Carpenter, "Exodus 18," 107; Reiss, "Jethro the Convert," 89. Regarding the thematic function of Exod 18:1–27, Cassuto notes the development of the numerous thematic connections between Exod 18:1–27 and the Amalekite scene immediately preceding it in Exod 17:8–16 (see Cassuto, *Exodus*, 211–12). See also Childs, *Exodus*, 322; Sarna, *Exploring Exodus*, 128–29; Alexander, *Exodus*, 345–46, 353; Reiss, "Jethro the Convert," 89–90; Sarna, "Exodus, Book of," *ABD* 2:696. As recognizing the literary connection between Exod 18:1–12 and 17:8–16 with a contrast theme, Sarna also notes the anticipation of Exod 18:13–27 with a theme of giving Yahweh's statutes and laws at Mount Sinai (see Sarna, *Exploring Exodus*, 129). See also Sarna, *Exodus*, 98; Bailey, *Exodus*, 32; Sarna, "Exodus, Book of," *ABD* 2:696. Furthermore, regarding the theological function of Exod 18:1–27, Durham notes that because of theological reasons, compilers place Exod 18:1–27 in its current location before the revelatory events at Mount Sinai (see Durham, *Exodus*, 252). See also Alexander, *Exodus*, 346.

they set out from Rephidim, and they came into the wilderness of Sinai, and they encamped in the wilderness. There Israel encamped in front of the mountain" (Exod 19:1–2).[18] (2) Jethro brought "a burnt offering and sacrifices" to Yahweh, and Aaron came with all the elders of the Israelites to eat bread with Jethro in the presence of Yahweh (Exod 18:12); whereas the laws about altars had not been given yet (Exod 20:22–26), and also the altar of burnt offering and the tabernacle had not been built yet (Exod 38:1–7; 40:1–33).[19] (3) Moses made known to the Israelites "the statutes of God and his laws" (Exod 18:16, 20), but no statutes or laws had been given yet (Exod 20:1–23:19).[20] (4) Jethro advised Moses to appoint the chiefs (or judges) over the Israelites (Exod 18:21, 25), but other biblical books narrated the appointment of the judges of the Israelites occurring before the departure of the Israelites from Mount Sinai (Deut 1:9–18; 16:18–20; 17:8–13; cf. 2 Chr 19:4–11).[21] And (5) Jethro departed and went away to his own country (Exod 18:27) while Num 10 recorded the departure of Jethro happening after the appearance of Yahweh at Mount Sinai (Num 10:29–32).[22] These five strong internal evidences suggest that the present location of Exod 18 may not present a strict sequence of events, and that the scenes in Exod 18 would be after, rather than before, the Mount Sinai events according to chronological order.[23]

18. Sarna, *Exploring Exodus*, 127; Sarna, *Exodus*, 97; Jacob, *Exodus*, 494; Zweck, *Freed to Follow*, 161; Houtman, *Exodus*, 2:400; Propp, *Exodus*, 1:628; Alexander, *Exodus*, 346; Sarna, "Exodus, Book of," *ABD* 2:696.

19. Childs, *Exodus*, 322; Sarna, *Exploring Exodus*, 128; Kaiser, "Exodus," 2:411; Sarna, *Exodus*, 97; Jacob, *Exodus*, 494; Propp, *Exodus*, 1:628; Alexander, *Exodus*, 346; Sarna, "Exodus, Book of," *ABD* 2:696.

20. Sarna, *Exploring Exodus*, 127–28; Kaiser, "Exodus," 2:411; Sarna, *Exodus*, 97; Jacob, *Exodus*, 494; Houtman, *Exodus*, 2:400; Propp, *Exodus*, 1:628 ; Alexander, *Exodus*, 346; Sarna, "Exodus, Book of," *ABD* 2:696.

21. Sarna, *Exploring Exodus*, 127; Kaiser, "Exodus," 2:411; Sarna, *Exodus*, 97; Jacob, *Exodus*, 494; Houtman, *Exodus*, 2:400; Propp, *Exodus*, 1:628; Alexander, *Exodus*, 346; Sarna, "Exodus, Book of," *ABD* 2:696.

22. Sarna, *Exploring Exodus*, 128; Sarna, *Exodus*, 97; Jacob, *Exodus*, 494; Houtman, *Exodus*, 2:400; Bailey, *Exodus*, 31–32; Sarna, "Exodus, Book of," *ABD* 2:696.

23. According to Exod 18:5, it is apparent that the event of Exod 18 happens at "the mountain of God," that is, Mount Sinai (see Davies, *Exodus*, 147; Garrett, *Exodus*, 438, 448–49; Bacon, "JE in the Middle Books," 24) or between Exod 19 and Num 10 (see Dozeman, *Exodus*, 400). Furthermore, according to the five strong internal evidences, at least three places have been proposed for the original place of Exod 18: (1) after the arrival of the Israelites at Mount Sinai (see Murphy, *Exodus*, 120; Hyatt, *Exodus*, 186–87; Enns, *Exodus*, 368; Walton, Matthews, and Chavalas, *IVP Bible Background Commentary*, 93); (2) after the self-revelation of Yahweh at Mount Sinai, including the giving of Yahweh's statutes and laws and the establishment of the covenant (see Sarna,

However, a number of commentators consider the recent place of Exod 18 as the proper chronological place in the book of Exodus, as W. H. Gispen states:

> Chapter 18 describes Jethro's visit to Moses, on which occasion he gave wise counsel to Moses (vv. 13–26). All indications point to the fact that this chapter is placed in the proper historical context, and that the visit did indeed take place between the battle of Rephidim and the giving of the law at Sinai.[24]

Concerning the preceding account of Exod 18 in Exod 17:8–16 about the war with the Amalekites, Douglas K. Stuart insists that Exod 18 should be placed as it is:

> The placement of this story [Exod 18] at this point in the book [the Book of Exodus] makes good sense in light of the fact that the Midianites and Amalekites were closely related; the defeat of the Amalekites (17:8–16), followed by the conversion of a Midianite (high?) priest (18:1–12) both demonstrate Yahweh's truth and power and his superiority over false gods and their adherents.[25]

Regarding the mountain of God, Mount Sinai, in Exod 18:5, Dean Zweck stresses that Exod 18 is properly in its current position:

> Jethro brings Zipporah and the two children with him to meet Moses at *the mountain of God* where Israel was camped. Chronologically there is a problem here: 19:2 records that they set out from Rephidim, came to the wilderness of Sinai, and camped before the mountain.... On the other hand, chapter 18 is appropriate in its present position because the narrative has come full circle. After fleeing from Pharaoh, Moses was in Midian, where he married one of Jethro's daughters and lived in Jethro's household (2:15–22). This time in Midian was a period of quiet preparation before the theophany at Sinai and Moses'

Exploring Exodus, 127–28; Durham, *Exodus*, 242, 245; Houtman, *Exodus*, 2:400; Bailey, *Exodus*, 31–32, 198–99; Alexander, *Exodus*, 346; Bacon, "JE in the Middle Books," 24; Sarna, "Exodus, Book of," *ABD* 2:696); and (3) before the departure of the Israelites from Mount Sinai, especially in Num 10 (see Davies, *Exodus*, 147; Childs, *Exodus*, 321–22; Kaiser, "Exodus," 2:411; Jacob, *Exodus*, 494; Propp, *Exodus*, 1:627–28).

24. Gispen, *Exodus*, 171. See also Kaiser, "Exodus," 2:411; Jacob, *Exodus*, 494; Zweck, *Freed to Follow*, 161; Propp, *Exodus*, 1:627; Dozeman, *Exodus*, 400; Alexander, *Exodus*, 347.

25. Stuart, *Exodus*, 402. See also Jacob, *Exodus*, 494; Houtman, *Exodus*, 2:400–401; Johnstone, *Exodus*, 1:374.

commission to return to Egypt (chapter 3). Now Moses has returned from Egypt, and, leading the rescued people of Israel, is en route to Sinai, where, as promised, he will again "serve God upon this mountain" (3:12). It is fitting that Moses be reunited with Jethro and his family at this point—before the second and greater theophany on Sinai. The scene of reunion provides a pause in the narrative, time for grateful remembrance.[26]

Concerning a burnt offering and sacrifices in Exod 18:12 and Yahweh's statutes and laws in Exod 18:16, 20, Walter C. Kaiser contends that Exod 18 has been placed in its appropriate sequence:

> In fact, we have already seen that portions of the law were already known before they were formalized at Sinai (see Notes on 16:4; and notice the loose wording of Deut 1:9–15, along with the presence of sacrifices almost from the beginning of the human race in Gen 4:3–4 and later in 8:20–21). This chapter, then, is in its proper chronological order.[27]

Whether or not the scenes with Jethro in Exod 18 are placed in their strict chronological sequence, scholars generally agree that Exod 18 is logically placed in its present place because of its literary features and theological themes,[28] and that it does not interrupt the whole Exodus narrative.[29]

The Divisions of the Book of Exodus

Commentators divide the book of Exodus into various major sections. Nahum M. Sarna divides the Exodus narrative into four sections:

> The work does not easily lend itself to separation into clear-cut major divisions, though a rough arrangement broadly partitions the book [the Book of Exodus] into the following sections: 1. Chapters 1–15:21, the story of Israel in Egypt, the oppression, the struggle for freedom, and the final liberation; 2. Chapter 15:22 to Chapter 18, the account of the journey from the Reed

---

26. Zweck, *Freed to Follow*, 161. See also McEntire, *Struggling with God*, 104–5.

27. Kaiser, "Exodus," 2:411. See also Houtman, *Exodus*, 2:400–401; Alexander, *Exodus*, 347; Sailhamer, *Pentateuch as Narrative*, 281.

28. Cassuto, *Exodus*, 211–12; Durham, *Exodus*, 252.

29. Murphy, *Exodus*, 120, notes, "The record of this collateral occurrence [Exod 18] is placed here, at a convenient pause, that it may not interfere with the main current of the narrative [the Book of Exodus]." See also Brueggemann, "Exodus," 1:824.

Sea to Sinai; 3. Chapters 19–24, the covenant at Sinai and prescriptions of the law; 4. Chapters 25–40, the command to erect the Tabernacle, and its implementation.[30]

Sarna emphasizes *four major events* within the Exodus narrative: (1) Israel's *oppression* and *liberation* in Egypt (Exod 1:1–15:21), (2) Israel's *journey* in the wilderness to Mount Sinai (Exod 15:22–18:27), (3) Yahweh's *covenant*, including his *laws* at Mount Sinai (Exod 19:1–24:18), and (4) Yahweh's *command* for the tabernacle at Mount Sinai and its *fulfillment* (Exod 25:1–40:38).

John I. Durham divides the Exodus narrative into three sections:

> The outline of the Book of Exodus is deceptively simple, given the complexity of the book's contents. I have divided the text into three major parts on the basis of the location of the people of Israel in the narrative sequence, so: Part One: Israel in Egypt (1:1–13:16); Part Two: Israel in the Wilderness (13:17–18:27); Part Three: Israel at Sinai (19:1–40:38).[31]

Durham highlights *three major locations* within the Exodus narrative: (1) Israel's persecution in and exodus from *Egypt* (Exod 1:1–13:16), (2) Israel's journey through *the wilderness* beyond the Red Sea (Exod 13:17–18:27), and (3) Yahweh's presence, laws and covenant, and instructions for the tabernacle at *Mount Sinai* (Exod 19:1–40:38).

William H. C. Propp divides the Exodus narrative into two sections by pointing out, "Exodus is a bipartite work whose center is somewhat difficult to determine. . . . In short, the Song of the Sea [Exod 15:1–21] both concludes the first half of Exodus [Exod 1:1–14:31] and opens the second half [Exod 15:22–40:38]."[32] Essential in Propp's statement is that there are *two major events* within the Exodus narrative: (1) *Yahweh's deliverance* for Israel from Egypt (Exod 1:1–15:21) and (2)

---

30. Sarna, *Exploring Exodus*, 6–7. See also Wells, "Exodus," 54.

31. Durham, *Exodus*, xxx. See also Lessing and Steinmann, *Prepare the Way*, 76–77. Furthermore, Durham notes, "It is an outline that emerges from the text, rather than one superimposed upon it, and it gives some indication of the whole Book of Exodus as a unified composite moving from the promise and the proof of Yahweh's Presence to the revelation and advent of that Presence, incorporating the involvement of that Presence in the solemnization of covenant relationship, recalling the threatened withdrawal of the Presence because of disobedience, and presenting with relief the reconciliation of Yahweh's Presence and his settlement in Israel's midst." Durham, *Exodus*, xxx.

32. Propp, *Exodus*, 1:37–38. See also Keil and Delitzsch, *Pentateuch*, 1:416–17; Gispen, *Exodus*, 1–2, 3; Steinmann, *Called to Be*, 132–33.

Yahweh's reign over Israel throughout the wilderness journey to Mount Sinai (Exod 15:22–40:38).

Thomas B. Dozeman observes "a division in Exodus between the themes of divine power (1:1–15:21) and divine presence (15:22–40:38)."[33] In other words, Dozeman points to *two major theological themes* within the Exodus narrative: (1) the *power of Yahweh* in Egypt (Exod 1:1–15:21) and (2) the *presence of Yahweh* in the wilderness (Exod 15:22–40:38).

Eugene Carpenter also divides the Exodus narrative into two sections by concluding, "It [Exod 18] separates Exodus into two parts, but at the same time unites the two parts in such a way that the significance of the events in chs. 1–17 is caught up in a new way and carried on into chs. 19–40."[34] Basically, Carpenter stresses *two major theological themes* within the Exodus narrative: (1) *Yahweh's deliverance* (נצל, "to deliver") (Exod 1:1–18:27) and (2) *Yahweh's judgment* (שפט, "to judge") (Exod 19:1–40:38).[35]

Finally, Thomas J. Egger divides the Exodus narrative into two sections:

> In my view, the strongest case can be made for viewing chs. 1–18 and 19–40 as the two narrative arcs within Exodus, with Exod 18 drawing part one to its close and 19:1 introducing a second, distinct movement.... Exodus falls into two major movements: the deliverance narrative in Exod 1–18 and the narrative of covenant and divine presence in Exod 19–40.[36]

Egger accents *two major theological themes* within the Exodus narrative: (1) *Yahweh's deliverance* (Exod 1:1–18:27) and (2) *Yahweh's presence* and *covenant* (Exod 19:1–40:38).

In summary, commentators have divided the Exodus narrative into four major sections based on key events,[37] three major sections based on key locations,[38] or two major sections based on key theological themes.[39]

---

33. Dozeman, *Exodus*, 52. See also Dozeman, *Exodus*, 44–47; Dozeman, *Pentateuch*, 285–86.

34. Carpenter, "Exodus 18," 108. See also Carpenter, "Exodus 18," 91.

35. Carpenter, "Exodus 18," 98–100. See also Erdman, *Exodus*, 7; Jacob, *Exodus*, xxxv; Zweck, *Freed to Follow*, 8, 14–16; Gavigan, McCarthy, and McGovern, *Navarre Bible*, 235–38; Menezes, *God of Israel*, 106–7.

36. Egger, "Visiting Iniquity," 448–58.

37. Sarna, *Exploring Exodus*, 6–7.

38. Durham, *Exodus*, xxx.

39. Propp, *Exodus*, 1:37–38; Dozeman, *Exodus*, 52; Carpenter, "Exodus 18," 108;

Scholars in Favor of Exodus 15 as the Main Transition in the Book of Exodus

Several scholars who approach the Exodus narrative as a two-part narrative see Exod 15:1–21 (or 1b–18), the Song of the Sea, as the main transition in the book of Exodus. Brevard S. Childs argues that the poem of Exod 15:1b–18 functions as the main transition in the book of Exodus:

> The movement of the poem from the deliverance at the sea to the land interprets the significance of Yahweh's redemptive intervention. He not only redeems a people for himself, but he leads them into his land. Whereas the first part of the hymn [Exod 15:1b–12] revolved about Yahweh's victory at the sea, the focus of the second half [Exod 15:13–18] is on Yahweh's sanctuary.[40]

In addition, Propp argues that the Song of the Sea (Exod 15:1–21) functions as the main transition in the book of Exodus, summarizing, "In short, the Song of the Sea [Exod 15:1–21] both concludes the first half of Exodus [Exod 1:1–14:31] and opens the second half [Exod 15:22–40:38]."[41]

Dozeman also argues that the Song of the Sea (Exod 15:1b–18) functions as the main transition in the book of Exodus:

> The two victory hymns [the Song of the Sea (15:1b–18) and the Song of Miriam (15:21b)] are also pivotal to the structure of Exodus, connecting the two themes of divine power and presence. Exodus 1:1–15:21 explores the power of Yahweh to save the Israelites from Egyptian slavery. The plot is centered on the conflict between Yahweh and Pharaoh and the setting is the land of Egypt. Exodus 15:22–40:38 shifts the theme to the presence of Yahweh with the Israelite people. The plot progresses from the conflict between Yahweh and Pharaoh to the pilgrimage of the Israelite people, and the setting changes from the land of Egypt to the wilderness and the mountain of God. . . . Both hymns celebrate the display of divine power, when Yahweh hurled the horse and its rider into the sea, providing commentary on the exodus. The Song of the Sea, in particular, provides a transition

---

Egger, "Visiting Iniquity," 448–58.

40. Childs, *Exodus*, 252.

41. Propp, *Exodus*, 1:38. Further, he notes, "Exod 15:1b–18 in effect epitomizes the Book of Exodus. It begins with Pharaoh's forces sinking in the Sea and climaxes with Israel's arrival at Yahweh's holy mountain, where God's new abode is constructed and his kingship commences." Propp, *Exodus*, 1:562.

to the theme of divine presence in the second half of Exodus. The final strophe of the hymn, 15:13–18, includes a confession about Yahweh's leading of the Israelites and planting then in the place of divine rule.[42]

Dozeman explains that as the main transitional narrative in the Exodus narrative, Exod 15:1b–18 gives the conclusion of Yahweh's deliverance at the Red Sea (Exod 13:17–14:31) and also the advance announcement of Yahweh's presence at Mount Sinai (Exod 15:22–40:38).

Robert L. Shreckhise also argues for the Song (Exod 15:1–21) as the main transition in the book of Exodus:

> In the Song [Exod 15:1–21], we see that God acts, and his people respond. Moses and Israel looked back at what had been done for them in celebration. They looked forward at what he had promised to do for them in anticipation.... One last time a diagram helps us to picture how the function of the Song as a hinge patterns our own response to the ongoing story of God's ישועה and חסד for his people.[43]

Shreckhise concludes that by concentrating on Yahweh's actions, Exod 15:1–21 looks backward to what Yahweh had done for Israel and also forward to what Yahweh had promised for Israel. Moreover, this Song functions as the turning point of the Exodus narrative from the theme of Yahweh's ישועה to the theme of Yahweh's חסד for Israel.

Similarly, Brian D. Russell argues:

> The Song of the Sea (15:1–21) celebrates Yahweh's victory over the Egyptians and the subsequent guidance of Yahweh's people to the mountain sanctuary at Sinai/Horeb. It stands at the center of the structure and theology of Exodus. It serves as the climax of Exod 1–14 and as an introduction to the themes and movement of Exod 15:22–40:38.[44]

Consequently, when approaching the final form of the Exodus narrative as a two-part narrative, several scholars emphasize Exod 15:1–21 (or 1b–18) as the main transition of the Exodus narrative with key theological themes.

---

42. Dozeman, *Exodus*, 332–33.
43. Shreckhise, "I Will Sing," 244–45.
44. Russell, *Song of the Sea*, 149.

The Role of Exodus 18 as the Main Transition in the Book of Exodus

In spite of the prevalence of the former view, a few other commentators have suggested that Exod 18:1–27 functions as the major transition in the book of Exodus. Carpenter discusses this significant role of Exod 18:1–27:

> It [Exod 18] is a major transitional chapter that serves both as an epilogue (vv. 1–12) to the first half of Exodus (chs. 2–17) and as a prologue (vv. 13–27) to the second half of Exodus (chs. 19–40). It takes up and resolves, gathers and adumbrates major issues on earlier/later chapters.[45]

Carpenter concludes that Exod 18:1–27 is a major transitional account in the Exodus narrative, and that it functions as both the conclusion of its preceding chapters (Exod 2–17) and the introduction of its following chapters (Exod 19–40). By claiming that, Carpenter also observes Exod 18:1–27 as a major transition of the book of Exodus in six specific considerations: (1) it "both unites and divides" the Exodus narrative;[46] (2) it "helps the reader grasp the overall content and meaning of the book";[47] (3) it "helps to emphasize and make clear two ways of knowing Yahweh" by both the exodus account and Yahweh's way through Yahweh's Torah;[48] (4) it "provides a respite (שׁלם is used twice) between two storms" at the Red Sea and Mount Sinai;[49] (5) it "moves all of the actors and action into 'the vicinity of Sinai, the Mountain of God' (18.5)" as the sacred place, where the sacred Torah of Yahweh is given;[50] and (6) its first half (Exod 18:1–12) "brings the exodus deliverance motif of the preceding chapters to a meaningful conclusion (τελός) but also addresses the issues raised by the Midianite traditions, both essential and incidental, found in chs. 2–4"; and its second half (Exod 18:13–27) "points forward to the dissemination of *mišpaṭ* (משׁפט) and therefore, to Sinai."[51]

---

45. Carpenter, "Exodus 18," 107.
46. Carpenter, "Exodus 18," 92.
47. Carpenter, "Exodus 18," 92.
48. Carpenter, "Exodus 18," 92.
49. Carpenter, "Exodus 18," 92–93.
50. Carpenter, "Exodus 18," 93.
51. Carpenter, "Exodus 18," 93.

Carpenter's work has been criticized by Waldemar Janzen,[52] and Janzen gives at least five examples for why he disagrees with Carpenter: (1) the "reciprocity" between Jethro and Moses' role in Exod 2–4 and 18:[53] Janzen argues that in both Midianite accounts, Exod 2–4 and 18, Jethro plays a continuing role as a host to Moses, Aaron, and all the elders of Israel,[54] but Carpenter sees Jethro playing changing roles, first, as a host to Moses in Exod 2–4 and, second, as a guest of Moses in Exod 18;[55] (2) the interpretation of "the tent" (Exod 18:7) "as an anticipation of the Tent of Meeting (= tabernacle) of chaps. 19–40, without any textual or other basis":[56] Janzen suggests "the tent" is simply Moses' tent,[57] but Carpenter approaches "the tent" as the developed tent of meeting in Exod 25–31;[58] (3) the reference of common words in Exod 18:13–27 to Exod 19–40, "such as *špṭ*" (six times in Exod 18:13–27 and nine times in Exod 19–40):[59] Janzen cannot see how a common root שׁפט, "to judge, to govern," refers to Exod 19–40 because it occurs about one hundred and eighty times in the OT,[60] but Carpenter sees it contributing toward a general motif of מִשְׁפָּט, "judgment," along with other key words in Exod 18:13–27, for example, דָּבָר, "speech, word," ידע, "to know," חֹק, "something prescribed, a statute or due," תּוֹרָה, "direction, instruction, law," יעץ, "to advise, to counsel," זהר, "to instruct, to teach, to warn," דֶּרֶךְ, "way, road, distance, journey," and צוה, "to lay charge (upon), to give charge (to), to charge, to command, to order";[61] (4) the significance of "the 10 occurrences of *dābār* in [Exod] 18:13–27" to the Ten Words, the Ten Commandments at Mount Sinai (Exod 20:1):[62] Janzen is not sure that in Exod 18:13–27, the ten uses of the noun דָּבָר, "speech, word," anticipate the Ten Commandments in Exod 20 because of the varied meanings of דָּבָר in Exod 18;[63] and (5) the references of "'statutes' (*ḥuqqîm*) and 'instructions' (*tôrōt*) in

---

52. Janzen, "Jethro," 159–72.
53. Janzen, "Jethro," 168.
54. Janzen, "Jethro," 163–68.
55. Carpenter, "Exodus 18," 100, 106.
56. Janzen, "Jethro," 169n34.
57. Janzen, "Jethro," 166n25.
58. Carpenter, "Exodus 18," 105.
59. Janzen, "Jethro," 169n34. See also Carpenter, "Exodus 18," 104.
60. Janzen, "Jethro," 169n34.
61. Carpenter, "Exodus 18," 99, 104.
62. Janzen, "Jethro," 169n34.
63. Janzen, "Jethro," 169n34.

v. 16; see also v. 20" to the exclusive law at Mount Sinai:[64] Janzen suggests that the two nouns, חֹק, "something prescribed, a statute or due," and תּוֹרָה, "direction, instruction, law," are used "within traditional case law,"[65] that is, they carry a general sense but do not specifically anticipate or allude to God's revelation at Mount Sinai.

Egger also sees Exod 18 (and Exod 15:22–18:27, more generally) as playing a significant role as the major transition in the book of Exodus:

> Thus, Exodus can be seen as a two-part narrative, with the closing chapters of the first movement (15:22–18:27) serving also an intermediate and transitional function as they anticipate major themes to be developed in the second movement [Exod 19–40].[66]

Egger especially emphasizes the concluding function of Exod 18 within Exod 1–18. Three of his twelve observations serve to illustrate: (1) Its focus on "*accomplished deliverance*" serves as "a fitting conclusion to the first narrative arc, recounting and praising not only Yahweh's deliverance of Israel out from Egypt, but also from the hardships encountered in the wilderness."[67] (2) It removes the "undercurrent of ambivalence or even skepticism regarding the departure from Egypt" in Exod 14–17.[68] And (3) it creates "a double inclusio" between Exod 2 and 18: The first inclusio is between Exod 2:13–14 and 18:13–27, which narrate one of Moses' roles as the judge and prince over Israel through the question and the answer, respectively. And the second inclusio is between Exod 2:15–22 and 18:1–12, which narrate the same characters and elements, for example, "Midian, Jethro, Zipporah, son(s); deliverance report; bread."[69]

Consequently, in analyzing the final form of the Exodus narrative as a two-part narrative, a few other commentators underline Exod 18:1–27 as the main transition of the Exodus narrative with key theological themes.

---

64. Janzen, "Jethro," 169n34.
65. Janzen, "Jethro," 169n34.
66. Egger, "Visiting Iniquity," 464.
67. Egger, "Visiting Iniquity," 449.
68. Egger, "Visiting Iniquity," 452–53.
69. Egger, "Visiting Iniquity," 455–58.

The Relationships of Exodus 18 in the Book of Exodus

Various commentators appreciate the literary and theological functions of Exod 18:1–27 by proposing its relationships within the Exodus narrative in different approaches.

The Relationship of Exodus 18 with the Midianite Accounts (Exod 2–4)

Exodus 18 is connected with Exod 2–4 in the account of Moses' judicial role (Exod 2:11–14),[70] in the accounts of Moses' Midianite family (Exod 2:16–22; 4:18–26),[71] and in the account of Yahweh's appearance at Mount Horeb (Exod 3:1–4:17).[72]

Childs specifically comments about the Midianite stories in the Exodus narrative:

> In spite of the complex history of traditions problems which lie behind the Midian stories, these chapters now perform a simple and straightforward function within the Exodus narrative. Chapter 2 pictures the quiet period of preparation. Moses pastures sheep for forty years in the wilderness. It is the quiet before the storm which erupts in ch. 3 and drives him back to Egypt. Now ch. 18 functions as a concluding scene. Once again the writer pictures an idyllic family scene, reminiscent of the patriarchs in Genesis. In ch. 3 Moses had received the sign that he would not only deliver the people, but that he would worship with them on the holy mountain (3.12). Ch. 18 comes to a climax with the common meal which was led by Jethro and shared by Aaron and the elders of the people.[73]

Carpenter, likewise, comments about the Midianite accounts within the book of Exodus by concluding, "It [Exod 18] brings the Midianite foci to a satisfactory conclusion, but signals the continuing contribution

---

70. Fox, *Now These Are the Names*, 99. See also Carpenter, "Exodus 18," 100–101.

71. Noth, *Exodus*, 148–49. See also Wendland, *Exodus*, 118; Alexander, *Exodus*, 345, 348; Carpenter, "Exodus 18," 105.

72. Larsson, *Bound for Freedom*, 123. See also Carpenter, "Exodus 18," 100.

73. Childs, *Exodus*, 327. See also Childs, *Exodus*, 325; Carpenter, "Exodus 18," 91; Carpenter, *Exodus*, 1:603.

to Israel by one of the ancestors of the Midianites, thus opening up room for continued peaceful relationships between the two peoples."[74]

The Relationship of Exodus 18 with the Preceding Chapters (Exod 1–17)

Childs observes that Exod 18:1–12 connects with the previous chapters (Exod 1–17):

> The first part of ch. 18 [Exod 18:1–12] offers a moment of grateful remembrance. It looks back at what has happened and what God has done for Israel. Not yet at least is there any hint of the momentous event of Sinai which lies just ahead. Just for a moment the writer pauses in the story to look backward and to rejoice.[75]

Walter Brueggemann mentions the relationship between Exod 18:8–12 and its previous chapters (Exod 1–17) by reflecting, "The exodus celebration of vv. 8–12 clearly looks back to the exodus and the beginning of the sojourn with its 'hardships.' It exults in God's stunning, sovereign act of liberation."[76]

When considering Exod 18:1–27 as the main transition in the Exodus narrative, Carpenter states, "Exodus 18 is perhaps the major transitional chapter in the book of Exodus, summarizing the past events (Exod. 1–17)."[77]

---

74. Carpenter, "Exodus 18," 107. See also Carpenter, "Exodus 18," 93. For more details on the connection between Exod 2–4 and 18, see Carpenter, "Exodus 18," 100–101, 105–6.

75. Childs, *Exodus*, 327. See also Burns, *Exodus, Leviticus, Numbers*, 137; Wendland, *Exodus*, 121; Houtman, *Exodus*, 2:395, 401; Janzen, *Exodus*, 224; Bailey, *Exodus*, 196–97. Furthermore, Blackburn, *God Who Makes Himself Known*, 77, notes, "In addition, Moses' language of 18:16 concerning 'the statutes of God and his laws' looks back to language already encountered in the wilderness section ('statutes' in 15:25–26 and 'law' in 16:4)."

76. Brueggemann, "Exodus," 1:829.

77. Carpenter, "Exodus 18," 91. See also Carpenter, "Exodus 18," 93, 107; Carpenter, *Exodus*, 1:603; Meyers, *Exodus*, 136; Alexander, *Exodus*, 345, 346; Blackburn, *God Who Makes Himself Known*, 77. For more details on the connection between Exod 1–17 and 18, see Carpenter, "Exodus 18," 101–4, 106–7.

The Relationship of Exodus 18 with the Preceding Scene (Exod 17:8–16)

Umberto Cassuto sees Exod 18:1–27 as a narrative contrast of the previous account (Exod 17:8–16) by saying, "This section [Exod 18:1–27] constitutes an antithesis to what is narrated at the end of the preceding part with regard to the war with the Amalekites [Exod 17:8–16]."[78] In other words, Cassuto sees the contrast between Exod 18:1–27 and 17:8–16 according to "the evolution of the tradition and the arrangement of the sections."[79] First, the evolution of the tradition is concerning the different actions between the Amalekites and the Kenites (or the Midianites), and how Saul, the first Israelite king, let the Kenites depart from among the Amalekites before attacking the Amalekites (1 Sam 15:6).[80] Secondly, the arrangement of the sections highlights various contrasting words between Exod 18:1–27 and 17:8–16, for example, "Then Amalek *came and fought* with Israel" (Exod 17:8) and "Then Jethro, the father-in-law of Moses, with his sons and his wife, *came* to Moses . . ., and they asked one to another about (their) *welfare*" (Exod 18:5, 7).[81]

Besides Cassuto, Sarna considers Exod 18:1–12 as standing in contrast to the previous account (Exod 17:8–16):

> Seen in this light [the friendly relationship between Israel and the Kenites in 1 Sam 15 and Num 24:20–21], the story of the visit of Moses' father-in-law affords a striking contrast between the relationship and behavior toward Israel of the two neighbors, Amalek and the Kenites. The one was viciously hostile and treacherous, the other friendly and helpful. The contrast is heightened by the literary juxtaposition.[82]

---

78. Cassuto, *Exodus*, 211. See also Childs, *Exodus*, 322; Propp, *Exodus*, 1:628, 634; Enns, *Exodus*, 367, 368; White, *Exodus*, 129; Alexander, *Exodus*, 345. Furthermore, a number of scholars acknowledge Exod 17 and 18 as a whole with their literary features (see Robinson, "Israel and Amalek," 16–17; Robinson, "Acknowledging One's Dependence," 139–40; Motyer, *Exodus*, 173).

79. Cassuto, *Exodus*, 211.

80. Cassuto, *Exodus*, 212. See also Sarna, *Exploring Exodus*, 128; Sarna, *Exodus*, 98; Bailey, *Exodus*, 198; Alexander, *Exodus*, 346; Sarna, "Exodus, Book of," *ABD* 2:696.

81. Cassuto, *Exodus*, 212. See also Propp, *Exodus*, 1:634; Enns, *Exodus*, 367; Motyer, *Exodus*, 173; Alexander, *Exodus*, 345–46; Robinson, "Israel and Amalek," 16–17; Robinson, "Acknowledging One's Dependence," 139–40.

82. Sarna, *Exploring Exodus*, 128–29. See also Sarna, *Exodus*, 98; Houtman, *Exodus*, 2:401; Carpenter, *Exodus*, 1:602; Alexander, *Exodus*, 353; Leveen, "Inside Out," 404–5; Reiss, "Jethro the Convert," 90; Sarna, "Exodus, Book of," *ABD* 2:696.

The Relationship of Exodus 18 with the Following Scene (Exod 19–20)

Cassuto explains the connection between Exod 18:1–27 and 19:1–20:21:

> The numerical schematism has a special character in this section [Exod 18:1–27]; it is now mainly based on the number ten. The word דָּבָר *dābhār* ['word', 'thing', 'matter'] occurs again and again in different meanings, particularly in the dialogue between Moses and Jethro, and finally even in the narrative; in all it is found ten times in the singular and once in the plural. Possibly this decade is to be regarded as a preliminary allusion to the Decalogue [עֲשֶׂרֶת הַדְּבָרִים *'ăsereth hadd^ebhārīm*], which is to form the main theme of the next section [Exod 19:1–20:21].[83]

According to the numerical symmetry, Cassuto sees that in Exod 18:1–27, especially in verses 13–27, the text employs the noun דָּבָר, "speech, word," ten times (Exod 18:14, 16, 17, 18, 19 (pl.), 22 [twice], 23, 26 [twice]), in order to allude to the following account, which is the revelation of Yahweh on Mount Sinai with the Decalogue or the Ten Commandments (Exod 20:1–21).

The Relationship of Exodus 18 with the Following Chapters (Exod 19–40)

Cassuto further suggests that Exod 18:1–27 functions as a prologue to the chapters which follow it (Exod 19–24). "With fine artistic understanding, the Torah prefaces the account of the central theme of this part of the Book of Exodus [Exod 18–24] with a prologue, the purpose of which is to prepare the reader's mind for the narrative that follows."[84] Cassuto, thus, considers Exod 18:1–27 as an occasion for Israel and for the reader to prepare their minds for the following great event, the revelation of Yahweh on Mount Sinai with Yahweh's statutes and laws (Exod 19–40).

---

83. Cassuto, *Exodus*, 222. See also Propp, *Exodus*, 1:631; Meyers, *Exodus*, 140; Dozeman, *Exodus*, 407–8; Hamilton, *Exodus*, 282–83; Carpenter, *Exodus*, 1:616; Alexander, *Exodus*, 352; Carpenter, "Exodus 18," 99, 104.

84. Cassuto, *Exodus*, 211. See also Wendland, *Exodus*, 121; Sarna, *Exploring Exodus*, 126, 129; Fox, *Now These Are the Names*, 99, 101; Durham, *Exodus*, 242, 252; Enns, *Exodus*, 373; Carpenter, "Exodus 18," 91, 107; Carpenter, *Exodus*, 1:603, 625. For more details on the connection between Exod 18 and 19–40, see Carpenter, "Exodus 18," 104–5, 106–7.

Brueggemann mentions the relationship between Exod 18:17–23 and its following chapters (Exod 19–40; Deut 1–34) by reflecting, "The judicial initiative of vv. 17–23, by contrast, looks forward to the Sinai covenant and its legal provisions for a covenantal ordering of society in the books of Exodus and Deuteronomy."[85]

Besides Cassuto and Brueggemann, Cornelis Houtman also sees a strong anticipatory function in Exod 18. In particular, Houtman focuses on the roles of Moses in Exod 18:13–27 in connection with the following chapters (Exod 19–40):

> The depiction of the restructuring of the administration of justice (18:13–27) results in a sharp delineation of Moses' position. As the highest judge, he is the mediator between God and man and the lawgiver (18:15–16, 19–20). In short, Moses is given the role he will occupy in Exod. 19ff. The new structure legitimizes his position as mediator and lawgiver, and enables him to devote himself completely to the tasks which, according to Exod. 19ff., will take up all his time.[86]

Thus, Houtman draws attention to the roles of Moses as the mediator and lawgiver of Yahweh for Israel in Exod 18:13–27, which will dominate Exod 19–40.

The Book in the Context of Current Scholarship

The issue of chronology in Exod 18:1–27 in the present form of the book of Exodus discussed above raises an important point. If one accepts that Exod 18 is placed in a non-chronological sequence, why did the author, compiler, or redactor put it in this particular location? Why did they place it after the redemptive events, especially right after the Amalekite battle (Exod 17:8–16) and before the revelatory events at Mount Sinai, especially right before the great revelation of Yahweh on Mount Sinai in the sights of the Israelites (Exod 19:1–15)? Such questions suggest an even more fundamental question this book will raise: As Exod 18 stands, how does it function in the Exodus narrative? This will be the main question for this book.

---

85. Brueggemann, "Exodus," 1:829. See also Childs, *Exodus*, 327; Bailey, *Exodus*, 197; Sarna, "Exodus, Book of," *ABD* 2:696.

86. Houtman, *Exodus*, 2:401. See also Houtman, *Exodus*, 2:395–96; Larsson, *Bound for Freedom*, 123; McEntire, *Struggling with God*, 105.

This book will examine and consider how Exod 18:1–27 functions literarily and theologically as the key transitional midpoint in the Exodus narrative, in dialogue with previous scholarship on the book of Exodus, especially Exod 18.[87]

Carpenter, Durham, and Sarna have divided the Exodus narrative into two,[88] three, and four major sections, respectively. However, in their divisions of the book of Exodus, all of them have pointed to Exod 18 as a significant transitional account.

As discussed above, a number of scholars, including Childs, Propp, Dozeman, Shreckhise, and Russell, consider Exod 15:1–21 as the primary transition in the Exodus narrative. However, other scholars view Exod 18 as functioning in this way. Carpenter and Egger consider Exod 18 and Exod 15:22–18:27, respectively, as the major transition in the Exodus narrative. Regarding Exod 15:1–21, this book will agree that its theological themes are transitional within the Exodus narrative, exhibiting a shift between, for example, Yahweh's victory and sanctuary,[89] Yahweh's liberation and covenant,[90] Yahweh's power and presence,[91] Yahweh's ישועה and חסד

---

87. As clarified above, Cassuto, Childs, Sarna, Durham, Propp, Enns, Stuart, Dozeman, and Carpenter explain that Exod 18:1–27 has been placed intentionally and deliberately in its current place with its literary features and theological themes. For example, Cassuto considers that Exod 18:1–27 as it stands is literarily placed in the book of Exodus, "a literary masterpiece" (see Cassuto, *Exodus*, 3). See also Cassuto, *Exodus*, 211–12; Childs, *Exodus*, 322; Sarna, *Exploring Exodus*, 128–29; Durham, *Exodus*, 242–43; Sarna, *Exodus*, 97–98; Propp, *Exodus*, 1:628; Enns, *Exodus*, 367; Stuart, *Exodus*, 402; Dozeman, *Exodus*, 399–400; Carpenter, *Exodus*, 1:602. Furthermore, Durham approaches that Exod 18:1–27 as recently placed is theologically located in the book of Exodus, "a whole piece of theological literature" (see Durham, *Exodus*, xx). See also Durham, *Exodus*, 252.

88. In Carpenter's view on the division of the book of Exodus in his Exodus commentary, Carpenter divides the book of Exodus into three sections: "The Multiplication, Oppression, and Liberation of Yahweh's people (1:1–15:21); Transition: Testing from the Reed Sea to the Sinai Region (15:22–18:27); Arrival and Encampment at Sinai and Theophany at the Mountain of God (19:1–40:38)" (See Carpenter, *Exodus*, 1:42). However, I think that even though Carpenter broadly recognizes the Exodus narrative as three basic sections, he specifically considers it as a two-part narrative as seen in his article on Exod 18 which emphasizes the two sections of the Exodus narrative with two major theological themes: (1) Yahweh's deliverance and (2) Yahweh's judgment (see Carpenter, "Exodus 18," 98–100).

89. Childs, *Exodus*, 252.

90. Propp, *Exodus*, 1:37–38.

91. Dozeman, *Exodus*, 327.

for Israel,[92] and Yahweh's victory and guidance.[93] This book will confirm that Exod 15:1–21 is itself a significant climax and transition in the Exodus narrative but will also argue that it functions as a key transition *within* the deliverance narrative (Exod 1–17), rather than *between* the two main parts of the Exodus narrative as Exod 18 does. Thus, this book will argue that Exod 15:1–21 is not the main transitional midpoint of the book of Exodus because its songs recount specifically what Yahweh did for Israel at the Red Sea (Exod 15:1–12, 19–21), and, indeed, it does not explicitly reference the preceding redemptive events in Egypt.

In addition to *not* seeing Exod 15:1–21 as the main transitional midpoint in the Exodus narrative, this book will agree with Carpenter and Egger that Exod 18 is the major transition of the book of Exodus, a two-part narrative, relating back to the first half of the book (Exod 1–17) and forward to the second half of the book (Exod 19–40). Exodus 18 is not merely *a* transition but *the key transitional midpoint* in the Exodus narrative. Carpenter argues that Exod 18 functions as a major transition of the Exodus narrative, but this book will go beyond his limited description of how Exod 18 fits in the whole Exodus narrative. Moreover, while this book is in harmony with some of Egger's claims, he only explores briefly how Exod 15:22–18:27 plays a significant role in the Exodus narrative, which causes him to confirm that the Exodus narrative is "a two-part narrative," consisting of Exod 1–18 and 19–40.[94] Therefore, this book will build on Carpenter's work[95] but avoid certain weaknesses, as identified by Janzen above, while also going beyond Egger's work.

Five connections between Exod 18 and the surrounding Exodus narrative have been discussed above: (1) with the introductory scene of the Midianite accounts (Exod 2–4), (2) with the preceding chapters (Exod 1–17), (3) with the preceding violent episode (Exod 17:8–16), (4) with the following revelatory episode (Exod 19–20), and (5) with the following chapters (Exod 19–40).

First, in connection with the introductory scene of the Midianite accounts (Exod 2–4), this book will agree with Childs and Carpenter, as cited above, that Exod 18—which prominently features Jethro, the priest of Midian—serves as a conclusion to the Midianite accounts in Exod 2–4.

---

92. Shreckhise, "I Will Sing," 244–45.
93. Russell, *Song of the Sea*, 149.
94. Egger, "Visiting Iniquity," 445–64.
95. Carpenter, "Exodus 18," 91–108.

Second, in connection with the preceding chapters (Exod 1–17), this book will agree with Childs, Brueggemann, and Carpenter, as cited above, that the first half of the chapter (Exod 18:1–12) summarizes the preceding redemptive events in Exod 1–17 by looking backward to what Yahweh had done for Israel in Egypt, at the Sea, and in the wilderness. Moreover, this book will consider the whole chapter of Exod 18 as the conclusion of the previous chapters (Exod 1–17).

Third, in connection with the preceding scene (Exod 17:8–16), this book will agree with Cassuto, as cited above, that the whole chapter of Exod 18 stands as an intentional contrast with Exod 17:8–16 with the literary characteristics not only the first half of the chapter (Exod 18:1–12) as seeing in Sarna's comment. Moreover, this contrast shows the differences between two neighboring nations, the Amalekites and the Midianites (or the Kenites), in order to describe the Israelite relationships with the Midianites (or the Kenites) as the friendly and peaceful neighbor and the Amalekites as the hostile and violent neighbor.

Fourth, in connection with the following scene (Exod 19–20), this book will agree with Cassuto, as cited above, that in Exod 18:13–27, the ten Hebrew nouns דָּבָר, "speech, word," anticipate and introduce the revelation of Yahweh's words, the Decalogue or the Ten Commandments, on Mount Sinai (Exod 20:1–21). Moreover, it is interesting that two occurrences of the verb דבר, "to speak," appear in prominent places in Exod 20, at the beginning and ending of the Ten Commandments scene, "Then God spoke (דבר) all these words, saying," and "and they [Israel] said to Moses, 'You, speak (דבר) with us, . . .'" (Exod 20:1 and 19, respectively), and also that the plural noun דְּבָרִים occurs at the opening of the Ten Commandments scene, "Then God spoke all these words (הַדְּבָרִים), saying . . ." (Exod 20:1).

And fifth, in connection with the following chapters (Exod 19–40), this book will agree with Cassuto, Brueggemann, and Houtman, as cited above, that the second half of the chapter (Exod 18:13–27) prepares the reader for the following revelatory events in Exod 19–40 by looking forward to what Yahweh is going to do for Israel at Mount Sinai through Yahweh's statutes and laws, and to Moses' central role in these revelatory events. Moreover, this book will consider the whole chapter of Exod 18 as the introduction or preparation of the following chapters (Exod 19–40).

Most significantly, this book will identify Exod 18, rather than Exod 15:1–21, as the key transitional midpoint of the Exodus narrative, because Exod 18 looks backward to all the previous events by concluding, "all which God had done for Moses and for Israel, his people" (Exod 18:1; cf. 18:8, 9) and "all the hardship which had come upon them [Israel] on the way" (Exod 18:8). These two all-encompassing clauses include the redemptive deeds of Yahweh for Israel in the land of Egypt, at the Red Sea, and on the wilderness journey to Mount Sinai, while Exod 15:1–21 recounts only Yahweh's redemptive deeds for Israel at the Red Sea. Moreover, Exod 18 looks forward to following events by introducing the revelation of Yahweh's statutes and laws and the roles of Moses as the mediator, the instructor, and the judge. Thus, Exod 18 as a whole plays a significant role within the Exodus narrative as a dramatic concluding summary of what Yahweh did for Israel in Egypt, at the Red Sea, and in the wilderness (Exod 1–17) and also as a strong anticipation of what Yahweh is going to do for Israel at Mount Sinai (Exod 19–40).

Finally, four purposes define the need for and value of this book.

The first purpose is to explain the location of Exod 18 as it stands in the final form of the book of Exodus. The non-chronological location of Exod 18 is a significant problem in the scholarly discussion that demands explanation. This book will examine and present how the author, compiler, or redactor put it in its present place in the final form of the book of Exodus with its literary features and theological themes within the Exodus narrative in order to exhibit it as the key transitional midpoint in the Exodus narrative.

The second purpose is to orient the reader of the book of Exodus to the importance of Exod 18 in the Exodus narrative. Various major events happen in the book of Exodus which its reader pays attention to and acknowledges, for example, the oppression in the land of Egypt, the birth of Moses, the burning bush at Mount Horeb, the ten plagues in the land of Egypt, the crossing at the Red Sea, the grumblings on the wilderness journey to Mount Sinai, but the typical reader likely regards Exod 18 as a minor episode in comparison to the great revelation of Yahweh at Mount Sinai and the golden calf episode. Thus, this book will help the reader of the book of Exodus realize the account of Exod 18 as one of the significant events in the book of Exodus by exhibiting Exod 18 as the key transitional midpoint in the Exodus narrative.

The third purpose is to exhibit that Yahweh's salvation is not only for the Israelites but also for the Gentiles, all the nations. The book of Exodus narrates the history of Yahweh's people, the Israelites. However, as narrated in the episode of Exod 18, Jethro, the priest of Midian, the father-in-law of Moses, hears of all Yahweh's salvation of the Israelites, comes with Moses' family to meet Moses at Mount Sinai, and directly hears from Moses about all Yahweh's mighty acts of deliverance in the land of Egypt, at the Red Sea, and on the wilderness journey to Mount Sinai. Then Jethro rejoices in, praises, and confesses Yahweh as the greatest and incomparable God, and, finally, worships Yahweh with the Israelite representatives in the presence of Yahweh. Consequently, this book will call attention to the function of Exod 18 in highlighting that Yahweh brings salvation to both the Israelites and the Gentiles, all the nations.

And the fourth purpose is to provide other implications of the account of Exod 18 for scholars, pastors, and even biblical students. Every sermon on Exod 18 which I have heard is preached by using only two implications—(1) the administration among people at church or workplace and (2) the obedience from the godly person's words or advices. This book will demonstrate other possible and proper implications on the account of Exod 18, which are more deeply rooted in the themes and theology of the Exodus narrative.

The Methodological Procedure to Be Employed

This book approaches the present form of the book of Exodus as a whole and, to some extent, as a self-contained story. This approach will employ narrative analysis, which focuses on literary elements including the narrator, the characters, the plot, time and space, and style. Thomas W. Mann introduces his comments on the book of Exodus, "The most important factor in our interpretation of Exodus is the way the text itself forces us to read it as unity."[96] Regarding the Exodus story as a unified narrative, Helmut Utzschneider and Wolfgang Oswald explain, "Notwithstanding the fact that the exodus narrative [Exod 1:1–15:21] has been integrated into the narrative continuum of the Old Testament narrative traditions, there are good literary reasons for viewing and interpreting it as an independent entity."[97] While the book of Exodus is indeed part of a larger

---

96. Mann, *Book of the Torah*, 78. Further, he notes, "The traditioning process has accomplished this by collecting all the material together within one 'book' that renders a narrative without any major divisions. It has also accomplished this unity by a number of critical references both prospective and retrospective." Mann, *Book of the Torah*, 78. See also Egger, "Visiting Iniquity," 324–27.

97. Utzschneider and Oswald, *Exodus 1–15*, 23. Further, they note, "its narrative unity (not 'isolation') finds expression in a series of signals and structures: in the clear opening and concluding signals, which are nevertheless open to those texts that are adjacent to them (to the following texts more than to the preceding); in the theme words, which bridge and permeate the narrative; through the ancient literary form that underlines the narrative; in the narrative's plot." Utzschneider and Oswald, *Exodus*

narrative, the Torah, it also stands as a self-contained unit within that larger narrative, with its own clear beginning (Exod 1:1–7) and end (Exod 40:34–38) and with its coherent plot development and resolution. Thus, it is legitimate and common among recent scholars to analyze the role of the narrative context of Exod 18 within the Exodus narrative, the narrative context of Exod 1–40.

In addition to considering Exod 18 within the final form of the book of Exodus as a whole, a number of scholars discern a literary unit within the book of Exodus and advocate for the theological value of reading it as a unified work. Durham, for example, approaches the book of Exodus as a whole in terms of its theological function:

> The Book of Exodus must be read as a whole. Despite the strands of narrative and legal and sacerdotal source-material that are clearly visible in the forty chapters that make up this book, and despite the fact that it is a compilation whose layers are still at least partly visible and to a degree recoverable, the Book of Exodus must be considered as a whole piece of theological literature, quite deliberately put into the form in which we have it, for very specific purposes.[98]

Moreover, this book will employ narrative analysis, which focuses on literary elements, including the narrator, the characters, the plot, time and space, and style, in order to analyze Exod 18 within the entire Exodus narrative. Shimon Bar-Efrat argues:

> The various historical approaches have undoubtedly contributed greatly to our knowledge of the world and literature of the Bible. The literary approach and methods are no less important than the historical ones, however, since the *being* of biblical narrative is equally as interesting as its *becoming*. Anyone who wishes to study its being must use the avenue of literary analysis, for it is impossible to appreciate the nature of biblical narrative fully, understand the network of its component elements or penetrate into its inner world without having recourse to methods and tools of literary scholarship.[99]

1–15, 23. See also Egger, "Visiting Iniquity," 324–27.

98. Durham, *Exodus*, xx. As the final form of the book of Exodus, Durham urges the reader to consider and read the Exodus narrative as a whole because of its theological role throughout its narrative which is all about Yahweh, for example, the appearance of Yahweh on Mount Sinai to Moses (Exod 3 and 4), to Israel (Exod 19, 20, and 24), and to Moses representing Israel (Exod 32, 33, and 34) (see Durham, *Exodus*, xxi–xxii).

99. Bar-Efrat, *Narrative Art in the Bible*, 10.

To study biblical narrative, one must employ narrative analysis. In other words, this is no less true for the narrative of Exod 18, which can be studied and considered by employing narrative analysis. Greater understanding of Exod 18 will be aided by paying attention to its literary component elements.[100]

This book will then examine Exod 18 as a whole by focusing on several interrelated and overlapping questions based on the main question for this book: As Exod 18 stands, how does it function in the Exodus narrative?

1. What literary elements contribute to the narrative and theology of Exod 18?

2. What is the function of the figure of Jethro in Exod 18 and in the Exodus narrative, and how does this relate to the function of Exod 18 as the key transitional midpoint?

3. How does Exod 18, as a whole, connect with and summarize the previous chapters (Exod 1–17)?

4. How does Exod 18, as a whole, connect with and anticipate the following chapters (Exod 19–40)?

5. Within the consideration of the preceding and following narrative connections, how does Exod 18 serve as the key transitional midpoint for some key narrative themes?

Therefore, this book will acknowledge that, among scholars, the precise transition of the two-part Exodus narrative has always been and will continue to be debatable, and that I am not making the case that Exod 18 is the indisputable and only possible key transition, but rather that its transitional role has often been overlooked, that it is a strong candidate as the key transitional midpoint in the Exodus narrative, and that reading it as such gives rise to important narrative and theological observations.

---

100. Bar-Efrat, *Narrative Art in the Bible*, 10–11. Further, he analyzes biblical narrative with five main literary elements: (1) the narrator, (2) the characters, (3) the plot, (4) time and space, and (5) style (see Bar-Efrat, *Narrative Art in the Bible*, 11). Nevertheless, Fewell and Gunn point to six elements of narrative: (1) plot structure, (2) character, (3) narrator's point of view, (4) language and meaning, (5) irony, and (6) reader's point of view (see Fewell and Gunn, "Narrative, Hebrew," *ABD* 4:1024–27). See also Hawk, "Literary/Narrative Criticism," *DOTP* 539–43.

Chapter 2
An Original Translation and Textual Notes on Exodus 18

THIS CHAPTER WILL PRESENT an original translation and textual notes on Exod 18:1–27, based on the MT. These original translation and textual notes will be used as a background in demonstrating Exod 18 as the key transitional midpoint in the Exodus narrative in terms of both literary features and theological themes.

An Original Translation on Exodus 18

¹ Now, Jethro, the priest of Midian, the father-in-law of Moses, heard all which God had done for Moses and for Israel, his people, that Yahweh had brought Israel out of Egypt. ² Then Jethro, the father-in-law of Moses, took Zipporah, the wife of Moses, after she had been sent away, ³ and her two sons. The name of the one was Gershom because he said, "I have been *a sojourner* in a foreign land," ⁴ and the name of the other was Eliezer because (he said),¹ "The God of my father was my help, and he delivered me from the sword of Pharaoh." ⁵ Then Jethro, the father-in-law of Moses, with his sons and his wife, came to Moses, to the wilderness where he was encamping (at)² the mountain of God,

---

1. This expression is omitted in the MT, but it is added to clarify this sentence (see *GBHS* §5.3.6, 204–5; Williams §582–98, 208–11).

2. The preposition does not appear in the MT, but it is added to clarify this sentence (see *GKC* §118 *d–g*, 373–74).

⁶ and he said to Moses, "I, your father-in-law, Jethro, am coming to you (s.), with your wife and her two sons with her." ⁷ Then Moses went out to meet his father-in-law, and he bowed down, and he kissed him, and they asked one to another (אִישׁ־לְרֵעֵהוּ) about (their)³ welfare (שָׁלוֹם), and they went to the tent. ⁸ Then Moses recounted to his father-in-law all which Yahweh had done to Pharaoh and to the Egyptians because of Israel, (and)⁴ all the hardship which had come upon them on the way; and Yahweh had delivered them! ⁹ Then Jethro rejoiced concerning all the good which Yahweh had done for Israel, whom he had delivered from the hand of the Egyptians. ¹⁰ Then Jethro said, "Blessed be Yahweh who has delivered you (pl.) from the hand of the Egyptians and from the hand of Pharaoh, (and)⁵ who has delivered the people from under the hand of the Egyptians, ¹¹ now, I know that Yahweh is *greater* than all gods, because in the thing (דָּבָר), they acted presumptuously against them." ¹² Then Jethro, the father-in-law of Moses, took a burnt offering and sacrifices to God, and Aaron with all the elders of Israel came to eat bread with the father-in-law of Moses in the presence of God.

¹³ On the next day, Moses sat to judge the people, and the people stood around Moses from morning until evening. ¹⁴ Then the father-in-law of Moses saw all which he was doing for the people, and he said, "What is this thing (דָּבָר) which you (s.) are doing for the people? Why are you (s.) sitting alone and all the people standing around you (s.) from morning until evening?" ¹⁵ Then Moses said to his father-in-law, "The people come to me to inquire of God. ¹⁶ When they have a case (דָּבָר), which comes to me, I judge between one (אִישׁ) and another (רֵעֵהוּ), and I make known the statutes of God and his laws." ¹⁷ Then the father-in-law of Moses said to him, "The thing (דָּבָר) which you (s.) are doing is *not good*. ¹⁸ Both you (s.) and this people who are with you (s.) will surely languish. Because the thing (דָּבָר) is too heavy for you (s.), you (s.) are not able to do it alone. ¹⁹ Now, obey me; I will advise you (s.), and may God be with you (s.). *You* (s.), be as the people in front of God, and, *you* (s.), bring the cases (דָּבָר) to God. ²⁰ Then teach them the statutes and the laws, and make known to them the way in which they should walk and the work which they should do. ²¹ Then, *you* (s.), provide from all the people men of ability who fear God, men of faithfulness who hate unjust gain, and set

---

3. The possessive pronoun does not appear in the MT, but it is added to clarify this sentence.

4. The conjunction does not appear in the MT, but it is added to clarify this sentence.

5. The conjunction does not appear in the MT, but it is added to clarify this sentence.

AN ORIGINAL TRANSLATION AND TEXTUAL NOTES ON EXODUS 18

over them chiefs of thousands, chiefs of hundreds, chiefs of fifties, and chiefs of tens. ²² Then let them judge the people at all times, and it will be that, every great case (דָּבָר), they can bring to you (s.), but every small case (דָּבָר), they can judge themselves, and thus lighten (the load)⁶ from upon you (s.), and they will carry (it)⁷ with you (s.). ²³ If you (s.) do *this thing* (דָּבָר), and God commands you (s.), then you (s.) will be able to endure, and also all this people will go to their place in peace (שָׁלוֹם). ²⁴ Then Moses obeyed his father-in-law, and he did all which he had said. ²⁵ Then Moses chose men of ability from all Israel, and he set them heads over the people, chiefs of thousands, chiefs of hundreds, chiefs of fifties, and chiefs of tens, ²⁶ and thus they kept on judging the people at all times. The hard case (דָּבָר), they would bring to Moses, but every small case (דָּבָר), they would judge themselves. ²⁷ Then Moses sent away his father-in-law, and he went to his own country.

Textual Notes on Exodus 18

Textual notes on Exod 18:1–27 will comment as appropriate verse by verse, and each verse will be divided into two parts according to the *'aṭnaḥ* accent in the MT.⁸

Exodus 18:1

וַיִּשְׁמַ֞ע יִתְר֨וֹ כֹהֵ֤ן מִדְיָן֙ חֹתֵ֣ן מֹשֶׁ֔ה אֵת֩ כָּל־אֲשֶׁ֨ר עָשָׂ֤ה אֱלֹהִים֙⁹ לְמֹשֶׁ֔ה וּלְיִשְׂרָאֵ֖ל עַמּ֑וֹ כִּֽי־הוֹצִ֧יא יְהוָ֛ה אֶת־יִשְׂרָאֵ֖ל מִמִּצְרָֽיִם׃

18:1a וַיִּשְׁמַ֞ע יִתְר֨וֹ כֹהֵ֤ן מִדְיָן֙ חֹתֵ֣ן מֹשֶׁ֔ה אֵת֩ כָּל־אֲשֶׁ֨ר עָשָׂ֤ה אֱלֹהִים֙ לְמֹשֶׁ֔ה וּלְיִשְׂרָאֵ֖ל עַמּ֑וֹ

In the MT, the *qal* imperfect *waw* consecutive form וַיִּשְׁמַע, "now, he heard," is placed in a new line, and its previous line ends with the symbol פ, which is an abbreviation for *pǝtûḥā'*, "open," to indicate the beginning of a new line or paragraph.¹⁰ Because this form stands on its own in a

---

6. The noun does not appear in the MT, but it is added to clarify this sentence.

7. The pronoun does not appear in the MT, but it is added to clarify this sentence.

8. Scott, *Simplified Guide to BHS*, 27–28.

9. A reading of one or several Hebrew manuscripts from the Cairo Geniza and the Greek version of the Old Testament (Septuagint) read the proper noun יהוה, "Yahweh," instead of the noun אֱלֹהִים, "God."

10. Scott, *Simplified Guide to BHS*, 1.

new line, it is used as narratively to introduce an independent narrative or to begin a new section of narrative.[11] Therefore, in this case, the *waw* consecutive וַ is translated "now" to introduce a new section in the Exodus narrative while still maintaining continuity with the preceding section (Exod 17:8–16).

The verb שָׁמַע, "to hear,"[12] occurs three times in Exod 18 (vv. 1, 19, 24). Here the verb שָׁמַע introduces the scene of Jethro's hearing of Yahweh's deliverance of Israel in the land of Egypt, at the Red Sea, and on the wilderness journey to Mount Sinai (Exod 18:1). This function is also consistent with the use of the verb שָׁמַע to mark other important scenes where Yahweh heard Israel's affliction in the land of Egypt (Exod 2:24; 3:7; 6:5) and their grumbling in the wilderness (Exod 16:7, 8, 9, 12).

The verb עָשָׂה, "to do, to make," occurs ten times in Exod 18 (vv. 1, 8, 9, 14 [twice], 17, 18, 20, 23, 24), and here its subject is the noun אֱלֹהִים, "God." In this case, this verb is used in a sense of deliverance by portraying Yahweh's saving and mighty acts for Israel (cf. Exod 18:1, 4, 8, 9, 10).[13] The preposition לְ, "for," is used to indicate for whose advantage Yahweh had acted.[14] In this case, Yahweh acted for the benefit of Moses and Israel.

18:1b כִּי־הוֹצִיא יְהוָה אֶת־יִשְׂרָאֵל מִמִּצְרָיִם׃

The conjunction כִּי, "that," is used as the object of perception, which follows the verb שָׁמַע to describe what Jethro heard. This conjunction introduces its following subordinate or substantival clause הוֹצִיא יְהוָה אֶת־יִשְׂרָאֵל מִמִּצְרָיִם, "Yahweh had brought Israel out of Egypt."[15] This subordinate clause also stands in apposition to its previous noun clause כָּל־אֲשֶׁר

---

11. *GBHS* §3.5.1 (*c*), 99–100. See also *GKC* §111 *f*, 327; Gibson §80, 97–100.

12. Rütersworden, "שָׁמַע; שֵׁמַע; שְׁמוּעָה," *TDOT* 15:259, notes, "1. *With Accusative Object*. a. *General*. The meaing 'hear' (in the sense of auditory perception) is present when the object specifies what is heard." Further, concerning its usages, he notes, "[Š]āma' (*et*) qôl (54 times) means 'hear a sound/noise/voice'," and, "The object of šāma' can also be a subordinate clause, introduced by *kî* or *ʾăšer*. שמע כי expresses a unique deictic cognizance of a report or message. A list, an entire message, or a universally acknowledged act or truth is expressed by שמע אשר." Rütersworden, "שָׁמַע; שֵׁמַע; שְׁמוּעָה," *TDOT* 15:259–60.

13. Ringgren, "עָשָׂה; מַעֲשֶׂה," *TDOT* 11:392, notes, "5. *God as Subject*. Frequently ʿāśâ refers to something God brings to pass in his governance of the world. His doing is characterized by abstract objects describing the nature of his actions."

14. Joüon §133 *d*, 487–89. See also *IBHS* §11.2.10 *d*, 206–9; *GBHS* §4.1.10 (*e.1*), 125; Williams §271 *a*, 107.

15. *GBHS* §4.3.4 (*j*), 164. See also *GKC* §157 *a*, 491; *IBHS* §38.8, 644–46; Joüon §157, 589–91; Williams §451 *a*, 159.

AN ORIGINAL TRANSLATION AND TEXTUAL NOTES ON EXODUS 18

עָשָׂה אֱלֹהִים לְמֹשֶׁה וּלְיִשְׂרָאֵל עַמּוֹ, "all which God had done for Moses and for Israel, his people," in order to clarify what Yahweh had done for Moses and Israel by bringing them out of Egypt.

The *hiphil* of the verb יָצָא, "to cause to go out, to cause to come out" or "to bring out, to lead out," occurs once in Exod 18, and here its subject is the proper noun יהוה, "Yahweh." In this case, this verb is used to describe Yahweh's delivering and powerful acts for Israel (cf. Exod 18:4, 8, 9, 10).[16]

Exodus 18:2

וַיִּקַּח יִתְרוֹ חֹתֵן מֹשֶׁה אֶת־צִפֹּרָה אֵשֶׁת מֹשֶׁה אַחַר שִׁלּוּחֶיהָ׃

18:2a וַיִּקַּח יִתְרוֹ חֹתֵן מֹשֶׁה אֶת־צִפֹּרָה אֵשֶׁת מֹשֶׁה

The verb לָקַח, "to take," occurs twice in Exod 18 (vv. 2, 12), and here its subject is the proper noun יִתְרוֹ, "Jethro." This verb is used here in the sense of leading someone.[17] In this case, it can mean that Jethro leads Zipporah and her two sons "to be united with Moses,"[18] portrayed as "a family reunion."[19]

18:2b אַחַר שִׁלּוּחֶיהָ׃

The clause אַחַר שִׁלּוּחֶיהָ, "after she had been sent away," functions temporally. The noun שִׁלּוּחֶיהָ, "she had been sent away," literally means,

---

16. Preuss, "יָצָא; מוֹצָא; תּוֹצָאוֹת," *TDOT* 6:233, notes, "The clear relationship of *yṣ'* to the description of Yahweh's liberating act begins with the book of Exodus. Yahweh sets his oppressed people free from their slavery in Egypt." See also Preuss, "יָצָא; מוֹצָא; תּוֹצָאוֹת," *TDOT* 6:238. Furthermore, Carpenter, "Exodus 18," 98, notes, "The verb יצא is found in v. 1 (and once in v. 7), then followed by נצל five times as the deliverance of Yahweh is recounted.... יצא and נצל both contain the sibilant צ and the equation of 'going out' (יצא) = 'deliverance' נצל is evident." See also Carpenter, *Exodus*, 1:608.

17. BDB, s.v. לָקַח, 7, 543.

18. Sarna, *Exploring Exodus*, 126, notes that a reason for Jethro to lead Zipporah, Gershom, and Eliezer is "to be reunited with Moses." See also Davis, *Moses and Gods of Egypt*, 197; Durham, *Exodus*, 243; Stuart, *Exodus*, 404; Cohen, "Jethro/Hobab's Detainment," 115; Lawlor, "The 'At-Sinai Narrative," 27. Nevertheless, it is interesting that Houtman notes that because Jethro is impressed by Yahweh and by the blessing upon Yahweh's people, Israel, through hearing all Yahweh's salvation for Israel, "the bringing back of Zipporah and her sons was a means to take up contact with Moses and Israel rather than the purpose of the journey." Houtman, *Exodus*, 2:403.

19. Enns, *Exodus*, 368, notes a simply picture of "a family reunion in the desert." See also Janzen, *Exodus*, 224; Ber, "Moses and Jethro," 158.

"her sending away," and it is derived from the *piel* of the verb שָׁלַח, "to send off, to send away," (cf. Exod 18:27).²⁰ This noun is the construct noun of the noun שִׁלּוּחִים, "sending away, parting gift," with the pronominal suffix third person feminine singular יהָ ֶ , and it occurs once in the book of Exodus (Exod 18:2). The pronominal suffix third person feminine singular יהָ ֶ refers to Zipporah whom Moses had sent away to Jethro, perhaps, before Moses and Aaron went to Pharaoh (cf. Exod 5:1), because the text omits any reference to Zipporah and her sons after the scene of Exod 4:24-26 until here in Exod 18.²¹

Exodus 18:3

וְאֵת שְׁנֵי בָנֶיהָ אֲשֶׁר שֵׁם הָאֶחָד גֵּרְשֹׁם כִּי אָמַר גֵּר הָיִיתִי בְּאֶרֶץ נָכְרִיָּה׃

18:3b אֲשֶׁר שֵׁם הָאֶחָד גֵּרְשֹׁם כִּי אָמַר גֵּר הָיִיתִי בְּאֶרֶץ נָכְרִיָּה׃

The relative pronoun אֲשֶׁר appears in the MT, but it is not translated here. This relative pronoun is used to name two persons, who are גֵּרְשֹׁם, "Gershom," and אֱלִיעֶזֶר, "Eliezer," in a pattern of ... אֲשֶׁר שֵׁם ... וְשֵׁם הָאֶחָד הָאֶחָד, "the name of the one . . ., and the name of the other . . .," so there is no need to translate it.²²

The proper noun ²³גֵּרְשֹׁם appears twice in the book of Exodus (Exod 2:22; 18:3). Here the proper name "Gershom" reappears, which may suggest "a recapitulation of [Exod] 2:22."²⁴

20. Nevertheless, Mendenhall, "Midian," *ABD* 4:816, observes that the noun שִׁלּוּחֶיהָ can mean, "she had been divorced." See also Propp, *Exodus*, 1:629; Ber, "Moses and Jethro," 158–59; Leveen, "Inside Out," 411.

21. It is interesting that the text does not say when Moses sends away Zipporah to Jethro, but among a number of scholars, there are three possibilities: (1) before going back to Egypt (see Kaiser, "Exodus," 2:411; Stuart, *Exodus*, 402, 404–8; Sailhamer, *Pentateuch as Narrative*, 280; Cohen, "Jethro/Hobab's Detainment," 115; Lawlor, "The 'At-Sinai Narrative," 27; Hughes, "Jethro," *DOTP* 468); (2) during the dangerous events in Egypt (see Cassuto, *Exodus*, 213; Sarna, *Exploring Exodus*, 126; Davis, *Moses and Gods of Egypt*, 197; Sarna, *Exodus*, 98; Jacob, *Exodus*, 495; Carpenter, *Exodus*, 1:608; Janzen, *Exodus*, 224); and (3) after going out of Egypt (see Brueggemann, "Exodus," 1:824–25). For different views, see Houtman, *Exodus*, 2:404; Enns, *Exodus*, 367–68.

22. Gibson §12 *Rem.* 2., 11–12.

23. Brueggemann, "Exodus," 1:704, notes, "The term גרשם (*gēršōm*) appears to be a combination of the word גר (*gēr*, 'alien') with the adverb שם (*šām*, 'there'). The narrative, which culminates in the term *alien*, is reinforced by the final word of the narrative, *foreigner* (נכרי *nākĕrî*)." See also Stuart, *Exodus*, 101–2, 404; Dozeman, *Exodus*, 91; Carpenter, *Exodus*, 1:170–71; Leveen, "Inside Out," 399.

24. Van Seters, *Life of Moses*, 210.

The clause כִּי אָמַר גֵּר הָיִיתִי בְּאֶרֶץ נָכְרִיָּה, "because he said, 'I have been *a sojourner* in a foreign land,'" functions causally. In the MT, the subject of the verb אָמַר, "to utter, to say," does not appear here, but in Exod 2:22, the sentence גֵּר הָיִיתִי בְּאֶרֶץ נָכְרִיָּה, "I have been *a sojourner* in a foreign land," had been said first by Moses when Zipporah bore the first son, Gershom. Thus, the subject of the verb אָמַר is Moses who gave the reason or meaning of his first son's name.[25]

Normally, a Hebrew sentence follows the sequence of verb, subject, and prepositional phrase. Here the sentence גֵּר הָיִיתִי בְּאֶרֶץ נָכְרִיָּה is begun with the noun גֵּר, "sojourner," as the subject, and then the noun גֵּר is followed by the verb הָיָה, "to become, to be," and the prepositional phrase בְּאֶרֶץ נָכְרִיָּה, "in a foreign land," respectively. Therefore, the noun [26]גֵּר is used as emphatic, and this emphasizes that Moses as a sojourner was in a foreign land.[27] The unexpressed subject of the verb הָיָה is Moses who spoke about his experience through his first son's name.[28]

---

25. Wagner, "מֵאמַר; מַאֲמָר; אֲמָרָה; אִמְרָה; אֵמֶר; אֹמֶר; אָמַר," *TDOT* 1:332, notes, "2. A Term That Signifies. '*amar* is used in the OT in connection with giving the meaning of something.... It is connected with giving names, by means of which it is possible to understand the nature of a thing or of a person and the relationship of that which is named to the one giving the name and his frame of reference (cf. Gen. 2:23 and the preceding verse, which explains the *vayyo'mer* of v. 23)."

26. Cassuto, *Exodus*, 214, notes, "The word גֵּר *gēr* ['sojourner'] in particular is used, even as God had said to Abraham (Gen. xv 13): 'that your descendants will be sojourners in a land that is not theirs'; and as the brothers of Joseph had said to Pharaoh (Gen. xlvii 4): 'We have come to sojourn in the land.'" See also Sarna, *Exodus*, 12–13.

27. Propp, *Exodus*, 1:177, notes, "Moses' statement also proves to be prophetic. 'Sojourner in a foreign land' would be an eloquent epitaph for one who was a stranger in Egypt, in Midian and in the wilderness, who was never fully accepted by his own people, who died before reaching Canaan and who was buried, not in ancestral soil, but in an unknown grave." See also Houtman, *Exodus*, 1:317–18.

28. A number of scholars comment on naming Moses' sons, reflecting on his spiritual and physical life: (1) regarding Moses' spiritual life, Davis, *Moses and Gods of Egypt*, 197, notes, "The names which Moses gave to his two sons born to him in Midian probably reflects something of his spiritual experiences while in that land." And (2) concerning Moses' physical life, Brueggemann, "Exodus," 1:825, notes, "The name of the two sons together witness to the shape and destiny of Moses' life." See also Leveen, "Inside Out," 399, 401, 406; Reiss, "Jethro the Convert," 90–91; Hughes, "Jethro," *DOTP* 468. Furthermore, the names of Moses' sons do not merely portray the experience of Moses but also the experience of Israel. Brueggemann, "Exodus," 1:825, notes, "The name of each son is essential to the characterizations of both Moses and Israel, a people that is both 'alien' (גר *gēr*) and 'helped' (עזר *'āzar*)." Further, Janzen, *Exodus*, 225, notes, "In [Exod] 2:23–25, Moses' rescue was contrasted with Israel's continued slavery. In retrospect, the names of the two sons characterize Moses' experience and also embrace Israel's story of salvation." See also Janzen, *Exodus*, 227.

The adjective נָכְרִיָּה, "foreign," is the feminine adjective of the adjective נָכְרִי, "foreign, alien," which occurs three times in the book of Exodus (Exod 2:22; 18:3; 21:8), and here it modifies the noun אֶרֶץ, "land." "A foreign land" which Moses mentioned is either the land of Egypt where Moses as an Israelite (cf. Exod 2:1, 6) was born (cf. Exod 2:2) and grew up (cf. Exod 2:10, 11) or the land of Midian where Moses as an Egyptian (cf. Exod 2:19) stayed with Jethro (cf. Exod 2:21), married Zipporah (cf. Exod 2:21), and had sons (cf. Exod 2:22; 4:20).[29]

Exodus 18:4

וְשֵׁם הָאֶחָד אֱלִיעֶזֶר כִּי־אֱלֹהֵי אָבִי בְּעֶזְרִי וַיַּצִּלֵנִי מֵחֶרֶב פַּרְעֹה׃

18:4a וְשֵׁם הָאֶחָד אֱלִיעֶזֶר

The proper noun אֱלִיעֶזֶר, "Eliezer," occurs once in the book of Exodus (Exod 18:4). Like the name of his other son, the appearance of the proper name "Eliezer" is important as a review of Moses' experience and exhibits the accomplishment of Yahweh's promises through Moses's life.[30]

18:4b כִּי־אֱלֹהֵי אָבִי בְּעֶזְרִי וַיַּצִּלֵנִי מֵחֶרֶב פַּרְעֹה׃

The clause כִּי־אֱלֹהֵי אָבִי בְּעֶזְרִי וַיַּצִּלֵנִי מֵחֶרֶב פַּרְעֹה, "because (he said), 'The God of my father was my help, and he delivered me from the sword of Pharaoh,'" functions causally. The construct noun and the noun with the pronominal suffix first person common singular אֱלֹהֵי אָבִי, "the God of my father," occur twice in the book of Exodus (Exod 15:2; 18:4), and the pronominal suffix first person common singular י, "my," refers to

---

29. Among many commentators, there are two explanations concerning "a foreign land": (1) "a foreign land" refers to the land of Egypt because "The 'land' is Egypt, not Midian, and Moses speaks of 'there' not 'here,' [a composite of *ger sham*, 'a stranger there'] as well as referring to the past." Sarna, *Exodus*, 13. See also Cassuto, *Exodus*, 214; Durham, *Exodus*, 243; Jacob, *Exodus*, 42; Brueggemann, "Exodus," 1:704; Janzen, *Exodus*, 224; Leveen, "Inside Out," 402. And (2) "a foreign land" refers to the land of Midian because of the two etiologies of the name "Gershom": (a) "Gershom includes the consonants of the verb 'to drive out' (*gāraš*), the action of the shepherds against the daughters of Reuel, prompting the rescue of Moses"; and (b) Moses' status is "as a resident alien in Midian." Dozeman, *Exodus*, 91. See also Davis, *Moses and Gods of Egypt*, 197; Enns, *Exodus*, 368.

30. As seeing the significance of the first appearance of Eliezer's name and description, Janzen, *Exodus*, 225, notes, "His [Eliezer's] name, not mentioned till now, completes the story of Moses' salvation." See also Dozeman, *Exodus*, 402; Van Seters, *Life of Moses*, 210.

Moses who reflected on his experience through the vehicle of his second son's name.³¹ However, the first time which refers to the God of Moses' father occurs in Exod 3:6 in the construct noun and the noun with the pronominal suffix second person masculine singular אֱלֹהֵי אָבִיךָ, "the God of your father," instead, and it refers to the God of Abraham, Isaac, and Jacob (cf. Exod 3:15, 16; 4:5). Therefore, Moses' "father" is Abraham, Isaac, and Jacob.³²

The preposition בְּ, here translated as "was," commonly means, "in." This preposition is used as essence to describe the predicate between two nouns, which are אֱלֹהֵי אָבִי, "the God of my father," and עֶזְרִי, "my help."³³ The noun with the pronominal suffix first person common singular עֶזְרִי, "my help," occurs once in the book of Exodus (Exod 18:4), and it reflects on Moses' relationship to the God of his "father."

The *hiphil* of the verb נָצַל, "to snatch away, to deliver," occurs eleven times in the book of Exodus (Exod 2:19; 3:8; 5:23 [twice]; 6:6; 12:27; 18:4, 8, 9, 10 [twice]), and here its subject is the construct noun and the noun with the pronominal suffix first person common singular אֱלֹהֵי אָבִי. The object of the *hiphil* of the verb נָצַל is indicated by the object suffix first person common singular נִי, "me," and it refers to Moses who gave the reason or meaning of his second son's name.³⁴

The noun חֶרֶב, "sword," occurs eight times in the book of Exodus (Exod 5:3, 21; 15:9; 17:13; 18:4; 20:25; 22:24; 32:27). "The sword of Pharaoh"³⁵ which Moses mentioned refers to the event in which Moses

---

31. See n28.

32. The divine name, "the God of my father," recalls the revelation of Yahweh at the burning bush at Mount Horeb where Yahweh first makes himself known to Moses (Exod 3:6) (see Cassuto, *Exodus*, 214; Childs, *Exodus*, 327; Dozeman, *Exodus*, 402). Furthermore, this divine name recalls the revelation of Yahweh in the book of Genesis when Yahweh gives his promises to Abraham, Isaac, and Jacob. Carpenter, *Exodus*, 1:609, notes, "'The God of my father' indicates the connection between the God who cared for Moses and delivered Israel, but who was the God who preserved and gave the promises that are now being realized to Abraham, Isaac, and Jacob. The events of the book of Exodus cannot be understood even in part without the connections the author-editor establishes with Genesis."

33. Williams §249, 100. See also Davidson §101 *Rem. 1.* (*a*), 139; GKC §119 i, 379; Joüon §133 *c*, 486–87; Gibson §118 (*c*) *Rem. 2.*, 149–50; GBHS §4.1.5 (*h*), 119; Williams §564, 199.

34. See n25.

35. In connection between the sword of Pharaoh and the hand of Pharaoh, Cassuto, *Exodus*, 214, notes, "This statement of Moses [the explanation of the second son's name] is well suited to our chapter [Exod 18:1–27], which uses the expression 'delivered' a number of times, and once in particular in connection with Pharaoh (v. 8: 'and

had fled from Pharaoh who sought to kill Moses after Pharaoh heard that Moses had killed an Egyptian (cf. Exod 2:11–15).[36]

Exodus 18:5

וַיָּבֹא יִתְרוֹ חֹתֵן מֹשֶׁה וּבָנָיו וְאִשְׁתּוֹ אֶל־מֹשֶׁה אֶל־הַמִּדְבָּר אֲשֶׁר־הוּא חֹנֶה שָׁם הַר הָאֱלֹהִים׃

18:5b אֶל־הַמִּדְבָּר אֲשֶׁר־הוּא חֹנֶה שָׁם הַר הָאֱלֹהִים׃

The noun מִדְבָּר, "wilderness," occurs twenty-seven times in the book of Exodus (Exod 3:1, 18; 4:27; 5:1, 3; 7:16; 8:27, 28; 13:18, 20; 14:3, 11, 12; 15:22 [twice]; 16:1, 2, 3, 10, 14, 32; 17:1; 18:5; 19:1, 2 [twice]; 23:31). Here "the wilderness" refers to the area which "encompasses Israel's experiences from the crossing of the Red Sea to its arrival at the mount of God (Ex. 3:12; 4:27; 18:5; 19:2)."[37]

The construct and proper nouns הַר הָאֱלֹהִים, "the mountain of God," occur four times in the book of Exodus (Exod 3:1; 4:27; 18:5; 24:13). Exodus 3:1 identifies the name of the mountain of God, and the mountain of God is called, "Horeb" (cf. Exod 17:6; 33:6) or "Sinai" (cf. Exod 19:11, 18, 20, 23; 24:16; 31:18; 34:2, 4, 29, 32) where Yahweh is present.[38]

---

how the Lord had delivered them'; *v.* 9: 'in that He had delivered them out of the hand of the Egyptians'; *v.* 10: 'who has delivered you out of the hands of the Egyptians and out of the hand of Pharaoh')."

36. Kaiser, "Exodus," 2:413. See also Davis, *Moses and Gods of Egypt*, 197; Durham, *Exodus*, 243; Jacob, *Exodus*, 495; Houtman, *Exodus*, 2:405; Carpenter, *Exodus*, 1:609. Furthermore, the reference of delivering from the sword of Pharaoh does not only point to Moses' experience of fleeing from Pharaoh in Exod 2:15 but also to the Israelites' experience of being brought out of Egypt (see Sarna, *Exodus*, 98; Brueggemann, "Exodus," 1:825; Enns, *Exodus*, 368).

37. Talmon, "מִדְבָּר; עֲרָבָה," *TDOT* 8:111. Further, he notes, "The finale and high point of this period are God's covenant with Israel 'on the third new moon [stereotypical time frame] after the Israelites had gone out of the land of Egypt' (Ex. 19:1ff.), the Sinai theophany, and the giving of the law (Ex. 20:1ff.; 34:27ff.; Dt. 5)." Talmon, "מִדְבָּר; עֲרָבָה," *TDOT* 8:111.

38. Durham, *Exodus*, 243. See also Talmon, "הַר; גִּבְעָה," *TDOT* 3:443–44; Kaiser, "Exodus," 2:411; Sarna, *Exodus*, 14; Jacob, *Exodus*, 495–96; Houtman, *Exodus*, 2:405; Propp, *Exodus*, 1:629; Janzen, *Exodus*, 224; Stuart, *Exodus*, 402. Furthermore, many commentators see the four connections of the usage of "the mountain of God" within the Exodus narrative: (1) where Yahweh first revealed himself to Moses at the burning bush (Exod 3:1); (2) where Moses met Aaron before going back to Egypt (Exod 4:27); (3) where Moses was encamping (Exod 18:5); and (4) where Yahweh will give Moses the law and the commandment (Exod 24:13). They agree that these four references of the mountain of God in the Exodus narrative are the same place (see Cassuto, *Exodus*,

Exodus 18:6

וַיֹּאמֶר֙[39] אֶל־מֹשֶׁ֔ה אֲנִ֛י[40] חֹתֶנְךָ֥ יִתְר֖וֹ בָּ֣א אֵלֶ֑יךָ וְאִ֨שְׁתְּךָ֔ וּשְׁנֵ֥י בָנֶ֖יהָ עִמָּֽהּ׃

18:6b וְאִ֨שְׁתְּךָ֔ וּשְׁנֵ֥י בָנֶ֖יהָ עִמָּֽהּ׃

The conjunction וְ, "with," commonly means, "and." This conjunction is used as accompaniment to describe with whom Jethro is coming to Moses.[41] In this case, Jethro with Moses' wife and two sons is coming to Moses.

Exodus 18:7

וַיֵּצֵ֨א מֹשֶׁ֜ה לִקְרַ֣את חֹֽתְנ֗וֹ וַיִּשְׁתַּ֙חוּ֙[42] וַיִּשַּׁק־ל֔וֹ וַיִּשְׁאֲל֥וּ אִישׁ־לְרֵעֵ֖הוּ לְשָׁל֑וֹם וַיָּבֹ֖אוּ[43] הָאֹֽהֱלָה׃

18:7a וַיֵּצֵ֨א מֹשֶׁ֜ה לִקְרַ֣את חֹֽתְנ֗וֹ וַיִּשְׁתַּ֙חוּ֙ וַיִּשַּׁק־ל֔וֹ וַיִּשְׁאֲל֥וּ אִישׁ־לְרֵעֵ֖הוּ לְשָׁל֑וֹם

214–15; Durham, *Exodus*, 243; Jacob, *Exodus*, 495–96; Janzen, *Exodus*, 224; Stuart, *Exodus*, 409; Carpenter, *Exodus*, 1:609). Interestingly, Durham, *Exodus*, 243, notes that the mountain of God is "the mountain of the supreme revelation of Yahweh's Presence." See also Houtman, *Exodus*, 2:405; Enns, *Exodus*, 369.

39. The Greek version of the Old Testament (Septuagint) and the Syriac version of the Old Testament read the *qal* imperfect *waw* consecutive form וַיֹּאמֶר in the passive voice, "and it was said," instead of the active voice, "and he said."

40. The Samaritan Pentateuch, the Greek version of the Old Testament (Septuagint), and the Syriac version of the Old Testament read the demonstrative particle הִנֵּה, "behold," instead of the independent personal pronoun אֲנִי, "I."

41. Williams §436, 154. See also *GKC* §154 *a*, 484n1; *GBHS* §4.3.3 (*b*), 157.

42. The Samaritan Pentateuch reads the *hishtaphel* imperfect *waw* consecutive third person masculine plural form with the preposition with the proper noun, וישתחו למשה, "and they bowed down to Moses," instead of the *hishtaphel* imperfect *waw* consecutive third person masculine singular form וַיִּשְׁתַּחוּ, "and he bowed down." The third person masculine plural refers to Jethro, Zipporah, and her two sons who bowed down to Moses.

43. The Samaritan Pentateuch, *codex Vaticanus*, *codex Coislinianus*, and *codices minusculis scripti* read the *hiphil* imperfect *waw* consecutive form with the object suffix third person masculine singular וַיְבִאֵהוּ, "and he brought him," (*codex Alexandrinus*, *codex Ambrosianus*, and *codices minusculis scripti* read the object suffix in plural, "and he brought them") instead of the *qal* imperfect *waw* consecutive form וַיָּבֹאוּ, "and they went." The subject of the *hiphil* of the verb בּוֹא, "to bring in, to bring," is Moses. The object suffix third person masculine singular הוּ, "him," refers to Jethro, but the object suffix plural, "them," refers to Jethro, Zipporah, and her two sons.

The preposition with the *qal* infinitive construct form לִקְרַאת, "to meet," is used as purpose to describe why Moses went out.⁴⁴ Therefore, in this case, Moses went out to meet Jethro.⁴⁵

The subject of the verbal form וַיִּשְׁתַּחוּ, "and he bowed down," is the proper noun מֹשֶׁה, "Moses." Thus, in this case, Moses bowed down to Jethro, his father-in-law.⁴⁶

The *qal* imperfect *waw* consecutive form with the preposition with the pronominal suffix third person masculine singular וַיִּשַּׁק־לֹו, "and he kissed him," is derived from the verb נָשַׁק, "to kiss."⁴⁷ In this case, Moses' action of kissing recalls and parallels the action in Exod 4:27 when Moses met and kissed Aaron at the mountain of God.⁴⁸

---

44. *GBHS* §3.4.1 (c), 83. See also *GKC* §114 *f–h*, 348; *IBHS* §36.2.3 *c–d*, 606–8; Joüon §124 *l*, 436–37; Williams §197, 83.

45. Significantly, Fretheim sees Jethro as the representative of Moses' family, including Zipporah and her two sons whom the narrator drops into the background (see Fretheim, *Exodus*, 196). See also Stuart, *Exodus*, 409. As pointing to the reaction of Moses, Jacob considers Moses' action as "an honor" to Jethro (see Jacob, *Exodus*, 496). Furthermore, commentators approach a parallel between Moses' meeting with Jethro (Exod 18:7–8) and with Aaron (Exod 4:27–28). Enns, *Exodus*, 369, notes, "The meeting between Moses and Jethro in verses 7–8 should jar our memory a bit. Moses here experiences a second reunion with a family member in the desert (cf. the reunion with Aaron in 4:27–28). Moses kisses his father-in-law, just as earlier he kissed Aaron. There is a fine literary (chiastic) symmetry here. As Moses had earlier met the Lord at Mount Horeb and then left, meeting Aaron in the desert, here he meets another relative, which is then followed by the climatic encounter with God on the mountain. Also, 4:28 parallels somewhat 18:8–9: In both places, Moses recounts 'everything' God has done or said." Further, Dozeman, *Exodus*, 402, notes, "Moses' meeting with Jethro recalls his rendezvous with Aaron in 4:27–31. Both stories take place in the wilderness at the mountain of God (4:27; 18:5). The encounter includes a kiss (4:27; 18:7). And in each case Moses recounts a past experience of God to a family member. But the parallel between the two stories ceases when Moses leads Jethro into 'the tent.'"

46. Preuss, "חוה; הִשְׁתַּחֲוָה," *TDOT* 4:251, notes, "One person would bow before another to greet him respectfully or to acknowledge his higher rank (Gen. 18:2; 19:1 [in both passages, however, it is ultimately Yahweh with whom Abram is dealing; cf. Nu. 22:31; Josh 5:14, the angel of Yahweh and the commander of the army of Yahweh]; but cf. also Gen. 23:7; 24:26; 33:3, 6f.; Ex. 4:31; 11:8; 18:7—common in all the pentateuchal sources)."

47. Beyse, "נָשַׁק; נְשִׁיקָה," *TDOT* 10:74–75, notes, "b. *Kinship*. Kissing as a sign of bonds of kinship takes up considerable space, such bonds being especially underscored when taking leave or seeing one another again.... The occasion of reunion, usually after a longer separation, is also a situation at which one exchanges kisses ([Gen] 33:4: Jacob and Esau; 45:15: Joseph and his brothers; Ex. 4:27: Moses and his brother Aaron; Ex. 18:7: Moses and his father-in-law Jethro; 2 S. 14:33b: David and his son Absalom after the latter's flight and exile)."

48. See n45.

The subject of the verb שָׁאַל, "to ask, to inquire," refers to Moses and Jethro. The noun phrase אִישׁ־לְרֵעֵהוּ, translated here as "one to another," literally means, "a man to his friend."[49] The noun שָׁלוֹם, "completeness, soundness, welfare, peace,"[50] occurs three times in the book of Exodus (Exod 4:18; 18:7, 23). Therefore, in this case, Moses and Jethro asked one to another about their welfare.[51]

18:7b וַיָּבֹאוּ הָאֹהֱלָה׃

The noun אֹהֶל, "tent," occurs sixty-two times in the book of Exodus. This tent is Moses' tent[52] and possibly anticipates the tent of meeting (cf. Exod 33:7) and the tabernacle (cf. Exod 40:18).[53]

Exodus 18:8

וַיְסַפֵּר מֹשֶׁה לְחֹתְנוֹ אֵת כָּל־אֲשֶׁר עָשָׂה יְהוָה לְפַרְעֹה וּלְמִצְרַיִם עַל אוֹדֹת יִשְׂרָאֵל אֵת[54] כָּל־הַתְּלָאָה אֲשֶׁר מְצָאָתַם בַּדֶּרֶךְ וַיַּצִּלֵם יְהוָה׃

---

49. BDB, s.v. אִישׁ, 35–36. Furthermore, Jacob, *Exodus*, 497, notes, "*Ish l're-e-hu* as equal friends."

50. BDB, s.v. שָׁלוֹם, 3, 1022–23. Furthermore, Carpenter, *Exodus*, 1:609, notes, "The word שָׁלוֹם is used three times in Exodus (4:18; 18:7, 23). All of the usages are in the Midianite material and communicate the שָׁלוֹם that existed between Moses and Jethro [Exod 4:18; 18:7], and hence between Israel, her God, and Jethro [Exod 18:23]." See also Carpenter, "Exodus 18," 106.

51. Fuhs, "שָׁאַל; שְׁאֵלָה; שְׁאֵלָה; מָשׁאוּל," *TDOT* 14:255–56, notes, "b. *šā'al (lᵉ)šālôm*. In connection with a greeting, the formulaic expression *šā'al lᵉšālôm* inquires how a person is doing. Whereas the greeting asks directly about the *šālôm*, in the inquiry this occurs indirectly. Such a query aims at establishing community. Unlike a greeting, an inquiry regarding a person's welfare is never merely noncommittal, always expressing rather a person's sincere concern for the life and fate of the person addressed.... In Ex. 18:7 mutual inquiry concerning the *šālôm* ends a phase of burdened relationships between Moses and Jethro." Furthermore, Carpenter, *Exodus*, 1:609, notes, "'The other's welfare' (לְרֵעֵהוּ לְשָׁלוֹם) indicates the continuing peace (שָׁלוֹם) that existed between them [Moses and Jethro]."

52. Cassuto, *Exodus*, 215. See also Childs, *Exodus*, 328; Sarna, *Exploring Exodus*, 126; Durham, *Exodus*, 244; Jacob, *Exodus*, 497; Janzen, *Exodus*, 226. Further, Propp considers the tent as "Moses' home" (see Propp, *Exodus*, 1:630).

53. Carpenter, "Exodus 18," 99, 105. See also Fretheim, *Exodus*, 196; Stuart, *Exodus*, 410; Dozeman, *Exodus*, 402–3; Carpenter, *Exodus*, 1:609–10.

54. A reading of one or several Hebrew manuscripts from the Cairo Geniza, a few *codices manuscripti*, the Greek version of the Old Testament (Septuagint), the Syriac version of the Old Testament, and the Vulgate read the conjunction with the direct object marker וְאֵת, "and," instead of the direct object marker אֵת.

18:8a וַיְסַפֵּר מֹשֶׁה לְחֹתְנוֹ אֵת כָּל־אֲשֶׁר עָשָׂה יְהוָה לְפַרְעֹה וּלְמִצְרַיִם עַל אוֹדֹת יִשְׂרָאֵל

The *piel* of the verb סָפַר, "to recount, to relate," occurs only four times in the book of Exodus (Exod 9:16; 10:2; 18:8; 24:3). Here Moses recounted to Jethro all Yahweh's deliverance of Israel.[55]

The noun clause כָּל־אֲשֶׁר עָשָׂה יְהוָה לְפַרְעֹה וּלְמִצְרַיִם עַל אוֹדֹת יִשְׂרָאֵל, "all which Yahweh had done to Pharaoh and to the Egyptians because of Israel," is Moses' brief speech as a summary of all Yahweh's redemptive deeds for Israel[56] in the land of Egypt and at the Red Sea, including saving Israelite children through the Hebrew midwives (cf. Exod 1:15–22), saving the child Moses through his mother and Pharaoh's daughter (cf. Exod 2:1–10), and saving Israel from Pharaoh and the Egyptians throughout the ten plagues in Egypt (cf. Exod 7:14–12:36) and through the crossing of the Red Sea (cf. Exod 14:1–31).[57]

---

55. Conrad, "סָפַר; מִסְפָּר," *TDOT* 10:312, notes, "The most frequent content of such recounting, however, is Yahweh's mighty salvific deeds; this is especially the case in the psalms. Such recounting is not, however, a simple retelling in the sense of a reporting of one's experiences (so in Ex. 18:8). The salvific deeds one has either experienced oneself or learned from tradition are related in order to evoke and proclaim Yahweh's salvific activity in the broader sense. This means, however, that Yahweh is praised, and such recounting is thus commensurately attested especially in hymnic (in part usually eschatological) statements (Ps. 75:2[1]; 96:3 [= 1 Ch. 16:24]; Ps. 145:6 [emended text], then expressly as a statement regarding the future in Ps. 102:[19], 22[(18), 23]; cf. Isa. 43:21), and especially in the vow of the individual as an element of the thanksgiving hymn and related statements (cohortative in the sg. Ps. 9:2, 15[1, 14]; 22:23[22]; 66:16; Sir. 51:1 [cf. Ps. 26:7]; Ps.71:15; 73:28 [here also as a defense against being tempted to speak blasphemously about God, v. 15; cf. vv. 8–11]; 118:17; jussive in the pl. in 107:22; differently in the lament; 88:12[11])." Nevertheless, as approaching the fulfillment of Yahweh's declaration on his name recounted in all the earth, Carpenter, *Exodus*, 1:612, notes, "'Then Moses recounted' employs the verb וַיְסַפֵּר. It signals the fulfillment of Yahweh's goal reported in [Exod] 9:16, in the prologue to the seventh plague, that his name would be 'recounted' (סַפֵּר שְׁמִי) in all the earth. In Exod 10:2 (cf. 12:26–28; 13:14–16) Yahweh desires that the parents tell (סַפֵּר) their children how Yahweh performed his signs among the Egyptians to deliver Israel. The verb is used in modern Heb. in the piel emphatic form to report a narrative of events. . . . Based on Jethro's reaction, Moses recounted orally essentially what we now read in Exod 1–17. Similarly, Moses delivered an account of Yahweh's deliverance of his laws to him at Sinai (24:3)."

56. Brueggemann, "Exodus," 1:825, notes, "Moses' brief speech is an abbreviated form of the narrative credo recital of Israel (v. 8)." See also Dozeman, *Exodus*, 403.

57. The words "all which Yahweh had done to Pharaoh and to the Egyptians because of Israel" highlight all Yahweh's salvation of Israel, especially punishing Pharaoh and the Egyptians in the land of Egypt and at the Red Sea. See also Childs, *Exodus*, 328; Jacob, *Exodus*, 497.

The subject of the verb עָשָׂה, "to do, to make," is the proper noun יְהוָה, "Yahweh." In this case, this verb is used in a sense of judgment by portraying Yahweh's delivering and powerful deeds for Israel to judge Pharaoh and the Egyptians (cf. Exod 18:1, 4, 8, 9, 10).

18:8b אֵת כָּל־הַתְּלָאָה אֲשֶׁר מְצָאָתַם בַּדֶּרֶךְ וַיַּצִּלֵם יְהוָה:

The noun clause כָּל־הַתְּלָאָה אֲשֶׁר מְצָאָתַם בַּדֶּרֶךְ, "all the hardship which had come upon them on the way," is Moses' concise word as a conclusion of all Yahweh's redemptive deeds for Israel[58] on the wilderness journey to Mount Sinai, including delivering Israel from the lack of water at Marah (cf. Exod 15:22–25), from the lack of food (cf. Exod 16:1–36), from the lack of water at Massah and Meribah (cf. Exod 17:1–7), and from the war with the Amalekites (cf. Exod 17:8–16).[59]

The noun תְּלָאָה, "weariness, hardship,"[60] occurs once in the book of Exodus (Exod 18:8). "The hardship" includes thirst, hunger, thirst, and war during the wilderness journey.[61] The verb מָצָא, "to attain to, to find," occurs once in Exod 18 (v. 8), and here its subject is the noun הַתְּלָאָה, "the hardship." According to the BDB, when this verb is used with the noun תְּלָאָה as its subject, it means, "to come upon, to light upon."[62]

The *hiphil* imperfect *waw* consecutive form with the object suffix third person masculine plural וַיַּצִּלֵם, "and he had delivered them," is used as epexegetical to clarify its preceding clauses.[63] In this case, this form clarifies the two preceding noun clauses, כָּל־אֲשֶׁר עָשָׂה יְהוָה לְפַרְעֹה וּלְמִצְרַיִם עַל אוֹדֹת יִשְׂרָאֵל and כָּל־הַתְּלָאָה אֲשֶׁר מְצָאָתַם בַּדֶּרֶךְ. The *hiphil* of the verb נָצַל, "to snatch away, to deliver," occurs five times in Exod 18 (vv. 4, 8, 9, 10 [twice]), and here its subject is the proper noun יְהוָה.[64] The object of

---

58. See n56.

59. The words "all the hardship which had come upon them on the way" emphasize all Yahweh's salvation of Israel, especially providing water, food, water, and victory on the wilderness journey to Mount Sinai. See also Propp, *Exodus*, 1:630. Nevertheless, other scholars include the crossing at the Sea. For example, Cassuto comments that all the hardship refers to the events "after the exodus from Egypt—the pursuit of the Egyptians, the division of the Sea of Reeds, the lack of water, the dearth of food, and the war with Amalek" (see Cassuto, *Exodus*, 215). See also Childs, *Exodus*, 328; Kaiser, "Exodus," 2:412; Jacob, *Exodus*, 497.

60. For further study on the noun תְּלָאָה, see Lerner, "Redefining התלאה," 402–11.

61. Propp, *Exodus*, 1:630. See also n59.

62. BDB, s.v. מָצָא, 3e, 593.

63. *GBHS* §3.5.1 (*d*), 100. See also *IBHS* §33.2.2 *a*, 551; Joüon §118 *j*, 392–93.

64. As considering Yahweh as the subject of the verb נָצַל, Houtman, *Exodus*, 2:407, notes, "YHWH always proved himself Israel's saviour." See also Stuart, *Exodus*, 411.

the *hiphil* of the verb נָצַל is indicated by the object suffix third person masculine plural ם ֵ, "them," and it refers to Israel. Therefore, in this case, Yahweh delivered Israel both from the oppression and death in Egypt and at the Red Sea and from the hardship in the wilderness.

Exodus 18:9

וַיִּחַדְּ[65] יִתְרוֹ עַל כָּל־הַטּוֹבָה אֲשֶׁר־עָשָׂה יְהוָה לְיִשְׂרָאֵל אֲשֶׁר הִצִּילוֹ מִיַּד מִצְרָיִם:

18:9a וַיִּחַדְּ יִתְרוֹ עַל כָּל־הַטּוֹבָה אֲשֶׁר־עָשָׂה יְהוָה לְיִשְׂרָאֵל

The verb חָדָה, "to rejoice," occurs only once in the book of Exodus (Exod 18:9). The preposition עַל, "concerning," commonly means, "on." This preposition is used as specification to describe about what Jethro rejoiced.[66] In this case, Jethro rejoiced concerning all Yahweh's good deeds for Israel.[67]

The noun clause כָּל־הַטּוֹבָה אֲשֶׁר־עָשָׂה יְהוָה לְיִשְׂרָאֵל, "all the good which Yahweh had done for Israel," refers to (1) his protection for Israel with security from Pharaoh and the Egyptians in Egypt and at the Red Sea and (2) his provision for Israel with water, food, water, and victory in the wilderness.[68]

The subject of the verb עָשָׂה, "to do, to make," is the proper noun יְהוָה, "Yahweh," (see Textual Notes on Exod 18:1a). The preposition לְ,

---

65. The Greek version of the Old Testament (Septuagint) reads the aorist form with the conjunction ἐξέστη δέ, "and he was amazed," instead of the *qal* imperfect *waw* consecutive form וַיִּחַדְּ, "then he rejoiced."

66. *IBHS* §11.2.13 g, 218. See also Williams §289, 113.

67. Stuart, *Exodus*, 411, notes, "In other words, he [Jethro] was not merely 'delighted to hear about all the good things' but personally delighted by the facts themselves—because they answered questions he himself had about this God Yahweh who had appeared to his son-in-law and promised such great things for a certain enslaved people in Egypt." See also Janzen, *Exodus*, 226. Furthermore, as seeing the contrast between blessing and curse, Carpenter, *Exodus*, 1:612, notes, "Jethro's response was not that of the nations who feared and trembled before Yahweh's acts as at the Reed Sea, but rather one of happy rejoicing and belief. The covenant blessings were therefore on him (Gen 12:1–3), not the curses, as in the case of Israel's enemies. Pharaoh had asked for Yahweh's blessing when the tenth plague struck, but had not received it (Exod 12:29–32). In contrast, in Gen 47:7–8 it is reported that Jacob blessed the pharaoh of his time. Now Jethro hears the story, responds favorably, is blessed, and in turn 'blesses' Yahweh (Exod 18:11–12)."

68. Durham, *Exodus*, 244. See also Jacob, *Exodus*, 497.

"for," is used to indicate for whose advantage Yahweh had acted.⁶⁹ In this case, Yahweh acted for the benefit of Israel. Moses' recounting of Yahweh's deliverance and Jethro's rejoicing in the good which Yahweh has done for Israel stand as the exact inverse of Moses' complaint to Yahweh back in Exod 5:22–23, "O Lord, why have you done evil (רָעַע) to this people?... and you have certainly not delivered (נָצַל) your people."

18:9b אֲשֶׁר הִצִּילוֹ מִיַּד מִצְרָיִם׃

The noun יָד, "hand," occurs four times in Exod 18 (vv. 9, 10 [three times]). Here this noun refers to "the hand of the Egyptians" (cf. Exod 18:10 [twice]) and also "the hand of Pharaoh" (cf. Exod 18:10). "The hand of Pharaoh and the Egyptians" from which Yahweh had delivered Israel recalls "the sword of Pharaoh" from which Yahweh delivered Moses (cf. Exod 18:4).⁷⁰ This portrays death which Pharaoh brought to Moses by seeking to kill Moses when Pharaoh heard that Moses killed an Egyptian (cf. Exod 2:11–15). In the first half of the Exodus narrative, "the hand of Pharaoh and the Egyptians" illustrates the oppression of Israel as slaves of Pharaoh and the Egyptians (cf. Exod 1:10–14; 5:4–23) and the death of Israel as enemies of Pharaoh and the Egyptians (cf. Exod 1:15–16, 22; 14:6–9, 23).⁷¹ In this case, Yahweh had delivered Israel from the hand of Pharaoh and the Egyptians, that is, from burdens (סִבְלָה), harshness (פֶּרֶךְ), hard service (עֲבוֹדָה), and death which had come from Pharaoh and the Egyptians.

Exodus 18:10

וַיֹּאמֶר יִתְרוֹ בָּרוּךְ יְהוָֹה אֲשֶׁר הִצִּיל אֶתְכֶם מִיַּד מִצְרַיִם וּמִיַּד פַּרְעֹה אֲשֶׁר הִצִּיל אֶת־הָעָם מִתַּחַת יַד־מִצְרָיִם׃

18:10a וַיֹּאמֶר יִתְרוֹ בָּרוּךְ יְהוָֹה אֲשֶׁר הִצִּיל אֶתְכֶם מִיַּד מִצְרַיִם וּמִיַּד פַּרְעֹה

---

69. Joüon §133 d, 487–89. See also IBHS §11.2.10 d, 206–9; GBHS §4.1.10 (e.1), 125; Williams §271 a, 107.

70. Cassuto, *Exodus*, 216, notes, "The words at the end of the verse, *in that he had delivered them out of the hand of the Egyptians*, are a repetition to give emphasize to the thought and to establish the nexus, referred to above, with the clause: 'and delivered me from the sword of Pharaoh' (v. 4)."

71. Carpenter, *Exodus*, 1:612–13, notes, "'From the arm of Pharaoh' underlines that Israel's servitude in Egypt was not voluntary but forced. Indeed, it was Pharaoh's desire that they remain in slavery."

The subject of the verb אָמַר, "to utter, to say," is the proper noun יִתְרוֹ, "Jethro," who spoke to Yahweh with "praise and thanksgiving."[72]

The *qal* passive participle form בָּרוּךְ, "blessed," is used as predicate to modify the proper noun יְהוָה, "Yahweh," and to describe an action of the proper noun יְהוָה.[73] The verb בָּרַךְ, "to kneel, to bless," occurs six times in the book of Exodus (Exod 12:32; 18:10; 20:11, 24; 23:25; 39:43). Here this verb is used in a sense of praise and thanksgiving.[74]

Exodus 18:11

עַתָּה יָדַעְתִּי כִּי־גָדוֹל יְהוָה מִכָּל־הָאֱלֹהִים כִּי בַדָּבָר אֲשֶׁר זָדוּ עֲלֵיהֶם:[75]

18:11a עַתָּה יָדַעְתִּי כִּי־גָדוֹל יְהוָה מִכָּל־הָאֱלֹהִים

The verb יָדַע, "to know," occurs once in Exod 18 (v. 11). Here, through his experience of hearing all Yahweh's protection and provision for Israel, Jethro now knows Yahweh as the greatest and incomparable God (Exod

---

72. Wagner, "אָמַר; אֹמֶר; אֵמֶר; אִמְרָה; אֲמָרָה; מַאֲמָר; מֵאמַר," *TDOT* 1:341, notes, "3. Man Speaking to God. In sketching the theological use of *'amar* it is necessary to include not only the idea of God speaking to man, but also the idea of man speaking to God. In the OT, men speak so that God is the one addressed and the object of what they say. This can take place in a variety of ways, such as through prayer, song or hymn, praise and thanksgiving, but also through lament, and even accusation, discussion, objection, assent, etc. As surely as all these speech types have their own unique terminology (→ פלל *pālal*, 'to pray'; → הלל *hālal*, 'to praise'; → זעק *zā'aq*, 'to cry out'; → שיר *shîr*, 'to sing'; → ברך *bārakh*, 'to bless'; → ידה *yādhāh*, 'to thank'; etc.), they are all connected with an *'amar*-event."

73. *GBHS* §3.4.3 (*b*), 92–94. See also *IBHS* §37.6, 623–28; Joüon §121 *c*, 409; Williams §215 *b*, 88–89.

74. Cassuto, *Exodus*, 216, notes, "*And Jethro said, Blessed be YHWH* ['the Lord']— that is, praise and thanks be to the God whom you call by the name of *YHWH* (for the connotation of the word בָּרוּךְ *bārūkh* [rendered 'blessed'] as an expression of praise and thanks, compare Gen. xiv 20: 'and blessed be God the most High, who has delivered your enemies into your hand')." See also Childs, *Exodus*, 328; Davis, *Moses and Gods of Egypt*, 198; Kaiser, "Exodus," 2:412; Fretheim, *Exodus*, 196; Enns, *Exodus*, 369; Stuart, *Exodus*, 412. Furthermore, as seeing the verb בָּרַךְ as used in a sense of benediction, Jacob, *Exodus*, 497, notes, "After Jethro had delivered his judgment about these events, he recapitulated them in order to clothe them in a festive benediction (see my comments to Gen 9.26). The first benediction known to us was pronounced by Noah over Shem, the second by the foreign priest Melchizedek over Abraham (Gen 14.20). Here the third was spoken by Jethro over Israel. Jethro was not called father-in-law of Moses in either instance, nor priest of Midian, but only Jethro. When he rejoiced with Israel, fell down to its God, and recognized Him, he was called only Jethro."

75. The MT assumes that there is a gap (*lacuna*) in the clause.

18:11).⁷⁶ In the preceding narrative, Yahweh expresses his intention that people come to "know" him and "know" things about him. Jethro stands as the first explicit fulfillment of the divine intention in the Exodus narrative, the only character in the story who says, "Now I know . . . ." However, Pharaoh and the Egyptians have known Yahweh through their experiences of both hearing and seeing all which Yahweh had done to them (Exod 5:2; 7:5, 17; 8:10, 22; 9:14, 29; 11:7; 14:4, 18), but they do not acknowledge who Yahweh is.⁷⁷

The object of the verb יָדַע is the noun clause כִּי־גָדוֹל יְהוָה מִכָּל־הָאֱלֹהִים, "that Yahweh is *greater* than all gods," literally, "that Yahweh is *great* from all gods." The conjunction כִּי, "that," is used as the object of perception, which follows the verb יָדַע to describe what Jethro knows. This conjunction introduces its following subordinate or substantival clause גָדוֹל יְהוָה מִכָּל־הָאֱלֹהִים, "Yahweh is *greater* than all gods."⁷⁸ This is the confession of Jethro, the priest of Midian, who is "a non-Israelite."⁷⁹ Indeed, after hearing all Yahweh's saving and mighty deeds for Israel, Jethro responds to Yahweh by rejoicing in, praising, and confessing Yahweh as the greatest and incomparable God (Exod 18:11; cf. 8:10; 9:14; 15:11).⁸⁰ Later, Jethro worships Yahweh (cf. Exod 18:12).

---

76. Sarna considers the formula, "now, I know," either as introducing new discovered knowledge or as reaffirming accepted knowledge (see Sarna, *Exodus*, 99). See also Childs, *Exodus*, 329. As arguing about Jethro's conversion, Enns, *Exodus*, 369, notes, "What is happening here? Is he [Jethro] a convert to 'Yahwism'? Perhaps so, but at the very least we can say that he has had a shift in thinking based on what God has done for Israel, ironically a realization that Israel itself is often slow to learn." Furthermore, a number of commentators approach Jethro's acknowledgement as new knowledge which Jethro discovers according to his experience of hearing all Yahweh's saving and mighty acts for Israel (see Propp, *Exodus*, 1:630). See also Cassuto, *Exodus*, 216; Fretheim, *Exodus*, 196; Dozeman, *Exodus*, 403–4. Other commentators see Jethro's acknowledgement as the fulfillment of Yahweh's purpose in the Exodus narrative (see Blackburn, *God Who Makes Himself Known*, 77). See also Carpenter, *Exodus*, 1:613.

77. Enns, *Exodus*, 369.

78. GBHS §4.3.4 (j), 164. See also GKC §157 a, 491; IBHS §38.8, 644–46; Joüon §157, 589–91; Williams §451 a, 159.

79. Blackburn, *God Who Makes Himself Known*, 77. See also Carpenter, *Exodus*, 1:613.

80. Stuart, *Exodus*, 412, notes, "As a result, Yahweh became for Jethro at that moment the supreme God, 'greater than all other gods'—the only supernatural being that in modern English usage would be called 'God.'" Interestingly, Jacob, *Exodus*, 497, notes, "[S]o Jethro's *ga-dol y-h-v-h* brought him spiritually close to Israel's beliefs." Further, he notes, "*Y-h-v-h* presented a contrast to every other *e-lo-him*; he was *the God who had brought Israel out of Egypt and had saved them*. For this non-Israelite HE could not have been the 'God of the fathers' who had been motivated by love to rescue their

18:11b כִּי בַדָּבָר אֲשֶׁר זָדוּ עֲלֵיהֶם:

The clause כִּי בַדָּבָר אֲשֶׁר זָדוּ עֲלֵיהֶם, "because in the thing (דָּבָר), they acted presumptuously against them," functions causally. The noun דָּבָר, "speech, word, thing,"[81] here translated as "the thing," refers to the unjust act which causes Israel to suffer and die in Egypt.[82]

The relative pronoun אֲשֶׁר appears in the MT, but it is not translated here. However, the clause כִּי בַדָּבָר אֲשֶׁר זָדוּ עֲלֵיהֶם is difficult to read, and it may be a textual problem in the MT.[83]

The subject of the verb זִיד, "to boil up, to seethe, to act proudly, presumptuously, rebelliously," refers to Pharaoh and the Egyptians.[84] The preposition עַל, "against," commonly means, "on." This preposition is used as adversative to describe against whom Pharaoh and the

---

children, nor could this man have penetrated the essence of this God as the only holy being. For Jethro, the salvation of Israel was a display of *might* through which HE (v. 12) had shown Himself superior to all other *e-lo-him*. For this reason Jethro later used the designation *y-h-v-h* only in reference to this divine deed (vv. 8, 10, 11); elsewhere he continued to use *e-lo-him* (vv. 12, 19, 21, 23). When Jethro called Him greater than all other *e-lo-him* (v. 11), he did not reject the others." Jacob, *Exodus*, 505.

81. BDB, s.v. דָּבָר, IV, 183–84.
82. Carpenter, *Exodus*, 1:616.
83. Childs, *Exodus*, 320. See also Durham, *Exodus*, 240; Houtman, *Exodus*, 2:409.
84. Scharbert, "זוּד*; זִיד; זֵד; זָדוֹן," *TDOT* 4:50, notes, "Beginning with E (Ex. 18:11), the term was used for the arrogance of the heathen nations in claiming rights over Israel to which they were not entitled." Furthermore, there are two different opinions on the reference of the subject of the verb זִיד: (1) its subject refers to "all gods." For example, Cassuto, *Exodus*, 216, notes, "כִּי בַדָּבָר אֲשֶׁר זָדוּ עֲלֵיהֶם *kī bhaddābhār 'ăšer zādhū 'ălēhem*. All the various interpretations and emendations that have been proposed with regard to these obscure words are improbable. Perhaps the word *gods*, which occurs in the verse, is to be regarded as the subject of the verb זָדוּ *zādhū* ['act proudly', 'boast'], and the sense is: precisely [this is the meaning of the word כִּי *kī* below, in xxxii 29: 'precisely [כִּי *kī*] because every man was against his son and against his brother'] in respect of these things of which the gods of Egypt boasted, for example, the divine power of the Nile, the divine light of the sun, the divine might of the sea, He [Yahweh] is greater *than they* [עֲלֵיהֶם *'ălēhem*], and His power exceeds their power, and He executed judgements on all the gods of Egypt. [The clause should be rendered: 'excelling them in the very things to which they laid claim']." See also Durham, *Exodus*, 244; Kaiser, "Exodus," 2:412–13; Janzen, *Exodus*, 226; Stuart, *Exodus*, 412. And (2) its subject refers to "Pharaoh and the Egyptians." For instance, Jacob, *Exodus*, 497–98, notes, "The final words of our verse are difficult. *Za-du* (derived from *zud*) could only have referred to the plotting of the Egyptians (Neh 9.10 *he-zi-du*). Here the divine retribution (*talion*) which occurred was confirmed. Precisely what they had plotted against others now occurred to them (Onk., Mid.); Pharaoh had wished to drown each newborn Israelite child in the Nile and now they themselves perished in the sea." See also Houtman, *Exodus*, 2:409; Propp, *Exodus*, 1:630; Dozeman, *Exodus*, 407–8.

Egyptians acted presumptuously.[85] The object of the preposition עַל is indicated by the pronominal suffix third person masculine plural הֶם ,, "them," and it refers to Israel. Therefore, in this case, Pharaoh and the Egyptians acted presumptuously against Israel, for example, (1) oppressing Israel to serve (עָבַד) Pharaoh and the Egyptians with burdens (סִבְלָה), with harshness (פֶּרֶךְ), and with hard service (עֲבוֹדָה) (cf. Exod 1:10–14); (2) killing every male child born to Israel (cf. Exod 1:15–16, 22); (3) oppressing Israel again with heavy service (עֲבוֹדָה) by no longer giving Israel straw to make bricks, forcing Israel to gather straw for themselves, and not reducing the number of bricks as Israel made in the past (cf. Exod 5:4–23); and (4) pursuing Israel with Pharaoh's numerous and powerful army to the Red Sea (cf. Exod 14:6–9, 23).

Exodus 18:12

וַיִּקַּח[86] יִתְרוֹ חֹתֵן מֹשֶׁה עֹלָה וּזְבָחִים לֵאלֹהִים וַיָּבֹא אַהֲרֹן וְכֹל | זִקְנֵי[87] יִשְׂרָאֵל לֶאֱכָל־לֶחֶם עִם־חֹתֵן מֹשֶׁה לִפְנֵי הָאֱלֹהִים׃

18:12a וַיִּקַּח יִתְרוֹ חֹתֵן מֹשֶׁה עֹלָה וּזְבָחִים לֵאלֹהִים

The *qal* imperfect *waw* consecutive form וַיִּקַּח, "then he took," is derived from the verb לָקַח, "to take." In this case, it means that Jethro brings or offers a burnt offering and sacrifices to Yahweh.[88]

---

85. Joüon §133 *f*, 489–90. See also *GKC* §119 *dd*, 383–84; *IBHS* §11.2.13 *c*, 217; *GBHS* §4.1.16 (*f*), 135; Williams §288 *a*, 112–13.

86. The Syriac version of the Old Testament (the Targum(s) and the Vulgate) reads *wqrb*, "and he offered," (cf. Gen 14:18) instead of the *qal* imperfect *waw* consecutive form וַיִּקַּח, "then he took."

87. The Samaritan Pentateuch reads וּמִזְ' (= וּמִזְּקְנֵי), "with some of the elders of," instead of the conjunction with the construct noun and adjective וְכֹל זִקְנֵי, "with all the elders of."

88. Concerning Jethro as a priest, Davis, *Moses and Gods of Egypt*, 198, notes, "In special praise to God, Jethro, a priest, offered sacrifices to the Lord (v. 12). The idea of sacrifice, of course, was already well known as evidenced by Genesis 3:21; 4:3–4; 8:20; 12:7–8; and 22:13." See also Cohen, "Jethro/Hobab's Detainment," 115. Furthermore, regarding the meanings of the verb לָקַח with a contrast between "to bring" and "to offer," Kaiser, "Exodus," 2:412, notes, "Jethro then 'took' or 'brought' (*wayyiqqaḥ*) a burnt offering ('*ōlāh*) and fellowship offerings (*zᵉḇāḥîm*; NIV, 'other sacrifices') to 'Elohim' (v. 12). 'Brought' is the customary word for proffering or providing an animal for sacrifice; it is never used in the OT in the sense of 'to offer' (see Bubar, p. 141; see the Notes for further discussion). It is the very same verb used in [Exodus] 25:2 and Leviticus 12:8. Accordingly, those scholars are wrong who wish to see the Midianite priest officiating here; he did not 'offer' these sacrifices, but he did worship and fellowship with Moses

The object of the verb לָקַח is the nouns עֹלָה וּזְבָחִים, "a burnt offering and sacrifices." The meaning of the noun עֹלָה is literally "ascending offering"[89] which is burned completely on the altar and ascends to Yahweh.[90] This burnt offering establishes "a relationship of acceptance and appreciation between the offerer and God."[91] The noun זְבָחִים is the plural noun of the noun זֶבַח, "sacrifice." Generally, the noun זֶבַח means "slaughter sacrifice"[92] which is offered to Yahweh and, unlike the burnt offering, is shared among worshipers.[93] This sacrifice emphasizes "the communal sharing and celebration of the worshipers."[94]

Significantly, in the book of Exodus, the noun עֹלָה occurs first, along with the noun זֶבַח in Exod 10:25. In that context, Pharaoh did not let Moses and young Israel's flocks and herds go with them. Moses argued against Pharaoh about giving them "sacrifices (זֶבַח) and burnt offerings (עֹלָה)" to sacrifice to Yahweh. Second, in Exod 18:12, the noun עֹלָה occurs again, along with the noun זֶבַח, and this time displays the first "burnt offering and sacrifices" to Yahweh[95] by Jethro, eating bread along with "the representatives of Israel,"[96] Aaron and all the elders of Israel (and, presum-

---

and Aaron 'in the presence of God.'" Nevertheless, Cody argues that the verb לָקַח specifically means, "to accept," so Jethro does not offer a burnt offering and sacrifices, but he receives them from either Moses or the elders of Israel and accepts them (see Cody, "Exodus 18,12," 159–61, 165).

89. Propp, *Exodus*, 1:631. See also Dozeman, *Exodus*, 405.

90. Propp, *Exodus*, 1:631. See also Dozeman, *Exodus*, 405; Carpenter, *Exodus*, 1:613.

91. Carpenter, *Exodus*, 1:613. Furthermore, Jacob, *Exodus*, 498, notes, "*O-lah* was in the singular to honor God first." Stuart, *Exodus*, 413, also notes, "A 'burnt offering' was understood to atone for past sins and to appeal for forgiveness and acceptance."

92. Propp, *Exodus*, 1:631. See also Dozeman, *Exodus*, 405; Carpenter, *Exodus*, 1:613.

93. Propp, *Exodus*, 1:631. See also Jacob, *Exodus*, 498; Dozeman, *Exodus*, 405; Carpenter, *Exodus*, 1:613.

94. Carpenter, *Exodus*, 1:613. Furthermore, Stuart, *Exodus*, 413, notes, "'Other sacrifices' were offered by Jethro to be sure to cover for any inadequacies in approaching such a powerful and, indeed, omnipotent God as Yahweh was, to ensure that Jethro would be accepted in genuine fellowship with God himself."

95. Enns, *Exodus*, 369, notes, "This is the first 'sacrifice in the desert' to which Moses referred in his earlier audiences with Pharaoh (3:18; 5:3; 8:27). Exodus 10:25 is especially relevant, since there burnt offerings and sacrifices are mentioned together: 'You must allow us to have sacrifices and burnt offerings to present to the LORD our God.' This is what begins to happen in 18:12. Of course, this is not the last sacrifice. In 20:24 and throughout the remainder of the book, we have many references to sacrifices. Moreover, 18:12 should not be thought of as the fulfillment of 10:25, but perhaps as a first installment on the importance placed on sacrifice in subsequent chapters."

96. Durham, *Exodus*, 244, 245. See also Houtman, *Exodus*, 2:410; Propp, *Exodus*, 1:631; Carpenter, *Exodus*, 1:614. It is interesting that Brueggemann, "Exodus," 1:825,

ably, Moses),[97] in the presence of God. And third, these two nouns, עֹלָה and זֶבַח, again appear together in Exod 24:5. The young men of Israel brought up "burnt offerings (עֹלָה) and sacrifices (זֶבַח)" to Yahweh in order that Yahweh might make the covenant with Israel (cf. Exod 24:8) and that later, Moses, Aaron, Nadab, Abihu, and the elders of Israel might eat and drink in the presence of Yahweh (cf. Exod 24:11).

18:12b וַיָּבֹא אַהֲרֹן וְכֹל ׀ זִקְנֵי יִשְׂרָאֵל לֶאֱכָל־לֶחֶם עִם־חֹתֵן מֹשֶׁה לִפְנֵי הָאֱלֹהִים׃

The preposition with the *qal* infinitive construct form לֶאֱכָל, "to eat," is used as purpose to describe why Aaron with all the elders of Israel came.[98] In this case, Aaron with all the elders of Israel came to eat bread with Jethro in the presence of God. To eat bread[99] in the presence of God possibly refers to a holy meal rather than a covenant meal.[100]

---

notes, "It is curious that Aaron and the elders, until now absent in the narrative, appear for the official sacrifice." Furthermore, Stuart, *Exodus*, 413, "Then 'Aaron came with all the elders of Israel to eat bread with Moses' father-in-law in the presence of God,' which signified the formal admission of Jethro into Israel." See also Houtman, *Exodus*, 2:410.

97. The text does not specifically mention Moses' presence or any action during the worship time. Among a number of commentators, there are two arguments about Moses' presence: (1) Moses was not there, for example, Jacob, *Exodus*, 498, notes, "Jethro here brought a sacrifice as if he himself had belonged to those saved. In elegant fashion he provided a meal and invited Aaron as well as the elders. Moses, whose office made him always available to the people, could not participate. We might better explain his absence through the fact that he had already entertained Jethro upon his arrival (v. 7); he also could not let himself be invited in his own encampment." See also Propp, *Exodus*, 1:631. And (2) Moses was there (see Kaiser, "Exodus," 2:412; Enns, *Exodus*, 370; Janzen, *Exodus*, 223, 225–26; Dozeman, *Exodus*, 405; Carpenter, *Exodus*, 1:614).

98. *GBHS* §3.4.1 (c), 83. See also *GKC* §114 *f–h*, 348; *IBHS* §36.2.3 *c–d*, 606–8; Joüon §124 *l*, 436–37; Williams §197, 83.

99. Interestingly, Enns, *Exodus*, 370, asks, "Where does this bread come from? A few short chapters earlier, it seemed necessary for God to provide manna from heaven or else the Israelites would starve (16:3). Is manna (their main food during the desert years; cf. Josh 5:11–12) meant here? If so, one would think it would be made clear. Perhaps Jethro has brought the bread with him, or at least the ingredients to bake bread. Or are we to assume that the Israelites themselves have the ingredients handy to bake bread? If so, their earlier complaint makes no sense. This element of the story is difficult to explain."

100. Among many commentators, there are two arguments concerning the reference of the action of eating bread in the presence of God: (1) It refers to a holy/sacred/cultic, that is, common/communal/communion meal (see Cassuto, *Exodus*, 217; Childs, *Exodus*, 327; Durham, *Exodus*, 244; Jacob, *Exodus*, 498; Janzen, *Exodus*, 226–27; Dozeman, *Exodus*, 403; Carpenter, *Exodus*, 1:614; Blackburn, *God Who Makes Himself Known*, 76). And (2) it refers to a covenant/treaty/solemn meal (see Avishur, *Studies in Biblical Narrative*, 159–72; Kaiser, "Exodus," 2:412; Sarna, *Exodus*, 99; Enns, *Exodus*, 370–71; Stuart, *Exodus*, 413; Cody, "Exodus 18,12," 155–58, 165; Robinson,

Exodus 18:13

וַיְהִי֙ מִֽמָּחֳרָ֔ת וַיֵּ֥שֶׁב מֹשֶׁ֖ה לִשְׁפֹּ֣ט אֶת־הָעָ֑ם וַיַּעֲמֹ֤ד הָעָם֙ עַל־מֹשֶׁ֔ה מִן־הַבֹּ֖קֶר עַד[101]־הָעָֽרֶב:

18:13a וַיְהִי֙ מִֽמָּחֳרָ֔ת וַיֵּ֥שֶׁב מֹשֶׁ֖ה לִשְׁפֹּ֣ט אֶת־הָעָ֑ם

The *qal* imperfect *waw* consecutive form וַיְהִי appears in the MT, but it is not translated here. In the MT, this form is placed in a new line or paragraph. Because it stands on its own in a new line, this form is used once again as narratival tool to introduce an independent narrative or to begin a new section of narrative.[102] Therefore, in this case, the *waw* consecutive ־וַ is not translated, but this new section will begin with the prepositional phrase מִמָּחֳרָת, "on the next day,"[103] which functions as an adverb of time in order to indicate a continuing time, shifting from one day to another day in the narrative.[104]

The preposition with the *qal* infinitive construct form לִשְׁפֹּט, "to judge,"[105] is used as purpose to describe why Moses sat.[106] The act of sitting to judge Israel[107] portrays Moses as the judge over Israel.[108] This

---

"Acknowledging One's Dependence," 140; Lerner, "Redefining התלאה," 402).

101. Many *codices manusrcipti*, the Samaritan Pentateuch, and the Syriac version of the Old Testament read the conjunction with the preposition וְעַד, "and until," instead of the preposition עַד, "until."

102. *GBHS* §3.5.1 (c), 99–100. See also *GKC* §111 *f*, 327; Gibson §80, 97–100.

103. The prepositional phrase מִמָּחֳרָת literally means, "on the morrow." This prepositional phrase occurs four times in the book of Exodus (Exod 9:6; 18:13; 32:6, 30) to specify an ongoing time, which changes from one day to another day in the narratives. See also André, "מָחָר; מָחֳרָת," *TDOT* 8:237–41.

104. Dozeman, *Exodus*, 408. See also Carpenter, *Exodus*, 1:616.

105. As approaching Exod 18:13–27 as an anticipation to the following great revelatory event at Mount Sinai, Carpenter, *Exodus*, 1:616, notes, "The word לִשְׁפֹּט occurs six times in vv. 13–27 and is suggested (ellipsis) a seventh time in v. 14. Other words from this section foreshadow and anticipate the coming events at Sinai (תּוֹרָה). This portion of the chapter is a prologue, a transition, to the events at Sinai."

106. *GBHS* §3.4.1 (c), 83. See also *GKC* §114 *f–h*, 348; *IBHS* §36.2.3 *c–d*, 606–8; Joüon §124 *l*, 436–37; Williams §197, 83.

107. It is interesting that Jacob, *Exodus*, 498, notes, "The judge sat like a king while the parties involved stood."

108. Dozeman, *Exodus*, 408. Furthermore, concerning Moses as the chief judge, Mann, *Book of the Torah*, 97–98, notes, "The need for divine confirmation of Moses' role is all the more pressing because Moses *is* already acting as the people's legislator and 'judge' (18:13–17). Note the counsel of Jethro (Moses' father-in-law): 'You shall represent the people before God, and bring their cases to God; and you shall teach

role recalls the question from one of the two struggling Hebrews: "Who set you [Moses] a prince (שַׂר) and a judge (שֹׁפֵט) over us?" (Exod 2:14), and, finally, this question is apparently answered here through Moses' judicial role.[109]

Exodus 18:14

וַיַּרְא חֹתֵן מֹשֶׁה אֵת כָּל־אֲשֶׁר־הוּא עֹשֶׂה לָעָם וַיֹּאמֶר מָה־הַדָּבָר הַזֶּה אֲשֶׁר אַתָּה עֹשֶׂה לָעָם מַדּוּעַ אַתָּה יוֹשֵׁב לְבַדֶּךָ וְכָל־הָעָם נִצָּב עָלֶיךָ מִן־בֹּקֶר עַד־[110]עָרֶב:

18:14a וַיַּרְא חֹתֵן מֹשֶׁה אֵת כָּל־אֲשֶׁר־הוּא עֹשֶׂה לָעָם

The verb רָאָה, "to see," occurs once in Exod 18 (v. 14).[111] Here Jethro as the father-in-law of Moses saw that Moses was sitting to judge Israel all day (Exod 18:14), and later, Jethro helped Moses with advice based on what he had seen (cf. Exod 18:17–23).

The noun clause כָּל־אֲשֶׁר־הוּא עֹשֶׂה לָעָם, "all which he was doing for the people,"[112] points to everything which Jethro saw, for example, that Moses was sitting alone to judge Israel, and Israel was standing around Moses from morning until evening (cf. Exod 18:13).

The verb עָשָׂה, "to do, to make," is used in a sense of judgment by displaying Moses as the judge for Israel (cf. Exod 18:13). The preposition לְ, "for," is used as advantage to describe for whom Moses was acting.[113]

---

them the statutes and the laws (*torot*), and make them know the way in which they must walk and what they must do' (18:19–20). The point of Jethro's advice, of course, is to designate Moses as the 'chief justice' and thus to spare him all of the relatively petty legal cases, which his newly appointed assistant judges will decide. The story also concludes with Moses enacting the recommended policy. However, the context of the story points again to what will happen at Sinai, for only there will Moses' new role as legislator be publicly confirmed by Yahweh and formally accepted by the people."

109. Mann, *Book of the Torah*, 97. See also Carpenter, *Exodus*, 1:616–17.

110. Many *codices manusrcipti*, the Samaritan Pentateuch, and the Syriac version of the Old Testament read the conjunction with the preposition וְעַד, "and until," instead of the preposition עַד, "until."

111. Cassuto, *Exodus*, 218, notes, "The phrasing is intended to form a parallelism between the beginning of this paragraph [Exod 18:14] and the commencement of the first paragraph (v. 1): first he [Jethro] heard all that God had done for Israel; now he sees all that Moses is doing for Israel."

112. Propp, *Exodus*, 1:631, notes, "18:14. *all that he was doing*. The echo of vv 1, 8, 9 may compare Yahweh's salvation of Israel to Moses' judging of Israel."

113. Joüon §133 d, 487–89. See also *IBHS* §11.2.10 d, 206–9; *GBHS* §4.1.10 (e.1), 125; Williams §271 a, 107.

18:14b וַיֹּאמֶר מָה־הַדָּבָר הַזֶּה אֲשֶׁר אַתָּה עֹשֶׂה לָעָם מַדּוּעַ אַתָּה יוֹשֵׁב לְבַדֶּךָ וְכָל־הָעָם נִצָּב עָלֶיךָ מִן־בֹּקֶר עַד־עָרֶב:

The subject of the verb אָמַר, "to utter, to say," refers to Jethro who inquired of Moses with the two following questions.[114]

The first question is מָה־הַדָּבָר הַזֶּה אֲשֶׁר אַתָּה עֹשֶׂה לָעָם, "What is this thing (דָּבָר) which you (s.) are doing for the people?"[115] Here "the thing" refers to the just act which brings peace and life among Israel.[116] Interestingly, in the second half of Exod 18 (vv. 13–27), the noun דָּבָר occurs ten times which "foreshadow the ten words"[117] at Mount Sinai in Exod 20:1–17.

The second question is מַדּוּעַ אַתָּה יוֹשֵׁב לְבַדֶּךָ וְכָל־הָעָם נִצָּב עָלֶיךָ מִן־בֹּקֶר עַד־עָרֶב, "Why are you (s.) sitting alone and all the people standing around you (s.) from morning until evening?"[118] The preposition with

---

114. Wagner, "אָמַר; אֹמֶר; אֵמֶר; אִמְרָה; אֲמָרָה; מַאֲמָר; מַאֲמַר," *TDOT* 1:331, notes, "1. A Communication Term. ʾamar is used to denote communication between two personal entities (or entities regarded as personal). The goal of ʾamar is that another person (or persons) might hear and understand, and might reply, in the broadest sense of the word (reaction)."

115. Carpenter, *Exodus*, 1:617, notes, "'What is this procedure?' (מָה־הַדָּבָר הַזֶּה) is a sincere attempt to learn more about the purpose and reason for Moses' practice. That Moses was working himself to death to fulfill his function (לְבַדֶּךָ) as judge for the people is the major concern of the enquiry, but also that many of the people were not served adequately because of time constraints."

116. Carpenter, *Exodus*, 1:616.

117. Carpenter, "Exodus 18," 99, 104. Further, he notes, "[T]he word דָּבָר ('case, matter, issue') is employed ten times in vv. 13–27 (onec in the pl.). It had been used only once in vv. 1–12, where it referred to the 'unjust treatment' (v. 11) that Israel had received at the hands of Egypt. In Israel, the דְּבָרִים of the people are to be handled differently. In chapters 19 and 20 it is the דְּבָרִים of Yahweh, 'the words of Yahweh,' that will decide the issues; in fact the use of דָּבָר ten times in these verses foreshadows the coming great 'Ten Words' in chapter 20." Carpenter, *Exodus*, 1:616. See also Propp, *Exodus*, 1:631; Dozeman, *Exodus*, 407–8.

118. Counting the question here as an expression of Exod 18:13, Cassuto, *Exodus*, 219, notes, "A general, preliminary question with which to open the discussion. *Why do you sit alone*, without any one to assist you, *and all the people stand about you from morning to evening*, and are fatigued thereby? There recur here, with the usual variations, the expressions used in the preceding verse [Exod 18:13]." Jacob, *Exodus*, 499, also notes, "The second question (*ma-du-a*) explained the first (*mah*) = I mean. We should note three matters emphasized in Jethro's statement: (1) Moses sat *alone* and judged; (2) the *entire* people (*kol*) stood around waiting for him; (3) this continued through the entire day (v. 13). This represented too much concern with the people (*o-seh la-am*)." Furthermore, interestingly, as approaching Moses' lone judicial role as a prophet, Stuart, *Exodus*, 415, notes, "But the most important reason for Moses' going it [to judge] alone was that he functioned as a prophet, who dispensed God's revelation,

the noun with the pronominal suffix second person masculine singular לְבַדֶּךָ, "alone," literally means, "by yourself."

Exodus 18:15

וַיֹּאמֶר מֹשֶׁה לְחֹתְנוֹ כִּי־יָבֹא אֵלַי הָעָם לִדְרֹשׁ אֱלֹהִים:

18:15b כִּי־יָבֹא אֵלַי הָעָם לִדְרֹשׁ אֱלֹהִים:

In verses 15–16, all verbs in the direct quotation are translated as present tense to denote actions in the present.[119]

The conjunction כִּי is used as recitative to introduce direct speech.[120] The *qal* imperfect form יָבֹא, "he comes," is used as customary to describe that Israel customarily comes to Moses to inquire of Yahweh, so it is translated in the present.[121] The preposition with the *qal* infinitive construct form לִדְרֹשׁ, "to inquire of," is used as purpose to describe why the people come.[122] According to the BDB, when the verb דָּרַשׁ, "to resort to, to seek," is used with the noun אֱלֹהִים, "God," as its object, it means, "to inquire of."[123] The picture, "the people come to me [Moses]

---

and that was the reason for his answer in the next verse [Exod 18:15]."

119. Gibson §63 (*b*), 73–75.

120. *GBHS* §4.3.4 (*l*), 165. See also Williams §452, 159.

121. Davidson §44 (*a*), 65–66. See also *GKC* §107 g, 315–16; *IBHS* §31.3 *b* and *e*, 504–6; Joüon §113 *c*, 366–67; *GBHS* §3.2.2 (*b*), 71; Williams §168, 70.

122. *GBHS* §3.4.1 (*c*), 83. See also *GKC* §114 *f–h*, 348; *IBHS* §36.2.3 *c–d*, 606–8; Joüon §124 *l*, 436–37; Williams §197, 83.

123. BDB, s.v. דָּרַשׁ, 2a, 205.

to inquire of God,"¹²⁴ illustrates that Moses plays an important role as the mediator between Yahweh and Israel.¹²⁵

Exodus 18:16

כִּי־יִהְיֶ֨ה לָהֶ֤ם דָּבָר֙ בָּ֣א ¹²⁶ אֵלַ֔י וְשָׁ֣פַטְתִּ֔י בֵּ֥ין אִ֖ישׁ וּבֵ֣ין רֵעֵ֑הוּ וְהוֹדַעְתִּ֛י אֶת־חֻקֵּ֥י הָאֱלֹהִ֖ים וְאֶת־תּוֹרֹתָֽיו׃

18:16a כִּי־יִהְיֶ֨ה לָהֶ֤ם דָּבָר֙ בָּ֣א אֵלַ֔י וְשָׁ֣פַטְתִּ֔י בֵּ֥ין אִ֖ישׁ וּבֵ֣ין רֵעֵ֑הוּ

The clause כִּי־יִהְיֶ֨ה לָהֶ֤ם דָּבָר֙ בָּ֣א אֵלַ֔י, "when they have a case (דָּבָר), which comes to me," functions temporally due to the presence of the conjunction כִּי, "when."¹²⁷

The sentence יִהְיֶ֨ה לָהֶ֤ם דָּבָר֙, "they have a case (דָּבָר)," literally means, "there is a case (דָּבָר) belonging to them." The *qal* imperfect form יִהְיֶ֨ה is used with the preposition לְ to denote possession.¹²⁸ According to the BDB, the noun דָּבָר can also mean, "case" for judicial investigation¹²⁹ (see also Textual Notes on Exod 18:14b).

In verse 16, both perfect *waw* consecutive forms . . . וְהוֹדַעְתִּ֛י . . . וְשָׁ֣פַטְתִּ֔י, "I judge . . ., and I make known . . .," which are preceded by

---

124. Discussing the expression "to inquire of God" here and in the Old Testament, Childs, *Exodus*, 330, notes, "Verse 15 suggests that the people have come to him 'to inquire of God'. This is a technical expression, used often in the Old Testament, which has its historical setting in the dispensing of oracles. Usually the sanctuary is the place designated for the pratice. Particularly in times of perplexity or embarrassment, a person sought a divine oracle (I Sam. 9.9; II Kings 22.18; Jer. 37.7). Ex. 33.7ff. mentions Moses' role in connection with the tent of meeting when it served as a sacred place outside the camp to which people went 'to seek Yahweh.'" Sarna, *Exodus*, 100, notes, "This biblical phrase [to inquire of God] originally meant to seek divine guidance in a situation in which human wisdom has unavailingly exhausted itself. Here it has acquired a legal nuance with the sense of 'seeking a judgment or decision,' 'making judicial inquiry.' This usage reflects the conception of true justice as being ultimately the expression of the will of God communicated through the human judge." See also Kaiser, "Exodus," 2:412; Brueggemann, "Exodus," 1:827; Houtman, *Exodus*, 2:414.

125. Dozeman, *Exodus*, 408. Furthermore, Stuart, *Exodus*, 416, notes, "Moses was not merely a judge. He was a prophet who conveyed God's will when it was sought. . . . A better translation would be 'the people come to me to inquire of God,' which connotes better Moses' intermediary role."

126. The Greek version of the Old Testament (Septuagint) reads καὶ ἔλθωσι, "and they come," instead of the *qal* participle form בָּא, "come."

127. GBHS §4.3.4 (e), 161–62. See also GKC §164 d, 502; IBHS §38.7 a, 643–44; Joüon §167 o, 627; Williams §445, 157.

128. GBHS §4.4.2 (b), 167. See also Williams §478, 170.

129. BDB, s.v. דָּבָר, IV 5, 183.

the *qal* imperfect form יִהְיֶה, are introducing a main clause and used in present tense.¹³⁰

The prepositional phrase בֵּין אִישׁ וּבֵין רֵעֵהוּ, "between one (אִישׁ) and another (רֵעֵהוּ)," literally means, "between a man (אִישׁ) and between his friend (רֵעֵהוּ)."¹³¹ The language of אִישׁ, "man," and רֵעַ, "friend, companion, fellow," corresponds with Exod 18:7, which represents peaceful relations between neighbors, and with Moses' interaction with the guilty Hebrew man in Exod 2:13-14. This is an example of the kind of contentious situation which Moses sits resolving in Exod 18:13-27.

Besides his action of sitting to judge Israel all day (cf. Exod 18:13), Moses answered Jethro's questions by saying, "When they have a case (דָּבָר), which comes to me, I judge between one (אִישׁ) and another (רֵעֵהוּ)." This makes it clear that Moses plays a role as the judge over Israel.¹³²

18:16b וְהוֹדַעְתִּי אֶת־חֻקֵּי הָאֱלֹהִים וְאֶת־תּוֹרֹתָיו׃

The *hiphil* perfect *waw* consecutive form וְהוֹדַעְתִּי, "and I make known," is derived from the *hiphil* of the verb יָדַע, "to make known, to declare." Here Moses makes known to Israel Yahweh's statutes and laws (Exod 18:16). Similarly, through Jethro's advice, Moses makes known to Israel the way in which they should walk and the work which they should do (Exod 18:20). Later, this word will appear in another significant context, where after Israel has sinned a great sin against Yahweh by making the golden calf, Moses asks Yahweh to make known his ways to find favor in his sight (Exod 33:13).

The statutes and laws of Yahweh which are being made known by Moses as the instructor for Israel¹³³ are presented here in a general

---

130. Gibson §75, 93-94. See also *GKC* §112 *ff* and *hh*, 336; *IBHS* §32.2.1 *b*, 526.

131. BDB, s.v. אִישׁ, 35-36.

132. Cassuto points to "one of two forms" which causes Israel to come to Moses to inquire of Yahweh (Exod 18:15): here, he notes, "[A] judicial form: *when they have a matter*—that is, a judgement, a dispute—the matter *comes to me, and I judge between a man and his neighbour*." Cassuto, *Exodus*, 219. Furthermore, Sarna, *Exploring Exodus*, 127, notes, "Moses himself is to act as the court of last resort for difficult cases." Further, he notes, "Moses, who acts as the supreme judicial authority, functions as the mediator of divine will, but not as lawmaker or as one who dispenses justice by virtue of superior wisdom." Sarna, *Exodus*, 100. See also Sarna, *Exodus*, 101; Stuart, *Exodus*, 416; Carpenter, *Exodus*, 1:617.

133. Cassuto expresses "one of two forms" which causes Israel to come to Moses to inquire of Yahweh (Exod 18:15): here, he notes, "[W]hen they come to ask for instruction and guidance, and I answer in God's name, *and I make them know the statutes of God and His directions.*" Cassuto, *Exodus*, 219. Furthermore, Sarna, *Exploring Exodus*,

sense rather than in a specific sense as in the great revelation of Yahweh at Mount Sinai (cf. Exod 20:1–17, 22–23:33).[134] Significantly, Yahweh's statutes and laws first recall the prior statute (חֻקָּה/חֹק) of the Passover (Exod 12:14, 17, 24, 43) and the law (תּוֹרָה) of the Passover (Exod 12:49), and they also anticipate specific statutes and laws in Yahweh's great revelatory event at Mount Sinai.[135]

Exodus 18:17

וַיֹּאמֶר חֹתֵן מֹשֶׁה אֵלָיו לֹא־טוֹב הַדָּבָר אֲשֶׁר אַתָּה עֹשֶׂה׃

18:17b לֹא־טוֹב הַדָּבָר אֲשֶׁר אַתָּה עֹשֶׂה׃

The noun דָּבָר, again, means "thing"[136] (see Textual Notes on Exod 18:14b). The independent personal pronoun אַתָּה, "you (s.)," refers to Moses. The verb עָשָׂה, "to do, to make," is used to describe Moses' responsibilities as the mediator, the judge, and the instructor for Israel (cf. Exod 18:15–16).

126, notes, "Moses is to act as teacher to the people." See also Sarna, *Exodus*, 101; Stuart, *Exodus*, 416; Carpenter, *Exodus*, 1:617.

134. Davis, *Moses and Gods of Egypt*, 199, notes, "On the basis of the expression 'ordinances and laws' found in verse 20 some have attempted to place the visit of Jethro after the law had been given at Sinai, but this is not necessary, for the ordinances and laws mentioned here are regulations of the most general sense and not necessarily related to the special revelation given at Sinai."

135. Blackburn, *God Who Makes Himself Known*, 77, notes, "In addition, Moses' language of 18:16 concerning 'the statutes of God and his laws' looks back to language already encountered in the wilderness section ('statutes' in 15:25–26 and 'law' in 16:4). As with the earlier wilderness material, 18:13–27 anticipates the giving of the law." Furthermore, as considering Yahweh's statutes and laws as both a proleptic and a preparation, Stuart, *Exodus*, 416, notes, "But do not 'God's decrees and laws' come only later, in chap. 20 and following, with the formal revelation of the covenant? The answer must be no; some of the decrees and laws of God were being proleptically revealed to the people for their benefit even before the unveiling of the Sinai covenant because answers were needed to important questions during the three months while the people were on their way to Sinai/Horeb and also because by dispensing decrees and laws in advance of Sinai, God was able to continue shaping his people's thinking in the direction of his eventual covenant relationship with them. Good education involves preparatory (prepaedeutic) instruction as well as concomitant instruction and follow-up instruction." Whereas Janzen, *Exodus*, 228, notes, "Again, the expressions used here seem to anticipate the covenant and law of Sinai, as already in 15:25–26." See also Carpenter, *Exodus*, 1:617.

136. BDB, s.v. דָּבָר, IV, 183–84.

Exodus 18:18

נָבֹל תִּבֹּל גַּם־אַתָּה גַּם־הָעָם הַזֶּה אֲשֶׁר עִמָּךְ כִּי־כָבֵד מִמְּךָ הַדָּבָר לֹא־תוּכַל עֲשֹׂהוּ[137] לְבַדֶּךָ:

18:18a נָבֹל תִּבֹּל גַּם־אַתָּה גַּם־הָעָם הַזֶּה אֲשֶׁר עִמָּךְ

The *qal* infinitive absolute form נָבֹל, "surely," which is followed by the *qal* imperfect form תִּבֹּל, "you (s.) will languish," is used as emphatic to affirm that an action or event is certainly to happen, and it also uses the same root with its following finite verb.[138] Therefore, in this case, this construction is translated with the adverb "surely" to emphasize an action which indeed happens.

18:18b כִּי־כָבֵד מִמְּךָ הַדָּבָר לֹא־תוּכַל עֲשֹׂהוּ לְבַדֶּךָ:

The causal clause כִּי־כָבֵד מִמְּךָ הַדָּבָר, "because the thing (דָּבָר) is too heavy for you (s.)," woodenly means, "because the thing (דָּבָר) is heavy from you (s.)" or "because the thing (דָּבָר) is heavier than you (s.)."[139]

The subject of the verb יָכֹל, "to be able, to have power, to prevail, to endure," refers to Moses. The *qal* infinitive construct form with the object suffix third person masculine singular עֲשֹׂהוּ, "to do it," is used as nominal in accusative case to describe what Moses is not able to do, and it also serves as a complement of the verb יָכֹל.[140]

Exodus 18:19

עַתָּה שְׁמַע בְּקֹלִי אִיעָצְךָ וִיהִי אֱלֹהִים עִמָּךְ הֱיֵה אַתָּה לָעָם מוּל הָאֱלֹהִים וְהֵבֵאתָ אַתָּה אֶת־הַדְּבָרִים[141] אֶל־הָאֱלֹהִים:

---

137. The Samaritan Pentateuch reads a different form, the *qal* infinitive construct form with the object suffix third person masculine singular עֲשׂוֹתוֹ, "to do it," instead of the *qal* infinitive construct form with the object suffix third person masculine singular עֲשֹׂהוּ, "to do it."

138. Williams §205, 85. See also *GKC* §113 *l–n*, 342; *IBHS* §35.3.1 *f*, 585–86; Joüon §123 *e*, 422; *GBHS* §3.4.2 (*b*), 87–89.

139. Davidson §34 *Rem.* 2., 48–49. See also *GKC* §133 *c*, 430; Joüon §141 *i*, 523–24; Gibson §44 *Rem.* 1., 45–46.

140. *GBHS* §3.4.1 (*a*), 80–82. See also *GKC* §114 *c*, 347; *IBHS* §36.2.1 *d*, 602; Joüon §124 *c*, 433; Williams §193, 81–82.

141. The Greek version of the Old Testament (Septuagint), the Syriac version of the Old Testament, and *Targum Pseudo-Jonathae secundum M. Ginsburger, Pseudo-Jonathan 1903* add the pronominal suffix third person masculine plural after the noun הַדְּבָרִים, "the cases."

18:19a עַתָּה שְׁמַע בְּקֹלִי אִיעָצְךָ וִיהִי אֱלֹהִים עִמָּךְ

The *qal* imperative form שְׁמַע is used as a command to express Jethro's desire to Moses.[142] The verb שָׁמַע, "to hear," is used with the prepositional phrase בְּקוֹל as a set idiom, שָׁמַע בְּקוֹל, meaning, "to obey."[143] To obey means to do what someone is told or expected to do.[144] This stands stark contrast to Pharaoh's refusal in Exod 5:2: "Who is Yahweh that I should obey him (אֶשְׁמַע בְּקֹלוֹ) by letting Israel go?" It also anticipates the demand which Israel obeys Yahweh's direction and instruction through Moses (Exod 19:5; 23:21–22). All three of these other passages use the same idiom שָׁמַע בְּקוֹל.

The conjunction with the *qal* jussive form וִיהִי, "and may he be," is used as a benediction.[145] The subject of the verb הָיָה, "to become, to be," is the noun אֱלֹהִים, "God." Jethro begins his advice to Moses with this: "and may God be with you (s.)." This shows that Jethro thinks of Yahweh who is "the source of revelation"[146] through Jethro's advice, which is under the direction and instruction of Yahweh and which will be approved and confirmed by Yahweh.[147]

---

142. Joüon §114 *m*, 378. See also *GKC* §110 *a*, 324; *IBHS* §34.4 *b*, 571–72; *GBHS* §3.3.2 (*a*), 76; Williams §188, 80.

143. BDB, s.v. שָׁמַע, 1m, 1034.

144. Rütersworden, "שָׁמַע; שֵׁמַע; שְׁמוּעָה," *TDOT* 15:265, notes, "3. With bᵉ. a. General. Far and away the commonest use of *šāmaʿ* with the prep. *bᵉ* is in the expression *šāmaʿ bᵉqôl*, 'heed someone's voice' (Gen. 21:12; 27:8, 13, 43; Ex. 4:1; 18:19; 23:21–22; Dt. 21:18, 20; Josh. 22:2; Jgs. 2:2; 20:13; 1 S. 8:7, 9, 19, 22; 12:1; 15:24; 19:6; 25:35; 28:21–22; 2 S. 12:18; 13:14; Isa. 50:10; Jer. 35:8; Prov. 5:13])."

145. *GBHS* §3.3.1 (*c*), 75. See also *GKC* §109 *b*, 321; *IBHS* §34.3 *c*, 569; Joüon §114 *h*, 376–77; Williams §184 *a*, 79.

146. Jacob, *Exodus*, 500. See also Durham, *Exodus*, 250.

147. Kaiser, "Exodus," 2:413, notes, "Jethro warned that his plan needed to be executed only if God was pleased with his advice ('and may God be with you,' v. 19, and 'If you do this and God so commands,' v. 23)." See also Cassuto, *Exodus*, 219; Stuart, *Exodus*, 417; Carpenter, *Exodus*, 1:621–22. Furthermore, Houtman explains that "וִיהִי אֱלֹהִים עִמָּךְ" means "if the advice is heeded, it will go well with Moses and he will no longer be burdened by physical and mental pressures (cf. 18:18); ... וִיהִי ... עִמָּךְ has been taken as Jethro's call to consult YHWH about the advice (*Mek.* II, 182; Rashi; cf. 18:23)." Houtman, *Exodus*, 2:416. Nevertheress, Propp, *Exodus*, 1:632, notes, "[*M*]*ay Deity be with you*. Jethro's intent is unclear. Is he blessing Moses (Luzzatto)? Is he predicting, 'Pursue my plan and Yahweh will be with you' (ibn Ezra; Rashbam)? Or does he caution, 'Pursue my plan only if Yahweh permits' (*Exod. Rab.* 27:6; *Mek. ʿămālēq* 4; cf. v 23)? By any interpretation, his interjection would be germane. When Moses judges, he especially requires divine assistance (cf. 1 Kgs 3:9). And Yahweh presumably must approve Moses' delegation of authority and inspire the lesser judges with wisdom."

18:19b הֱיֵה אַתָּה לָעָם מוּל הָאֱלֹהִים וְהֵבֵאתָ אַתָּה אֶת־הַדְּבָרִים אֶל־הָאֱלֹהִים׃

The *qal* imperative form הֱיֵה, "be," is used as command to express Jethro's desire to Moses.[148] The preposition לְ, "as," is used as comparison to describe that Moses represents Israel in front of God.[149]

The *hiphil* perfect *waw* consecutive form וְהֵבֵאתָ, "and bring," is preceded by the *qal* imperative form הֱיֵה, so it is used as volitional to express a command or wish.[150] The object of the *hiphil* of the verb בּוֹא, "to cause to come in, to cause to come" or "to bring in, to bring," is the noun הַדְּבָרִים, which in this instance means "the cases (דָּבָר)."[151]

Regarding Moses as the mediator between Yahweh and Israel, Jethro speaks of Moses as Israel in the presence of Yahweh, so that Moses alone may bring their cases to Yahweh.[152] In other words, Moses as the representative of Israel will go up to Mount Sinai and appear before Yahweh to bring their cases to Yahweh, and after that, Moses will go down from Mount Sinai and bring Yahweh's solutions to them.

---

148. Joüon §114 *m*, 378. See also GKC §110 *a*, 324; IBHS §34.4 *b*, 571–72; GBHS §3.3.2 (*a*), 76; Williams §188, 80.

149. Williams §274 *b*, 109. See also IBHS §11.2.10 *d*, 206–7.

150. GBHS §3.5.2 (*c*), 102–3. See also Davidson §55 (*a*), 81; GKC §112 *r*, 333; IBHS §32.2.2 *a–b*, 529–30; Joüon §119 *l*, 399–400; Gibson §76 (*a*), 94; Williams §179, 75–76.

151. BDB, s.v. דָּבָר, IV 5, 183. Cassuto, *Exodus*, 220, notes, "[A]nd you by yourself bring the words—that is, the petitions of your people—to God."

152. Propp, *Exodus*, 1:632, notes, "[O]pposite the Deity. That is, Moses alone will continue as Israel's intermediary before Yahweh." Further, he notes, "Ramban takes the text literally: once the Tabernacle is erects, Moses is to remain inside, perpetually in Yahweh's presence (contrast 33:7–11)." Propp, *Exodus*, 1:632. Furthermore, by giving a clear picture of "the practice of the heathen priests," Cassuto, *Exodus*, 219, notes, "The words, *you be for the people in front of God*, can well be explained in the light of the practice of the heathen priests, who came before the idols to offer the petitions of the worshippers, such as a request for healing from sickness or for deliverance from any trouble." See also Cassuto, *Exodus*, 219–20.

Exodus 18:20

וְהִזְהַרְתָּ֣ה אֶתְהֶ֔ם אֶת־הַֽחֻקִּ֖ים[153] וְאֶת־הַתּוֹרֹ֑ת[154] וְהוֹדַעְתָּ֣ לָהֶ֗ם אֶת־הַדֶּ֙רֶךְ֙[155] יֵ֣לְכוּ בָ֔הּ וְאֶת־הַֽמַּעֲשֶׂ֖ה אֲשֶׁ֥ר יַעֲשֽׂוּן׃

18:20a וְהִזְהַרְתָּ֣ה אֶתְהֶ֔ם אֶת־הַֽחֻקִּ֖ים וְאֶת־הַתּוֹרֹ֑ת

The *hiphil* perfect *waw* consecutive form וְהִזְהַרְתָּה, "then teach," is preceded by the *qal* imperative form הֱיֵה, "be," in verse 19, so it is used as volitional to express a command or wish.[156] The verb זָהַר, "to instruct, to teach, to warn," occurs only here in the book of Exodus.[157]

Regarding Moses as the instructor for Israel with Yahweh's statutes and laws, Jethro speaks of Moses playing a role as the instructor by teaching Israel Yahweh's statutes and laws.[158] In other words, Moses will fulfill a unique role in helping Israel learn Yahweh's statutes and laws which will come directly from Yahweh through Moses alone.[159]

---

153. The Greek version of the Old Testament adds τοῦ θεοῦ, "of God," (= הָאֱלֹהִים (חֻקֵּי)) after the noun הַחֻקִּים, "the statutes."

154. The Samaritan Pentateuch reads the singular noun הַתּוֹרָה, "the law," instead of the plural noun הַתּוֹרֹת, "the laws." The Greek version of the Old Testament reads the singular noun with the genitive personal pronoun τὸν νόμον αὐτοῦ, "his law," (cf. v. 16) instead of the plural noun הַתּוֹרֹת.

155. Some *codices manuscripti* adds the relative pronoun אֲשֶׁר, "which," after the noun הַדֶּרֶךְ, "the way."

156. *GBHS* §3.5.2 (*c*), 102–3. See also Davidson §55 (*a*), 81; *GKC* §112 *r*, 333; *IBHS* §32.2.2 *a*–*b*, 529–30; Joüon §119 *l*, 399–400; Gibson §76 (*a*), 94; Williams §179, 75–76.

157. Carpenter, *Exodus*, 1:622, notes, "Hebrew זהר here means to 'clarify, caution, inform,' rather than 'warn,' as it does in other contexts. It may be akin to the root זהר in Dan 12:3, meaning 'shine.'" Furthermore, Görg, "זָהַר; זֹהַר," *TDOT* 4:43, notes, "1. *Use Outside the Prophets*. In Ex. 18:13–27, a 'smooth, self-contained narrative sequence,' probably Elohistic, v. 20 begins with the hiphil of *zhr* in climactic suffix conjunction (here in the sense of a certain future), continuing an exhortation on the part of Moses' father-in-law. The advice pertains to a future function of the mediator between the people and God (v. 19), who is also to be the mediator between God and the people (v. 20). A double object here characterizes the force of the verb: what is meant in the first instance is undoubtedly the function of 'informing' the people (*ethhem*) about 'statutes' (*ḥuqqîm*) and 'decisions' (*tôrôth*) of God. . . . The term *zhr* (hiphil) and *yd'* (hiphil) now stand in correspondence (v. 20): 'enlightening' instruction parallels making known the way men must walk and act."

158. Görg, "זָהַר; זֹהַר," *TDOT* 4:43, notes, "In any case, Moses' adviser expects him to exercise the function of a 'teacher' who is required to do more than merely make formal pronouncements." Furthermore, as seeing the repetition of the two nouns, חק and תּוֹרָה, in Moses's answer (Exod 18:16) and in Jethro's advice here, Jacob, *Exodus*, 500, notes, "In this repetition Jethro associated himself with Moses' statement through '*ḥu-qîm* and *to-rot*.'"

159. López, "תּוֹרָה," *TDOT* 15:615, notes, "The laws were communicated directly to

18:20b וְהוֹדַעְתָּ לָהֶם אֶת־הַדֶּרֶךְ יֵלְכוּ בָהּ וְאֶת־הַמַּעֲשֶׂה אֲשֶׁר יַעֲשׂוּן׃

The *hiphil* perfect *waw* consecutive form וְהוֹדַעְתָּ, "and make known," is preceded by the *qal* imperative form הֱיֵה in verse 19, so it is used as volitional to express a command or wish.[160] The *hiphil* perfect *waw* consecutive form וְהוֹדַעְתָּ is derived from the *hiphil* of the verb יָדַע, "to make known, to declare."

The first object of the *hiphil* of the verb יָדַע is the noun clause הַדֶּרֶךְ יֵלְכוּ בָהּ, "the way[161] in which they should walk." The *qal* imperfect form יֵלְכוּ, "they should walk," is used as obligation.[162]

The second object of the *hiphil* of the verb יָדַע is the noun clause הַמַּעֲשֶׂה אֲשֶׁר יַעֲשׂוּן, "the work which they should do." The *qal* imperfect form with the paragogic *nun* יַעֲשׂוּן, "they should do," is used again as obligation.[163]

Exodus 18:21

וְאַתָּה תֶחֱזֶה [164] מִכָּל־הָעָם אַנְשֵׁי־חַיִל יִרְאֵי אֱלֹהִים אַנְשֵׁי אֱמֶת שֹׂנְאֵי בָצַע וְשַׂמְתָּ עֲלֵהֶם שָׂרֵי אֲלָפִים שָׂרֵי [165] מֵאוֹת שָׂרֵי חֲמִשִּׁים וְשָׂרֵי עֲשָׂרֹת׃

Moses by God through revelation, without the need for oracular media. The precepts and laws that he taught the people were a direct promulgation of divine laws."

160. *GBHS* §3.5.2 (*c*), 102–3. See also Davidson §55 (*a*), 81; *GKC* §112 *r*, 333; *IBHS* §32.2.2 *a–b*, 529–30; Joüon §119 *l*, 399–400; Gibson §76 (*a*), 94; Williams §179, 75–76.

161. Regarding the way of Yahweh, Koch, "הֲלִיכָה; הָלִיךְ; מְסִלָּה; חוּק; שׁוּק; דֶּרֶךְ; דָּרַךְ; אֹרַח; שְׁבִיל; נְתִיבָה; נָתִיב; מַעְגָּל," *TDOT* 3:284, notes, "The use of *derekh* in the prayer of Moses in Ex. 33:12–14 is more figurative. Moses asks Yahweh to show (*hodhia'*) him his way in order that he might find favor in his sight to lead the people. Here the way of God includes not only the fixing of a route from Egypt to Canaan but also the successful following of the route through 'the one whom thou sendest with me,' God granting his own presence (*panim*)." Furthermore, Carpenter, *Exodus*, 1:622, notes, "'The way they should live' is literally 'the way (הַדֶּרֶךְ) they should walk/go (יֵלְכוּ בָהּ).' This term becomes the 'way of Yahweh' (cf. Exod 32:8; 33:13; Deut 5:33; 8:2; 10:12; 11:22; 32:4) and indicates life lived according to Yahweh's instructions, his words, his acts. When they know God's way, they are expected to follow it. This terminology was picked up as the Way in the NT as a bridge to God's acts in Christ in the book of Acts. The Way described the beliefs and lifestyle of the Christians (Acts 9:2; 19:23; 22:4; 24:22, ἡ ὁδός)."

162. *IBHS* §31.4 *g*, 508–9. See also *GKC* §107 *n*, 317; *GBHS* §3.2.2 (*d*.3), 72; Williams §172, 71–72.

163. *IBHS* §31.4 *g*, 508–9. See also *GKC* §107 *n*, 317; *GBHS* §3.2.2 (*d*.3), 72; Williams §172, 71–72.

164. The Samaritan Pentateuch and the Greek version of the Old Testament (Septuagint) add לְךָ, "for yourselves," after the *qal* imperfect form תֶחֱזֶה, "provide."

165. A reading of one or several Hebrew manuscripts from the Cairo Geniza, many

18:21a וְאַתָּה תֶחֱזֶה מִכָּל־הָעָם אַנְשֵׁי־חַיִל יִרְאֵי אֱלֹהִים אַנְשֵׁי אֱמֶת שֹׂנְאֵי בָצַע

The independent personal pronoun אַתָּה, "you (s.)," refers to Moses. The *qal* imperfect form תֶחֱזֶה, "provide," is preceded by the *qal* imperative form הֱיֵה, "be," in verse 19, so it is used as volitional to express the speaker's will in a positive request or command.[166] According to the BDB, the verb חָזָה, "to see, to behold," can also mean, "to provide."[167]

As it concerns Moses as the judge over Israel, Jethro encourages Moses to provide "men of ability who fear God, men of faithfulness who hate unjust gain"[168] from all Israel with Yahweh's revelation which helps Moses choose who are the right ones.[169] "Men of ability who fear God" are those whom Moses will provide from all Israel through Yahweh's direction and instruction, who have skills in both speech and action as influential leaders,[170] and who fear Yahweh.[171] "Men of faithfulness who

---

codices manuscripti, the Samaritan Pentateuch, the Greek version of the Old Testament (Septuagint), the Syriac version of the Old Testament, *codex manuscriptus vel editio secundum apparatum criticum Sperberi*, and the Vulgate read the conjunction with the construct noun וְשָׂרֵי, "and chiefs of," instead of the construct noun שָׂרֵי, "chiefs of."

166. *IBHS* §31.5 a–b, 509–10.

167. BDB, s.v. I. חָזָה, 3c, 302. Furthermore, Jacob, *Exodus*, 500, notes, "Here we also had a phrase taken from the prophetic language—*te-he-zeh*, which was used only in 24.11 in the *Torah* and as *ma-he-zeh* in Nu 24.4, 16 where it refers to the divine vision. A prophetic gaze which penetrated the inner being would be necessary to discover who was right (Rashi: *b'ru-ah ha-qo-desh she-a-le-kha*)." See also Houtman, *Exodus*, 2:418.

168. Interestingly, Houtman, *Exodus*, 2:418–19, notes, "For the four-fold requirement see e.g. Deut. 1:16f.; 16:18ff.; 1 Sam. 12:3ff.; 2 Chr. 19:6. Wisdom is not cited among the requirements (by contrast see Deut. 1:13; 1 Kgs. 3:9, 28), evidently because complex matters are to be submitted to Moses."

169. Dozeman, *Exodus*, 409, notes, "The Hebrew verb translated 'to select' in v. 21 (*ḥāzâ*) is a technical term for prophetic clairvoyance (see Amos 1:1; Isa 1:1; Mic 1:1). The advice is that Moses 'perceive' the qualities of justice and truth in the judges he appoints." Furthermore, Carpenter, *Exodus*, 1:622, notes, "'You yourself discern' (תֶחֱזֶה) uses a strong word whose ptc., חֹזֶה, is used to designate a 'seer,' or priviledged visionary: one who sees God's vision given to his people for discernment. Here, in a purely social context, the word indicates Moses' ability to discern those who have certain intangible qualities, but whose qualities are also visible to those who are sensitive to them." See also Houtman, *Exodus*, 2:418.

170. Propp, *Exodus*, 1:632, notes, "[M]*en of competence*. My translation is inspired by Ramban. *'îš ḥayil* can connote a warrior, a rich man or a citizen of deserved respect and social influence. While the last dominates here, the judges also require physical stamina and material prosperity (cf. ibn Ezra; next NOTE)." See also Jacob, *Exodus*, 500; Houtman, *Exodus*, 2:418; Dozeman, *Exodus*, 409; Carpenter, *Exodus*, 1:622.

171. Carpenter, *Exodus*, 1:623, notes, "The 'fear of God' (יִרְאֵי אֱלֹהִים) was a *sine qua non* in these men and helps define the aspect of these persons being emphasized in this context. They shared this moral quality with the midwives (Exod 1:17), and God

hate unjust gain" are those whom Moses will provide from all Israel through Yahweh's direction and instruction, who love truth, justice, and righteousness,[172] and who hate lies, injustice, and unrighteousness.[173]

18:21b וְשַׂמְתָּ עֲלֵהֶם שָׂרֵי אֲלָפִים שָׂרֵי מֵאוֹת שָׂרֵי חֲמִשִּׁים וְשָׂרֵי עֲשָׂרֹת:

The *qal* perfect *waw* consecutive form וְשַׂמְתָּ, "and set," is preceded by the *qal* imperative form הֱיֵה in verse 19, so it is used as volitional to express a command or wish.[174]

The noun שַׂר, "chieftain, chief, ruler, official, captain, prince," occurs in significant contexts prior to its appearance here. First, this noun occurs in Exod 1:11 to refer to the taskmasters (שָׂרֵי מִסִּים) whom Pharaoh and the Egyptians set (שִׂים) over Israel to afflict (III. עָנָה) Israel with burdens (סִבְלָה). Second, this noun is used in the question from one of the two struggling Hebrews: "Who set (שִׂים) you [Moses] a prince (שַׂר) and a judge (שֹׁפֵט) over us?" (Exod 2:14). Finally, here in Exod 18, this noun is used eight times to emphasize "chiefs of thousands, chiefs of hundreds, chiefs of fifties, and chiefs of tens"[175] whom Moses set (שִׂים/נָתַן) over

---

desired that even the Egyptians fear him, and some did (9:20; 10:7). Indeed, Israel, without the fear of God to guide them, would be useless and ultimately as corrupt and rebellious as Pharaoh and Amalekites—even the Amorites. The fear of God, axiomatic in Israel (Prov 1:7), ensured their ethical, moral, and religious integrity, and Yahweh would appear at Sinai for the express purpose of turning his people away from sinning (Exod 20:20). The fear of God helped establish them as men of character and truth (אֱמֶת), for they would not corrupt through bribery (בֶּצַע) the jurisprudence system they were being called on to establish." Furthermore, significantly, Jacob, *Exodus*, 500, notes, "*Yir-ei e-lo-him* who feared God, not men, in their judgments; 'for the judgment belongs to God' (Deut 1.17)."

172. Jacob, *Exodus*, 500, notes, "*An-shei e-met*—who always stood with truth and righteousness because it was an essential part of their being; Rashi explained it as upright, reliable, and straightforward; men whose judgments would be readily accepted. Ibn Ezra—those who did not lie." Furthermore, Cassuto, *Exodus*, 220, notes, "[M]*en of truth*—seekers of truth, who realize that the task of the judge is none other than to give true judgement."

173. Houtman, *Exodus*, 2:418, notes, "[T]hose who place their own interests and the betterment of their own position first easily succumb to the temptation of accepting gifts and resorting to extortion, and may be less than scrupulous about justice; the maintenance of a just society is not in good hands with them (cf. 1 Sam. 8:3; Isa. 56:11; Jer. 22:17; Hab. 2:9 et al.); justice is in good hands with those who do not put themselves first and are not greedy for gain (cf. Isa. 33:15; Ps. 119:36; Prov. 1:19; 15:27; 28:16)." See also Jacob, *Exodus*, 500; Propp, *Exodus*, 1:632.

174. *GBHS* §3.5.2 (*c*), 102–3. See also Davidson §55 (*a*), 81; *GKC* §112 *r*, 333; *IBHS* §32.2.2 *a–b*, 529–30; Joüon §119 *l*, 399–400; Gibson §76 (*a*), 94; Williams §179, 75–76.

175. Cassuto, *Exodus*, 220, notes, "[T]o serve as *rulers of thousands, rulers of hundreds, rulers of fifties, and rulers of tens*—these numbers are not to be interpreted with

Israel[176] (cf. Exod 18:25) to lighten (קָלַל) his load (cf. Exod 18:22) and to establish peace (שָׁלוֹם) for Israel (cf. Exod 18:23).

Exodus 18:22

וְשָׁפְטוּ אֶת־הָעָם֮ בְּכָל־עֵת֒ וְהָיָ֞ה כָּל־הַדָּבָ֤ר הַגָּדֹל֙ יָבִ֣יאוּ אֵלֶ֔יךָ וְכָל־הַדָּבָ֥ר הַקָּטֹ֖ן יִשְׁפְּטוּ־הֵ֑ם וְהָקֵל֙ מֵֽעָלֶ֔יךָ וְנָשְׂא֖וּ אִתָּֽךְ׃

18:22a וְשָׁפְטוּ אֶת־הָעָם֮ בְּכָל־עֵת֒ וְהָיָ֞ה כָּל־הַדָּבָ֤ר הַגָּדֹל֙ יָבִ֣יאוּ אֵלֶ֔יךָ וְכָל־הַדָּבָ֥ר הַקָּטֹ֖ן יִשְׁפְּטוּ־הֵ֑ם

The *qal* perfect *waw* consecutive form וְשָׁפְטוּ, "then let them judge," is preceded by the *qal* imperative form הֱיֵה, "be," in verse 19, so it is used as volitional to express a command or wish.[177] The subject of the verb שָׁפַט, "to judge, to govern," refers to men of ability who fear God, men of faithfulness who hate unjust gain or chiefs of thousands, chiefs of hundreds, chiefs of fifties, and chiefs of tens.

Jethro urges Moses to reduce his lone load by letting the chiefs of thousands, hundreds, fifties, and tens judge Israel's cases at all times. This means apparently that Israel no longer needs to wait for Moses all day because of their chiefs.[178]

---

mathematical exactitude, but as various ranks of rulers, one senior to the other." Furthermore, among many commentators, there are two arguments concerning the characteristic of "chiefs of thousands, chiefs of hundreds, chiefs of fifties, and chiefs of tens": (1) civil administration is that, for example, Stuart, *Exodus*, 418, notes, "These terms [thousands, hundreds, fifties and tens] are used elsewhere to denote military units, but here they delineate civilian groupings of various sizes. It is not any more likely that the terms are to be taken literally in this context than in a military context.... In other words, the expression 'thousands, hundreds, fifties and tens' seems to be essentially a figure of speech by which is meant 'all the various population groupings.'" See also Jacob, *Exodus*, 500–501; Houtman, *Exodus*, 2:419. And (2) military organization is that, for instance, Childs, *Exodus*, 331, notes, "The division of the people into units of thousands, hundreds, fifties, and tens reflects the military organization of the nation (I Sam. 29.2; II Sam. 18.1, etc.)." Further, Sarna, *Exploring Exodus*, 127, notes, "This ranking [chiefs of thousands, hundreds, fifties, and tens] by population division is unclear and better fits a military rather than civil administration." See also Davis, *Moses and Gods of Egypt*, 199; Durham, *Exodus*, 250–51; Sarna, *Exodus*, 101; Janzen, *Exodus*, 228; Niehr, "שָׂרַר; שָׂר; מִשְׂרָה," *TDOT* 14:205–6.

176. Propp, *Exodus*, 1:632, notes, "[P]lace over them. Although the language is somewhat ambiguous, the sense must be 'over the Israelites,' not 'over the judges' (cf. LXX)." See also Houtman, *Exodus*, 2:419.

177. *GBHS* §3.5.2 (c), 102–3. See also Davidson §55 (a), 81; *GKC* §112 r, 333; *IBHS* §32.2.2 a–b, 529–30; Joüon §119 l, 399–400; Gibson §76 (a), 94; Williams §179, 75–76.

178. Houtman, *Exodus*, 2:419, notes, "בכל־עת (see 9:18), the lengthy wait (18:13,

The *qal* perfect *waw* consecutive form וְהָיָה, "and it will be that," is used as impersonal and a linking word to introduce a new and important development.[179]

The *hiphil* imperfect form יָבִיאוּ, "they can bring," is used as a modal to express the ability to do something.[180]

The *qal* imperfect form יִשְׁפְּטוּ, "they can judge," is used as a modal to express the ability to do something.[181] The independent personal pronoun הֵם, "themselves," is used as emphatic with the *qal* imperfect form יִשְׁפְּטוּ.[182]

As it concerns Moses as the judge who would now set lesser chiefs (or judges) over Israel,[183] Jethro explains to Moses how justice should work: Every great case, they are to bring to Moses, so that Moses as the chief judge may judge it. However, every small case, they are to judge themselves.[184]

18:22b וְהָקֵל מֵעָלֶיךָ וְנָשְׂאוּ אִתָּךְ׃

The conjunction וְ, translated "and thus," is used as consequential to describe a logical consequence of an action or event which results from its preceding action or event,[185] "*and thus* lighten (the load)."

Here Jethro shows Moses two related results of setting the chiefs of Israel: (1) They will lighten (קָלַל) the load from Moses' lone responsibilities. And (2) they will carry (נָשָׂא) that load as Moses' helpers.

---

14) is over; with such a large number of judges grievances will be heard right away."

179. Gibson §72, 88–91.

180. Williams §169, 70–71. See also *GKC* §107 *r–s, w*, 318–19; *IBHS* §31.4 *b–c*, 507; Joüon §113 *l*, 370–71.

181. Williams §169, 70–71. See also *GKC* §107 *r–s, w*, 318–19; *IBHS* §31.4 *b–c*, 507; Joüon §113 *l*, 370–71.

182. *GKC* §32 *b*, 105. See also *GKC* §135 *a*, 437; *IBHS* §16.3.2 *a*, 293; Joüon §146 *a*, 538–40; Williams §106, 46.

183. Propp, *Exodus*, 1:632, notes, "[R]ulers. The term *śar* takes us back to 2:14 (J): 'Who set you [Moses] as a man, ruler (*śar*) and judge (*šōpēṭ*) over us?' Moses himself is now the one who appoints rulers and judges."

184. Regarding the administration of the chiefs of Israel, Cassuto, *Exodus*, 220, notes, "[I]n all normal cases: if the dispute affects a family, it should be brought before a ruler of ten; if a wider circle, it should be tried by a ruler of fifty or of a hundred; and if a still large group is involved, the case should be judged by a ruler of a thousand." See also Houtman, *Exodus*, 2:420.

185. Williams §181 *a*, 77. See also *GKC* §110 *f*, 324–25; Joüon §116 *a*, 381; Gibson §87, 106–7.

Exodus 18:23

אִם אֶת־הַדָּבָר הַזֶּה תַּעֲשֶׂה וְצִוְּךָ אֱלֹהִים וְיָכָלְתָּ עֲמֹד וְגַם כָּל־הָעָם הַזֶּה עַל־[186]
מְקֹמוֹ יָבֹא בְשָׁלוֹם:

18:23a אִם אֶת־הַדָּבָר הַזֶּה תַּעֲשֶׂה וְצִוְּךָ אֱלֹהִים וְיָכָלְתָּ עֲמֹד

The protasis or "if" clause is אִם אֶת־הַדָּבָר הַזֶּה תַּעֲשֶׂה וְצִוְּךָ אֱלֹהִים, "if you (s.) do *this thing* (דָּבָר), and God commands you (s.)."[187]

Here Jethro ends his advice to Moses with this: "and God commands you (s.)." This demonstrates that Jethro still respects the approval and confirmation of Yahweh, and that it is through such advice which Yahweh leads and guides Moses.[188]

The apodosis or "then" clause is וְיָכָלְתָּ עֲמֹד, "then you (s.) will be able to endure." The *qal* perfect *waw* consecutive form וְיָכָלְתָּ, "then you (s.) will be able," is used as apodictic to introduce the apodosis or "then" clause.[189] The *qal* infinitive construct form עֲמֹד, "to stand," or in this case "to endure,"[190] is used as nominal in the accusative case to describe what Moses will be able to do, and it also serves as a complement of the verb יָכֹל, "to be able, to have power, to prevail, to endure."[191]

The first result of acting according to Jethro's advice is that Moses will be able to endure his lone responsibilities by sharing his load with the chiefs of Israel.[192]

18:23b וְגַם כָּל־הָעָם הַזֶּה עַל־מְקֹמוֹ יָבֹא בְשָׁלוֹם:

The continued apodosis or "then" clause is וְגַם כָּל־הָעָם הַזֶּה עַל־מְקֹמוֹ יָבֹא בְשָׁלוֹם, "and also all this people will go to their place in peace (שָׁלוֹם)."

---

186. The Samaritan Pentateuch reads the preposition אֶל, "to," instead of the preposition עַל, "to."

187. *GBHS* §4.3.2 (a), 154. See also *GKC* §159 *l*, 494–95; *IBHS* §38.2 *d*, 636–38; Joüon §167 *c*, 629; Williams §453, 160.

188. Propp, *Exodus*, 1:633, notes, "18:23. *Deity commands*. Jethro seemingly returns to his proviso of v 19: the system will function only if God approves. Or the sense might be: God will guide Moses' judgment (Rashbam)." See also Cassuto, *Exodus*, 220–21; Houtman, *Exodus*, 2:420–21; Stuart, *Exodus*, 419; Carpenter, *Exodus*, 1:623.

189. *GBHS* §3.5.2 (d), 103–4. See also *GKC* §112 *ff*, 336; Gibson §71 (a), 86–87.

190. BDB, s.v. עָמַד, 3d, 764.

191. *GBHS* §3.4.1 (a), 80–82. See also *GKC* §114 *c*, 347; *IBHS* §36.2.1 *d*, 602; Joüon §124 *c*, 433; Williams §193, 81–82.

192. Houtman, *Exodus*, 2:421, notes, "Moses will stay healthy physically and mentally (cf. 18:18 for contrast)."

The second result of doing according to Jethro's advice is that Israel will go to their place in peace because they do not need to suffer prolonged conflict or disputing, or to spend all day long waiting for Moses' judgment.[193]

Exodus 18:24

וַיִּשְׁמַע מֹשֶׁה לְקוֹל חֹתְנוֹ וַיַּעַשׂ כֹּל אֲשֶׁר אָמָר:

18:24a וַיִּשְׁמַע מֹשֶׁה לְקוֹל חֹתְנוֹ

The sentence וַיִּשְׁמַע מֹשֶׁה לְקוֹל חֹתְנוֹ, "then Moses obeyed his father-in-law," literally means, "then Moses heard the voice of his father-in-law." Here, after hearing all Jethro's advice, Moses obeys Jethro, his father-in-law. In other words, Moses listens to Jethro because Jethro's advice is Yahweh's command.[194]

18:24b וַיַּעַשׂ כֹּל אֲשֶׁר אָמָר:

The subject of the verb עָשָׂה, "to do, to make," refers to Moses, and its object is the noun phrase כֹּל אֲשֶׁר אָמָר, "all which he had said." The subject of the verb אָמַר, "to utter, to say," refers to Jethro who had spoken to Moses with his advice.[195] Besides obeying Jethro, Moses does all which

---

193. Jacob, *Exodus*, 507, notes, "The last word spoken by this worthy priest [Jethro] was peace; with this he left Israel and Moses, whom he had once permitted to depart with the same word of blessing (4.18)." See also Propp, *Exodus*, 1:633. Furthermore, Stuart, *Exodus*, 419, notes, "Jethro's goal in this advice, which he assumed God would endorse, was that both Moses and the people would have relief: Moses from his huge workload ('you will be able to stand the strain') and the people's morale ('and all these people will go home satisfied')." See also Houtman, *Exodus*, 2:421.

194. Enns, *Exodus*, 372, notes, "Moses listens to his father-in-law and puts the plan into operation; we can assume it works well (vv. 24–26). It seems that the reason why Moses obeys Jethro is not to be polite or to try it to see if it works. Rather, as a number of commentators have mentioned, Jethro's advice is also God's command." See also Fretheim, *Exodus*, 199; Houtman, *Exodus*, 2:420–21. Furthermore, Propp, *Exodus*, 1:633, notes, "18:24. *listened*. Moses' obedience to Jethro implies divine confirmation of the plan (cf. vv 19, 23)."

195. Wagner, "אָמַר; אֹמֶר; אֵמֶר; אִמְרָה; אֲמָרָה; אֲמָר; מַאֲמָר; מֵאמַר," *TDOT* 1:331, notes, "1. *A Communication Term*. *'amar* is used to denote communication between two personal entities (or entities regarded as personal). The goal of *'amar* is that another person (or persons) might hear and understand, and might reply, in the broadest sense of the word (reaction)."

Jethro had said. In other words, Moses does all according to Jethro's advice as he has done all Yahweh's direction and instruction.[196]

Exodus 18:25

וַיִּבְחַ֨ר מֹשֶׁ֤ה אַנְשֵׁי־חַ֙יִל֙ מִכָּל־יִשְׂרָאֵ֔ל וַיִּתֵּ֥ן אֹתָ֛ם רָאשִׁ֖ים עַל־הָעָ֑ם שָׂרֵ֤י אֲלָפִים֙ שָׂרֵ֣י מֵא֔וֹת שָׂרֵ֥י חֲמִשִּׁ֖ים וְשָׂרֵ֥י עֲשָׂרֹֽת׃

18:25a וַיִּבְחַ֨ר מֹשֶׁ֤ה אַנְשֵׁי־חַ֙יִל֙ מִכָּל־יִשְׂרָאֵ֔ל וַיִּתֵּ֥ן אֹתָ֛ם רָאשִׁ֖ים עַל־הָעָ֑ם

Verses 25–26 are the repetition of "Jethro's words with a few changes" (cf. Exod 18:21–22).[197]

According to the BDB, the verb נָתַן, "to give, to put, to set," can also mean, "to set, to appoint."[198] The noun רָאשִׁים, "heads," is derived from the noun רֹאשׁ, "head," which in this context means, "chief (man)."[199] According to Jethro's advice, Moses chooses "men of ability" from all Israel, and he sets them heads to be leaders over Israel.[200]

---

196. Carpenter, *Exodus*, 1:623, notes, "The statement 'and he did everything just as he had said' indicates that Moses considered the advice as if it were from Yahweh. The phrase is used throughout Exodus to describe the obedience of Moses to Yahweh's instructions."

197. Cassuto, *Exodus*, 221.

198. BDB, s.v. נָתַן, 2c, 680. Furthermore, Lipiński, "אֶתְנָה; מַתַּת; מַתָּנָה; מַתָּן; נָתַן; מַתָּן; אֶתְנַן/אֶתְנָן," *TDOT* 10:93, notes, "2. *Set, Put*. The verb *nātan* is frequently used with the meaning 'set, put, place,' often accompanied by the preps. b^e, l^e, '*al*, or '*el* to indicate the place.... The semantic proximity with verbs of 'putting, placing' is also evident in numerous idiomatic expressions similarly constructed with → שִׂים *śîm*, sometimes → שִׁית *šît* and *nātan*, as if these verbs were synonyms."

199. BDB, s.v. I. רֹאשׁ, 3a, 911. Furthermore, Propp indicates "heads" as leaders (see Propp, *Exodus*, 1:633). See also Beuken, "רֹאשׁ I; רָאשָׁה; רֵאשָׁה; רֵאשִׁית; מְרַאֲשׁוֹת," *TDOT* 13:254.

200. It is interesting that a few scholars argue that this event does not take place now but in Deut 1:9–18. For example, Jacob, *Exodus*, 502, notes, "Moses agreed with his [Jethro's] analysis, but delayed the execution of this plan [the organization of the people] till the following year just prior to breaking camp at Sinai." Furthermore, a number of commentators consider that this event relates to Deut 17:8–13 and 2 Chr 19:4–11. For instance, Brueggemann, "Exodus," 1:828–29, notes, "Deut 17:8–13 as the establishment of a judiciary system with a central high court and 2 Chr 19:4–11 as an important judicial reform in Jerusalem (see also Deut 16:18–20)."

Exodus 18:26

וְשָׁפְט֣וּ[201] אֶת־הָעָם֮ בְּכָל־עֵת֒ אֶת־הַדָּבָ֤ר הַקָּשֶׁה֙ יְבִיא֣וּן אֶל־מֹשֶׁ֔ה וְכָל־הַדָּבָ֥ר הַקָּטֹ֖ן יִשְׁפּוּט֥וּ הֵֽם׃

18:26a וְשָׁפְט֣וּ אֶת־הָעָם֮ בְּכָל־עֵת֒

The *qal* perfect *waw* consecutive form וְשָׁפְט֣וּ, "and thus they kept on judging," is used as consequential to describe a logical consequence of an action or event which results from its preceding action or event.[202] Therefore, in this case, the *waw* consecutive וְ is translated "and thus" to describe a resulting action of its previous action. This form is used as iterative to describe that the chiefs of Israel habitually judged Israel.[203]

18:26b אֶת־הַדָּבָ֤ר הַקָּשֶׁה֙ יְבִיא֣וּן אֶל־מֹשֶׁ֔ה וְכָל־הַדָּבָ֥ר הַקָּטֹ֖ן יִשְׁפּוּט֥וּ הֵֽם׃

The *hiphil* imperfect form with the paragogic *nun* יְבִיא֣וּן, "they would bring," and the *qal* imperfect form יִשְׁפּוּט֥וּ, "they would judge," are preceded by the *qal* imperfect *waw* consecutive forms, וַיִּבְחַ֥ר, "then he chose," and וַיִּתֵּ֥ן, "and he set," in verse 25, and they are translated in past tense to fit the past time context.[204]

The independent personal pronoun הֵֽם, "themselves," is used as emphatic with the *qal* imperfect form יִשְׁפּוּט֥וּ which is the third person masculine plural, in order to focus on the subject of the *qal* imperfect form יִשְׁפּוּט֥וּ.[205]

Exodus 18:27

וַיְשַׁלַּ֥ח מֹשֶׁ֖ה אֶת־חֹתְנ֑וֹ וַיֵּ֥לֶךְ ל֖וֹ אֶל־אַרְצֽוֹ׃ פ

18:27a וַיְשַׁלַּ֥ח מֹשֶׁ֖ה אֶת־חֹתְנ֑וֹ

The subject of the *piel* of the verb שָׁלַח, "to send off, to send away," is the proper noun מֹשֶׁה, "Moses." Moses' act of sending Jethro away is portrayed

---

201. The Samaritan Pentateuch reads the *qal* imperfect *waw* consecutive form וַיִּשְׁפְּטוּ, "and they judged," instead of the *qal* perfect *waw* consecutive form וְשָׁפְט֣וּ, "and thus they kept on judging."

202. *GBHS* §3.5.2 (*b*), 102. See also *GKC* §112 *a*, 330; Gibson §69, 83–85.

203. *GBHS* §3.5.2 (*e*), 104–5. See also *GKC* §112 *e*, 331–32; Joüon §119 *v*, 402–3.

204. *IBHS* §32.2.3 *e*, 533–34. See also *GKC* §112 *g*, 332; Joüon §119 *v*, 402–3.

205. *GKC* §32 *b*, 105. See also *GKC* §135 *a*, 437; *IBHS* §16.3.2 *a*, 293; Joüon §146 *a*, 538–40; Williams §106, 46.

as a happy conclusion.²⁰⁶ This recalls Exod 4:18–20 when Moses with his family went back to the land of Egypt.²⁰⁷

18:27b וַיֵּלֶךְ לוֹ אֶל־אַרְצוֹ׃ פ

The subject of the verb הָלַךְ, "to go, to come, to walk," refers to Jethro. The preposition with the pronominal suffix third person masculine singular לוֹ is used as possessive to describe that Jethro has his own country, which refers to the land of Midian.²⁰⁸ This is the last time in which Jethro appears in the Exodus narrative.²⁰⁹

---

206. Stuart, *Exodus*, 419, notes, "Moses' sending 'his father-in-law on his way' does not connote any such overtone as 'getting rid of Jethro' but suggests a warm, happy parting." Furthermore, Carpenter, *Exodus*, 1:624, notes, "The sending of Moses' father-in-law constitutes the second half of the inclusio found in vv. 2 and 5."

207. As narrated in verses 2–6, Moses reunites his family, Zipporah, Gershom, and Eliezer, and later, they are absent from the narrative until here, at the end of the narrative, for the entirety of the OT. Many scholars think that Jethro alone went to his own country, and Moses' wife and two sons still were with Moses. For example, Enns, *Exodus*, 373, notes, "Jethro and Moses part company in verse 27, as they had done earlier in 4:19–20, but now for the last time. Presumably Moses' family remains behind, since Gershom's descendants serve as priests (Judg. 18:30), although Zipporah is not mentioned again. Interestingly, according to Numbers 12:1, Moses had a Cushite wife. This may be a second wife in addition to Zipporah, or a wife after the death of Zipporah (not recorded); any suggestion is conjecture. The fact that 18:27 stresses that '*Jethro* returned' should, I feel, be taken at face value: he and he alone." See also Stuart, *Exodus*, 419.

208. *GBHS* §4.1.10 (*f*), 126. See also Joüon §130 *g*, 476–77; Williams §270, 106–7.

209. Jacob, *Exodus*, 505, notes, "His [Jethro's] farewell was final, and he never again appears in the history of Israel." Furthermore, Propp, *Exodus*, 1:633, "[W]ent him . . . *to his land*. Rather than join Israel, Jethro returns to minister among his own people – to what god(s) is unclear. Conceivably, he will be a missionary for Yahweh." See also Stuart, *Exodus*, 419.

Chapter 3
Narrative Analysis of Exodus 18

THIS CHAPTER WILL PRESENT, in two parts, an initial analysis of the narrative features and theological themes of Exod 18:1–27. Part 1, "The Structure of Exodus 18," will present, and then modify, a symmetrical outline of Exod 18, which Carpenter offers.[1] Part 2, "Other Narrative Elements of Exodus 18," will examine Exod 18 by employing narrative analysis and by focusing on literary elements, including (1) the narrator, (2) the characters, (3) the plot, (4) time and space, and (5) style.[2]

The Structure of Exodus 18

Eugene Carpenter states, "Exodus 18 is perhaps the major transitional chapter in the book of Exodus, summarizing the past events (Exod. 1–17) and preparing for the coming revelations at Sinai (Exod. 19–40)."[3] He observes, "It is a skillfully constructed, unified chapter that both unites and divides Exodus."[4] He also explains:

---

1. Carpenter, "Exodus 18," 96. See also Carpenter, *Exodus*, 1:604–5.

2. Bar-Efrat, *Narrative Art in the Bible*, 10–11.

3. Carpenter, "Exodus 18," 91. Further, he notes, "But ch. 18 seems to be the major hinge in the structure of the total composition, serving both as a prologue *and* an epilogue." Carpenter, "Exodus 18," 91–92. See also Carpenter, "Exodus 18," 107.

4. Carpenter, "Exodus 18," 92. See also Carpenter, "Exodus 18," 108.

The first half of the chapter (vv. 1–12) brings the exodus deliverance motif of the preceding chapters to a meaningful conclusion (τελός), but also addresses the issues raised by the Midianite traditions, both essential and incidental, found in chs. 2–4. The second half of the chapter (vv. 13–27) points forward to the dissemination of *mišpaṭ* (משפט) and therefore, to Sinai. The second half creates a totally new ambience appropriate to the ongoing activities of Sinai.[5]

Consequently, this chapter will consider and examine the structure of Exod 18 which will build upon Carpenter's symmetrical outline of Exod 18 and will extend and revise it.

When considering Exod 18 as "a whole," that is, "a literary unit,"[6] Carpenter presents a symmetrical outline of Exod 18 as follows:

Symmetrical Outline of Exodus 18

Flashback (v. 1)

On the next day (v. 13)

First Section (vv. 1–12)	Second Section (vv. 13–27)
Scenario (vv. 2–7)	Scenario (vv. 13–16)
First half of inclusio (vv. 2/5)* (Parenthetical report/repetition (vv. 3–4))	
Moses relates the story (v. 8)	Jethro relates his advice (vv. 17–23) (large direct speech balances introduction/conclusion to vv. 1–12; direct speech indicates importance of material)
Jethro responds (vv. 9–12)	Moses responds (vv. 24–27)
(report/repetition)	
—in attitude (v. 9)	—in attitude (v. 24)
—in word (vv. 10–11)	—in word (v. 25)
—in action (v. 12) —(direct speech indicates importance of material)	—in action (v. 26)
	Second half of inclusio (v. 27)*

---

5. Carpenter, "Exodus 18," 93.
6. Carpenter, "Exodus 18," 94.

* Everything between the inclusio takes place in the holy space and time, at the Mountain of God.⁷

According to Carpenter's symmetrical outline of Exod 18 above, he divides Exod 18 chronologically into two parts (vv. 1–12 and 13–27) divided by the prepositional phrase מִֽמָּחֳרָ֔ת, "on the next day," which functions as an adverb of time. Each part has the introduction—v. 1 functions as a "flashback" for the reader and as a "transition" to Exod 18. Each of these two parts contains the scenarios (vv. 2–7 and 13–16), the reports (vv. 8 and 17–23), and the concluding responses to the reports (vv. 9–12 and 24–27). Moreover, the beginning elements in the first part and the final verse of the second part form an inclusio for Exod 18 as a whole: "Then Jethro, the father-in-law of Moses, took Zipporah, the wife of Moses, after she had been sent away, . . . Then Jethro, the father-in-law of Moses, with his sons and his wife, came to Moses, to the wilderness where he was encamping at the mountain of God" (vv. 2, 5) and "Then Moses sent away his father-in-law, and he went to his own country" (v. 27).⁸

First, regarding the scenarios (vv. 2–7 and 13–16), Carpenter observes that the first half of Exod 18 (vv. 1–12) contains "the parenthetical comment" concerning Moses' two sons (vv. 3–4) which is between the two statements (vv. 2, 5) as the inclusio to the first half of Exod 18. Similarly, he discerns that the second half of Exod 18 (vv. 13–27) contains "Jethro's direct speech" (vv. 17–23) which parallels the first half of Exod 18. Interestingly, he notes that each of these two major parts begins with "a parallel phrase": v. 1 begins with, "Jethro heard," and v. 14 begins with, "Jethro saw."⁹

Second, concerning the reports (vv. 8 and 17–23) and the concluding responses to the reports (vv. 9–12 and 24–27), Carpenter explains that the first part (vv. 1–12) shows the main dialogue between Moses and Jethro. Moses "recounts the exodus story" while Jethro "listens" and "responds" in attitude (v. 9), in word (vv. 10–11), and in action (v. 12). In the second part (vv. 13–27), the main dialogue between Moses and Jethro happens again, but there is a reversal. Jethro gives advice as Moses listens and responds in attitude (v. 24), in word (v. 25), and in action (v. 26).¹⁰

---

7. Carpenter, "Exodus 18," 96. See also Carpenter, *Exodus*, 1:604–5.
8. Carpenter, "Exodus 18," 94. See also Carpenter, *Exodus*, 1:603.
9. Carpenter, "Exodus 18," 94–95. See also Carpenter, *Exodus*, 1:603–4.
10. Carpenter, "Exodus 18," 95. See also Carpenter, *Exodus*, 1:604.

Finally, regarding the inclusio to Exod 18 (vv. 2, 5 and 27), Carpenter points to "the action" of Exod 18 "in the vicinity of the Mountain of God, the place of holy space and holy time (worship and instruction)."[11] However, he clarifies, "The inclusio does not include the material in vv. 1 and 3–4 because that material does not reflect events that took place in the holy space of the vicinity of the Mountain of Yahweh, nor during the two days of holy time there."[12]

In addition to reflecting on and analyzing Carpenter's symmetrical outline of Exod 18 above, the book will develop and modify it in order to express how Exod 18 functions literarily and theologically as the key transitional midpoint in the Exodus narrative:

Developed and Modified Symmetrical Outline of the Episode of Exodus 18

The First Scene (vv. 1–12):	The Second Scene (vv. 13–27):
Now (v. 1):	On the next day (v. 13):
—The present day or the first day	—The next day or the second day
The narrator introduces the first scene (vv. 1–4):	The narrator introduces the second scene (vv. 13–14a):
	—Moses sits to judge Israel (v. 13)
—Jethro hears all which Yahweh had done for Moses and Israel (v. 1)	—Jethro sees all which Moses is doing alone for Israel (v. 14a)
—Jethro takes Zipporah and her two sons, Gershom and Eliezer (vv. 2–4)	
The narrator tells the first scene (vv. 5–12):	The narrator tells the second scene (vv. 14b–27):
—Jethro comes with Zipporah and her two sons, Gershom and Eliezer, to Moses (vv. 5–6)	—Jethro asks Moses (v. 14b)
—Moses meets Jethro (v. 7)	—Moses answers Jethro (vv. 15–16)
—Moses recounts to Jethro concerning the salvation of Yahweh (v. 8)	—Jethro advises Moses concerning the responsibilities of Moses (vv. 17–23)
—Jethro responds (vv. 9–12):	—Moses responds (vv. 24–26):
• Jethro rejoices in Yahweh (in attitude) (v. 9)	• Moses obeys Jethro (in attitude) (v. 24a)

---

11. Carpenter, "Exodus 18," 95. See also Carpenter, *Exodus*, 1:604.
12. Carpenter, "Exodus 18," 95–96. See also Carpenter, *Exodus*, 1:604.

- Jethro praises and confesses Yahweh (in word) (vv. 10–11)

- Jethro worships Yahweh (in action) (v. 12)
- Moses does all which Jethro has advised Moses (in action) (vv. 24b–26)

—Moses sends away Jethro (v. 27a)

—Jethro goes to his own country (v. 27b)

According to the developed and modified symmetrical outline of the episode of Exod 18 above, it is clear that the episode of Exod 18 contains two main parts or scenes (vv. 1–12 and 13–27).[13] These two main scenes are divided by the prepositional phrase מִמָּחֳרָת (v. 13) which serves as an adverb of time in order to indicate a continuing time. This continuing time shifts from one day to another day in the narrative.[14] Here Exod 18 has been divided into two days: (1) Now, that is, the present day or the first day happens in vv. 1–12. And (2) the next day, that is, the second day happens in vv. 13–27. Each scene consists of the introduction to the scene (vv. 1–4 and 13–14a), the key actions in the scene (vv. 5–12 and 14b–27), and the inclusio (vv. 5 and 27b).

First, concerning the introduction to the scene (vv. 1–4 and 13–14a), the narrator introduces both scenes with Jethro who is one of the main characters in Exod 18: Jethro *hears* all that Yahweh had done for Moses and Israel (v. 1), and Jethro *sees* all that Moses is doing alone for Israel (v. 14a). Both phrases parallel each other with the verbs of perception, that is, "to hear" (v. 1) and "to see" (v. 14a).[15] Indeed, Jethro both hears of all

---

13. Regarding the part or scene, the book will consider Exod 18 as two distinct scenes (vv. 1–12 and 13–27) which involve "a small number of active characters," that is, Jethro and Moses and "*short* speeches," that is, the small conversation between Jethro and Moses (see Utzschneider and Oswald, *Exodus 1–15*, 26). Furthermore, concerning the episode, the book will consider Exod 18 as an episode within the Exodus narrative which includes two distinct scenes with Jethro and Moses' speeches and actions (see Utzschneider and Oswald, *Exodus 1–15*, 26–29).

14. Noth, *Exodus*, 146, realizes the two scenes of Exod 18 as "two consecutive days." See also Janzen, "Jethro," 165–66; Dozeman, *Exodus*, 408; Johnstone, *Exodus*, 1:373, 377; Carpenter, "Exodus 18," 94; Carpenter, *Exodus*, 1:603, 616; Ber, "Moses and Jethro," 154; André, "מָחָר; מׇחֳרָת," *TDOT* 8:237–41.

15. Cassuto, *Exodus*, 218, notes, "The phrasing is intended to form a parallelism between the beginning of this paragraph [Exod 18:14] and the commencement of the first paragraph (v. 1): first he heard all that God had done for Israel; now he sees all that Moses is doing for Israel." See also Carpenter, "Exodus 18," 95; Carpenter, *Exodus*, 1:604; Ber, "Moses and Jethro," 155.

Yahweh's saving acts for Israel and sees all Moses' solitary responsibilities for Israel. In other words, Jethro *hears* all Yahweh's saving acts for Israel which is narrated in Exod 1–17. Likewise, Jethro *sees* all Moses' lone responsibilities for Israel, which have begun here in Exod 18, and will be prominent in Exod 19–40. Thus, when approaching Exod 18 as the key transitional midpoint in the Exodus narrative, both introductions in the episode of Exod 18 show a main turning point. This main turning point changes from Jethro's hearing of all Yahweh's delivering and powerful acts for Israel narrated in Exod 1–17 to Jethro's seeing of all Moses' lone deeds for Israel being dominant in Exod 19–40.

Second, regarding the key actions in the scene (vv. 5–12 and 14b–27), the narrator tells both scenes with the reactions between Jethro and Moses: In the first scene, *Jethro* comes to Moses (vv. 5–6), and *Moses* goes out to meet Jethro (v. 7). *Moses* recounts to Jethro concerning the salvation of Yahweh (v. 8), and then *Jethro* responds by rejoicing in Yahweh (in attitude) (v. 9), by praising and confessing Yahweh (in word) (vv. 10–11), and by worshiping Yahweh (in action) (v. 12). In the second scene, *Jethro* asks Moses (v. 14b), and *Moses* answers Jethro (vv. 15–16). *Jethro* advises Moses concerning the lone responsibilities of Moses (vv. 17–23), and then *Moses* responds by obeying Jethro (in attitude) (v. 24a) and by doing all which Jethro has advised Moses (in action) (vv. 24b–26). These reactions between Jethro and Moses parallel each other with the two main characters who exchange their responses.[16] On the one hand, *Moses* recounts to Jethro all Yahweh's great deeds for Israel, and then *Jethro* responds to Yahweh in attitude, word, and action, but, on the other hand, *Jethro* advises Moses concerning all Moses' lone deeds for Israel, and then *Moses* responds to Jethro in attitude and action. Consequently, in relation to Exod 18 as the key transitional midpoint in the Exodus narrative, both key actions exchanged between Jethro and Moses in the episode of Exod 18 demonstrate a major pivot. This pivot shifts from the end or conclusion of the fulfillment of Yahweh's promises for Israel to deliver Israel from Egypt, so that Israel will serve (or worship) Yahweh on the mountain of God expressed in Exod 3:7–12 to the beginning or anticipation of the great revelation of Yahweh on Mount Sinai through Moses alone in Exod 19–40.

Finally, concerning the inclusio (vv. 5 and 27b), the narrator highlights Jethro as one of the main characters in the episode of Exod

---

16. Carpenter, "Exodus 18," 95. See also Carpenter, *Exodus*, 1:604.

18. First, Jethro *comes* with Zipporah and her two sons, Gershom and Eliezer, to Moses (v. 5), and, finally, Jethro *goes* to his own country (v. 27b). This plot makes apparent the inclusio to Exod 18 in the holy time and at the holy place with, first, coming to Moses at the mountain of God and, finally, going to the land of Midian.[17] In other words, on the first day, Jethro *comes* to the episode of Exod 18, and at the end, that is, on the second day, he *goes* out of the episode of Exod 18. Therefore, as seeing Exod 18 as the key transitional midpoint in the Exodus narrative, the inclusio of Jethro's actions in the episode of Exod 18, that is, "coming (in)" (v. 5) and "going (out)" (v. 27b), displays a main bridge. This main bridge moves from the fulfillment of Yahweh's purpose on his sacred name recounted in all the earth in Exod 9:16 through Jethro's coming to the mountain of God, the holy place, to the anticipation of Yahweh's purpose on his holy people among all the nations in Exod 19:5–6 through Jethro's going to the land of Midian, that is, the earth.

In conclusion, as discussed above, Carpenter's work on Exod 18 as "the major transitional chapter in the book of Exodus"[18] is helpful. Exodus 18 looks backward to what Yahweh had done for Israel through Jethro's hearing of all Yahweh's saving acts for Israel (v. 1; cf. v. 8) and to what Yahweh had promised through Jethro's coming to worship Yahweh at Mount Sinai (v. 12). Likewise, it looks forward to what Yahweh is going to do for Israel through the prominence of Moses (v. 14a) and to the holy location of Mount Sinai and all which will take place there, accented by Jethro's arrival (v. 5) and departure (v. 27b). Carpenter's work directly supports the thesis of the book: Exod 18:1–27 functions literarily and theologically as the key transitional midpoint in the Exodus narrative.

---

17. Coats, *Exodus 1–18*, 147, notes, "Element IV [Conclusion: v. 27] stands in parallel with element I [Exposition: vv. 1–7]. Just as the opening notes Jethro's arrival, so the closing notes his departure (on the parallel with Gen 26:31, cf. Brekelmans)." Motyer, *Exodus*, 170, notes, "The whole chapter [Exod 18] is bracketed by the arrival and the departure of Jethro (1, 27)." Johnstone, *Exodus*, 1:373, notes, "The arrival of Jethro, Moses' father-in-law, in vv. 1–7 and his departure in v. 27 demarcate Exod 18 as a single episode (MT marks it as one unit)." See also Carpenter, "Exodus 18," 95–96; Carpenter, *Exodus*, 1:604; Preuss, "בּוֹא; אָתָה," *TDOT* 2:22–25. Furthermore, a number of commentators approach the scene of Jethro's departure to his own country as the end of the episode of Exod 18 (see Cassuto, *Exodus*, 221; Childs, *Exodus*, 331; Brueggemann, "Exodus," 1:828; Enns, *Exodus*, 373; Thompson, *Origin Tradition*, 150).

18. Carpenter, "Exodus 18," 91. See also Carpenter, "Exodus 18," 107.

Other Narrative Elements of Exodus 18

As discussed above, the developed and modified symmetrical outline of the episode of Exod 18 demonstrates its literary quality. This leads the book to employ narrative analysis in order to analyze the episode. L. D. Hawk explains narrative criticism (or narrative analysis):

> Central to the method is an interest in the ways that a story is shaped into a narrative. Narrative criticism commonly distinguishes between "story" and "narrative," story being an abstraction that becomes concrete when given utterance through the medium of narrative. Since a story may be told, or narrated, in any number of ways, narrative critics undertake a close reading of texts in order to discern the narrator's strategies and message. Through analysis of the techniques and devices that configure a narrative, the critic attempts to discern the interests, perspectives and purposes of the narrator.[19]

Hawk clarifies that narrative is narrated through the communication of the narrator, for example, Hebrew literary features and significant themes,[20] and that the critic reads closely the narrative by employing narrative analysis to acknowledge how fascinated, thoughtful, and purposeful the narrator is.

Regarding constructive literary approaches, Dennis T. Olson argues:

> Many literary studies of biblical texts in the 1970s and 1980s shared a commitment to what might be called "constructive" literary readings of biblical texts. They often sought to highlight the artfulness, sophistication and meaningfulness of biblical literature, both prose and poetry. Literary scholars often assumed a basic unity, structure, and coherence in the text.[21]

Olson focuses on the literary features which the author utilizes. This literary work of the biblical texts expresses how artful, sophisticated, and meaningful it is.

Likewise, Umberto Cassuto approaches the book of Exodus as a whole in terms of both its theological themes and literary features:

> The Book of Exodus is not only a sublime religious document; it is also a literary masterpiece, and our understanding of any

---

19. Hawk, "Literary/Narrative Criticism," *DOTP* 537–38.
20. Hawk, "Literary/Narrative Criticism," *DOTP* 538.
21. Olson, "Literary and Rhetorical Criticism," 16.

literary work depends on our understanding of the artistic criteria which governed its composition, and on our appreciation of the beauty with which it is imbued.[22]

Besides the theological quality of the book of Exodus, Cassuto observes the literary quality within the book of Exodus which displays artistry and beauty work throughout the book of Exodus.

In discussing narrative analysis and the literary design within the biblical texts, especially within the book of Exodus, Shimon Bar-Efrat lists five main narrative elements: (1) the narrator, (2) the characters, (3) the plot, (4) time and space, and (5) style.[23] A consideration of each of these elements will serve to further demonstrate narrative analysis of Exod 18 and to lay a foundation for the book's case for Exod 18 as the key transitional midpoint in the Exodus narrative.

The Narrator

The narrator's voice is a constituent part of the narrative and is located, in real sense, inside the narrative.[24] Throughout the episode of Exod

---

22. Cassuto, *Exodus*, 3. Further, he describes the book of Exodus as "a literary masterpiece" by paying attention to "the literary techniques of the ancient Orient," for example, "the sequence of the sections, the repetitions of words, phrases, paragraphs, or complete sections, the numerical symmetry, the symbolical of the numbers," and so on (see Cassuto, *Exodus*, 3).

23. Bar-Efrat, *Narrative Art in the Bible*, 10–11. Nevertheless, Fewell and Gunn point to six elements of narrative: (1) plot structure, (2) character, (3) narrator's point of view, (4) language and meaning, (5) irony, and (6) reader's point of view (see Fewell and Gunn, "Narrative, Hebrew," *ABD* 4:1024–27). See also Hawk, "Literary/Narrative Criticism," *DOTP* 539–43. Furthermore, Siebert-Hommes, *Let the Daughters Live!*, 17–18, notes, "The architecture of a text is multifaceted and complex. In attempting to bring to light as many features of the architecture of a biblical text as possible, various aspects require attention: 1. features relating to its inherent auditory character; 2. peculiarities reflecting its basic Hebrew nature; 3. segmentational units within the story; 4. word repetition; 5. textual structure; [and] 6. polysemy." For more details, see Siebert-Hommes, *Let the Daughters Live!*, 18–29. Other scholars stress three main narrative components: Powell, *What Is Narrative Criticism?*, 35, notes, "Every story encompasses three elements: events, characters, and settings. Somebody does something to someone, somewhere, at some time. The 'something' that is done is an event, the 'somebody' and 'someone' are characters, and the 'somewhere' and 'sometime' are settings." Gunn and Fewell describe narrative constructed by three elements: (1) character, (2) plot, and (3) wordplay (see Gunn and Fewell, *Narrative in the Hebrew Bible*, 1–3). Walsh indicates three narrative components: (1) place, (2) time, and (3) characters (see Walsh, *Style and Structure*, 119–20).

24. Bar-Efrat, *Narrative Art in the Bible*, 13–14. Further, he notes, "It is also

18, the voice of the narrator (Exod 18:1, 2–4, 5–6a, 7, 8, 9, 10a, 12, 13, 14a, 15a, 17a, 24, 25–26, 27) appears and plays a role as "the omniscient narrator"[25] and "the manifesting narrator."[26] The omniscient narrator is the one who seems to know everything about the characters and the details in the episode.[27] The narrator knows about Jethro, the priest of Midian, the father-in-law of Moses, about the family of Moses, including his wife, Zipporah, and two sons, Gershom and Eliezer, where Moses was encamping, and even every speech and action of the characters throughout the episode. He also knows the hidden details which are not told in the episode, for instance, how Jethro heard all redemptive deeds of Yahweh for Israel, when Zipporah, the wife of Moses, was sent away, when Eliezer, the second son of Moses, was born, how the report of the coming of Jethro reached Moses, and even when Jethro came to Moses and went to his own country. Moreover, the manifesting narrator is the

---

customary to make a distinction between the (implied) author and the narrator. It is the latter who tells us what is happening and which character is speaking at any given time. The former becomes known to us through what the narrator says, through the speech of the characters (which is formulated by the author) and through the organization of the narrative materials, plot, time, space, etc." Bar-Efrat, *Narrative Art in the Bible*, 14. Furthermore, as considering the differences between the author and the narrator, Hawk, "Literary/Narrative Criticism," *DOTP* 542, notes, "The narrator can be thought of simply as the one through whom the story is told, as distinguished from the author(s) who produced the text. The 'narrator' is thus an abstract entity who renders the story into a whole, suggests connections and invests events and characters with significance." Concerning the narrator's point of view, Fewell and Gunn, "Narrative, Hebrew," *ABD* 4:1025, note, "The narrator's point of view can be detected in direct narration, comment, and explanation. Alternatively, the narrator may step aside and allow the characters to speak for themselves and so to convey their own point of view." For more details and examples of the narrator, see Gunn and Fewell, *Narrative in the Hebrew Bible*, 52–63; Walsh, *Style and Structure*, 124–25, 140–43; Walsh, *Old Testament Narrative*, 97–105.

25. Bar-Efrat, *Narrative Art in the Bible*, 17–23. See also Hawk, "Literary/Narrative Criticism," *DOTP* 542–43. Nevertheless, Fokkelman, *Reading Biblical Narrative*, 56, notes, "The first sentences of the Bible [Genesis 1] immediately betray one of the main characteristics of the narrator: he is *omniscient*—but in a literary rather than a theological sense." Further, he notes, "The writer of Genesis 1 tells us about events at which nobody was present, and yet he tells them with authority. This authority is a result of his position as narrator." Fokkelman, *Reading Biblical Narrative*, 56. For more details on the writer's license and authority, see Fokkelman, *Reading Biblical Narrative*, 57–59.

26. Bar-Efrat, *Narrative Art in the Bible*, 23–41.

27. Bar-Efrat, *Narrative Art in the Bible*, 14. Further, he notes, "The former [narrators who know everything about the characters] see through solid walls into secret corners, even penetrating the hidden recesses of people's minds." Bar-Efrat, *Narrative Art in the Bible*, 14. See also Hawk, "Literary/Narrative Criticism," *DOTP* 540.

one who exists everywhere in the episode.[28] The narrator is in the episode by seeing all which Yahweh had done for Moses and Israel in Egypt, at the Red Sea, and in the wilderness and also by hearing and seeing all which Jethro and Moses had said and done in the episode.

Consequently, the episode of Exod 18 is marked by a consistent omniscient narrative point of view. The narrator who knows everything and is present everywhere in the episode shows the episode as a unified account and makes it flow coherently by connecting the details in the past (or *analepses*)[29] with the details in the present and future (or *prolepses*).[30] For example, the narrator narrates the details in the past about all redemptive deeds of Yahweh for Israel in Egypt, at the Red Sea, and in the wilderness, about Moses' family, including his wife, Zipporah, and first son, Gershom, and so on, and the details in the present and future about Moses' second son, Eliezer, about Jethro's rejoicing in, praising, confessing, and worshiping Yahweh, about Jethro's advice, and so on. The details in the past told by the narrator in the episode assist the reader in recalling the significant deeds in the preceding incidents, especially all of Yahweh's delivering and powerful acts for Israel as internal *analepses*.[31] Similarly, the details in the present and future reported by the narrator in the episode help the reader anticipate the important actions in the following events, especially Yahweh's great self-revelation at Mount Sinai as mixed *prolepses*.[32] This illustrates clearly that the narrator holds the two

---

28. Bar-Efrat, *Narrative Art in the Bible*, 14. Further, he notes, "The latter [narrators who are present everywhere] observe things from the outside, seeing what people do and hearing what they say, leaving it to us to draw conclusions about their inner lives." Bar-Efrat, *Narrative Art in the Bible*, 14. See also Hawk, "Literary/Narrative Criticism," *DOTP* 540.

29. Concerning the details in the past (or *analepses*), the book will point to the past or preceding events which are narrated by the narrator fully in the past and again and briefly in the episode of Exod 18 in order to draw the reader's attention to a conclusion or a recall of the significant events. See also Powell, *What Is Narrative Criticism?*, 36–38.

30. Concerning the details in the present and future (or *prolepses*), the book will point to the future or following events which are narrated by the narrator briefly in the episode of Exod 18 and later and fully in the future in order to draw the reader's attention to an introduction or an anticipation of the significant events. See also Powell, *What Is Narrative Criticism?*, 36–38.

31. In the episode of Exod 18, the narrator tells concisely the past incidents which occurred within the book of Exodus, that is, the preceding chapters (see Powell, *What Is Narrative Criticism?*, 37).

32. In the episode of Exod 18, the narrator tells concisely the future incidents which will occur within the book of Exodus, that is, the following chapters and outside of it, that is, the rest of the Pentateuchal narratives (see Powell, *What Is Narrative Criticism?*, 37–38).

major scenes of the episode together with the key transition through both conclusion of the past and anticipation of the future.

The Characters

The characters in the narrative are developed mainly through their speeches and actions.[33] The episode of Exod 18 has both main characters

---

33. Bar-Efrat, *Narrative Art in the Bible*, 47–48. Further, he explains how the narrator uses "the principal techniques" to shape the characters in the narrative (see Bar-Efrat, *Narrative Art in the Bible*, 48). There are two principal techniques: (1) The direct shaping of the characters includes: (a) outward appearance, that is, the details of the physical and external appearance of the characters, for example, a hairy man and a smooth man, weak eyes and beautiful and lovely eyes, tall and short, and so on (see Bar-Efrat, *Narrative Art in the Bible*, 48–53); and (b) inward personality, that is, the descriptions of the characterizations of the characters, for instance, a righteous man and wicked, great sinners, a blameless and upright man, the man who revered God and feared God, and so on (see Bar-Efrat, *Narrative Art in the Bible*, 53–64). And (2) the indirect shaping of the characters includes: (a) speech, that is, the interactions between the speaker and the interlocutor expresses the character, thoughts, feelings, and status of the speaker and the interlocutor (see Bar-Efrat, *Narrative Art in the Bible*, 64–77); (b) actions, that is, the means of the characterizations present and build the characters (see Bar-Efrat, *Narrative Art in the Bible*, 77–86); and (c) minor characters, that is, the personal relationships through both speech and actions clarify the personalities of the main characters (see Bar-Efrat, *Narrative Art in the Bible*, 86–92). Hawk, "Literary/Narrative Criticism," *DOTP* 542, also notes, "The reader's perception of a character is shaped by a number of factors: descriptions and commentary provided by the narrator, the names or titles ascribed to the character, the character's actions and words, and comments made by other characters in the narrative." For more examples, see Hawk, "Literary/Narrative Criticism," *DOTP* 542. Likewise, Fewell and Gunn, "Narrative, Hebrew," *ABD* 4:1025, note, "A reader's reconstruction of character involves observing, assessing, comparing and contrasting what the characters do, what they say, what the narrator says about them, how other characters respond to them and what other characters say about them." Further, they note interestingly, "We may usually take what the narrator says about a character as a serious guide to aid us in our understanding of a character, but the narrator seldom tells us all we want to know. Rarely does the narrator describe external appearances or present internal thoughts and emotions. Moreover, what other characters say cannot always be relied upon since characters in biblical narrative, mimicking real life, convey only limited human viewpoints, frequently prejudiced and self-serving." Fewell and Gunn, "Narrative, Hebrew," *ABD* 4:1025. See also Fokkelman, *Reading Biblical Narrative*, 67–68; Powell, *What Is Narrative Criticism?*, 51–53. For more details and examples of the characters, see Gunn and Fewell, *Narrative in the Hebrew Bible*, 63–89; Walsh, *Style and Structure*, 120–21, 125–31; Walsh, *Old Testament Narrative*, 23–41.

and minor characters.³⁴ The main characters are Jethro and Moses.³⁵ The minor characters are Moses' wife, Zipporah, and his two sons, Gershom and Eliezer, Aaron and all the elders of Israel, and Israel.³⁶ Moreover, there are more characters of whom the narrator speaks, for example, Yahweh, Pharaoh³⁷ and the Egyptians, all gods, men of ability who fear Yahweh, and men of faithfulness who hate unjust gain.

The main characters are narrated in the episode of Exod 18 to demonstrate the significant roles through their speeches and actions. Jethro is on-stage in Exod 2–4 but has been off-stage for quite some time. Now, suddenly, Jethro is one of the main characters again throughout the episode.³⁸ In the first scene (Exod 18:1–12), Jethro comes with Moses' wife, Zipporah, and two sons, Gershom and Eliezer, to meet Moses because

---

34. Regarding the main characters in the book of Exodus, Kürle, *Appeal of Exodus*, 2, notes, "In Exodus the three main characters—God, Moses, and Israel—dominate all of the text." See also Mann, *Book of the Torah*, 79; Propp, *Exodus*, 1:32; Wells, "Exodus," 57–58. Further, Kürle expresses two characterizations of literary characters for the reader: (1) Direct characterization is "rare in biblical narrative" but serves "a summarial function." It is described through "epithets of the divine and of human characters." For example, the characterization of Yahweh is directly told "during his first encounter with Moses (Exod. 3), in the song at the *yam-suf* (Exod. 15), and after the sin of the people in Exod. 34." The characterization of Moses is directly expressed "in Exod. 3–4 with something like an epithet ('Who am I?', 'I am not eloquent' . . .)." The characterization of Pharaoh is directly said through "a stubborn heart." The characterization of Israel is directly spoken through "stiff-necked without any hope of improvement (Exod. 32–34)." Kürle, *Appeal of Exodus*, 4. And (2) indirect characterization is common in biblical narrative. It is described through "the characters' actions," for instance, Moses' anger and Yahweh's patience. Kürle, *Appeal of Exodus*, 4–5. See also Powell, *What Is Narrative Criticism?*, 52–53.

35. Carpenter, *Exodus*, 1:605, notes, "The two leading characters, Moses and Jethro his father-in-law, dominate the chapter [Exod 18]." See also Houtman, *Exodus*, 2:393, 401.

36. Discussing the relationship between Exod 18:1–12 and 18:13–27, Houtman, *Exodus*, 2:401, notes, "The role played by the leading figures, Moses and his father-in-law, in the first part [vv. 1–12] augmented by Moses' wife and sons and Aaron and the elders, in the second part [vv. 13–27] by the people, is the connecting factor."

37. Interestingly, Kürle argues that as studying the main characters of the book of Exodus, Pharaoh plays "the major role" as "Yahweh's adversary" by "the hardening of his heart" (see Kürle, *Appeal of Exodus*, 50–60). See also Ford, *God, Pharaoh and Moses*, 4–5, 113.

38. Many scholars claim that Jethro plays a significant role in the episode of Exod 18 (see Sailhamer, *Pentateuch as Narrative*, 281; Burns, *Exodus, Leviticus, Numbers*, 136; Durham, *Exodus*, 240; Ber, "Moses and Jethro," 153, 158). Furthermore, Jethro plays an important role not only in Exod 18 but also in the book of Exodus (see Carpenter, *Exodus*, 1:171).

of hearing of all which Yahweh had done for Israel in the land of Egypt, at the Red Sea, and on the wilderness journey to Mount Sinai. Jethro rejoices in, praises, and confesses Yahweh as the greatest and incomparable God. Then Jethro worships Yahweh by taking a burnt offering and sacrifices to Yahweh and eating bread with Aaron and all the elders of Israel (and, presumably, Moses) in the presence of Yahweh. In the second scene (Exod 18:13–27), on the next day, because of seeing all which Moses is doing alone for Israel with heavy duties, Jethro advises Moses concerning the responsibilities of Moses for Israel, and after that, he goes to his own country. Therefore, Jethro as a main character appears predominantly throughout the whole episode.

Moses' role as the other main character throughout the episode of Exod 18[39] also unifies the chapter. In the first scene (Exod 18:1–12), while Moses is encamping at Mount Sinai, Moses meets his father-in-law, Jethro, wife, Zipporah, and two sons, Gershom and Eliezer, and then he recounts to Jethro all about Yahweh's deliverance of Israel from Pharaoh and the Egyptians in Egypt and at the Red Sea and from the hardship in the wilderness. In the second scene (Exod 18:13–27), on the next day, Moses sits to judge Israel from morning until evening, and then Jethro sees all which Moses is doing alone for Israel and advises Moses. Moses obeys Jethro's advice about the lone responsibilities of Moses: (1) being as Israel in the presence of Yahweh to inquire of Yahweh, (2) making known and teaching Yahweh's statutes and laws to Israel, and (3) judging Israel's cases and setting lesser chiefs (or judges) over Israel. Clearly, Moses is a main character throughout the episode, a dominant role which, unlike Jethro, will carry through the remainder of the Exodus narrative.

In addition, even though there is no direct speech or direct action of Yahweh throughout the episode of Exod 18,[40] the characterization of Yahweh here also serves to unify the episode. In the episode, whereas Yahweh is portrayed as the "hidden yet active God,"[41] his actions, es-

---

39. Moses is not only a main character in the episode of Exod 18 but also in the Exodus narrative (see Erdman, *Exodus*, 7; Davies, *Exodus*, 51; Gispen, *Exodus*, 4, 5; Dozeman, *Exodus*, 47; McEntire, *Struggling with God*, 87; Kürle, *Appeal of Exodus*, 125).

40. Gowan, *Theology in Exodus*, 170, notes, "The account of the visit of Jethro in chapter 18 is a special case, for although God is referred to frequently, he neither speaks nor acts." See also Blackburn, *God Who Makes Himself Known*, 76; Ber, "Moses and Jethro," 150.

41. Motyer, *Exodus*, 24. See also Ber, "Moses and Jethro," 150. Furthermore, even though Yahweh is sometimes absent in some episodes, there are two ways to express his presence in those episodes: (1) Yahweh's representatives, for example, angels and persons

pecially his delivering and powerful acts for Israel are present in the episode through proclamation by others,[42] much as in Exod 1:1–2:25.[43] In those opening chapters, it is the narrator's voice which states, "Then God dealt well with the midwives . . ., he made households for them" (Exod 1:20–21) and "Then God heard their groaning, and God remembered his covenant with Abraham, with Isaac, and with Jacob, and God saw the sons of Israel, and God knew" (Exod 2:24–25). In Exod 18, it is the characters who recount Yahweh's mighty acts of deliverance (Moses) and praise and worship Yahweh for them (Jethro, Aaron, and all the elders of Israel). In the scene on the second day, Jethro and Moses speak further about Yahweh's character and way as God who reveals just statutes and laws, who is worthy of fear, who will be with Moses and direct him, and so forth. Accordingly, much like in Exod 1–2, Yahweh has a significant role as the ultimate character[44] in the whole episode even though he is not presently on-stage.

The Plot

The plot is orderly, that is, temporally and causally organized by the narrator, and it helps the reader grasp its meaning, connection, and development through the various events, especially through the speeches and actions of the characters in the narrative.[45] The continuing presence of

---

"stand in" for him (see Freedman, *God as an Absent Character*, 2). And (2) the narrator or characters "talk about" Yahweh (see Freedman, *God as an Absent Character*, 2–3).

42. Gowan, *Theology in Exodus*, 170.

43. Cole, *Exodus*, 19, notes, "God is the unseen controller of all history and all circumstances." Furthermore, Wells, "Exodus," 59, notes, "Though God appears absent in the first two chapters of Exodus, we find evidence of his work through the liberating actions of these strong women." Further, he notes, "It is often noted that only with the Israelites' cry to God at 2:23 does God become significantly present in the narrative (2:24–25), although there are less decisive references earlier, in 1:20–21." Wells, "Exodus," 59n23. Nevertheless, Brueggemann, *Introduction to the Old Testament*, 57, notes, "It is noteworthy that in all of chapters 1–2, YHWH plays no effective role, so that the narrative begins in a needy human world. From the outset, we are on notice of the drama to come because of the wonder of Hebrew births in defiance of Pharaoh (1:8–22), and because of the rage and passion of Moses who is a dangerous, violent agent of the slaves (2:11–22)."

44. Wells, "Exodus," 56, notes, "This [God's acts] is not to suggest that there are no other important players in story [the Book of Exodus]—Moses in particular is key—but God is the central character and the chief actor." See also Sarna, *Exodus*, xiii.

45. Bar-Efrat, *Narrative Art in the Bible*, 93–95. Further, he describes how the plot works within biblical narrative by giving the two kinds of the narrative: (1) The single

Moses as an actor in the episode of Exod 18 helps to connect Exod 18 with the plotline which precedes and the plotline which follows.[46] In the episode, the plot has its own beginning and end[47] signaled through Jethro's movements:[48] Jethro's *arrival* in the first scene (Exod 18:5) and

---

narrative appears two types in biblical narrative: (a) The units of the plot are that "the smallest narrative units" in biblical narrative have their functions: "components of the plot," "a means of characterizing the protagonists," and "ways of expressing meaning" (see Bar-Efrat, *Narrative Art in the Bible*, 95). For more descriptions and examples, see Bar-Efrat, *Narrative Art in the Bible*, 95–111. And (b) the stages of the plot point to "the situation existing at the beginning of the action" which supplies "the background information," introduces "the characters," informs the reader "of their names, traits, physical appearance, state in life and the relations obtaining among them," and provides "the other details needed for understanding the story" (see Bar-Efrat, *Narrative Art in the Bible*, 111). For more descriptions and examples, see Bar-Efrat, *Narrative Art in the Bible*, 111–32. And (2) collections of narratives are "a variety of connections between the individual narratives, some of them external and most of them internal" (see Bar-Efrat, *Narrative Art in the Bible*, 132). The external connection is identified by "the letter *waw* (and)," by the phrases: "And it came to pass," "After these things," "At that time," "After the death of . . . ," "After this," and "In those days," by the usage of "the same subject or words" at the end of the previous narrative and the beginning of the following narrative, and by "duplication or contradiction" (see Bar-Efrat, *Narrative Art in the Bible*, 132–35); whereas the internal connection is marked by sharing "the same principal character" as the hero in "a cycle of stories" (see Bar-Efrat, *Narrative Art in the Bible*, 135). For more examples, see Bar-Efrat, *Narrative Art in the Bible*, 135–40. Furthermore, Fewell and Gunn, "Narrative, Hebrew," *ABD* 4:1024, note, "Plot is the organizing force or principle through which narrative meaning is communicated. But not only is meaning expressed on a time continuum, it is conveyed through different and incomplete sources—the voice of the narrator, the speech and actions of characters. Presented with fragmented but potentially coherent information, the reader must observe, order, and amplify in order to force meaning." Further, they note, "A reader comprehends a plot both in terms of the simple sequence of action and in terms of the rise and fall of dramatic tension." Fewell and Gunn, "Narrative, Hebrew," *ABD* 4:1024. They also give the reader "three basic categories" to acknowledge "the dramatic structure of the plot": (1) exposition, (2) conflict, and (3) resolution (see Fewell and Gunn, "Narrative, Hebrew," *ABD* 4:1024). See also Fokkelman, *Reading Biblical Narrative*, 76–78. For more details and examples of the plot, see Gunn and Fewell, *Narrative in the Hebrew Bible*, 101–28; Walsh, *Old Testament Narrative*, 13–22.

46. Bar-Efrat, *Narrative Art in the Bible*, 135. As it comes to approaching the episode of Exod 18 as a unity within the Exodus narrative, at the beginning of the episode, v. 1 begins with the *waw* consecutive form which links it to its previous narrative (Exod 17:8–16); then v. 13 begins with the *waw* consecutive forms and the prepositional phrase which connect it with its previous scene (vv. 1–12); and, finally, Moses is still continuing to play a key character in the Exodus narrative.

47. Bar-Efrat, *Narrative Art in the Bible*, 94. See also Utzschneider and Oswald, *Exodus 1–15*, 23; Kürle, *Appeal of Exodus*, 20–27.

48. Coats, *Exodus 1–18*, 147. See also Motyer, *Exodus*, 170; Johnstone, *Exodus*, 1:373; Carpenter, "Exodus 18," 95–96; Carpenter, *Exodus*, 1:604; Preuss, "בּוֹא; אָתָה," *TDOT* 2:22–25.

departure in the second scene (Exod 18:27b) occur in a single two-day episode which unifies the two main scenes of the episode. Moreover, the consistent interactions of Jethro and Moses also serve to hold the two halves of the episode together and to relate the two major scenes in the episode:[49] Jethro *hears all* which Yahweh had done for Moses and Israel (Exod 18:1) and *sees all* which Moses is doing alone for Israel (Exod 18:14a).[50] Whereas Moses *recounts* to Jethro concerning the salvation of Yahweh (Exod 18:8), Jethro *advises* Moses concerning the lone responsibilities of Moses (Exod 18:17–23). After hearing of the salvation of Yahweh from Moses' lips, Jethro *responds* (Exod 18:9–12): Jethro rejoices in Yahweh (in attitude) (Exod 18:9), praises and confesses Yahweh (in word) (Exod 18:10–11), and worships Yahweh (in action) (Exod 18:12). Similarly, after listening to Jethro's advice, Moses *responds* (Exod 18:24–26): Moses obeys Jethro (in attitude) (Exod 18:24a) and does all which Jethro has advised Moses (in action) (Exod 18:24b–26).

Time and Space

The episode of Exod 18 consists of two scenes: (1) Exod 18:1–12 and (2) Exod 18:13–27. The narrator's connection of these two scenes with respect to time and space further illustrates narrative analysis of Exod 18.

Time

Time is an important part of a narrative with "a twofold relationship: it unfolds within time, and time passes within it."[51] Time depends on

49. Bar-Efrat, *Narrative Art in the Bible*, 93.

50. Cassuto, *Exodus*, 218. See also Carpenter, "Exodus 18," 95; Carpenter, *Exodus*, 1:604; Ber, "Moses and Jethro," 155.

51. Bar-Efrat, *Narrative Art in the Bible*, 141–43. Further, he notes, "This twofold link with time has significant implications for the nature, possibilities and limitations of the narrative as well as for the way it is interpreted." Bar-Efrat, *Narrative Art in the Bible*, 141. He also clarifies the two distinct kinds of time used in the narrative: (1) External/objective/narration time employed by the narrator is disclosed to the reader through the constructed and organized narrative, for example, "the words, collocations, sentences and paragraphs" (see Bar-Efrat, *Narrative Art in the Bible*, 141–42). The narrator uses the narration time in the narrative in order to tell continually and orderly the narrative to the reader "without interruptions, delays or accelerations" (see Bar-Efrat, *Narrative Art in the Bible*, 142). The narrator also tells the narration time in the narrative with easy and clear words on lines or pages for the reader in order to read and understand it (see Bar-Efrat, *Narrative Art in the Bible*, 143–44). And (2) internal/subjective/narrated

the narrator who tells it to the reader in order to make the narrative "a whole" and a "functional" narrative as coordinated with "the character, meaning and values of the entire narrative."[52] Regarding tenses throughout the episode of Exod 18, the *waw* consecutive form occurs forty-one times (Exod 18:1, 2, 4, 5, 6, 7 [five times], 8 [twice], 9, 10, 12 [twice], 13 [three times], 14 [twice], 15, 16 [twice], 17, 19, 20 [twice], 21, 22 [three times], 23 [twice], 24 [twice], 25 [twice], 26, 27 [twice]). These *waw* consecutive forms contribute to the sense that the episode is a unified narrative, narrated continually.

In addition, the episode of Exod 18 consists of two main scenes, the second of which (vv. 13–27) begins with the *qal* imperfect *waw* consecutive form וַיְהִי followed by the prepositional phrase מִמָּחֳרָת, "on the next day." The prepositional phrase מִמָּחֳרָת functions as an adverb of time in order to indicate an ongoing time from a day to another day in the episode.[53] This unifies two main scenes as a single two-day episode.

---

time used by the narrator is unfolded to the reader through the characters and events "in both the qualitative and the quantitative aspects" (see Bar-Efrat, *Narrative Art in the Bible*, 141–42). The narrator employs the narrated time in the narrative in order to tell disorderly the narrative to the reader with "gaps, delays and jumps" (see Bar-Efrat, *Narrative Art in the Bible*, 142). There are two types of the narrated time: (a) Tense is that in Hebrew tenses, time is expressed by an action which depends on an event in the narrative and indicates the past, present, or future of the event (see Bar-Efrat, *Narrative Art in the Bible*, 144). And (b) temporal expressions are that time is expressed by "the nouns, adverbs and prepositions denoting points, periods, relations and the movement or direction of time." These expressions have two kinds: (i) Duration is a period of time, for example, forty days and forty nights (Gen 7:12), seven years (Gen 29:20). And (ii) points of time are specific times, for instance, evening (Gen 24:11), the break of dawn (1 Sam 9:26) (see Bar-Efrat, *Narrative Art in the Bible*, 144–45). See also Fokkelman, *Reading Biblical Narrative*, 97–111; Powell, *What Is Narrative Criticism?*, 72–74. For more details and examples of time, see Walsh, *Style and Structure*, 122–24, 135–40; Walsh, *Old Testament Narrative*, 53–64.

52. Bar-Efrat, *Narrative Art in the Bible*, 142. Further, he notes, "Apart from its role within the narrative itself, such as providing emphases or implying connections between separate incidents, narrated time can fulfill direct functions for the reader, such as creating suspense or determining attitudes." Bar-Efrat, *Narrative Art in the Bible*, 142. Furthermore, Hawk, "Literary/Narrative Criticism," *DOTP* 540, notes, "Because human beings perceive events with a consciousness of their location in time, narratives utilize time as a means of organizing, explaining and evaluating experience. Telling a story thus requires decisions about how to situate it within time. Where and how will the story begin? How and when will it end? In what order will the events be presented? In addition, events must be connected so as to explain their significance and to impart a sense of the whole."

53. Noth, *Exodus*, 146. See also Janzen, "Jethro," 165–66; Dozeman, *Exodus*, 408; Johnstone, *Exodus*, 1:373, 377; Carpenter, "Exodus 18," 94; Carpenter, *Exodus*, 1:603, 616; Ber, "Moses and Jethro," 154; André, "מָחֳרָת; מִמָּחֳרָת," *TDOT* 8:237–41.

Therefore, both the *waw* consecutive forms and the prepositional phrase מִמָּחֳרָת join the two major scenes of the episode of Exod 18 together. A similar temporal narrative structure—one episode consisting of two scenes tied together with the transition "on the next day"—is found in Exod 2:11–15, a scene which has significant thematic ties to Exod 18.

Space

In most biblical narratives, space is depicted within "a well-defined framework."[54] There are two features shaping space in biblical narratives: (1) "the movement of characters" and (2) "the reference to places."[55] Both of them are often woven together in biblical narratives,[56] and they can be mentioned by a watchman, another character, or the narrator.[57] Thus, the episode of Exod 18, consisting of two major scenes (vv. 1–12 and 13–27), is continuous not only with respect to time but also with respect to space. Throughout the episode, the location is the encampment of Israel at the mountain of God, Mount Horeb or Sinai. According to Exod 18:5, concerning the movement of characters, Jethro comes with Moses' wife, Zipporah, and two sons, Gershom and Eliezer, to meet Moses at the mountain of God where Moses is encamping. After Moses has met Jethro, Moses and Jethro go to the tent, which is probably Moses' tent (Exod 18:7). The tent remains clearly at Mount Sinai where Moses is encamping as narrated in Exod 18:5. When Jethro worships Yahweh by bringing a burnt offering and sacrifices to Yahweh and eating bread with Aaron

---

54. Bar-Efrat, *Narrative Art in the Bible*, 184. In describing the relationship between time and space, he notes, "There are, however, appreciable differences between the dimensions of time and space in the narrative. First of all, there is no parallel relationship in the realm of space to that between narration time and narrated time. Space exists within the narrative but the narrative does not exist within space, and therefore the internal space of the narrative is realized not in external space (as is a painting) but in external time. The ways for shaping space in a narrative are also essentially different from those used for time." Bar-Efrat, *Narrative Art in the Bible*, 184. For examples of the relationship between time and space, see Bar-Efrat, *Narrative Art in the Bible*, 184–85. See also Fokkelman, *Reading Biblical Narrative*, 97–111; Powell, *What Is Narrative Criticism?*, 70–72. For more details and examples of space, see Walsh, *Style and Structure*, 122, 132–35; Walsh, *Old Testament Narrative*, 43–52.

55. Bar-Efrat, *Narrative Art in the Bible*, 185.

56. Bar-Efrat, *Narrative Art in the Bible*, 185.

57. For examples of space informed by a watchman or another character, see Bar-Efrat, *Narrative Art in the Bible*, 185–86. For examples of space informed by the narrator, see Bar-Efrat, *Narrative Art in the Bible*, 186–87. For more examples of space in biblical narratives, see Bar-Efrat, *Narrative Art in the Bible*, 187–96.

and all the elders of Israel in the presence of Yahweh, that is, likewise, at Mount Sinai. This location shows the fulfillment of Yahweh's promises in Exod 3:7–12 that when Moses has brought Israel out of Egypt, Moses will serve (or worship) Yahweh on this mountain (Exod 3:12). This initial scene of worship at Mount Sinai, thus, brings the narrative a full circle from Moses' previous experience there (Exod 3:1) and celebrates that the deliverance narrative of Exod 1–17 has reached its goal and conclusion. Thus, narrative space and location heighten the function of Exod 18 as a restropective summary and capstone of Exod 1–17.

The place where Moses sits to judge Israel, and Israel stands around Moses from morning until evening (Exod 18:13), also seems to be Mount Sinai because the narrator does not report any movement from Mount Sinai before this second day. Thus, the discussion between Jethro and Moses also takes place at Mount Sinai. Finally, as Exod 19 opens, the narrator does not mention the departure of Moses and Israel from Mount Sinai, but he reports retrospectively the previous departure from Rephidim and the arrival of Israel at Mount Sinai: "On the third new moon, after the sons of Israel had gone out of the land of Egypt, on that day, they came into the wilderness of Sinai. Then they set out from Rephidim, and they came into the wilderness of Sinai, and they encamped in the wilderness" (Exod 19:1–2a). Throughout Exod 19–40, Moses and Israel remain at Mount Sinai, continuing the narrative setting of both scenes in the episode. The continuity of the holy mountain location from Exod 18 on through Exod 19–40 is an important aspect of the prospective function of Exod 18.

Style

Besides the narrator, the characters, the plot, and time and space, style is the final main literary element in the narrative.[58] Some key components

---

58. Bar-Efrat, *Narrative Art in the Bible*, 197, notes, "In every narrative it is possible to discern three strata: 1. The stratum of language—the words and sentences of which the narrative is composed; 2. the stratum of what is represented by those words, namely the 'world' described in the narrative: the characters, events and settings; 3. the stratum of meanings, that is the concepts, views and values embodied in the narrative, which are expressed principally through the speech and actions of the characters, their fate and the general course of events." Further, he points that the second stratum is based on the first stratum, and the third stratum is based on the second stratum (see Bar-Efrat, *Narrative Art in the Bible*, 197).

of style in biblical narrative are "sound and rhythm,"[59] "the meaning of the word,"[60] "the repetition of words,"[61] and "word order."[62] The book will focus on the repetition of words in the episode of Exod 18 in which various words and phrases prominently appear.[63] The repetition of various words and phrases in the episode demonstrates both its two-scene structure and its literary and theological coherence.[64]

---

59. Bar-Efrat, *Narrative Art in the Bible*, 200, notes, "In poetry the sounds of words fulfill a far more important role than in prose, but in prose, too, and in narrative in particular, sound patterns which are worthy of attention sometimes occur." For examples of the repetition of sounds, see Bar-Efrat, *Narrative Art in the Bible*, 201–3.

60. Bar-Efrat states clearly that a word is not only used in its literal meaning but also in its non-literal meaning (see Bar-Efrat, *Narrative Art in the Bible*, 206–7). For examples of the non-literal meaning of the word, see Bar-Efrat, Narrative *Art in the Bible*, 207–11. Furthermore, Fewell and Gunn, "Narrative, Hebrew," *ABD* 4:1025, note, "All narrative information is, of course, communicated through the medium of language. The language of narrative is often multivalent, carrying more than one meaning at once." They also clarify "several different types of verbal ambiguity": a word read by the reader has two or more meanings with "unequal force," but "the characters usually perceive only one meaning to be intended" (see Fewell and Gunn, "Narrative, Hebrew," *ABD* 4:1025). And a word has two or more meanings with "equal force," but "the ambiguity may be recognized by the characters as well as by the reader" (see Fewell and Gunn, "Narrative, Hebrew," *ABD* 4:1025–26). See also Hawk, "Literary/Narrative Criticism," *DOTP* 541–42.

61. Bar-Efrat discern the repetition of words in biblical narrative by explaining various kinds of repetition, for instance, duplication of a word in a sentence (see Bar-Efrat, *Narrative Art in the Bible*, 211–12), a key word in a narrative (see Bar-Efrat, *Narrative Art in the Bible*, 212–15), resumption of a word or sentence in other following narratives (see Bar-Efrat, *Narrative Art in the Bible*, 215–16), and envelope of the same or slight changed words at the beginning and end of a narrative (see Bar-Efrat, *Narrative Art in the Bible*, 216). See also Gunn and Fewell, *Narrative in the Hebrew Bible*, 148–55; Fokkelman, *Reading Biblical Narrative*, 112–22; Walsh, *Style and Structure*, 145–53; Walsh, *Old Testament Narrative*, 81–95.

62. Normally, Hebrew word order begins with a verb and then followed by a noun (and then followed by a prepositional phrase). If it is not in the order, "it expresses a special significance, which should be determined in each instance by the content and the context" (see Bar-Efrat, *Narrative Art in the Bible*, 216–18).

63. Several scholars agree that there are repetitions employed in the episode of Exod 18, especially in vv. 1–12 (see Noth, *Exodus*, 146; Childs, *Exodus*, 321; Burns, *Exodus, Leviticus, Numbers*, 136; Zweck, *Freed to Follow*, 159). For examples of repetitions in Exod 18, see Cassuto, *Exodus*, 216, 219, 221–22; Meyers, *Exodus*, 140.

64. Bar-Efrat, *Narrative Art in the Bible*, 197–200. See also Hawk, "Literary/Narrative Criticism," *DOTP* 540–42; Walsh, *Style and Structure*, 7–11.

Three Verbs for the Salvation of Yahweh

The verb עָשָׂה, "to do, to make," occurs ten times (Exod 18:1, 8, 9, 14 [twice], 17, 18, 20, 23, 24).[65] Three of ten times have the noun אֱלֹהִים, "God," (Exod 18:1) and the proper noun יְהוָה, "Yahweh," (Exod 18:8, 9) functioning as their subjects, and they are used to indicate Yahweh's deeds,[66] for example, the deliverance of Yahweh which is a theme of the first scene (Exod 18:1–12).[67]

In addition, the *hiphil* of the verb נָצַל, "to snatch away, to deliver," occurs five times (Exod 18:4, 8, 9, 10 [twice]).[68] Its subjects are the construct noun and the noun with the pronominal suffix first person common singular אֱלֹהֵי אָבִי, "the God of my father," (Exod 18:4) and the proper noun יְהוָה, "Yahweh," (Exod 18:8, 9, 10 [twice]), and its objects are clearly Moses and Israel. All these verbs indicate Yahweh's deliverance.[69]

Besides the verb עָשָׂה (Exod 18:1, 8, 9) and the *hiphil* of the verb נָצַל (Exod 18:4, 8, 9, 10 [twice]), the *hiphil* of the verb יָצָא, "to cause to go out, to cause to come out" or "to bring out, to lead out," (Exod 18:1) indicates Yahweh's redemptive deeds.[70] Consequently, the narrator uses these three verbs, עָשָׂה, נָצַל, and יָצָא, to emphasize a theme of the first scene (Exod 18:1–12) about what Yahweh had done for Israel by bringing Israel out of Egypt and delivering Israel from the hand of Pharaoh and the Egyptians and from all the hardship which had come upon Israel on the way.[71] In other words, Yahweh makes himself known to the Israelites, Pharaoh, the Egyptians, the Amalekites, and even more all the nations through Yahweh's great deeds, the salvation of Yahweh for Yahweh's people. Thus, the three verbs, עָשָׂה, נָצַל, and יָצָא, unify the first scene (Exod 18:1–12) with a theological theme, the salvation of Yahweh.

---

65. Houtman, *Exodus*, 1:49–50.

66. Ringgren, "מַעֲשֶׂה ;עָשָׂה," *TDOT* 11:392.

67. Carpenter, "Exodus 18," 93. See also Carpenter, "Exodus 18," 98, 100, 106.

68. Houtman, *Exodus*, 1:311. See also Houtman, *Exodus*, 2:396; Dozeman, *Exodus*, 399.

69. Carpenter, "Exodus 18," 98. See also Carpenter, "Exodus 18," 100; Carpenter, *Exodus*, 1:608.

70. Carpenter, "Exodus 18," 98. See also Carpenter, "Exodus 18," 101; Preuss, "יָצָא; מוֹצָא ;תּוֹצָאוֹת," *TDOT* 6:233, 238; Houtman, *Exodus*, 1:32–33; Carpenter, *Exodus*, 1:608.

71. Gowan, *Theology in Exodus*, 170, notes, "There is a very prominent emphasis on God's deliverance of Israel from Egypt (*natsal*: 18:4, 8, 9, 10; *yatsa'*: 18:1; *'asah*: 18:1, 8, 9)."

One Verb for Arrival, Entry, and Bringing of Cases

The verb בּוֹא, "to come in, to come, to go in, to go," occurs ten times (Exod 18:5, 6, 7, 12, 15, 16, 19, 22, 23, 26). The first five times have Jethro (Exod 18:5, 6, 7), Aaron and all the elders of Israel (Exod 18:12), and Israel (Exod 18:15) functioning as their subjects, and they are used to refer to coming to the mountain of God, Mount Horeb or Sinai, where Yahweh dwells.[72] On Mount Sinai, Jethro, Aaron, all the elders of Israel, and even Israel come to praise and worship Yahweh (cf. Exod 3:12). Moreover, the *hiphil* of the verb בּוֹא, "to cause to come in, to cause to come" or "to bring in, to bring," has Moses (Exod 18:19) and men of ability and faithfulness (Exod 18:22, 26) functioning as its subjects, and it is used to refer to bringing the cases to someone.[73] Regarding Moses as the subject of the *hiphil* of the verb בּוֹא, Moses as the mediator brings Israel's cases to Yahweh. Regarding men of ability and faithfulness as the subject of the *hiphil* of the verb בּוֹא, men of ability and faithfulness bring Israel's hard cases to Moses as the chief judge. Consequently, the narrator repeatedly uses the verb בּוֹא to emphasize a theme of the Exodus narrative, especially of the episode of Exod 18 about the presence of Yahweh on Mount Sinai according to Yahweh's promises in Exod 3:7–12. In other words, the Israelites and even more all the nations have experienced by hearing and seeing what Yahweh had done for the Israelites, and they will come to Mount Sinai to praise and worship in the presence of Yahweh and to bring their cases to Yahweh. Moreover, the usage of the verb בּוֹא in both halves of Exod 18 further binds together its two distinct scenes (Exod 18:1–12 and 13–27).

Two Verbs for the Activity of Mediating the Knowledge of Yahweh

The verb עָשָׂה, "to do, to make," occurs ten times (Exod 18:1, 8, 9, 14 [twice], 17, 18, 20, 23, 24). The first three occurrences, already discussed, come in the first scene where the verb עָשָׂה is used in reference to Yahweh's acts of deliverance. The other seven times have Moses (Exod 18:14 [twice], 17, 18, 23, 24) and Israel (Exod 18:20) functioning as their subjects, and they refer to human deeds under Yahweh's commands and

---

72. Preuss, "בּוֹא; אָתָה," *TDOT* 2:22–25.
73. Preuss, "בּוֹא; אָתָה," *TDOT* 2:25.

instructions, for example, Moses' activity of conveying the knowledge of Yahweh as narrated in the second scene (Exod 18:13–27).

Besides the verb עָשָׂה (Exod 18:14 [twice], 17, 18, 20, 23, 24), the verb שָׁפַט, "to judge, to govern," occurs six times (Exod 18:13, 16, 22 [twice], 26 [twice]). The first two times have Moses (Exod 18:13, 16) functioning as their subject, and they are used to refer to judging someone's case. Moses, as the judge, judges Israel's hard cases (Exod 18:23). Moreover, four times have men of ability and faithfulness (Exod 18:22 [twice], 26 [twice]) functioning as their subjects, and they are used to refer to judging someone's case. Men of ability and faithfulness chosen by Moses judge Israel's small cases to establish "peace (שָׁלוֹם)" for Israel (Exod 18:23). Both kinds of cases are still under Yahweh's commands and instructions through Yahweh's statutes and laws. Consequently, the narrator uses these two verbs, עָשָׂה and שָׁפַט, to emphasize a theme of the Exodus narrative concerning the knowledge of Yahweh through the statutes and laws of Yahweh from which all the nations may learn to know the justice and righteousness of Yahweh. Yahweh has revealed himself concerning his justice and righteousness by judging and punishing Pharaoh and the Egyptians (Exod 7:14–14:31), the Amalekites (Exod 17:8–16), and even the Israelites (Exod 32:1–34:35). Now, in Exod 18, Yahweh is pictured as revealing his justice and righteousness *through his statutes and laws and through the judging of Moses and the appointed magistrates.*[74]

Two Verbs for Denoting the Knowledge of Yahweh

The verb יָדַע, "to know," occurs three times (Exod 18:11, 16, 20). The first time has Jethro (Exod 18:11) functioning as its subject, and it is used to indicate the knowledge of Yahweh in a sense of knowing Yahweh by hearing about the deliverance of Yahweh from Moses.[75] This builds upon a theme of the Exodus narrative that Yahweh makes himself known to all the nations through his saving and mighty deeds for his people, Israel, in Egypt, at the Red Sea, and in the wilderness (cf. Exod 9:16; 18:1, 8). Moreover, the *hiphil* of the verb יָדַע, "to make known, to declare," has Moses (Exod 18:16,

---

74. Nevertheless, concerning the usage of the verb שָׁפַט in the second scene (Exod 18:13–27), Carpenter considers a theological theme of the second scene as "the dissemination of *mišpaṭ* (משפט)" (see Carpenter, "Exodus 18," 93, 99, 104).

75. Carpenter, "Exodus 18," 92. See also Carpenter, "Exodus 18," 101, 108; Houtman, *Exodus*, 1:30–31.

20) functioning as its subject, and it is used to indicate the knowledge of Yahweh in a sense of knowing Yahweh by learning his statutes and laws from Moses as the instructor.[76] This introduces a theme of the Exodus narrative that Yahweh makes himself known to Yahweh's people through Yahweh's statutes and laws at Mount Sinai. Consequently, the verb יָדַע is used in these two scenes in such a way as to both tie them together and to distinguish them from one another. The distinct usage of the verb יָדַע in Exod 18:1–12 and 13–27 also heightens its retrospective and prospective functions, as will be discussed in the following chapters.

Besides the verb יָדַע, the verb זָהַר, "to instruct, to teach, to warn," (Exod 18:20) has Moses (Exod 18:20) functioning as its subject, and it is used to refer to teaching someone something.[77] Moses is portrayed as the instructor, teaching Israel the statutes and laws of Yahweh, so that Israel may learn and know "the way in which they should walk and the work which they should do" (Exod 18:20). Both the way and the work, which Israel should walk in and do, are revealed through Yahweh's statutes and laws, mediated by Moses. Consequently, the narrator uses these two verbs, יָדַע and זָהַר, to emphasize a theme of the Exodus narrative concerning the knowledge of Yahweh through the mighty deliverance of Yahweh and through the statutes and laws of Yahweh, so that all the nations may learn and know that "Yahweh is *greater* than all gods" (Exod 18:11).

Frequent Repetition of the Noun דָּבָר

The noun דָּבָר, "speech, word," occurs eleven times (Exod 18:11, 14, 16, 17, 18, 19, 22 [twice], 23, 26 [twice]). In Exod 18:11, 14, 17, 18, and 23, the noun דָּבָר means, "thing."[78] In Exod 18:16, 19, 22 [twice], and 26 [twice], the noun דָּבָר has the more precise sense of "case" for judicial investigation.[79] In the second scene (Exod 18:13–27), the noun דָּבָר occurs

---

76. Carpenter, "Exodus 18," 92. See also Carpenter, "Exodus 18," 108; Houtman, *Exodus*, 1:30–31.

77. Görg, "זֹהַר; זָהַר," *TDOT* 4:43. See also Houtman, *Exodus*, 2:417; Carpenter, *Exodus*, 1:622.

78. BDB, s.v. דָּבָר, IV, 183–84. See also Houtman, *Exodus*, 1:15; Carpenter, "Exodus 18," 99, 101, 104.

79. BDB, s.v. דָּבָר, IV 5, 183. See also Houtman, *Exodus*, 1:15; Carpenter, "Exodus 18," 99, 101, 104.

ten times which may anticipate the Decalogue[80] (the ten *words*) in Exod 20:1–17. Consequently, the frequent repetition of the noun דָּבָר serves to hold the two scenes of Exod 18 together.

Inclusio

The verb לָקַח, "to take," occurs twice (Exod 18:2, 12). These two times have Jethro (Exod 18:2, 12) functioning as their subject, and they are used to refer to taking someone or something to someone.[81] Jethro takes Moses' wife and two sons to Moses (Exod 18:2) and a burnt offering and sacrifices to Yahweh (Exod 18:12). Consequently, the narrator uses the verb לָקַח to show an inclusio of the first scene (Exod 18:1–12), and this inclusio serves to unify the first scene.

The noun שִׁלּוּחֶיהָ, "she had been sent away," literally means, "her sending away," and it is the construct noun of the noun שִׁלּוּחִים, "sending away, parting gift," with the pronominal suffix third person feminine singular יהָ. This noun occurs once in the book of Exodus (Exod 18:2), and it is derived from the verb שָׁלַח, "to send," which is the *piel* of the verb שָׁלַח, "to send off, to send away," (Exod 18:27).[82] Both the noun שִׁלּוּחֶיהָ and the verb שָׁלַח have Moses (Exod 18:2, 27) functioning as their subject. Moses had sent away Zipporah to Jethro (Exod 18:2) and then sends away Jethro to the land of Midian (Exod 18:27). Consequently, the narrator uses both the noun שִׁלּוּחֶיהָ and the verb שָׁלַח to form an inclusio around the episode of Exod 18,[83] and this inclusio further demonstrates that the two distinct scenes of Exod 18 are bound together as a literary unit.

The noun שָׁלוֹם, "completeness, soundness, welfare, peace," occurs twice (Exod 18:7, 23). In Exod 18:7, the noun שָׁלוֹם means, "welfare,"[84] about which Moses and Jethro asked. In Exod 18:23, the noun שָׁלוֹם means

---

80. Cassuto, *Exodus*, 222. See also Propp, *Exodus*, 1:631; Meyers, *Exodus*, 140; Dozeman, *Exodus*, 407–8; Hamilton, *Exodus*, 282–83; Carpenter, *Exodus*, 1:616; Alexander, *Exodus*, 352; Carpenter, "Exodus 18," 99, 104.

81. BDB, s.v. לָקַח, 7, 543. See also Houtman, *Exodus*, 1:37–38; Cassuto, *Exodus*, 222; Motyer, *Exodus*, 170.

82. Houtman, *Exodus*, 1:58. See also Cassuto, *Exodus*, 221–22; Hamilton, *Exodus*, 290; Ber, "Moses and Jethro," 155.

83. Carpenter, "Exodus 18," 94. See also Carpenter, *Exodus*, 1:603.

84. BDB, s.v. שָׁלוֹם, 3, 1022–23. See also Houtman, *Exodus*, 1:420; Cassuto, *Exodus*, 222.

"peace,"[85] in which all Israel will go to their place. In both cases, this comes out of Jethro's mouth.[86] Consequently, the narrator uses the noun שָׁלוֹם to exhibit an inclusio of Jethro and Moses' conversations,[87] and this inclusio also serves to bind the two halves of Exod 18 together.

Repeated Clauses

In the first scene (Exod 18:1–12), various duplicated clauses bind the first scene together.

Translation:		The MT:
... all which God had done for Moses and for Israel, his people, ...	Exod 18:1	כָּל־אֲשֶׁר עָשָׂה אֱלֹהִים לְמֹשֶׁה וּלְיִשְׂרָאֵל עַמּוֹ
... all which Yahweh had done to Pharaoh and to the Egyptians because of Israel, (and) all the hardship which had come upon them on the way; ...	Exod 18:8	אֵת כָּל־אֲשֶׁר עָשָׂה יְהוָה לְפַרְעֹה וּלְמִצְרַיִם עַל אוֹדֹת יִשְׂרָאֵל אֵת כָּל־הַתְּלָאָה אֲשֶׁר מְצָאָתַם בַּדֶּרֶךְ
... all the good which Yahweh had done for Israel, whom he had delivered from the hand of the Egyptians.	Exod 18:9	כָּל־הַטּוֹבָה אֲשֶׁר־עָשָׂה יְהוָה לְיִשְׂרָאֵל אֲשֶׁר הִצִּילוֹ מִיַּד מִצְרָיִם׃

In these noun clauses, the narrator repeats the nouns with the relative pronoun כָּל־אֲשֶׁר, "all which," (Exod 18:1, 8), כָּל־הַתְּלָאָה אֲשֶׁר, "all the hardship which," (Exod 18:8), and כָּל־הַטּוֹבָה אֲשֶׁר, "all the good which," (Exod 18:9), the nouns אֱלֹהִים, "God," (Exod 18:1) and יְהוָה, "Yahweh," (Exod 18:8, 9), the verb עָשָׂה, "to do, to make," (Exod 18:1, 8, 9), and the prepositional phrase לְיִשְׂרָאֵל, "for Israel," (Exod 18:1, 9).

---

85. BDB, s.v. שָׁלוֹם, 4, 1023. See also Stendebach, "שָׁלוֹם," *TDOT* 15:26; Houtman, *Exodus*, 1:420; 2:421; Cassuto, *Exodus*, 222.

86. Carpenter, "Exodus 18," 100. Concerning the usage of the noun שָׁלוֹם in the Midianite accounts (Exod 2–4 and 18), Carpenter argues, "An evident purpose for relating ch. 18 to chs. 2–4 is to demonstrate the fulfillment of issues first raised there [Exod 4:18]" Carpenter, "Exodus 18," 100. See also Carpenter, "Exodus 18," 106.

87. Carpenter, "Exodus 18," 97. See also Carpenter, "Exodus 18," 106; Carpenter, *Exodus*, 1:609.

Translation:		The MT:
... whom he [Yahweh] had delivered from the hand of the Egyptians.	Exod 18:9	אֲשֶׁ֥ר הִצִּיל֖וֹ מִיַּ֥ד מִצְרָֽיִם׃
... Yahweh who has delivered you from the hand of the Egyptians and from the hand of Pharaoh, (and) who has delivered the people from under the hand of the Egyptians, ...	Exod 18:10	יְהוָ֗ה אֲשֶׁ֨ר הִצִּ֥יל אֶתְכֶ֛ם מִיַּ֥ד מִצְרַ֖יִם וּמִיַּ֣ד פַּרְעֹ֑ה אֲשֶׁ֤ר הִצִּיל֙ אֶת־הָעָ֔ם מִתַּ֖חַת יַד־מִצְרָֽיִם׃

Here the narrator repeats the *hiphil* of the verb נָצַל, "to snatch away, to deliver," (Exod 18:9, 10 [twice]) and the prepositional phrase מִיַּד מִצְרַיִם, "from the hand of the Egyptians," (Exod 18:9, 10 [twice]).

Repeated Sentences

Likewise, many duplicated sentences serve to unify the second scene (Exod 18:13–27). Observations regarding repetition indicate both repeated clauses and sentences that: (1) there are literary features within the text which unify the first scene (Exod 18:1–12) and which unify the second scene (Exod 18:13–27); and (2) there are also literary features in the text which unify Exod 18 as a whole.

Translation:		The MT:
... Moses sat to judge the people, and the people stood around Moses from morning until evening.	Exod 18:13	וַיֵּ֤שֶׁב מֹשֶׁה֙ לִשְׁפֹּ֣ט אֶת־הָעָ֔ם וַיַּעֲמֹ֤ד הָעָם֙ עַל־מֹשֶׁ֔ה מִן־הַבֹּ֖קֶר עַד־הָעָֽרֶב׃
... Why are you [Moses] sitting alone and all the people standing around you [Moses] from morning until evening?	Exod 18:14	מַדּ֗וּעַ אַתָּ֤ה יוֹשֵׁב֙ לְבַדֶּ֔ךָ וְכָל־הָעָ֛ם נִצָּ֥ב עָלֶ֖יךָ מִן־בֹּ֥קֶר עַד־עָֽרֶב׃

These two verses again employ the repeated words and phrases, for instance, the verb יָשַׁב, "to sit, to remain, to dwell," (Exod 18:13, 14) and the prepositional phrase מִן־(הַ)בֹּקֶר עַד־(הָ)עֶרֶב, "from morning until evening," (Exod 18:13, 14).

Translation:		The MT:
Then let them judge the people at all times, and it will be that, every great case, they can bring to you [Moses], but every small case, they can judge themselves, and thus lighten (the load) from upon you [Moses], and they will carry (it) with you [Moses].	Exod 18:22	וְשָׁפְטוּ אֶת־הָעָם בְּכָל־עֵת וְהָיָה כָּל־הַדָּבָר הַגָּדֹל יָבִיאוּ אֵלֶיךָ וְכָל־הַדָּבָר הַקָּטֹן יִשְׁפְּטוּ־הֵם וְהָקֵל מֵעָלֶיךָ וְנָשְׂאוּ אִתָּךְ׃
... and thus they kept on judging the people at all times. The hard case, they would bring to Moses, but every small case, they would judge themselves.	Exod 18:26	וְשָׁפְטוּ אֶת־הָעָם בְּכָל־עֵת אֶת־הַדָּבָר הַקָּשֶׁה יְבִיאוּן אֶל־מֹשֶׁה וְכָל־הַדָּבָר הַקָּטֹן יִשְׁפּוּטוּ הֵם׃

These verses repeat the verb שָׁפַט, "to judge, to govern," (Exod 18:22 [twice], 26 [twice]) and the *hiphil* of the verb בּוֹא, "to cause to come in, to cause to come" or "to bring in, to bring," (Exod 18:22, 26), the objects אֶת־הָעָם, "the people," (Exod 18:22, 26) and הֵם, "themselves," (Exod 18:22, 26), the prepositional phrase בְּכָל־עֵת, "at all times," (Exod 18:22, 26), the noun הַדָּבָר, "case," (Exod 18:22 [twice], 26 [twice]), and the noun phrase וְכָל־הַדָּבָר הַקָּטֹן, "but every small case," (Exod 18:22, 26).

Translation:		The MT:
Then, you [Moses], provide from all the people men of ability who fear God, men of faithfulness who hate unjust gain, and set over them chiefs of thousands, chiefs of hundreds, chiefs of fifties, and chiefs of tens.	Exod 18:21	וְאַתָּה תֶחֱזֶה מִכָּל־הָעָם אַנְשֵׁי־חַיִל יִרְאֵי אֱלֹהִים אַנְשֵׁי אֱמֶת שֹׂנְאֵי בָצַע וְשַׂמְתָּ עֲלֵהֶם שָׂרֵי אֲלָפִים שָׂרֵי מֵאוֹת שָׂרֵי חֲמִשִּׁים וְשָׂרֵי עֲשָׂרֹת׃
Then Moses chose men of ability from all Israel, and he set them heads over the people, chiefs of thousands, chiefs of hundreds, chiefs of fifties, and chiefs of tens, ...	Exod 18:25	וַיִּבְחַר מֹשֶׁה אַנְשֵׁי־חַיִל מִכָּל־יִשְׂרָאֵל וַיִּתֵּן אֹתָם רָאשִׁים עַל־הָעָם שָׂרֵי אֲלָפִים שָׂרֵי מֵאוֹת שָׂרֵי חֲמִשִּׁים וְשָׂרֵי עֲשָׂרֹת׃

Here the narrator uses the repeated phrases אַנְשֵׁי־חַיִל, "men of ability," (Exod 18:21, 25) and שָׂרֵי אֲלָפִים שָׂרֵי מֵאוֹת שָׂרֵי חֲמִשִּׁים וְשָׂרֵי עֲשָׂרֹת, "chiefs of thousands, chiefs of hundreds, chiefs of fifties, and chiefs of tens," (Exod 18:21, 25).

Therefore, as demonstrated above, the narrative style of Exod 18 unifies Exod 18 and its two distinct scenes (Exod 18:1–12 and 13–27). The verb עָשָׂה is used repeatedly in both scenes with distinct subjects: (1) Yahweh in the first scene (Exod 18:1–12) to exhibit his saving and mighty acts for his people, Israel, and (2) Moses and Israel in the second scene (Exod 18:13–27) to show human acts according to the commands and instructions of Yahweh. The verb בּוֹא is also repeated in both halves of Exod 18 with a distinct sense in each: (1) Jethro, Aaron, all the elders of Israel, and even Israel come to praise and worship Yahweh; and (2) Moses and the appointed magistrates bring Israel's cases to Yahweh and Moses, respectively. The verb יָדַע is used repeatedly in both scenes with distinct senses: (1) Jethro knows Yahweh by hearing about Yahweh's redemptive deeds from Moses, acknowledging Yahweh as the greatest and incomparable God; and (2) Moses makes known Yahweh's statutes and laws to Israel. These three verbs, עָשָׂה, בּוֹא, and יָדַע, not only unify each half of Exod 18 but also unify Exod 18 as a whole. The repeated verbs, נָצַל and לָקַח, and clauses unify the first scene (Exod 18:1–12), and the repeated verb שָׁפַט, noun דָּבָר, and sentences unify the second scene (Exod 18:13–27). Inclusios formed with the verb לָקַח, with the noun שִׁלּוּחֶיהָ and the verb שָׁלַח, and with the noun שָׁלוֹם, as well as the general prominence of the noun דָּבָר throughout, further unify Exod 18. Moreover, one more literary feature demonstrating that Exod 18 is a unified work with two distinct scenes (Exod 18:1–12 and 13–27) concerns one of the titles of Jethro, חֹתֵן מֹשֶׁה, "the father-in-law of Moses." This will be discussed in the next chapter.

In conclusion, as discussed above, Exod 18:1–27 exhibits a symmetrical structure and expresses a literary and theological unity with parallel movements between two distinct scenes (vv. 1–12 and 13–27), especially the conversations between Jethro and Moses. This chapter has also examined other literary dimensions of Exod 18, such as the narrator, the characters, the plot, time and space, and style, especially the repetition of words and phrases. Observations arising from this narrative analysis will contribute to the argument in the following chapters of the strong retrospective and prospective functions of Exod 18, suggesting it as the key transitional midpoint in the Exodus narrative.

Chapter 4

The Figure of Jethro in Exodus 18 and in the Exodus Narrative

THIS CHAPTER WILL EXAMINE the figure of Jethro in Exod 18:1–27 and in the Exodus narrative through the exploration of three topics. The first, "The Names and Titles of Jethro in the Exodus Narrative," will describe the various names and titles of Jethro in the book of Exodus and establish that they refer to the same character. The second, "The Narrative Roles of Jethro in Exodus 18," will examine Jethro's six narrative roles in relation to other characters within Exod 18. And the third, "The Rhetorical Uses of Jethro in the Exodus Narrative as a Whole," will look at Jethro's function as an idealized figure who serves as (1) a model to contrast with all the nations and (2) a model to contrast with all the faithless Israelites in the Exodus narrative. In particular, this chapter will analyze the rhetorical uses of Jethro to exhibit Exod 18 as the key transitional midpoint of the Exodus narrative.

Throughout the Exodus narrative, Yahweh, Moses, and the Israelites are "the three main characters."[1] However, regarding the narrative of Exod 18, Cornelis Houtman observes that Moses and Jethro are "the leading figures"[2] and argues, "First he [the writer] calls attention to the man who, alongside Moses, will play the key role, an old acquaintance,

---

1. Kürle, *Appeal of Exodus*, 2. Further, he points that the three main characters— Yahweh, Moses, and the Israelites—are constructed by considering their existence, development, and interaction in the Exodus narrative (see Kürle, *Appeal of Exodus*, 2–6).

2. Houtman, *Exodus*, 2:401. See also Carpenter, *Exodus*, 1:605.

Jethro, the priest of Midian, Moses' father-in-law."[3] Jethro plays "a major role"[4] in Exod 18 in "the religious development of Israel"[5] and in "Moses' leadership over the people of Israel."[6] Jethro's influence, however, is not restricted to Exod 18. When analyzing the reactions between Jethro and Moses in Exod 2:16–22, Eugene Carpenter contends that Jethro plays an important part in the Exodus narrative:

> Thus Jethro becomes a key player in the narrative of Exodus, for through him God's goal of touching and reaching the nations begins, as he brings the nations and his people into contact. While Moses' own people reject him and Pharaoh rejects him, a Midianite priest receives him and shows him hospitality.[7]

Jethro, thus, plays a key role not only toward Moses and the Israelites throughout Exod 18 but also toward all the nations in the Exodus narrative.

The Names and Titles of Jethro in the Exodus Narrative

Jethro is first introduced by using the proper noun רְעוּאֵל, "Reuel," (Exod 2:18),[8] and then the proper noun רְעוּאֵל is changed to the proper noun

---

3. Houtman, *Exodus*, 2:393.

4. Sailhamer, *Pentateuch as Narrative*, 281. Furthermore, regarding the major role of Jethro in Exod 18, Durham expresses that Jethro, the father-in-law of Moses, "is presented by the narrative as (1) the caretaker of Moses' wife and two sons during Moses' absence in Egypt, (2) the glad recipient of the report of Yahweh's deliverance of Israel, (3) the confessor of Yahweh's supremacy among all gods, (4) the sacerdotal leader of all present, including even Moses and Aaron, and (5) Moses' counselor in the application to Israel of Yahweh's guidance for living in Covenant." Durham, *Exodus*, 240.

5. Dalglish, *Great Deliverance*, 78. Further, he speaks of critics who argue that Jethro's reactions—his joy, praise, confession, and worship—upon hearing the delivering and powerful acts of Yahweh for the Israelites display him as "a very significant part in the religious development of Israel." Dalglish, *Great Deliverance*, 78.

6. Meyer, *Message of Exodus*, 45. Sailhamer emphasizes that Jethro plays a significant role by "instructing Moses, the lawgiver himself, how to carry out the administration of God's Law to Israel." Sailhamer, *Pentateuch as Narrative*, 281. Dozeman, *Exodus*, 408, notes, "In Exod 18:13–27 Moses' unnamed Midianite father-in-law become the protagonist. He clarifies for Moses the need to have legal assistance in judging the people. He also fashions the solution in which there are levels of court proceedings."

7. Carpenter, *Exodus*, 1:171.

8. The proper noun רְעוּאֵל occurs again in Num 10:29. In Num 10:29 and Judg 4:11, another name which is perhaps used for Jethro is the proper noun חֹבָב, "Hobab," (see Cohen, "Jethro/Hobab's Detainment," 115; Sarna, *Exploring Exodus*, 36; Pixley, *On Exodus*, 12; Gurtner, *Exodus*, 194). Concerning the proper noun חֹבָב as another name

יִתְרוֹ, "Jethro," (Exod 3:1; 4:18b; 18:1, 2, 5, 6, 9, 10, 12). The proper noun יִתְרוֹ may function as a specifically *relational* alternative to Reuel, since it regularly appears alongside the noun phrase חֹתֵן מֹשֶׁה, "the father-in-law of Moses," (Exod 18:1, 2, 5, 12; cf. 3:1; 18:6).[9] In the MT, the proper noun יִתְרוֹ is "shortened"[10] to the proper noun יֶתֶר, "Jether" or "Jethro," in Exod 4:18a.[11] Therefore, the three proper nouns, רְעוּאֵל, יִתְרוֹ, and יֶתֶר, refer to the same character, Jethro, the priest of Midian, the father-in-law of Moses (Exod 18:1; cf. 3:1).[12]

In addition to his three names, Jethro has two titles: (1) the priest of Midian and (2) the father-in-law of Moses.[13] The first title is the noun phrase כֹּהֵן מִדְיָן, "the priest of Midian," (Exod 2:16; 3:1; 18:1).[14] This title is first introduced at the beginning of the Midianite accounts without giving his proper name. The text states that in the land of Midian, there is the priest of Midian who has seven daughters and a flock (Exod 2:16; cf. 3:1). The priest of Midian is then named Reuel who is the father of the seven daughters (Exod 2:18), and who also has Moses as his son-in-law and Gershom as his grandson (Exod 2:21–22). Two times in the MT, the title, "the priest of Midian," stands in apposition to the proper

---

of Jethro outside of the book of Exodus, some scholars think that Hobab is not Jethro, but he is the brother-in-law of Moses or the son of Jethro (see Jacob, *Exodus*, 503–11; Carpenter, *Exodus*, 1:624; Hughes, "Jethro," *DOTP* 469). Other scholars tend to argue that Reuel is "the clan name" and to emend the texts, so that they may read the texts that Jethro is the son of Reuel (cf. Exod 2:18), whereas Hobab is the son of Reuel and the son-in-law of Moses (cf. Num 10:29) (see Albright, "Jethro, Hobab and Reuel," 5–7; Hughes, "Jethro," *DOTP* 469; Knauf, "Reuel," *ABD* 5:693). Nevertheless, the issue has not been solved but has been proposed in various ways to deal with such different names of Jethro in various places (see Albright, "Jethro, Hobab and Reuel," 4; Durham, *Exodus*, 22; Propp, *Exodus*, 1:172–73; Stuart, *Exodus*, 99n146).

9. Jacob, *Exodus*, 508. Further, he points that the proper noun יִתְרוֹ is called not only for the sake of Moses but also for the outside of the land of Midian (see Jacob, *Exodus*, 509). See also Cassuto, *Exodus*, 30.

10. Sarna, *Exploring Exodus*, 36. See also Johnstone, *Exodus*, 1:56, 113.

11. Various commentators argue about the shortened name of Jethro, appearing in Exod 4:18a in three ways: (1) a grammatical form or an orthographic variation (see Cassuto, *Exodus*, 52; Childs, *Exodus*, 92; Kaiser, "Exodus," 2:333; Utzschneider and Oswald, *Exodus 1–15*, 136) and (2) an Israelite form (see Propp, *Exodus*, 1:197). However, for the purpose of the book, it is sufficient to simply note that the book of Exodus seems to use the two proper noun forms interchangeably, so that the variation seems to carry no rhetorical significance.

12. Gispen, *Exodus*, 61. See also Propp, *Exodus*, 1:197.

13. Leveen, "Inside Out," 405. See also Reiss, "Jethro the Convert," 90.

14. Leveen, "Inside Out," 405. See also Reiss, "Jethro the Convert," 90; Lawlor, "'At-Sinai Narrative," 28.

noun יִתְרוֹ, "Jethro," at the beginning of the burning bush event (Exod 3:1) and at the beginning of Exod 18 (v. 1).[15] Therefore, the two proper names, Reuel and Jethro, indicate "the same person"[16] as the priest of Midian who has seven daughters and a flock (Exod 2:16; cf. 3:1), and who later becomes the father-in-law of Moses and the grandfather of both Gershom and Eliezer (Exod 2:21–22; 18:2–4).

The second title of Jethro, the noun phrase חֹתֵן מֹשֶׁה, "the father-in-law of Moses,"[17] occurs in Exod 18 (vv. 1, 2, 5, 12 [twice], 14, 17).[18] Other references to this title appear in two forms of the noun חֹתֵן, "father-in-law," with the pronominal suffixes: חֹתְנוֹ, "his father-in-law," (Exod 3:1; 4:18; 18:7, 8, 15, 24, 27) and חֹתֶנְךָ, "your father-in-law," (Exod 18:6). The title is first introduced and stands in apposition to the proper noun יִתְרוֹ, "Jethro," at the beginning of the burning bush event (Exod 3:1) after Moses has married Zipporah. This pattern appears again when Moses returns to Jethro to ask for permission to go back to Egypt according to Yahweh's command (Exod 4:18).[19] Later, even though the pattern is

---

15. Janzen, *Exodus*, 48. See also Davies, *Exodus*, 66; Zweck, *Freed to Follow*, 29. Furthermore, Janzen, *Exodus*, 229, notes, "There are no references to Jethro outside of Exodus (but cf. Num. 10:29; Judg. 4:11) *[Narrative Technique: Unevenness]*." Cassuto, *Exodus*, 30, notes, "It seems more probable to suppose that there existed among the Israelites variant traditions concerning the man's name, which were well known to the people, and that the Torah deliberately chose the name Reuel when alluding to him only as the priest of Midian, but preferred to use here, when speaking of him as Moses' father-in-law, the name Jethro [יִתְרוֹ *Yithrō*, from a stem meaning 'abundance', 'superiority'], the more honoured designation, which points to his pre-eminent status." Nevertheless, Noth, *Exodus*, 37, notes, "Verse 18 gives the name of the priest as Reuel, a name which is given to him only once elsewhere, in Num. 10.29: in Ex. 3.1; 4.18; 18.1 ff. his name is Jethro. Now in the text of Ex. 2.18 the name Reuel looks very much like an addition, but when this addition was made—and this presumably happened at quite an early stage—the Midianite father-in-law of Moses was known in certain Israelite circles by the name Reuel. The different in names shows that the oldest tradition of Moses' relation by marriage with Midian gave no name for his father-in-law, who was originally described merely as the 'priest of Midian'. This is still the case even in the present text when he is introduced for the first time in Ex. 2.16. It is impossible to discover the origin of the different names given to the priest at a later date."

16. Keil and Delitzsch, *Pentateuch*, 1:434. See also Gispen, *Exodus*, 46, 49; Kaiser, "Exodus," 2:313; Osborn and Hatton, *Exodus*, 45, 53, 427.

17. The noun phrase חֹתֵן מֹשֶׁה occurs later in Num 10:29; Judg 1:16; and 4:11 (see Albright, "Jethro, Hobab and Reuel," 6–9; Cohen, "Jethro/Hobab's Detainment," 115–16; Hughes, "Jethro," *DOTP* 469; Launderville, "Hobab," *ABD* 3:235).

18. Janzen, *Exodus*, 224. See also Leveen, "Inside Out," 405; Reiss, "Jethro the Convert," 90; Garrett, *Exodus*, 442.

19. Concerning Moses' act of asking permission to go back to Egypt, Huey, *Exodus*, 33, notes, "God had already ordered Moses to go to Egypt, but he nevertheless

repeatedly used in Exod 18 (vv. 1, 2, 5, 6 (חֹתְנֶךָ), 12), the title also stands alone (vv. 7 (חֹתְנוֹ), 8 (חֹתְנוֹ), 12, 14, 15 (חֹתְנוֹ), 17, 24 (חֹתְנוֹ), 27 (חֹתְנוֹ)). The extensive use of the title in Exod 18[20] (vv. 1, 2, 5, 6, 7, 8, 12 [twice], 14, 15, 17, 24, 27) suggests that Jethro as the father-in-law of Moses has a close relationship with Moses through Zipporah, one of Jethro's seven daughters (Exod 2:21; 18:2) and even through Gershom and Eliezer, Jethro's grandsons (Exod 2:22; 18:3–4).

The Narrative Roles of Jethro in Exodus 18

Jethro fills six narrative roles in Exod 18: (1) a Midianite, (2) a priest, (3) the father-in-law of Moses, (4) a confessor of Yahweh, (5) an experienced fatherly advisor, and (6) a believer in Yahweh. These six narrative roles illustrate Jethro's role as a multifaceted character within Exod 18 and lay the groundwork for the narrator's rhetorical uses of Jethro in the whole Exodus narrative.

Jethro plays significant roles in relation to other characters within Exod 18. As *a Midianite*,[21] Jethro lives and serves as a priest for the

---

went to his father-in-law to ask permission to depart. The normal rules of deference to the head of the family in the ancient Near East had to be observed, as Moses was still under Jethro's authority." See also Meyer, *Devotional Commentary on Exodus*, 76, 79; Meyer, *Message of Exodus*, 57; Zweck, *Freed to Follow*, 46. Concerning Jethro's authority, Garrett, *Exodus*, 224, notes, "To his father-in-law, he [Moses] is a good son. He respectfully asks to be relieved of his shepherding duty so that he may go back to his people in Egypt." Furthermore, Alexander, *Exodus*, 104, notes, "On the basis of v. 18 alone it would be wrong to infer that Moses withheld from Jethro what YHWH had said at Horeb. In v. 18 the author merely seeks to show that Jethro willingly consented to Moses' return to Egypt.... Without repeating all that has been recorded concerning the theophany at Horeb, v. 18 establishes that Jethro supports Moses' return to Egypt. Jethro reappears later in Exod. 18, where once more he is supportive of his son-in-law."

20. Leveen, "Inside Out," 405–6. See also Reiss, "Jethro the Convert," 90; Alexander, *Exodus*, 348. Interestingly, Fox, *Now These Are the Names*, 99, notes, "The designation 'father-in-law' recurs throughout this chapter [Exod 18] (thirteen times), perhaps playing up the importance of the relationship in Israelite society." See also Hamilton, *Exodus*, 277.

21. Jacob, *Exodus*, 509, notes, "Also, we are not certain that Jethro was born a Midianite; he could have wandered into the land or perhaps was summoned to the office of priest there from Edom-Seir." Concerning Jethro as a Midianite, Garrett points the recent order of the texts between Exod 17:8–16 and Exod 18 to the close relationship between the Amalekites and the Midianites (see Garrett, *Exodus*, 438, 443–44). Furthermore, Lamsa, *Old Testament Light*, 102, notes, "The Midianites were the descendants of Abraham from his wife Kenturah, whom he married after the death of Sarah [Gen. 25:1–2]." Further, he points that the Midianites know about the God of their ancestors but worship other gods (see Lamsa, *Old Testament Light*, 102, 137–38). Even

Midianites in the land of Midian (cf. Exod 2:16; 3:1; 18:1). Umberto Cassuto emphasizes that Jethro is "a man of importance among his people."[22] Adriane Leveen describes the purpose of Jethro's coming to Moses at Mount Sinai by noting that Jethro is "a Midianite who comes to praise God,"[23] and that this action stands in contrast to insiders, that is, the Israelites, and other outsiders, that is, Pharaoh and the Egyptians, who neither come to praise nor acknowledge God.[24] Therefore, Jethro is a Midianite or a Gentile or a non-Israelite,[25] who recognizes the God of the Israelites.

---

though the texts do not state unequivocally about Jethro that he is a Midianite by born from a Midianite family, they tell his story by narrating that in the land of Midian, he is the priest of Midian, that is, a priest from/in the land of Midian or for the Midianites (see Childs, *Exodus*, 323, 329; Propp, *Exodus*, 1:633; Stuart, *Exodus*, 108), has seven daughters, including Zipporah, has a flock, has a house, and has a grandson, Gershom (cf. Exod 2:16, 18, 21–22).

22. Cassuto, *Exodus*, 213. See also Larsson, *Bound for Freedom*, 125. Furthermore, Reiss, "Jethro the Convert," 90, notes, "Whether the term *kohen* (priest) here denotes a religious or political leader, it is clear that Jethro had an important role in his Midianite community." See also Hughes, "Jethro," *DOTP* 467.

23. Leveen, "Inside Out," 408. See also Wells, *God's Holy People*, 175.

24. Leveen, "Inside Out," 407–9. See also Van Brugge, "Mentoring for the Kingdom's Sake," 9.

25. Van Brugge, "Mentoring for the Kingdom's Sake," 9. See also Ber, "Moses and Jethro," 164; Kaiser, "Exodus," 2:412; Bruckner, *Exodus*, 163, 165, 168. Concerning the usage of the divine names, Houtman, *Exodus*, 2:397, notes, "[T]he general name for God is used with a view to the non-Israelite Jethro; YHWH with a view to Israel." See also Johnstone, *Exodus*, 1:374, 377. Regarding the life of the church, Janzen, *Exodus*, 230, notes, "Jethro and events of chapter 18 have generated limited interest among Christian interpreters. Some follow the widely held Jewish position that Jethro models a non-Israelite converted to the true God." See also Bruckner, *Exodus*, 164–65. Furthermore, as approaching Jethro's confession as fulfilling Exod 9:14–16 and also as connecting to the knowledge of Yahweh, Blackburn, *God Who Makes Himself Known*, 77, notes, "That Jethro is a non-Israelite is particularly important given the scope of the Lord's commitment to be known, for Jethro's confession suggests that the intended goal of the plagues is being realized on an international scale, thereby fulfilling the Lord's goals in the exodus." See also Fretheim, *Exodus*, 196–97; Enns, *Exodus*, 369; Walton, Matthews, and Chavalas, *IVP Bible Background Commentary*, 93; Bruckner, *Exodus*, 165.

Jethro as *a priest*[26] speaks of שָׁלוֹם, "completeness, soundness, welfare, peace," two times in Exod 18:7, 23 (cf. Exod 4:18).[27] Jethro and Moses ask "one to another about their welfare (שָׁלוֹם)" (Exod 18:7). Later, Jethro closes his judicial advice to Moses by saying, "If you do this thing, and God commands you, then you will be able to endure, and also all this people will go to their place in peace (שָׁלוֹם)" (Exod 18:23).[28] In the Pentateuchal narratives, the noun שָׁלוֹם is used in two ways: (1) to speak of "welfare" (Gen 29:6 [twice]; 37:14 [twice]; 43:27 [twice], 28; Exod 18:7) and (2) to speak of "peace" (Gen 15:15; 26:29, 31; 28:21; 41:16; 43:23; 44:17; Exod 4:18; 18:23; Lev 26:6; Num 6:26; 25:12; Deut 2:26; 20:10, 11; 29:19). Aaron, the priest of Israel, only speaks the noun שָׁלוֹם in the Aaronic Benediction, "May Yahweh bless you and keep you; May Yahweh make his face shine upon you and be gracious to you; May Yahweh lift up his face upon you and give you peace (שָׁלוֹם)" (Num 6:24–26). Moreover, after his clear confession of Yahweh in Exod 18:11, Jethro functions in "a priestly role,"[29] bringing a burnt offering and sacrifices to Yahweh and

---

26. Childs, *Exodus*, 323, 329. Some commentators realize that in Exod 18:12, Jethro plays a role as a priest by bringing a burnt offering and sacrifices to Yahweh (see Erdman, *Exodus*, 84; Meyer, *Devotional Commentary on Exodus*, 207–8; Davis, *Moses and Gods of Egypt*, 198; Carpenter, *Exodus*, 1:165, 613). Furthermore, Murphy, *Exodus*, 24, notes, "As in primitive times the sacred and civil functions were generally united in one person, the priest of Midian was probably at least an elder in the state; but there is no reason to suppose that he was not a priest in the strict sense of the term, as the civil functionaries of Midian, we find, were designated by several other terms." See also Hyatt, *Exodus*, 67, 188, 193. Interestingly, Davis, *Moses and Gods of Egypt*, 65, notes, "The man with whom he [Moses] stayed (Reuel) may have been a priest of the true God (cf. 18:12–23)." See also Davis, *Moses and Gods of Egypt*, 198; Stuart, *Exodus*, 403. Keil and Delitzsch, *Pentateuch*, 1:434, note, "The name רְעוּאֵל (Reguel, friend of God) indicates that this priest served the old Semitic God *El* (אֵל)." However, the narratives of Genesis and Exodus consistently employ "*El*" as a common noun in reference to the one Creator God who made promises to Abraham (e.g., Gen 17:1–2) and who appears to Moses and rescues his people (e.g., Exod 20:5; 34:6).

27. Alexander, *Exodus*, 343. In Exod 4:18, after Moses has met Yahweh at Mount Horeb, he goes back to Jethro and asks him for permission to go back to the land of Egypt according to Yahweh's command, and then Jethro says to Moses, "Go in peace (שָׁלוֹם)." Furthermore, according to Jethro's speaking of שָׁלוֹם, Leveen, "Inside Out," 407, notes, "Jethro remains a safe figure to Moses, a figure of peace. The home and land in which Moses resided with Jethro was a safe haven. As a result, Moses can and does bring Jethro into his tent." See also Reiss, "Jethro the Convert," 91, 93.

28. Murphy, *Exodus*, 122, notes, "Prompt and impartial administration of justice will allay quarrels and beget that mutual confidence and good feeling which tends to peace."

29. Concerning the two Midianite accounts (Exod 4:24–26 and 18:1–12) which show "Moses' weaknesses and insufficiencies," Ber argues that in Exod 4:25, Zipporah

eating bread with Aaron and all the elders of Israel in the presence of Yahweh (Exod 18:12).[30] Therefore, Jethro acts as a priest by both bringing "peace"[31] and worshiping Yahweh.

Jethro is referred to as *the father-in-law of Moses*[32] thirteen times in Exod 18 (vv. 1, 2, 5, 6, 7, 8, 12 [twice], 14, 15, 17, 24, 27; cf. Exod 3:1;

---

presumably plays "a priestly role" instead of Moses, and that in Exod 18:12, Jethro presumably plays "a priestly role" because of Moses' absence (see Ber, "Moses and Jethro," 164). See also Dozeman, *Exodus*, 405. Furthermore, some commentators discern the similarity between the priestly roles of Jethro toward Moses (Exod 18) and Melchizedek toward Abraham (Gen 14–15) (see Sailhamer, *Pentateuch as Narrative*, 280–81; Janzen, *Exodus*, 227–28, 229; Bailey, *Exodus*, 197–98; Ber, "Moses and Jethro," 164). Nevertheless, Durham sees Jethro as a "presiding priest" who receives or accepts a burnt offering and sacrifices (see Durham, *Exodus*, 244–45). Kaiser disagrees with the priestly role of Jethro "officiating" in Exod 18:12 because he does not "offer" a burnt offering and sacrifices to Yahweh but joins "Moses and Aaron" to worship Yahweh in his presence (see Kaiser, "Exodus," 2:412).

30. As it comes to Jethro's act of offering a burnt offering and sacrifices to Yahweh, Rylaarsdam and Park describe Jethro's role in three ways: (1) Jethro acted for Moses because of their blood relationship. (2) Jethro became "a convert" to Yahweh and was ordained "a priest" in the service. And (3) Jethro was "a priest of Yahweh" in the land of Midian and taught Moses (see Rylaarsdam and Park, "Exodus," 1:963–65). Burns, *Exodus, Leviticus, Numbers*, 136, notes, "The fact that Jethro is represented as presiding at a Yahwist worship service (Exod 18:12) has given rise to the suggestion that Jethro was a worshipper of Yahweh (indeed, a Yahwistic priest) and that it was he who first introduced Moses to the God Yahweh. In support of this view, scholars point to the unusual endorsement implicitly given to Jethro when in Exod 18:13–27 the writer acknowledges that Israel was indebted to him for its system of justice. Jethro was a foreigner whose advice even Moses honored. This picture is supplemented by the witness of Exod 3 that Moses first learned Yahweh's name during the time he was a member of Jethro's household. This evidence has been brought together in what has come to be called the 'Kenite Hypothesis,' so called because Jethro is elsewhere described as a Kenite (see Judg 1:16; 4:11)." See also Gispen, *Exodus*, 46–47; Zweck, *Freed to Follow*, 162–63; Johnstone, *Exodus*, 1:56; Carpenter, *Exodus*, 1:166–67, 166n88. However, while Moses was pasturing the flock of Jethro in the wilderness, Yahweh first appeared to Moses at the burning bush at Mount Horeb (Exod 3:1–6) and revealed his sacred name to Moses (Exod 3:13–15). Later, Jethro heard of Yahweh's deliverance of Israel (Exod 18:1), and Moses recounted to Jethro concerning Yahweh's delivering and powerful acts (Exod 18:8). Of course, as narrated in the Exodus narrative, it is apparent that Moses first knows Yahweh and also makes known to Jethro Yahweh's saving and mighty acts and holy name. In other words, Moses does not learn anything about Yahweh from Jethro, but Moses certainly introduces Yahweh to Jethro.

31. The use of שָׁלוֹם, "welfare/peace," in Exod 18 functions in a retrospective and prospective aspect: Moses and Jethro ask one to another about their (past/present) welfare in v. 7, and then Jethro speaks of (future) peace for Israel in v. 23.

32. Garrett, *Exodus*, 442. See also Durham, *Exodus*, 240; Hamilton, *Exodus*, 277.

4:18).³³ This portrays Jethro in "close relationship"³⁴ with Moses through his daughter and grandsons. Jethro takes Zipporah, Gershom, and Eliezer (Exod 18:2–4), and they reunite with Moses at Mount Sinai (Exod 18:5–6).³⁵ This family reunion expresses "a relaxed and friendly family atmosphere"³⁶ (Exod 18:7–8) and a contrast to "the preceding stories of deprivation, grumbling, and danger from enemies."³⁷ Due to his close relationship with Moses as the father-in-law of Moses, Jethro also has an importance "among the Israelites"³⁸ through his judicial advice to Moses (Exod 18:17–23). Therefore, through his role as the father-in-law of Moses, Jethro influenced not only on Moses but also on the Israelites.

Jethro as *a confessor of Yahweh*³⁹ initially hears from report what Yahweh has done for Moses and Israel by bringing them out of Egypt (Exod 18:1).⁴⁰ Upon arriving, Jethro hears directly from Moses' mouth

33. Regarding the repetition of Jethro's title, the father-in-law of Moses, occurring thirteen times in Exod 18, Alexander, *Exodus*, 348, notes, "Jethro's standing within the chapter [Exod 18] rests primarily on his family relationship with Moses, and not on his religious status within Midian."

34. Carpenter, *Exodus*, 1:608. See also Cassuto, *Exodus*, 213; Fretheim, *Exodus*, 195; Alexander, *Exodus*, 348, 351. Furthermore, Childs, *Exodus*, 327, notes, "The repetition of his [Jethro's] kinship with Moses seven times in twelve verses produces an atmosphere of polite formality."

35. Many scholars agree that Jethro's act of taking Moses' wife and two sons to Moses expresses the family reunion of Moses (see Bailey, *Exodus*, 196, 197, 199, 200; Bruckner, *Exodus*, 163, 164; Alexander, *Exodus*, 349; Longman, *How to Read Exodus*, 115. Houtman, *Exodus*, 2:393, notes, "He [the writer] relates how Jethro, impressed by the great things YHWH had done for Moses and Israel, sets out with Moses' wife Zipporah and her sons to meet Moses; not first of all—as the sequel shows—to reunite the family, but primarily to hear from Moses' own mouth (18:8) that everything that had reached his ears was true." See also Houtman, *Exodus*, 2:403; Hyatt, *Exodus*, 188. Furthermore, Burns, *Exodus, Leviticus, Numbers*, 137, notes, "Contemporary readers might be surprised that Jethro, not Zipporah, Gershom or Eliezer, was the object of Moses' affection at this tender reunion." See also Coats, *Exodus 1–18*, 146; Bruckner, *Exodus*, 163; Dozeman, *Exodus*, 90; Garrett, *Exodus*, 442.

36. Janzen, *Exodus*, 224. See also Ber, "Moses and Jethro," 163.

37. Janzen, *Exodus*, 224.

38. Jacob, *Exodus*, 505–6.

39. Childs confirms that even though Jethro is a non-Israelite priest, he plays an important role throughout Exod 18 as "a faithful witness of Yahweh" by bearing witness to Yahweh through his joy, praise, confession, and worship (see Childs, *Exodus*, 329). See also Durham, *Exodus*, 240; Propp, *Exodus*, 1:171, 176. Reiss suggests that Jethro is "a convert" by blessing, taking a burnt offering and sacrifices to, and eating bread in the presence of Yahweh (see Reiss, "Jethro the Convert," 93). See also Wendland, *Exodus*, 18; Stuart, *Exodus*, 419; Hamilton, *Exodus*, 281.

40. Houtman, *Exodus*, 2:403, 407. See also Stuart, *Exodus*, 403–4; Hamilton, *Exodus*,

how Yahweh had delivered Israel from Pharaoh and the Egyptians in Egypt and at the Red Sea and from all the hardship in the wilderness (Exod 18:8).[41] Upon hearing this, Jethro rejoices in and praises Yahweh for this deliverance (Exod 18:9–10), and he makes a remarkable confession, "Now, I know that Yahweh is greater than all gods" (Exod 18:11).[42]

277; Johnstone, *Exodus*, 1:376. Interestingly, Murphy, *Exodus*, 120, notes, "The spread of intelligence is much more rapid among nomadic tribes than in a settled population." See also Cole, *Exodus*, 137; Larsson, *Bound for Freedom*, 124; Carpenter, *Exodus*, 1:608.

41. Houtman, *Exodus*, 2:407. See also Motyer, *Exodus*, 186, 187; Bruckner, *Exodus*, 164–65; Dozeman, *Exodus*, 403; Johnstone, *Exodus*, 1:376. Interestingly, Murphy, *Exodus*, 120, notes, "He [Moses] naturally rehearses to him [Jethro] the wonders of the short period during which they had been separated." Furthermore, Alexander, *Exodus*, 349–50, notes, "The reader of Exodus is expected to infer that Moses tells Jethro the substance of all that has been recorded in chs. 5–17."

42. Durham, *Exodus*, 244, notes, "Jethro's further confession moves from a repetition of Moses' summary to an assertion of his own. He declares his own faith on the basis of his own experience." See also Bailey, *Exodus*, 199–200. As it comes to Jethro's own faith, Fretheim, *Exodus*, 196, notes, "Whatever faith Jethro may have had before, there is now a new content to his confession in view of God's creation of a new people." See also Zweck, *Freed to Follow*, 162; Dozeman, *Exodus*, 403–4. Regarding Jethro's ambiguous confession, in consultation with Zimmerli, Childs, *Exodus*, 329, notes, "The confession is an acknowledgement of a new understanding of God which has resulted from his action. But the acknowledgement does not determine the status of the speaker before his confession. His new understanding can be a deepening of a prior knowledge (I Kings 17.24) or a totally new understanding which is fully discontinuous with the past (II Kings 5.15). In other words, from the formula [ʿattāh yādaʿtî (now I know)] alone Jethro's confession could indicate either that he was a previous worshipper of Yahweh, or that he was a new convert." See also Davies, *Exodus*, 149; Hyatt, *Exodus*, 189; Pixley, *On Exodus*, 112; Zweck, *Freed to Follow*, 162. Further, Childs refers to J. Tirinus who "argued that Jethro came as a believer in the true God and not as a pagan," and who "pointed out that he [Jethro] could not have lived forty years with Moses and not come to know the God of Israel." Childs, *Exodus*, 333. Furthermore, Kaiser, "Exodus," 2:412, notes, "The news evoked an instinctive 'Praise Yahweh' from Jethro (v. 10), thereby showing either that he had continued believing in the God of his fathers (since he, too, was a descendant of Abraham through Midian, Gen 25:2) or that he had spiritually benefited from Moses' forty-year stay in his house." In contrast, as it comes to seeing Jethro as a believer in Yahweh, Janzen, *Exodus*, 226, notes, "One need not assume a 'conversion' of Jethro to a God he has not known before. It makes better sense to understand his words as a confirmation of certainty regarding a God (Yahweh) he already knows, or as an enhanced view of Yahweh's greatness." See also Pixley, *On Exodus*, 112; Zweck, *Freed to Follow*, 162. With regard to the Midianites as the descendants of Abraham, Lamsa emphasizes that even though the Midianites worship "many gods," they acknowledge "the God of their ancestors" as the greatest and incomparable God (see Lamsa, *Old Testament Light*, 102, 137–38). See also Meyer, *Devotional Commentary on Exodus*, 207. Noth, *Exodus*, 149, notes, "With respect to the content of this confession the recognition of a 'polytheistic-comparative' exaltation of Yahweh over 'all gods' such as still occurs occasionally in traditional language, especially in the Psalms, is here put in the mouth of a Midianite whom the divine acts have led to 'enlightenment.'"

Finally, after his confession, Jethro worships Yahweh by taking a burnt offering and sacrifices to Yahweh and by eating bread with Aaron and all the elders of the Israelites in the presence of Yahweh (Exod 18:12). Therefore, Jethro plays a narrative role of a confessor of Yahweh through the acts of hearing-rejoicing-praising-confessing-worshiping.[43]

Esses, *Jesus in Exodus*, 102, notes, "Jethro realized, from Moses' account of all that had happened, that God is greater than all other gods, that there's only one Lord, only one God, only on King in the universe. Jethro forsook his idolatry, became a proselyte to Judaism, and accepted the living God as his Deliverer, his Redeemer, his Healer, and his Savior." Walton, Matthews, and Chavalas, *IVP Bible Background Commentary*, 93, note, "Jethro's acknowledgment of the superiority of Yahweh does not suggest that he was a worshiper of Yahweh or that he became a worshiper of Yahweh. The polytheism of the ancient world allowed for the recognition of the relative strengths of various deities and would expect each deity to be praised in superlative terms when there was evidence of his activity or displays of his power. Regardless of Jethro's religious persuasions, Yahweh was accomplishing his purpose that through his mighty acts 'all the world will know that I am Yahweh.'" For other concerns about Jethro's confession, see Childs, *Exodus*, 328–29; Dozeman, *Exodus*, 404; Blackburn, *God Who Makes Himself Known*, 76. However, as narrated in the Exodus narrative, it is not clear that Jethro is previously a believer in Yahweh, but it is obvious that Jethro knows Yahweh by first hearing of Yahweh's deliverance of Israel (Exod 18:1) and later by directly hearing of Yahweh's saving and mighty acts from Moses' mouth (Exod 18:8). This causes Jethro to confess Yahweh as the greatest and incomparable God (Exod 18:11), and his confession is a new acknowledgement of Yahweh. Even though there are many gods in the ancient Near East, Yahweh's delivering and powerful acts in the Exodus narrative are not just acts by any god. According to the Exodus narrative, Yahweh's mighty deeds are the decisive acts of the Creator God which demand acknowledgement from all the nations. The first commandment (Exod 20:3–6) and the command to drive out the inhabitants in the land of Canaan—lest their gods become a snare (Exod 23:23–24, 33)—bracket Yahweh's initial commands to Israel at Mount Sinai, and Yahweh's powerful deeds in the Exodus narrative have paved the way for such insistence on the confession and worship of Yahweh alone. It is apparent that as reading the book of Exodus as a whole, Jethro's confession and worship in Exod 18 should be read in this light, not against the typical background of a polytheistic mindset in the ancient Near East, as Walton, Matthews, and Chavalas are suggesting. Finally, according to Jethro's confession and worship of Yahweh, Jethro becomes a believer in Yahweh as seen in Jethro's advice (Exod 18:19–23).

43. Childs, *Exodus*, 323, notes, "[T]he climax of the chapter [Exod 18] now comes in v. 11 with the confession of Jethro. Verse 12 now forms the final element in a series of acts which proceed from hearing, rejoicing, blessing, confessing, and sacrificing." See also Childs, *Exodus*, 329; Meyer, *Message of Exodus*, 109; Motyer, *Exodus*, 170. As discerning the change of themes in Exod 18:1–12 from "the integration of Moses' family" to that of "Israel's new identity as the exodus community of faith," Fretheim describes eight "basic elements" for integrating into "the community of faith": (1) hearing, (2) visiting, (3) going, (4) declaring, (5) rejoicing, (6) giving thanks, (7) confessing, and (8) presenting an offering (see Fretheim, *Exodus*, 195–97). Furthermore, Motyer, *Exodus*, 170, notes, "We would say that Jethro came to faith, that he was converted—and the response of the Israelite leadership shows that Jethro was officially affirmed in the faith he had professed (12b)." See also Motyer, *Exodus*, 173, 186; Bruckner, *Exodus*, 164–65;

Jethro, as *an experienced fatherly advisor*,⁴⁴ sees Moses bearing judicial responsibilities all alone for Israel (Exod 18:14) and warns that this is not a realistic or sustainable situation (Exod 18:17–18). Therefore, Jethro advises Moses concerning his responsibilities as the mediator between Yahweh and Israel, as the instructor for Israel with Yahweh's statutes and laws, and as the judge, who would now judge Israel's cases and set lesser chiefs (or judges) over Israel (Exod 18:19–23). Jethro, as an experienced fatherly advisor, is portrayed as "older and more experienced than Moses in structuring the life of a community."⁴⁵

After his confession, Jethro, as *a believer in Yahweh*,⁴⁶ anchors his advice to Moses in his convictions about Yahweh. Jethro exhorts, "Now, obey

---

Garrett, *Exodus*, 445.

44. Houtman, *Exodus*, 2:395–96. See also Ber, "Moses and Jethro," 157; Leveen, "Inside Out," 405, 409–11; Osborn and Hatton, *Exodus*, 426. As demonstrating the relationship between Exod 18:1–12 and 18:13–27, Houtman, *Exodus*, 2:401–2, notes, "Also in another respect there is a connection: Jethro's acknowledgement of YHWH's greatness and the acceptance of Jethro by the representatives of Israel (18:10–12) make him a man of authority; so 18:1–12 can be regarded as preliminary to Moses' readily going along with Jethro's advice (18:17ff.)." See also Houtman, *Exodus*, 2:412. Furthermore, Stuart, *Exodus*, 414, notes, "Immediately after his conversion Jethro was able to play a helpful role in Israel by recommending the basic structure of the judicial system, a properly hierarchical arrangement that placed Moses at the top of the judicial pyramid as Israel's 'supreme court' and established inferior courts/judges under him."

45. Janzen, *Exodus*, 228. Further, he notes, "Jethro's advice is meant to relieve Moses from undue work stress and to provide more efficient judicial services for the people. It is accepted in the spirit in which it is given. *Moses listened to his father-in-law and did all that he had said* (18:24). In ancient times, the experience that comes with age was valued highly, rather than rejected as interfering with younger persons' independence." Janzen, *Exodus*, 228. See also Meyer, *Message of Exodus*, 110; Jacob, *Exodus*, 501, 505; Zweck, *Freed to Follow*, 165–66; Carpenter, *Exodus*, 1:618. Bruckner, *Exodus*, 168, notes, "This [Jethro's advice] was not special revelation, but nonetheless revelation given through Jethro's wisdom and experience (see also Acts 15:28)."

46. Wendland, *Exodus*, 118, notes, "It is interesting to note how the Amalekites fought against the Israelites, while Jethro, a Midianite priest, became a believer in the true God, the God of Israel." Whereas Jethro as a believer in Yahweh is unclear, Childs, *Exodus*, 323, notes, "[T]he tradition did not resort to the device of a 'conversion story' by which to render the older elements harmless (cf. exegesis). Jethro is nowhere pictured as a heathen who becomes a Yahwist. The contrast with Naaman (II Kings 5) is striking in this regard. Rather, Jethro is described praising the God of Israel in the language of faith and following the pattern of Ps. 135." See also Dozeman, *Exodus*, 404–5. Nevertheless, Keil and Delitzsch consider Jethro as "the first-fruits of the heathen" who seeks God and joins his people in "religious fellowship" after bringing back to Moses his wife and sons, acknowledging Yahweh and his delivering and powerful acts with joy and praise, and worshiping Yahweh with offerings and celebration (see Keil and Delitzsch, *Pentateuch*, 2:83). See also Knight, *Theology as Narration*, 126; Wendland, *Exodus*, 118.

me; I will advise you, and may God be with you" (Exod 18:19), and he concludes with the assurance, "If you do this thing, and God commands you, then you will be able to endure, and also all this people will go to their place in peace" (Exod 18:23). Jethro's advice here is grounded in his understanding of God's purposes for Israel and expresses his confidence in God.[47] Moreover, in his advice, Jethro directs Moses to choose as judges "from all the people men of ability who fear God, men of faithfulness who hate unjust gain" (Exod 18:21). Jethro realizes that one of the most vital characteristics of judges is the fear of Yahweh.[48] Therefore, Jethro, as a believer in Yahweh, expresses his faith in Yahweh as the greatest and incomparable God through his faithful advice for Moses.

The six narrative roles of Jethro in Exod 18, (1) a Midianite, (2) a priest, (3) the father-in-law of Moses, (4) a confessor of Yahweh, (5) an experienced fatherly advisor, and (6) a believer in Yahweh, establish Jethro as an important and complex character in Exod 18. Moreover, these roles directly relate to the rhetorical uses of Jethro in the Exodus narrative as a whole.

The Rhetorical Uses of Jethro in the Exodus Narrative as a Whole

In the whole Exodus narrative, Jethro is rhetorically employed by the narrator as an idealized figure who serves as (1) a model to contrast with all the nations and (2) a model to contrast with all the faithless Israelites.

---

47. Durham clarifies that Yahweh is "the source and the center" of Jethro's advice (see Durham, *Exodus*, 250). See also Jacob, *Exodus*, 500; Zweck, *Freed to Follow*, 165; Ashby, *Go Out and Meet God*, 79; Bruckner, *Exodus*, 168. Furthermore, Ber, "Moses and Jethro," 164, notes, "We must also be aware of the rhetorical effort to present this advice as in accord with God's will and God's plan for Israel. Jethro in his speech gives positive, rational, and wise arguments, and he shows concern for Israel, Moses, and for proper, just, and good administration in Israel." See also Meyer, *Message of Exodus*, 110; Fretheim, *Exodus*, 199; Stuart, *Exodus*, 419; Alexander, *Exodus*, 352–53.

48. Rylaarsdam and Park, "Exodus," 1:968, note, "They [the judges] must be men who *fear God*, i.e., take him seriously, and they must have personal character and integrity. The standards of moral conduct later exalted in Israel (cf. Ps. 15) are here attributed to the Midianite priest." Significantly, Jacob, *Exodus*, 500, notes, "*Yir-ei e-lo-him* who feared God, not men, in their judgments; 'for the judgment belongs to God' (Deut 1.17)." See also Blackburn, *God Who Makes Himself Known*, 77. Carpenter, *Exodus*, 1:623, notes, "The fear of God helped establish them [men of ability] as men of character and truth (אֱמֶת), for they would not corrupt through bribery (בֶּצַע) the jurisprudence system they were being called on to establish."

Viktor Ber addresses Jethro's act of taking a burnt offering and sacrifices to Yahweh as having an effect on the Israelites:

> I want to argue that Jethro's leading role during the sacrifice must be understood in regards to the narrative's overall rhetoric. One can understand Jethro's role as the climactic point in a chain of positive responses to the story of God's actions for Israel.[49]

Jethro as a Midianite or a Gentile or a non-Israelite functions retrospectively in the Exodus narrative as *a model to contrast with all the nations*.[50] Jethro hears general news about Yahweh's mighty deeds for Israel (Exod 18:1), prompting him to bring Moses' wife and two sons to Moses at the mountain of God (Exod 18:2–7). There Jethro hears directly from Moses about Yahweh's great name and saving acts for Israel (Exod 18:8). Having heard that, Jethro rejoices in, praises, and confesses Yahweh as the greatest and incomparable God (Exod 18:9–11).

Leveen notes the contrasting reactions of Jethro on the one hand and Pharaoh and the Egyptians on the other hand:

> Jethro draws the implication of what he has realized in a clear and highly public manner: 'Now I know that YHWH is greater than all the gods...' (Exod. 18:11). This type of public acknowledgement of God's superior might is precisely what God sought in inflicting the ten plagues on Pharaoh and the Egyptians. Yet Pharaoh was disastrously slow in grasping the power of this Israelite God. In contrast, upon hearing the news, Jethro immediately recognizes and acknowledges God's superiority.... Thus, as an outsider, a Midianite, Jethro stands in contrast with that other outsider, the Pharaoh, in acknowledging God.[51]

Jethro's role as a confessor of Yahweh stands in stark contrast with the reactions of Pharaoh, the Egyptians, and the Amalekites in the previous chapters (Exod 1–17). These other non-Israelites consistently show

---

49. Ber, "Moses and Jethro," 164.

50. Ber, "Moses and Jethro," 164. Furthermore, as seeing the parallels between the roles of Jethro (Exod 18) and Melchizedek (Gen 14–15), Sailhamer, *Pentateuch as Narrative*, 281, notes, "The purpose of these parallels appears to be to cast Jethro as another Melchizedek, the paradigm of the righteous Gentile." See also Ber, "Moses and Jethro," 164; Bruckner, *Exodus*, 166. Interestingly, Van Brugge, "Mentoring for the Kingdom's Sake," 9, notes, "Because of Moses mentoring Jethro, a Gentile is brought to faith, and Jethro actually breaks out into praise of the covenant Lord (v. 10)." See also Bruckner, *Exodus*, 164–65; Garrett, *Exodus*, 445.

51. Leveen, "Inside Out," 408. See also Reiss, "Jethro the Convert," 92.

hostility and stubborn resistance toward the Israelites and Yahweh's purposes for the Israelites.

In Egypt, Pharaoh and the Egyptians oppressed the Israelites with hard labor and killed every male child born to the Israelites. Their goal was to suppress the population of the Israelites, but Yahweh multiplied and preserved the children of the Israelites, including Moses (Exod 1:8–2:10). Later, when Moses went back to Egypt to talk to Pharaoh about Yahweh's saving plan for the Israelites, Pharaoh repeatedly refused to let the Israelites go out of Egypt. However, Yahweh saved the Israelites and brought the Israelites out of Egypt with many signs in the ten plagues before Pharaoh and the Egyptians through Moses and Aaron, the representatives of Yahweh (Exod 7:14–12:36). After the Israelites left Egypt, Pharaoh with his horses, chariots, horsemen, and army pursued the Israelites and encamped at the Red Sea. Pharaoh and his servants regretted "that we have let Israel go from serving us" (Exod 14:5). However, Yahweh delivered the Israelites from the hand of Pharaoh and the Egyptians with finality (Exod 14:1–31). Pharaoh and the Egyptians experienced Yahweh by both hearing and seeing, but they neither turned toward Yahweh nor confessed Yahweh as Jethro does,[52] after only hearing of Yahweh's salvation from Moses.[53] Likewise, the Amalekites, at Rephidim,

---

52. Leveen, "Inside Out," 408. See also Reiss, "Jethro the Convert," 92; Blackburn, *God Who Makes Himself Known*, 77. Houtman, *Exodus*, 2:394–95, notes, "Watching Jethro and the Israelites enjoy the meal to YHWH gives the reader warm feelings. He senses that not all non-Israelites are like Pharaoh and Amalek, and that there is another way than the ruin of non-Israelites to make people acknowledge the greatness of YHWH." In other words, Jethro, a non-Israelite, knows "YHWH's incomparable greatness" by "learning of Israel's redemptive blessings, the history of YHWH's mighty deeds" rather than by participating in the destruction of Pharaoh, the Egyptians, and the Amalekites, other non-Israelites. See also Houtman, *Exodus*, 2:395, 403. Enns, *Exodus*, 367, notes, "Unlike the nations of 15:14–16 who tremble at such news, Jethro is attracted to it, and so he comes to Moses." See also Fretheim, *Exodus*, 195; Ford, *God, Pharaoh and Moses*, 180; Russell, *Song of the Sea*, 52–53. Further, Enns notes, "Although neither the Egyptians nor the Amalekites get it, Jethro, the Midianite, has learned the lesson of the Exodus: 'The Lord is greater than all other gods.'" Enns, *Exodus*, 369. Bruckner, *Exodus*, 165, notes, "What the pharaoh and the Egyptians know (7:5; 14:4, 18) and the Israelites know firsthand (6:7; 10:2; 14:31), Jethro also claimed to know." Furthermore, Enns, *Exodus*, 369, notes, "But it is Jethro, not Pharaoh or the Amalekites, who gives the proper response: praise." See also Enns, *Exodus*, 374; Carpenter, *Exodus*, 1:613.

53. Bruckner, *Exodus*, 165, notes, "Jethro believed in the Lord as God on the basis of Moses' testimony although he did not see any of the dramatic historical events himself." See also Hamilton, *Exodus*, 280. Alexander, *Exodus*, 350, notes, "Whereas the Egyptians and the Israelites slowly came to a knowledge of YHWH through witnessing the events described in chs. 5–14, Jethro must rely upon the testimony of Moses, his son-in-law."

came and fought against the Israelites, but Yahweh, through Moses, gave the Israelites the victory (Exod 17:8–16). The Amalekites experienced Yahweh by both hearing and seeing, but they neither turned toward Yahweh nor acknowledged Yahweh's word and deed as Jethro does.[54] Thus, while Pharaoh, the Egyptians, and the Amalekites experienced Yahweh as a man of war (Exod 14:14; 15:3, 6–7; 17:16), Jethro's experience of Yahweh and the Israelites is one of *peace* (Exod 18:7, 23).

By functioning retrospectively, Jethro's reaction portrays Jethro as a model to contrast with all the nations.[55] Jethro, therefore, fulfills this purpose of Yahweh, "But because of this, I have raised you [Pharaoh] up to show you [Pharaoh] my power and to recount my name in all the earth" (Exod 9:16).[56] Indeed, Yahweh's great name and mighty deeds have been recounted and reported around the ancient Near Eastern territory and even reached out to Jethro (Exod 18:1), and now Jethro himself joins in acknowledging and recounting them (Exod 18:10–11).

On the other hand, Jethro, as a confessor of Yahweh who becomes, in a sense, an Israelite,[57] also thereby functions prospectively in the Exodus narrative as *a model to contrast with all the faithless Israelites*.[58] After Jethro

---

54. See n52, 53. White, *Exodus*, 129, notes, "If Amalek represents the adversity of the Gentile nations toward the election of Israel, Jethro represents not only the Gentile acceptance of this mystery of the covenant but also a non-Israelite contribution to the covenant. In this way, Israel appears here as a discreet but real centerpiece of human history, around which all other peoples or cultures stand. The claim that God has elected his people is to be transmitted throughout human history, dividing Gentiles on either side but also uniting them in the age of the Messiah. The mystery of Israel will shape the future religious history of the entire human race, throughout all time, in a discreet but remarkable and clear way."

55. Concerning the contradiction between the Israelites and the Midianites in Isa 10:26, Enns, *Exodus*, 374, notes, "But in Exodus 18 at least, Israel and Midian are allies, and the Midianites serve as models of how nations ought to respond to Israel's God, in contrast to Egypt and the Amalekites." Concerning Jethro's departure, Bruckner, *Exodus*, 166, notes, "He [Jethro] did not follow the presence of the Lord to Sinai, or 'serve' him with Israel. Instead he returned to Midian, believing in the Lord God. Jethro was a model of hope for Gentiles, very early in biblical tradition, that the promise God made to Abraham, Jethro's common ancestor with Moses, would be fulfilled."

56. Blackburn, *God Who Makes Himself Known*, 77. See also Fretheim, *Exodus*, 196, 197; Enns, *Exodus*, 369; Walton, Matthews, and Chavalas, *IVP Bible Background Commentary*, 93; Carpenter, *Exodus*, 1:612.

57. Cody, "Exodus 18,12," 161, notes, "So then, Jethro 'accepted the sacrifices (made) to God', in a gesture which consisted of his receiving the portion of the sacrificial victims proffered to him, which he ate as the representatives of the Israelites ate their portions. By doing so, he signified his acceptance of the covenant proffered to him."

58. Jethro's rhetorical function as "a model to contrast with all the faithless Israelites" portrays an example of a faithful and obedient Israelite to Yahweh according to

has rejoiced in, praised, and confessed Yahweh as the greatest and incomparable God, he joins in worshiping Yahweh, bringing a burnt offering and sacrifices to Yahweh, and eating bread with Aaron and all the elders of the Israelites, the representatives of the Israelites, in the presence of Yahweh (Exod 18:12). Later, Jethro as a believer in Yahweh advises Moses, grounding his advice in a concern for Yahweh's will and an awareness of Yahweh's presence (Exod 18:19, 23). Moreover, in his advice, Jethro directs Moses to choose judges "from all the people men of ability who fear God, men of faithfulness who hate unjust gain" (Exod 18:21). Jethro recognizes that one of the characteristics of chiefs (or judges) is to fear Yahweh as the two Hebrew midwives did before Yahweh (cf. Exod 1:17). Here Jethro speaks as a faithful and true Israelite.

As it pertains to Jethro's act of coming to worship Yahweh, Leveen expounds:

> Perhaps ironically, as a Midianite, Jethro's praise of God is also contrasted to that of the insiders, the Israelites themselves, in a way that throws a negative light on the Israelite behavior since their departure from Egypt. Jethro celebrates God's liberation of Israel from Egypt in pointed contrast to the Israelite desires to return to Egypt, as noted already in Exod 16.3 ('if only we had died in Egypt') and Exod 17.3 ('Why did you bring us up from Egypt. . .?'). Jethro sees clearly what Israel can only glimpse in fleeting moments punctuated by hunger, thirst, and complaint. . . . But it is also as an outsider that Jethro creates a shocking contrast with the Israelites. The contrast between his praise and their grumbling constitutes a withering critique of their complaints and preoccupations. This passage suggests a possible use of the figure of the outsider as one who heightens, by contrast, the failures of the Israelites.[59]

In his proper confession, worship, and faithful advice, Jethro stands in contrast with Aaron and the Israelites, especially with respect to the golden calf event at Mount Sinai (Exod 32–34).

Yahweh's declaration to his people, the Israelites, at Mount Sinai by stating, "Then, now, if you will surely obey me, and you will keep my covenant, then you shall be to me a treasured possession from all the peoples because all the earth belongs to me, and you shall be to me a kingdom of priests and a holy nation" (Exod 19:5-6). Nevertheless, as narrated in the golden calf episode at Mount Sinai (Exod 32–34), the Israelites are faithless and disobedient people to Yahweh by making a golden calf and worshiping it (Exod 32:1-6).

59. Leveen, "Inside Out," 408–9. See also Reiss, "Jethro the Convert," 91.

When the Israelites see that Moses delays to come down from the mountain of God (Exod 32:1), they ask Aaron to make them gods. Aaron makes a golden calf, and the Israelites confess, "These are your gods, O Israel, who brought you up out of the land of Egypt" (Exod 32:2–4). Aaron builds an altar, and the Israelites come and worship the golden calf by bringing burnt offerings and peace offerings and by sitting down to eat and drink and rising up to play (Exod 32:5–6). All this directly violates Yahweh's commandments, and Yahweh's wrath burns hot against Aaron and the Israelites (Exod 32:7–10). Aaron and the Israelites experience Yahweh by both hearing and seeing, but they quickly turn away from Yahweh and disobey Yahweh's commandments by making and serving the false gods.

Thus, by functioning prospectively, the character of Jethro, though an "Israelite" only in an "ingrafted" or "adopted" sense, stands as a model to contrast with all the faithless Israelites.[60] Yahweh promised Moses, "I will be with you, and this is the sign for you that I have sent you: when you have brought the people out of Egypt, you (pl.) shall serve God on this mountain" (Exod 3:12). Having brought the Israelites out, Yahweh declares his special purpose for them: "Then, now, if you will surely obey me, and you will keep my covenant, then you shall be to me a treasured possession from all the peoples because all the earth belongs to me, and you shall be to me a kingdom of priests and a holy nation" (Exod 19:5–6; cf. 15:26). Yahweh has come down to deliver his people, the Israelites, from their slavery under Pharaoh and the Egyptians, which has caused them to suffer and die, and to bring them into his service, which should cause them to rejoice in, praise, and confess Yahweh as Jethro does (Exod 18:9–11), so that they may serve (or worship) Yahweh as Jethro does as well (Exod 18:12; cf. 24:9–11). Yahweh wants his people, the Israelites and even all the nations, to obey him and keep his commandments, so that they may be his people, holy people, as Jethro does in his advice to Moses (Exod 18:19–23; cf. 19:5–6).

This also looks forward to Yahweh's promises and purpose for all the Israelites, and Jethro is an example what it means to be Yahweh's people, "a treasured possession from all the peoples," "a kingdom of priests," and

---

60. Wells, *God's Holy People*, 52, notes, "What does it mean for Israel, God's kingdom, to have a priestly character? The immediate context of Exod. 18 and 19 provides some clues concerning this identity. On a minimal understanding, it suggests those who are concerned with approaching God, who are 'consecrated' to him and his service, and who specialize in things sacred. Priesthood is both a status which is given and a function which is demanded. It is a special expression of separation and devotion."

"a holy nation" (Exod 19:5–6). Yahweh has brought his people out of their suffering and led them a place of peace in his presence, so that they may continue to hear about and acknowledge Yahweh, and also that they may serve and worship Yahweh and live as Yahweh's obedient people. This is the very picture of Jethro in Exod 18.

Therefore, in the Exodus narrative, the character of Jethro is rhetorically employed by the narrator as (1) a model to contrast with all the nations, who hears of and comes to Yahweh, and (2) a model to contrast with all the faithless Israelites, who comes into Yahweh's presence to serve Yahweh and to live in faith and obedience to Yahweh. These two rhetorical uses further establish that Exod 18 functions both retrospectively and prospectively as the key transitional midpoint of the Exodus narrative. Jethro also serves both retrospectively and prospectively by drawing to a close the contrasting Gentile responses to Yahweh—Jethro's acts of coming to praise Yahweh and of acknowledging Yahweh—in Exod 1–18[61] and anticipating the Israelites' often contrasting response to Yahweh—Jethro's acts of worshiping Yahweh and of living as a faithful and obedient person to Yahweh—in Exod 18–40.

In conclusion, as discussed above, Jethro, the priest of Midian, the father-in-law of Moses, plays six narrative roles in the narrative of Exod 18: (1) a Midianite, (2) a priest, (3) the father-in-law of Moses, (4) a confessor of Yahweh, (5) an experienced fatherly advisor, and (6) a believer in Yahweh. These narrative roles present Jethro in relation to other characters, especially Yahweh, Moses, and the Israelites within Exod 18. In the whole Exodus narrative, Jethro is also employed rhetorically by the narrator as (1) a model to contrast with all the nations and (2) a model to contrast with all the faithless Israelites. For example, the narrator uses

---

61. Eslinger, "Knowing Yahweh," 195n15, notes, "[T]here is nowhere in the entire exodus story, or even the entire Bible, where Yahweh's hope for recognition is fulfilled. There is no confirming, 'and X knew that he was Yahweh'—either for 'Jew or Greek'—anywhere in the Old Testament." In contrast, a key theme in the entire Exodus narrative is the knowledge of Yahweh, that is, Yahweh's making himself known. Throughout Exod 1–17, Yahweh has obviously made himself known to Moses and Aaron, the Israelites, Pharaoh and the Egyptians, and the Amalekites through Yahweh's saving and mighty deeds and sacred name in the land of Egypt, at the Red Sea, and on the wilderness journey to Mount Sinai. The theme of Yahweh's making himself known, which has dominated the entire Exodus narrative up to this point, does not find its explicit resolution until Jethro's confession in Exod 18: "Now, I know that Yahweh is greater than all gods" (v. 11). This is apparent that Jethro acknowledges Yahweh as the greatest and incomparable God by hearing of Yahweh's delivering and powerful deeds and holy name, and this acknowledgement exhibits the fulfillment of the acknowledgement of Yahweh which Eslinger has misread. See also Egger, "Visiting Iniquity," 472n65.

the characterization of Jethro to tell the audience about the knowledge of Yahweh, that is, Yahweh's making himself known. As a model to contrast with all the nations, Jethro has only heard of Yahweh's great redemptive deeds of Israel (Exod 18:1, 8) and then responds to Yahweh by rejoicing in, praising, and confessing Yahweh as the greatest and incomparable God (Exod 18:9–11). This rhetorical use pictures a proper acknowledgement of Yahweh by Jethro who stands in contrast with Pharaoh, the Egyptians, and the Amalekites (Exod 1–17). After his confession, Jethro as a model to contrast with all the faithless Israelites reacts promptly to Yahweh by serving (or worshiping) Yahweh (Exod 18:12) and speaks of Yahweh's will and presence in Jethro's advice for Moses (Exod 18:19–23). This rhetorical use portrays a faithful and obedient person to Yahweh in the person of Jethro who stands in contrast with Aaron and the Israelites (Exod 19–40). Thus, the rhetorical uses of Jethro employed by the narrator express Exod 18 as the key transitional midpoint of the Exodus narrative by bringing a conclusion of Yahweh's declaration on all the nations' hearing of Yahweh's great acts and holy name and on their coming to Yahweh with joy, praise, and confession, and by exhibiting an anticipation of Yahweh's announcement on Yahweh's own people who live in faith and obedience to serve (or worship) Yahweh.

Now that we have seen the retrospective and prospective functions of Jethro's character in Exod 18 for the whole Exodus narrative, the following chapter will explore the retrospective function of Exod 18 more generally to argue that Exod 18 is indeed the key transitional midpoint of the Exodus narrative.

Chapter 5

The Retrospective Function of Exodus 18

THIS BOOK SEEKS TO highlight the function of Exod 18:1–27 in drawing to a close the first narrative movement, the first half of the book of Exodus (Exod 1–17), in which Yahweh is seen and known through his mighty acts of deliverance, mediated through Moses. Exodus 18 also signals a shift, moving into the second narrative movement, the second half of the book of Exodus (Exod 19–40), to a self-revelation of Yahweh which will feature Israel's need to heed the word and will of Yahweh as mediated through Moses. We have argued that Exod 18's most prominent figure, Jethro, the priest of Midian, the father-in-law of Moses, offers a first strong indication of the chapter's retrospective and prospective interest. In what follows, we describe the strong retrospective function of Exod 18 more generally.

In demonstrating Exod 18 as the key transitional midpoint of the Exodus narrative, this chapter will outline significant ways in which Exod 18 as a whole connects with and summarizes the previous narratives in Exod 1–17. This summative, retrospective role of Exod 18 will be discussed under six themes: (1) the Jethro accounts, (2) Yahweh saving the Israelites from external threats through his mighty acts of deliverance, (3) the presence of Yahweh in various places, (4) the knowledge of Yahweh by Yahweh's self-revelation through his mighty acts of deliverance, (5) Moses as the judge, acting as "God" to Pharaoh and the Egyptians, and (6) the Israelites as the Egyptian slaves.

The Jethro Accounts

This book has already shown that the Jethro accounts consisting of Exod 2:16–4:26 and 18:1–27 present Jethro as the main character and also share other related elements.¹ The first narrative movement of the Exodus narrative comes a full circle as the themes in Exod 2–4 form an inclusio with Exod 18.² The episode of Exod 18 begins, "Now, Jethro, the priest of

---

1. Carpenter, "Exodus 18," 105, notes, "As is now clear, ch. 18 is especially closely related to the Midianite material in chs. 2–4. The heading of the chapter [Exod 18] in v. 1 serves beautifully to reintroduce us to Jethro, the priest of Midian and father-in-law of Moses, thus repeating all of the important information about him found in Exodus 2–4, the major block of Midianite traditions. . . . Zipporah and Moses' sons are reintroduced (vv. 2–6). The chapter answers the question of the religious relationship of Jethro to Moses and to Israel and satisfies the reader's questions that have arisen about Zipporah and Moses' sons (cf. 2.22 and 4.20)." Furthermore, regarding the relationship between Exod 2:16–4:26 and 18:1–27, Alexander, *Exodus*, 349, notes, "Jethro's journey ends when he comes to the wilderness in the region of Horeb. Although no specific name is given to the location of the Israelite camp, it was relatively close to the 'mountain of God', previously mentioned in 3:1. Whereas previously Moses encountered YHWH and was commissioned while shepherding the flock of Jethro in Horeb to lead the Israelites out of Egypt, now Jethro in Horeb learns of what YHWH has done for the Israelites. Whereas previously Jethro had sent Moses away in peace (4:18), now Moses receives him in peace (18:7; see note on v. 7). Whereas previously Jethro had brought Moses into his family (2:15–22), now he brings Moses' family to him (18:5–6). Jethro's prior kindness is reciprocated by Moses, who greets his father-in-law with appropriate respect and warmth." Furthermore, Carpenter, "Exodus 18," 106, notes, "The physical movement of Moses and Jethro in chs. 2–4 and 18 is interesting. In Exodus 2–4, Moses flees to the wilderness where he is welcomed and received hospitably by Jethro. Here Jethro is received likewise in the wilderness by Moses. In Exod. 4.18, Jethro sends off Moses in שלום. שלום is used three times in Exodus: 4.18; 18.7, 23. All usages are in the Midianite materials and involve Jethro and Moses. Here Moses receives Jethro in שלום and sends him off. The final usage in 18.23 includes Israel and God. The reception and blessings received by Moses, God's representative of his people, results in Moses, Israel, and their God blessing Jethro in return, a clear demonstration of covenant hospitality." See also Carpenter, "Exodus 18," 100. In contrast, Janzen, "Jethro," 163, notes, "In Jethro, in the role of a host in chaps. 2–4 and then again in chap. 18, I discovered the key markers for generating the structure of Exodus in my commentary." See also Janzen, "Jethro," 165, 166, 167, 168, 170. Further, he notes, "In both Midian sections, chaps 2–4 and chap. 18, Jethro functions as welcoming host and as a facilitator to settling down to traditional wilderness life after a turbulent escape." Janzen, "Jethro," 167.

2. Childs, *Exodus*, 327, notes, "In spite of the complex history of traditions problems which lie behind the Midian stories, these chapters [Exod 2:15–4:20 and Exod 18] now perform a simple and straightforward function within the Exodus narrative. Chapter 2 pictures the quiet period of preparation. Moses pastures sheep for forty years in the wilderness. It is the quiet before the storm which erupts in ch. 3 and drives him back to Egypt. Now ch. 18 functions as a concluding scene. . . . In ch. 3 Moses had received the sign that he would not only deliver the people, but that he would worship with them on the holy mountain (3.12). Ch. 18 comes to a climax with the common

Midian, the father-in-law of Moses" (Exod 18:1). The name and titles of Jethro are reintroduced here as first introduced in Exod 3:1; 4:18.[3]

The arrival of Jethro from the land of Midian to Mount Sinai along with Moses' wife, Zipporah, and his sons, Gershom and Eliezer (Exod 18:2–4)[4] ties the end of the deliverance narrative back to its beginning,

---

meal which was led by Jethro and shared by Aaron and the elders of the people. The first part of ch. 18 offers a moment of grateful remembrance. It looks back at what has happened and what God has done for Israel. Not yet at least is there any hint of the momentous event of Sinai which lies just ahead. Just for a moment the writer pauses in the story to look backward and to rejoice." See also Carpenter, *Exodus*, 1:603. Carpenter, "Exodus 18," 93, notes, "The first half of the chapter (vv. 1–12) . . . addresses the issues raised by the Midianite traditions, both essential and incidental, found in chs. 2–4." See also Carpenter, "Exodus 18," 100, 101, 107; Alexander, *Exodus*, 345; Janzen, "Jethro," 168. Ber, "Moses and Jethro," 158, notes, "It is legitimate to interpret the appearance of Jethro, Zippora, and her sons as an indication of a motif in Exodus called 'the Midianite motif.' In its context, Moses' family reunion in Exodus 18 represents the motif's harmonic conclusion." Lawlor, "'At-Sinai Narrative,'" 27, notes, "A 'positive' reading of the two movements of Exod 18 (18:1–12, 13–27) tends to draw attention to 18:1–12 as an 'epilogue' to the introduction of Jethro in Exod 2." Jeon, "Visit of Jethro," 291, notes, "Exodus 18 both thematically and structurally completes the Midianite narrative strand from Exod 2–4, functioning as a transitional hinge between the narratives of the wilderness and Sinai." Further, he notes, "The connection of Exod 18 with Exod 2–4 is obvious, yet this Moses-Midianite (Jethro) strand finishes at chapter 18 without further narrative consequence. Exodus 18, therefore, should be considered the completion of the Moses-Midianite cycle." Jeon, "The Visit of Jethro," 291. Nevertheless, he notes, "Verses 13–26 differ from the earlier story [vv. 1–12] in a number of ways: the subject matter of the second part of the chapter falls outside of the narrative framework of the 'family' story of Exod 2–4 and 18; Jethro's name is not mentioned in the second part; the role of Jethro as wise man or counselor on a national issue is quite different from his role in the previous Moses-Midianite cycle, where he is a family patron." Jeon, "The Visit of Jethro," 298.

3. Childs, *Exodus*, 326, notes, "The introduction of Jethro, priest of Midian, Moses' father-in-law, carries the reader back to the earliest period in the Exodus narrative. His name, his occupation, his country, and his relation to Moses, all serve to recall the beginning of the story. It reminds of that period of exile before Moses had begun his task of deliverance. The fact that the author intended to make this connection is further attested by the explicit reference in vv. 2ff. to Zipporah and her two sons (cf. Acts 7:29)." See also Meyer, *Message of Exodus*, 108; Fox, *Now These Are the Names*, 99; Dozeman, *Exodus*, 401; Janzen, "Jethro," 165. Furthermore, Meyers, *Exodus*, 136, notes, "The first part of the chapter (vv. 1–12) brings Moses' father-in-law Jethro back into the narrative and provides an ending to the exodus narrative." Further, she notes, "Jethro appears here for the third and last time in the exodus account. He is first mentioned when Moses flees from Egypt and marries his daughter Zipporah (3:1) and then a second time when Moses leaves him to begin his mission in Egypt (4:18). Now, having heard of the exodus, Jethro reappears." Meyers, *Exodus*, 136. Ber, "Moses and Jethro," 153, notes, "Obviously, Jethro's arrival in Exod. 18 calls to mind memories of Moses' stay in the land of Midian (Exod. 2,15–4, 26)."

4. Bailey, *Exodus*, 199, notes, "Verse 2 completes the information given in 2:21 and

when Moses fled from Pharaoh (Exod 2:15), settled in the land of Midian, married Zipporah, and had son(s) (Exod 2:16–4:26).[5] This reunion of Moses' Midianite family reprises a number of specific elements from the scenes in Exod 2:16–4:26.[6] When Moses fled from the land of Egypt

---

4:18–26, indicating that Jethro took care of his daughter and grandsons while their husband and father went back to Egypt."

5. Burns, *Exodus, Leviticus, Numbers*, 137, notes, "The focus on Jethro and Moses' family circle in Exod 18:1–12 affords an opportunity for us to pause and look back to the beginnings of the exodus." Wendland, *Exodus*, 118, notes, "We remember from our study of Exodus chapter 2 how Moses tended sheep for Jethro, the priest of Midian, in this same area where the Israelites had now come. It was here that Moses married Zipporah, Jethro's daughter, a marriage blessed with two sons, Gershom and Eliezer." Zweck, *Freed to Follow*, 161, notes, "On the other hand, chapter 18 is appropriate in its present position because the narrative has come full circle. After fleeing from Pharaoh, Moses was in Midian, where he married one of Jethro's daughters and lived in Jethro's household (2:15–22). This time in Midian was a period of quiet preparation before the theophany at Sinai and Moses' commission to return to Egypt (chapter 3). Now Moses has returned from Egypt, and, leading the rescued people of Israel, is en route to Sinai, where, as promised, he will again 'serve God upon this mountain' (3:12). It is fitting that Moses be reunited with Jethro and his family at this point—before the second and greater theophany on Sinai. The scene of reunion provides a pause in the narrative, time for grateful remembrance."

6. Fretheim, *Exodus*, 195, notes, "The family relationship is no doubt a factor (see 2:15–22; 4:18–26), . . . The narrator's emphasis on this relationship is shown by the repeated reference to Jethro as Moses' father-in-law (thirteen times; priest only once). The detail relating to Zipporah and Moses' two sons reinforces the interest in family. In particular, the attention given to the sons' names demonstrates an interest in family religious continuity." Further, he notes, "But there are now changes. This change is highlighted by the repeated reference to God's delivering Israel from Egypt (five times in vv. 1–12), virtually a refrain. To link these repetitions: the concern is *the integration of Moses' family into Israel's new identity as the exodus community of faith*." Fretheim, *Exodus*, 195. Jeon, "Visit of Jethro," 291, notes, "Exodus 2–4 and 18 have a number of corresponding elements that indicate a close literary connection between them." For more details, see Jeon, "Visit of Jethro," 291. See also Egger, "Visiting Iniquity," 455–57. Furthermore, concerning the reunion of Abraham's descendants, Osborn and Hatton, *Exodus*, 426, note, "Even with these technical problems, however, the chapter [Exod 18] serves a special function in the structure of the book [the Book of Exodus]. . . . Secondly, it shows how Moses was reunited with his family before having to give full attention to the establishment of law and order." Further, they note, "Finally, it shows how two lines of descendants from Abraham, through the Israelites and the Midianites, were reunited before the special revelation of Yahweh on the mountain. The Israelites were Abraham's descendants through his first wife, Sarah, and the Midianites were his descendants through his second wife, Keturah. (See Gen 25.1–2.) And Moses' wife, Zipporah, was a descendant of Keturah. This reunion is sealed with the special covenant described in verse 12." Osborn and Hatton, *Exodus*, 426. Osborn and Hatton, *Exodus*, 435, note, "This is because verse 12 not only describes a union of families in worshiping God, but also suggests a kind of reunion of tribes, since the Midianites and Israelites were all descended from one ancestor, Abraham (see Gen 25.1–2). . . .

to the land of Midian, he met the seven daughters of Reuel, the priest of Midian, with their flock at a well (Exod 2:16). Shepherds came and drove the seven women, along with their flock, away. Moses "stood up and saved (ישע) them" from the shepherds' threat, "and he watered their flock" (Exod 2:17). The seven women went home and reported to their father, "An Egyptian delivered (נצל) us from the hand of the shepherds (מִיַּד הָרֹעִים), and he also drew water for us, and he watered the flock" (Exod 2:19). Thus, Reuel summoned Moses, so that Moses might "eat (אכל) bread (לֶחֶם)" with them (Exod 2:20). Moses settled with Reuel and married one of his daughters, Zipporah, who bore a son, Gershom (Exod 2:21–22). Before Yahweh called Moses at the burning bush on Mount Horeb, Reuel, the priest of Midian, was introduced with another name, "Jethro," and another title, "the father-in-law of Moses" (Exod 3:1; cf. 4:18; 18:1). After meeting with Yahweh, Moses went back to Jethro and asked for permission to return to the land of Egypt (Exod 4:18). Later, Moses took his wife and sons to the land of Egypt (Exod 4:19). However, Moses' wife and sons remained absent and unmentioned throughout Exod 4:27–17:16, reappearing now here in Exod 18.[7]

Moses' second son is mentioned in Exod 4:20, but only here in Exod 18 is Eliezer's name given, along with its meaning, "The God of my father was my help, and he delivered (נצל) me from the sword of Pharaoh (מֵחֶרֶב

Moses is not mentioned as a participant, but we should assume that he was included. It is possible that this meal was the ritual celebration of the reunion of the Israelites with the Midianites." Regarding Moses as a bridge for a reunion of Abraham's descendants between two sides [Jethro and Aaron], Durham, *Exodus*, 240, notes, "The nuclear theme of the whole of Exod 18 is the integration of the traditions of the Sarah/Isaac/Jacob/Joseph side of Abraham's family with those of the Keturah/Midian side. Moses, the descendant of the Sarah-Isaac side, becomes the divinely chosen medium of connection with Jethro, the descendant of the Keturah-Midian side. Moses, bereft of his family in Egypt by his flight from the justice of Pharaoh, has found a family in Midian. By one of those remarkable connections so recurrent in the Bible, however, Moses' new family is, in a quite literal sense, just another branch of his old family. And Moses becomes the guide and the bridge-person who links the two parts of the family separated since Abraham's day (Gen 25:1–6)." Further, he points that Exod 18 "functions now as the conclusion of a division in the family of father Abraham," for example, Cain/Seth, Keturah/Sarah, Ishmael/Isaac, and Esau/Jacob (see Durham, *Exodus*, 241–42). See also Durham, *Exodus*, 245–46.

7. Meyer, *Message of Exodus*, 108, notes, "Nothing has been said to Moses' family since the end of Exodus 4. Now Jethro, the priest of Midian, Moses' father-in-law, again makes an appearance.... Because it has been so long since the members of the family have been mentioned, we are given a brief resume." See also Houtman, *Exodus*, 2:404; Osborn and Hatton, *Exodus*, 427; Garrett, *Exodus*, 441; White, *Exodus*, 130; Alexander, *Exodus*, 349.

פַּרְעֹה)" (Exod 18:4). After Moses had met Jethro, Moses recounted to Jethro about Yahweh's deliverance, "all which Yahweh had done to Pharaoh and to the Egyptians because of Israel, and all the hardship which had come upon them on the way; and Yahweh had delivered (נצל) them!" (Exod 18:8). Then Jethro rejoiced in Yahweh's deliverance, "all the good which Yahweh had done for Israel, whom he had delivered (נצל) from the hand of the Egyptians (מִיַּד מִצְרָיִם)" (Exod 18:9), and he praised Yahweh "who has delivered (נצל) you from the hand of the Egyptians (מִיַּד מִצְרַיִם) and from the hand of Pharaoh (מִיַּד פַּרְעֹה), and who has delivered (נצל) the people from under the hand of the Egyptians (מִתַּחַת יַד־מִצְרָיִם)" (Exod 18:10). After Jethro had acknowledged Yahweh, he took sacrifices to Yahweh, and Aaron and all the elders of Israel "came to eat (אכל) bread (לֶחֶם)"[8] with Jethro before Yahweh (Exod 18:12).

In addition, the Hebrew word שָׁלוֹם, "completeness, soundness, welfare, peace," occurs only three times in the Exodus narrative, with all three occurances in these Jethro scenes (Exod 4:18; 18:7, 23)[9] from the mouth of Jethro who is the priest of Midian: (1) when Jethro lets Moses go back to the land of Egypt, "Go in peace (שָׁלוֹם)" (Exod 4:18), (2) when Jethro and Moses meet and ask about "their welfare (שָׁלוֹם)" (Exod 18:7), and (3) when Jethro advises Moses to establish "peace (שָׁלוֹם)" for Israel (Exod 18:23).

Therefore, the Jethro accounts in Exod 2:16–4:26 and 18:1–27 serve additionally to show that Exod 18 functions retrospectively. These accounts share identical and related key elements: (1) the characters of Moses, Jethro, Zipporah, and son(s), who only appear at the beginning and at the end of the first narrative movement, the first half of the book

---

8. A commentator thinks of eating bread that the Passover in Exod 12:1–28 precedes and a meal in Exod 18:12 follows Yahweh's deliverance, and a meal in Exod 2:20 and another meal in Exod 18:12 precede Moses' encounter with Yahweh. Enns, *Exodus*, 370, notes, "Beyond the matter of bread, the meal has a number of theological implications for how we understand this stage of the story. Note that this is not the first meal referred to in Exodus. The most recent meal is the Passover, which takes place on the eve of Israel's deliverance. In both cases, a meal precedes a climactic redemptive event. More important, this is not the first meal Moses and Jethro have together, for in 2:20 they also eat *leḥem*. This first meal, from the point of view of the flow of the narrative, occurred just before Moses' first encounter with God on Mount Horeb (ch. 3). This second meal immediately precedes Moses' second and climatic encounter with God on Mount Sinai."

9. Carpenter, *Exodus*, 1:609, notes, "The word שָׁלוֹם is used three times in Exodus (4:18; 18:7, 23). All of the usages are in the Midianite materials and communicate the שָׁלוֹם that existed between Moses and Jethro, and hence between Israel, her God, and Jethro." See also Carpenter, "Exodus 18," 100, 101, 106.

of Exodus (Exod 2:16–4:26 and 18:1–27) and nowhere else in the book of Exodus;[10] (2) the actions of (a) saving (ישׁע)/delivering (נצל) Jethro's seven daughters from the hand of shepherds (מִיַּד הָרֹעִים) (Exod 2:17, 19) and delivering (נצל) Moses from the sword of Pharaoh (מֵחֶרֶב פַּרְעֹה) (Exod 18:4)/delivering (נצל) Israel from the hand of Pharaoh and the Egyptians (מִיַּד פַּרְעֹה/מִצְרָיִם) (Exod 18:8, 9, 10) and (b) eating (אכל) bread (לֶחֶם) (Exod 2:20; 18:12);[11] and (3) Jethro's concern regarding Moses' peace/welfare, indicated by his repetition of the word שָׁלוֹם (Exod 4:18; 18:7, 23).[12] These recurring elements in the Jethro accounts—elements which do not again appear in the Exodus narrative afterwards—serve to bring the Jethro and Midianite elements of the story to a complete conclusion as an inclusio and further evince the key transitional midpoint role of Exod 18 within the Exodus narrative.

Yahweh Saving the Israelites from External Threats through His Mighty Acts of Deliverance

Yahweh saves the Israelites from external threats—Pharaoh and the Egyptians, thirst, hunger, thirst, and the Amalekites—through his mighty acts of deliverance.[13] The episode of Exod 18 offers a brief

---

10. See Egger, "Visiting Iniquity," 455. Ber, "Moses and Jethro," 159, notes, "I think that the characters here (Moses' father-in-law, wife, children) embody a strong argument in favor of the connection between these texts [Exod 4:24–26 and 18]." For an example of Zipporah, see Ber, "Moses and Jethro," 159.

11. See Egger, "Visiting Iniquity," 455–56.

12. See Carpenter, "Exodus 18," 106; Carpenter, *Exodus*, 1:609.

13. Wendland, *Exodus*, 121, notes, "With this chapter [Exod 18] we bring Part I [Exod 1–18] of the book of Exodus to a close. The theme of the entire book, we recall, is 'Jehovah's Covenant with the People of Israel.' The first eighteen chapters have presented 'the deliverance of the covenant people out of Egypt.' What we have considered thus far—the birth and call of Moses, the negotiations between Moses and Pharaoh concerning Israel's release from bondage, the plagues, the Passover, the departure out of Egypt, the crossing of the Red Sea and Israel's early experiences in the desert on their journey to Mount Sinai—all this has been preparatory to 'the establishment of Jehovah's covenant with Israel' (Part II) [Exod 19–24]." Furthermore, Egger, "Visiting Iniquity," 450, notes, "the deliverance characterizing the Exod 1–18 narrative arc takes place in the face of *external* threats: bitter slavery and oppression, infanticide, military foes (Egypt and later Amalek), and life-threatening hunger and thirst in the wilderness." Further, he demonstrates "a chiastic structure to the external threats encountered by Israel" in Exod 14–17: the Egyptian army-thirst-hunger-thirst-the Amalekite army (see Egger, "Visiting Iniquity," 450–51).

summary of this salvation theme.[14] At the beginning of Exod 18, Jethro hears of Yahweh's salvation of the Israelites, "all which God had done for Moses and for Israel, his people, that Yahweh had brought Israel out of Egypt" (Exod 18:1). After Moses has met Jethro, Moses directly recounts to Jethro concerning Yahweh's salvation of the Israelites, "all which Yahweh had done to Pharaoh and to the Egyptians because of Israel, and all the hardship which had come upon them on the way; and Yahweh had delivered them!" (Exod 18:8). Then Jethro rejoices in Yahweh's salvation of the Israelites, "all the good which Yahweh had done for Israel, whom he had delivered from the hand of the Egyptians" (Exod 18:9), and he praises Yahweh "who has delivered you from the hand of the Egyptians and from the hand of Pharaoh, and who has delivered the people from under the hand of the Egyptians" (Exod 18:10). This theme is, likewise, highlighted with the name of Moses' second son, Eliezer, whose name is explained as "The God of my father was my help" (Exod 18:4), and it is clarified that Yahweh delivers Moses from the sword of Pharaoh (Exod 18:4; cf. 2:15).[15]

These redemptive clauses, especially the all-encompassing clauses "all which God had done for Moses and for Israel, his people" (Exod 18:1; cf. 18:8, 9) and "all the hardship which had come upon them [Israel] on

---

14. Meyers, *Exodus*, 136, notes, "The first part of the chapter [Exod 18] (vv. 1–12) ... provides an ending to the exodus narrative." Carpenter, *Exodus*, 1:603, notes, "The chapter [Exod 18] is best described as a magnificent transition piece that brings the earlier chapters of Exodus (1–17) to a conclusion that celebrates Yahweh's success in vv. 1–12." Further, he notes, "The first half of the chapter (vv. 1–12) brings the exodus deliverance motif of the preceding chapters to a meaningful conclusion (τέλος)." Carpenter, "Exodus 18," 93. See also Alexander, *Exodus*, 345; Janzen, "Jethro," 168. Furthermore, Egger, "Visiting Iniquity," 449, notes, "the emphasis on *accomplished deliverance* in Exod 18 stands as a fitting conclusion to the first narrative arc."

15. Murphy, *Exodus*, 120, notes, "Moses had a grateful remembrance of his deliverance from the sword of Pharaoh." Davies, *Exodus*, 148, notes, "SWORD OF PHARAOH occurs only here, but the reference could be to 2:15." Osborn and Hatton, *Exodus*, 429, note, "*From the sword of Pharaoh* is simply a descriptive way of saying 'from being killed by the king of Egypt' (TEV). An alternative model is 'who saved me from the king of Egypt, who intended to kill me.'" Carpenter, *Exodus*, 1:609, notes, "The name of the second son, Eliezer (אֱלִיעֶזֶר), 'God is my help,' is not a mere creation to fit the literary context. The exodus itself has inspired the name, which seems to indicate that the son was born and named after God called Moses to deliver his people in Midian. It is also possible that the child was named in remembrance of Yahweh's protection of Moses from Pharaoh when he fled Egypt after killing an Egyptian (2:10–15)." See also Alexander, *Exodus*, 348.

the way" (Exod 18:8), draw the accounts of Exod 1–17 to an emphatic conclusion.[16] Douglas K. Stuart explains:

> Moses probably spent a good many hours recounting to Jethro the entire story that we know in written form as Exod 4:27–17:16, and it is not at all improbable that such a full oral review may have been part of the process by which God prepared Moses to become the writer of the book of Exodus.[17]

T. Desmond Alexander argues, "The reader of Exodus is expected to infer that Moses tells Jethro the substance of all that has been recorded in chs. 5–17."[18]

The redemptive clauses also serve to emphasize the fulfillment of Yahweh's declaration to Moses at Mount Horeb, "and I have come down to deliver them [Israel] from the hand of the Egyptians" (Exod 3:8; cf. 3:10, 17; 6:6).[19] Thomas B. Dozeman discusses:

> Two themes stand out in Moses' interpretation of Eliezer's name. The first is the identification of Yahweh as the 'God of the father,' and the second is the declaration of salvation as a divine rescue (*nāṣal*). Both themes occur in the first revelation of Yahweh to Moses on the mountain of God (3:6–9). The phrase 'God of the father' stresses Yahweh's kinship with the Israelites, not the Midianites—an important point of clarification since Jethro will assume the leadership role in worship on the mountain of God. The declaration of divine rescue signals the fulfillment of the exodus from Egypt and, with it, the initial phase of Moses' commission.[20]

---

16. Durham, *Exodus*, 244, notes, "This recital [of Yahweh's mighty acts] is summarized concisely, with careful reference to purpose of these mighty acts: Moses recounted what Yahweh had done to Pharaoh and the Egyptians *on behalf of Israel*; he related the 'wearying difficulties' of the journey as a means of pointing out how *Yahweh had rescued Israel every time*." See also Dozeman, *Exodus*, 403. Interestingly, as considering Exod 18 as the completion of Yahweh's deliverance, Egger points to the name of Moses' second son, Eliezer, which the narrator keeps until here in Exod 18:4 unlike the name of Moses' first son, Gershom, which the narrator gives in Exod 2:22 and again here in Exod 18:3 (see Egger, "Visiting Iniquity," 449–50).

17. Stuart, *Exodus*, 410–11.

18. Alexander, *Exodus*, 349–50.

19. Concerning Exod 18:9, Gispen, *Exodus*, 174, notes, "Verse 9, cf. 3:8; the Lord's promise was fulfilled." Furthermore, concerning Eliezer's name in Exod 18:4, Bruckner, *Exodus*, 164, notes, "The reminder about Moses' son Gershom and the introduction of his son Eliezer also serve to briefly summarize Moses' personal experience."

20. Dozeman, *Exodus*, 402.

Waldemar Janzen comments:

> The name of the second son, *Eliezer*, means *My God [is my] helper*. His name, not mentioned till now, completes Moses' salvation. . . .; the name of the second encompasses the story of deliverance. . . . In retrospect, the names of the two sons characterize Moses' experience and also embrace Israel's story of salvation. . . . For the immediate participants in these stories, the children with their testifying names would, of course, continue to be reminders of the message carried by their names. Israel meets with Jethro at the mountain of God, in the presence of Moses' sons with their confessional names. Both the meeting and the sons' names work together to emphasize that Moses' commission to bring Israel out of Egypt (3:10) has been completed and Israel has 'arrived.'[21]

Two all-encompassing clauses summarize what Yahweh had done for Israel in the land of Egypt, at the Red Sea, and on the wilderness journey to Mount Sinai, as recorded in the first seventeen chapters of the book of Exodus.[22] The first clause, "all which God had done for Moses and for Israel, his people" (Exod 18:1; cf. 18:8, 9), indicates that Yahweh's great deeds for Israel are his delivering and powerful acts through which Yahweh had saved Israel from Egypt (Exod 18:1), from the hand of Pharaoh and the Egyptians (Exod 18:9, 10; cf. 18:4, 8). Yahweh's salvation of Israel from Pharaoh and the Egyptians happens both in the land of Egypt and at the Red Sea.[23] The second clause, "all the hardship which had come upon them [Israel] on the way" (Exod 18:8), marks that Yahweh had rescued Israel from all the sequenced

---

21. Janzen, *Exodus*, 225–26.

22. In contrast, other scholars discern two major places, Egypt and the wilderness, during the redemptive events. Erdman, *Exodus*, 84, notes, "Word reaches Jethro that Moses has brought the people, by divine help, out of the land of bondage, across the desert, to the foot of Mount Sinai." Rylaarsdam and Park, "Exodus," 1:964, note, "After the reunion Moses invited (Samar.) Jethro into his tent and gave him an account of the great acts of Yahweh both in Egypt and in the desert." See also Keil and Delitzsch, *Pentateuch*, 2:84; Meyer, *Devotional Commentary on Exodus*, 207; Brueggemann, "Exodus," 1:829; Coats, *Exodus 1–18*, 146.

23. Osborn and Hatton, *Exodus*, 427, note, "This [all that God had done] refers to all the plagues as well as to the miraculous crossing at the Red Sea." Stuart, *Exodus*, 403, notes, "The stories of the plagues and the Red Sea deliverance would also have surely impressed him [Jethro]."

hardship—thirst, hunger, thirst, and war with the Amalekites—which happens on the wilderness journey to Mount Sinai.[24]

In the land of Egypt, Yahweh acted as the Savior of the Israelites[25] through many great deeds of judgment and deliverance. When a new Pharaoh who did not know Joseph arose over the land of Egypt, the new Pharaoh planned to oppress the Israelites with hard labor and to kill every male child born to the Israelites, but Yahweh, nevertheless, multiplied and preserved the Israelite children, including the infant Moses (Exod 1:8–2:10).[26] Yahweh saved the Israelites and brought them out of the land of Egypt through signs and the ten plagues in front of Pharaoh and the Egyptians through Moses and Aaron, the representatives

---

24. Bruckner, *Exodus*, 165, notes, "He [Moses] described their protection through what the Lord *had done to Pharaoh and the Egyptians*. He also told about *all the hardships*, including the lack of water and food, the quarreling, and the Amalekite attack." Nevertheless, other scholars consider that the redemptive event at the Red Sea is included in the wilderness journey to Mount Sinai. Cassuto, *Exodus*, 215, notes, "*Then Moses told his father-in-law* all the details of the happenings of which the latter had received general reports: *all that the Lord had done . . . to Pharaoh and to the Egyptians for Israel's sake . . . and also all the hardship that had come upon them in the way* after the exodus from Egypt—the pursuit of the Egyptians, the division of the Sea of Reeds, the lack of water, the dearth of food, and the war with Amalek—and how everything ended happily: *and how the Lord delivered them.*" Kaiser, "Exodus," 2:412, notes, "As the psalmist exhorted (Ps 145:5–7, 12), so Moses acted, recounting the awesome work and abundant goodness of Yahweh both in Israel's rescue from Egypt and in their subsequent 'hardship' (v. 8) along the way: the Red Sea, thirst, lack of meat, and the war with Amalek." Jacob, *Exodus*, 497, notes, "Moses' report was divided into two sections; the first dealt with events till the defeat of Pharaoh and the Exodus from Egypt (chapters 5–14); the second from the Sea of Reeds to their meeting, *ba-de-rekh*. This meant the events of Marah, *manna*, and Amalek." Houtman, *Exodus*, 2:407, notes, "General terms are used for the events: first there is an allusion to the plagues and the doom of Pharaoh and his army; next to the dangers that threatened Israel, pursuit by the Egyptians, thirst, hunger, Amalek's threat." See also Johnstone, *Exodus*, 1:376.

25. Houtman, *Exodus*, 2:394, 407.

26. The deliverance of the infant Moses at the Nile foreshadows the deliverance of the Israelites in the land of Egypt and at the Red Sea. Furthermore, some commentators see Moses' other rescuing events foreshadowing the Israelites' rescuing events. As discerning the name of Moses' second son, Eliezer, Alexander, *Exodus*, 348, notes, "Although Eliezer's name is related to Moses' first flight from Egypt, it takes on added significance in the light of the exodus of the Israelites." Concerning Moses' saving act for Jethro's seven daughters at the well, Hughes, "Jethro," *DOTP* 467, notes, "Moses rises to the occasion and 'delivers' them [a group of seven women]—a microdeliverance that foreshadows the macrodeliverance of the exodus event itself." Nevertheless, regarding Jethro's role in Exod 18, Carpenter, "Exodus 18," 98, notes, "The fact and the purpose of the deliverance of Yahweh finds expression in microcosm in Jethro, a pagan priest of Midian, who is also Moses' father-in-law. The same thing in macrocosm occurs in Exodus 5–17 among Israel and the Egyptians."

of Yahweh (Exod 7:14–12:36). Yahweh delivered the Israelites from the oppressing hand of Pharaoh and the Egyptians, who had caused the Israelites to groan and cry out in their affliction (Exod 2:23–25; cf. 3:7, 9; 6:5). After Yahweh brought the Israelites out of Egypt, Yahweh saved the Israelites from the hand of Pharaoh and the Egyptians at the Red Sea (Exod 14:1–31). Moreover, on the wilderness journey to Mount Sinai, Yahweh delivered the Israelites from the lack of water at Marah (Exod 15:22–25), the lack of food (Exod 16:1–36), the lack of water at Massah and Meribah (Exod 17:1–7), and, finally, the battle with the Amalekites (Exod 17:8–16).

The two all-encompassing clauses also conclude what Yahweh had declared through his promises to Moses at Mount Horeb, "and I have come down to deliver (נצל) them [Israel] from the hand of the Egyptians (מִיַּד מִצְרַיִם)" (Exod 3:8; cf. 3:10, 17; 6:6). In Exod 18, the narrator brings the theme of the salvation of Yahweh to a prominent conclusion by repeating the same words in Exod 3:8. For example, the *hiphil* of the verb נצל, "to snatch away, to deliver," (Exod 18:4, 8, 9, 10 [twice]) and the synonymous prepositional phrases מִיַּד/מִתַּחַת יַד־מִצְרָיִם, "from the hand of/from under the hand of the Egyptians," (Exod 18:9, 10 [twice]), מִיַּד פַּרְעֹה, "from the hand of Pharaoh," (Exod 18:10), and מֵחֶרֶב פַּרְעֹה, "from the sword of Pharaoh," (Exod 18:4).

In Exod 3:8, Yahweh promised Moses at Mount Horeb that he will deliver Israel from the hand of the Egyptians (cf. Exod 3:10, 17; 6:6). In Exod 18, when Moses recounts to Jethro about Yahweh's salvation of Israel in the land of Egypt, at the Red Sea, and on the wilderness journey to Mount Sinai, he concludes, "and Yahweh had delivered them [Israel]!" (Exod 18:8). Exodus 18 recounts that Yahweh did for Israel as he had promised Moses at Mount Horeb. Indeed, Yahweh delivered Israel from the hand of Pharaoh and the Egyptians in the land of Egypt and at the Red Sea and also from all the hardship on the wilderness journey to Mount Sinai (Exod 18:8; cf. 3:8; 18:1, 4, 9, 10).

As discussed in chapter 4 concerning the rhetorical uses of Jethro in the Exodus narrative as a whole, Jethro is rhetorically depicted by the narrator as a model to contrast with all the nations in Exod 1–18. In Exod 18, the narrator retrospectively portrays Jethro as a model to contrast with all the nations whom the Israelites encountered up to that time. Even though all the nations, especially Pharaoh, the Egyptians, and the Amalekites heard about Yahweh's purpose for his people, the Israelites (Exod 5:1, 3), they refused Yahweh (Exod 5:2) and brought threats, affliction, oppression, and even death to the Israelites (Exod 1:9–16, 22; 5:5–21; 17:8). In contrast, Jethro initially hears a report about Yahweh's salvation of the Israelites (Exod 18:1) and then brings Moses' family, Zipporah, Gershom, and Eliezer (Exod 18:2–4) to be reunited with Moses at Mount Sinai (Exod 18:5–6). Jethro also makes this family reunion relaxed and friendly (Exod 18:7–8). After hearing of Yahweh's salvation of the Israelites, Jethro comes and brings friendship and peace to Moses and even to Yahweh's people. Thus, Pharaoh, the Egyptians, and the Amalekites acted with hostility and violence toward Yahweh's people. The Gentile Jethro, however, responds to Yahweh's mighty acts of deliverance with faith, resulting in friendship and peace with Yahweh's people.

Therefore, Exod 18, functioning retrospectively, summarizes the preceding narratives of Yahweh's mighty acts of deliverance in the first narrative movement, the first half of the Exodus narrative (Exod 1–17) and also fulfills the original declaration of Yahweh to Moses at Mount Horeb in Exod 3:8 with the theme of Yahweh's deliverance of the Israelites from external threats—Pharaoh and the Egyptians, thirst, hunger, thirst, and the Amalekites—through his mighty acts of deliverance. Jethro hears of "all which God had done for Moses and for Israel, his people" (Exod 18:1; cf. 18:8, 9), specifically how Yahweh had delivered Israel from "Pharaoh and the Egyptians" and from "all the hardship which had come upon them [Israel] on the way" (Exod 18:8).

The Presence of Yahweh in Various Places

Yahweh's presence, a major theme in the Exodus narrative, is manifested and localized in various places, such as the mountain of God/Mount Horeb, the burning bush, the land of Midian, the land of Egypt, the pillars of cloud and fire, the Red Sea, the wilderness, and the mountain of God/Mount Sinai.[27] Within the flow of the Exodus narrative and

---

27. Regarding the reminiscence of the same mountain of God, Burns, *Exodus, Leviticus, Numbers*, 137, notes, "We recall that Moses was in the wilderness at this 'mountain of God' (cf. Exod 18:5) tending his father-in-law's flock when he first came to know Yahweh and to perceive his own mission in mediating God's redeeming activity toward Israel." Wendland, *Exodus*, 118, notes, "We remember from our study of Exodus chapter 2 how Moses tended sheep for Jethro, the priest of Midian, in this same area where the Israelites had now come." Jacob, *Exodus*, 495–96, notes, "Jethro knew he could find Moses at Horeb, at the mountain of God, for Moses had, undoubtedly, told him about the revelation at the thornbush when he wished to leave. Moses must also have told Jethro about the promise of 3:12; he could then depart with the words that

the development of this theme, the episode of Exod 18 represents a strong and satisfying conclusion to theme of Yahweh's presence seeking out Israel in Egypt, journeying with them through the wilderness, and bringing them to the mountain of God. This is the first narrative movement of the Exodus narrative. From this point on, throughout the second narrative movement of the Exodus narrative, Yahweh's presence will be fixed and massively centered at Mount Sinai and, ultimately, in the Tabernacle. Thus, Exod 18 functions as a key transitional turning point with respect to this theme.

The presence of Yahweh is explicitly noted in both halves of Exod 18.[28] In the first scene (Exod 18:1–12), Jethro comes to meet Moses *at the mountain of God* (Exod 18:5) where Yahweh makes himself known to Moses and dwells with his people.[29] Jethro, Aaron, and all the elders

---

they would see each other again at Horeb. God's mountain! When Jethro learned that the stipulated events had occurred (*ki ho-tzi y-h-v-h*), he departed for that place. A person went or came into the desert *el ha-mid-bar* (*ha-mid-ba-rah*) and in it he came upon *har ha-e-lo-him* . . . These three designations represented the same place." Concerning Yahweh's presence in various places, Zweck, *Freed to Follow*, 161, notes, "On the other hand, chapter 18 is appropriate in its present position because the narrative has come full circle. After fleeing from Pharaoh, Moses was in Midian, where he married one of Jethro's daughters and lived in Jethro's household (2:15–22). This time in Midian was a period of quiet preparation before the theophany at Sinai and Moses' commission to return to Egypt (chapter 3). Now Moses has returned from Egypt, and, leading the rescued people of Israel, is en route to Sinai, where, as promised, he will again 'serve God upon this mountain' (3:12). It is fitting that Moses be reunited with Jethro and his family at this point—before the second and greater theophany on Sinai. The scene of reunion provides a pause in the narrative, time for grateful remembrance."

28. Fox, *Now These Are the Names*, 101, notes, "It has been noted (Cohn 1981) that the 'trek narratives' in Exodus and Numbers have been laid out evenly, with six 'stations' between Egypt and Sinai and another six between Sinai and the land of Israel. Thus here [Exod 18], Israel has come to the mid-point of its journey. In another perspective, Moshe himself has come full circle, returning to both the spot and the man in whose presence the mature adult phase of his life had begun." Zweck, *Freed to Follow*, 161, notes, "On the other hand, chapter 18 is appropriate in its present position because the narrative has come full circle."

29. Finegan, *Let My People Go*, 112–14, notes, "The revelation took place at the burning bush (Exodus 3:1 ff.). . . . The God who manifested himself to Abraham and went with him, and was similarly known to the succeeding patriarchs, will now also be mightily present with the whole people. He has manifested himself to Moses in the burning bush, and he will manifest himself to them in mighty deeds. He is present with Moses, and he will be present with the people." Durham, *Exodus*, 244, notes, "Moses' summary is a proof-of-Presence summary, a confession of Yahweh's powerful protection of and provision for Israel." Carpenter, "Exodus 18," 93, notes, "The chapter [Exod 18] moves all of the actors and action into 'the vicinity of Sinai, the Mountain of God' (18.5) where the sacred traditions of the acts of Yahweh can be recounted in sacred space (18.5, 7–8) and where provision for the dissemination of the sacred *tôrôt* (תורות),

of Israel (and, presumably, Moses) eat bread *in the presence of Yahweh* (Exod 18:12). The second scene (Exod 18:13–27) describes Israel coming to Moses *to inquire of Yahweh* (Exod 18:15). After confessing Yahweh, Jethro says, "and may God be with you" (Exod 18:19) and "and God commands you" (Exod 18:23), and he advises Moses, "You, be as the people" *in front of Yahweh* (Exod 18:19).

Yahweh reveals himself and dwells among his people at the mountain of God, that is, at Mount Sinai.[30] Thus, the presence of Yahweh in Exod 18 completes a "full circle"[31] with the original declaration of Yahweh to Moses at the mountain of God, that is, at Mount Horeb,[32] "I will be with you, and this is the sign for you that I have sent you: when you have brought the people out of Egypt, you shall serve God on this mountain" (Exod 3:12; cf. 3:18; 4:23; 5:1, 3; 7:16; 8:1, 20, 27; 9:1, 13; 10:3).[33]

---

instructions of Yahweh, can be made."

30. Larsson, *Bound for Freedom*, 125, notes, "The meeting between Jethro and Moses at the foot of Mount Sinai thus becomes a testimony of God's presence far beyond the borders of people, communities, and congregations, which all too often tend to become dividing walls. This biblical theme will continue to reverberate in the great miracle about to occur."

31. Fox, *Now These Are the Names*, 101. See also Zweck, *Freed to Follow*, 161.

32. Finegan, *Let My People Go*, 112, notes, "In our preceding chapter we judged Horeb and Sinai to refer to the same mountain; therefore, at this point [Exod 18] Moses was back over in the southern part of the Sinaitic peninsula." Fox, *Now These Are the Names*, 101, notes, "In another perspective, Moshe himself has come full circle, returning to both the spot and the man in whose presence the mature adult phase of his life had begun." Larsson, *Bound for Freedom*, 123, notes, "The people of Israel have now camped 'at the mountain of God' (18:5); that is, Moses has returned to the place where he once received the calling to lead the people of God out of Egypt. When he trembled before the tremendous task (3:11), God answered: 'I will be with you; and this shall be the sign for you that it is I who sent you: when you have brought the people out of Egypt, you shall worship God on this mountain' (see pp. 34f.). This chapter [Exod 18] looks back on the events in Moses' life between his first and second visits to 'the mountain of God.'"

33. Many scholars see Jethro' worshiping act in Exod 18:12 as the fulfillment of Yahweh's promises in Exod 3:12. Cole, *Exodus*, 138, notes, "Jethro must have known that this mountain [the mountain of God] was the goal of Israel's pilgrimage (Ex. 5:1) and that worship there was to be the sign of God's fulfillment of His promise (Ex. 3:12)." See also Bailey, *Exodus*, 199. Pixley, *On Exodus*, 111, notes, "The mention of the 'mountain of God' is reminiscent of the 'sign' that Yahweh had promised Moses—that when he had led the Israelites out of Egypt, they would worship Yahweh in this place (§2.1.3). Now the sign is fulfilled, and the dynamics that began on this very mountain are brought to completion." Nevertheless, other scholars approach the act of Jethro's worshiping Yahweh in Exod 18:12 as "the partial fulfillment" of Yahweh's sign in Exod 3:12. Propp, *Exodus*, 1:631, notes, "At any rate, Jethro's act is the partial fulfillment of 3:12, the command/prediction of Israel's worship at the mountain (see also 24:4–5)." See also

The theme of Yahweh's presence has been developed throughout Exod 1–18. In Exod 1:1–2:25, Yahweh's acts for Israel begin behind the scenes.[34] According to Yahweh's promises with Abraham, Isaac, and Jacob, Yahweh blesses Jacob's descendants in the land of Egypt (Exod 1:7). Through the midwives, Yahweh saves every male child born to Israel (Exod 1:17), and Yahweh also blesses the midwives with families (Exod 1:20–21). Yahweh rescues Moses from the Nile (Exod 2:1–10) and from Pharaoh (Exod 2:14–15; cf. 18:4), and Yahweh also blesses Moses with a new family in the land of Midian (Exod 2:21–22). Yahweh hears Israel's groaning, remembering his covenant with Abraham, Isaac, and Jacob, seeing Israel, and knowing (Exod 2:24–25).

In Exod 3:1–4:17, Yahweh is present in a new way in the Exodus narrative. While Moses is keeping the flock of Jethro and comes to the mountain of God, Mount Horeb, Yahweh reveals himself, appearing to Moses in the burning bush, a place which, thus, becomes holy ground (Exod 3:1–5). Moses then returns to the land of Midian to ask for permission from Jethro to go back to the land of Egypt, and then Yahweh speaks to Moses in the land of Midian (Exod 4:18–19). Yahweh will be with Moses to bring the Israelites out of the land of Egypt as Yahweh promised (cf. Exod 3:12; 4:12, 15). Yahweh's presence is explicitly noted in the land of Egypt throughout the plague narrative (Exod 7:17, 25; 8:2, 21–23, 24; 9:3–5, 6, 14–18, 23; 10:1–2, 4, 13; 11:1, 4; 12:12–13, 23, 27, 29), with the Israelites as they depart (Exod 13:21–22), between the Israelites and the Egyptians at the Red Sea (Exod 14:13–14, 19–20, 21–25, 27), and with the Israelites in the wilderness (Exod 15:25; 16:4, 7, 10, 15; 17:6–7, 16). Finally, Moses brings the Israelites back to the mountain of God, Mount Sinai (Exod 18:5).[35]

Propp, *Exodus*, 1:633–34. Dozeman, *Exodus*, 402, notes, "The setting of the mountain of God (18:5) reinforces this interpretation, recalling the divine sign to Moses during his commission (3:12). The sign was that after the exodus he would 'worship God on this mountain.'" Further, he notes, "The fulfillment of the divine sign will continue into chaps. 19–34 as the worship leadership of Jethro on the mountain of God is transferred to Moses." Dozeman, *Exodus*, 402.

34. Fretheim, "Exodus, Book of," *DOTP* 250, notes, "The journey of God in Exodus is also notable. God is hardly present at the beginning of the book, but at the end God has moved down from his distant abode at the top of the mountain to become an intense presence in the very midst of the community of faith."

35. Janzen, *Exodus*, 223, notes, "Moses has brought his people to the *mountain of God* (18:5), from which he was sent into Egypt to rescue them (3:1)." Further, he notes, "This [the mountain of God (18:5), Horeb/Sinai] is the mountain where Moses saw the burning bush, where he received his call, and from where he was sent on his mission to

Yahweh locates his saving and gracious presence in specific locations for the sake of his people. This begins at Mount Horeb, where Yahweh appears to Moses and promises, "I will be with you, and this is the sign for you that I have sent you: when you have brought the people out of Egypt, you shall serve God on this mountain" (Exod 3:12). After Yahweh has brought Israel out of Egypt, Yahweh's presence is manifested by the pillars of cloud and fire in which he "goes before" Israel (Exod 13:21–22).

Exodus 18 summaries the presence of Yahweh as he promised to Moses at Mount Horeb, "I will be with you, and this is the sign for you that I have sent you: when you have brought (יצא) the people out of Egypt, you shall serve (עבד) God on this mountain" (Exod 3:12; cf. 3:18; 4:23; 5:1, 3; 7:16; 8:1, 20, 27; 9:1, 13; 10:3). Moses related this promise to Pharaoh in three ways: (1) "Let my son [Israel] go (שלח), so that he may serve (עבד) me [Yahweh]" (Exod 4:23; cf. 7:16; 8:1, 20; 9:1, 13; 10:3, 26); (2) "and now, please let us go (הלך) a journey of three days into the wilderness, so that we may sacrifice (זבח) to Yahweh, our God" (Exod 3:18; cf. 5:3; 8:27, 29); and (3) "Let my people [Israel] go (שלח), so that they may keep a feast (חגג) to me [Yahweh] in the wilderness" (Exod 5:1; cf. 10:9).

Reminiscent of the promised sign at Mount Horeb in Exod 3:12, Jethro meets Moses at Mount Sinai,[36] hears of Yahweh's salvation from

---

Egypt." Janzen, *Exodus*, 224.

36. Some commentators consider the mountain of God as the meeting place between Moses and Jethro. Murphy, *Exodus*, 120, notes, "Moses had formerly led the flock of Jethro as far as 'the mount of God in Horeb.' As soon as he arrives at this point, therefore, he is in the neighborhood of Jethro, who accordingly pays him a visit, accompanied by Zipporah and her two sons." Noth, *Exodus*, 148, notes, "Now in any case in Ex. 18 this 'mountain of God' does not play the role of the scene of a theophany, but is a place where there was a meeting between Israel and the 'priest of Midian.'" Pixley, *On Exodus*, 110, notes, "Jethro, priest of Midian and father-in-law of Moses, comes to meet Moses at the 'mountain of God,' the place where Yahweh had appeared to Moses in the burning bush." See also Pixley, *On Exodus*, 112. Furthermore, a commentator approaches the mountain of God as the meeting place between Yahweh and individuals. Propp, *Exodus*, 1:634, notes, "We could also call Horeb a 'mountain of meeting.' There Moses encounters Yahweh, Aaron and Jethro; Israel meets God, and, centuries later, Elijah hears the small, still voice (1 Kgs 19:8–18). Exod 18:12; 24:5, 9–11, moreover, describe banquets on Horeb. And from Horeb, Israel bears the *ōhel mô'ēd* 'Meeting Tent,' where humans can commune with the divine." Nevertheless, concerning the mountain of God as the meeting place between Moses and Jethro, other commentators recommend the mountain of God as the meeting place between Moses and Aaron. Propp, *Exodus*, 1:627, notes, "Within E, Moses and Jethro's affectionate meeting at 'the Deity's mountain' recalls the previous reunion of Moses and Aaron on the same spot (4:27)." Enns, *Exodus*, 369, notes, "The meeting between Moses and Jethro in verses 7–8 should jar our memory a bit. Moses here experiences a second reunion with a family member in the desert (cf. the reunion with Aaron in 4:27–28)." See also Stuart, *Exodus*,

Moses, rejoices in Yahweh, praises Yahweh, and acknowledges Yahweh as the greatest and incomparable God (Exod 18:5–11). Jethro then worships Yahweh by taking a burnt offering and sacrifices to Yahweh and eating bread with Aaron and all the elders of Israel (and, presumably, Moses), the representatives of Israel, in the presence of Yahweh (Exod 18:12).[37] Exodus 18 brings Yahweh's promise that after Moses has brought Israel out of the land of Egypt, they will worship Yahweh at the mountain of God/Mount Horeb or Sinai (Exod 18:12; cf. 3:12; 18:5).

Therefore, the theme of Yahweh's presence in various places serves to illustrate the retrospective function of Exod 18. The significant account on Yahweh's presence in Exod 18, both in connection with the sacred mountain, Mount Sinai, and with Moses (cf. Exod 3:1; 18:5), resonates strongly with the theme of Yahweh's presence in the preceding narrative and brings this theme to a full circle at the same sacred place, the mountain of God. Yahweh, who revealed himself to Moses at the mountain of God (Exod 3:1–4:17), has been with Moses (cf. Exod 3:12a) and Israel through the ten plagues, the Red Sea, deprivations in the wilderness, and battle with the Amalekites. Now, Moses and Israel have come back to the mountain of God (cf. Exod 3:12b) where Yahweh's sign promised in Exod 3:12 has been fulfilled as they come in the presence of Yahweh (cf. Exod 18:12, 19) whose presence continues to be connected both with the sacred mountain and with Moses.

---

409. Dozeman, *Exodus*, 402, notes, "Moses' meeting with Jethro recalls his rendezvous with Aaron in 4:27–31. Both stories take place in the wilderness at the mountain of God (4:27; 18:5)." See also Dozeman, *Exodus*, 402–3.

37. Janzen, *Exodus*, 223, notes, "When Jethro, Moses, and the elders of Israel worship God together (18:12), the sign promised in 3:12 is fulfilled." Further, he notes, "Further, God gave him [Moses] a promise: *I will be with you; and this shall be the sign for you that it is I who sent you: when you have brought the people out of Egypt, you shall worship God on this mountain* (3:12). The worship in which Jethro, Moses, Aaron, and the elders engage brings this sign to fulfillment (18:12). Moses' immediate commission has been brought to completion." Janzen, *Exodus*, 224–25. See also Janzen, *Exodus*, 230. Janzen, "Jethro," 166, notes, "At the mention of the mountain of God, even the first-time reader may recall God's words to Moses at the burning bush (3:12) and realize that a significant sequence of events has come to its conclusion now, in keeping with God's promise here." Jeon, "Visit of Jethro," 292, notes, "In this vein, the sign mentioned in 3:12, worshiping God on the mountain of God, must be accomplished for the legitimation of Moses; consequently, the sacrifice at the conclusion of the first half of Exod 18 (v. 12), can be understood as the accomplishment of this sign."

The Knowledge of Yahweh by Yahweh's Self-revelation through His Mighty Acts of Deliverance

Yahweh makes himself known to Moses, Aaron, the Israelites, Pharaoh, the Egyptians, the Amalekites, and Jethro through his mighty acts of deliverance.[38] This knowledge is highlighted and brought to satisfying conclusion in the episode of Exod 18.[39] The narrator summarizes Yahweh's deliverance of Israel in the land of Egypt, at the Red Sea, and on the wilderness journey to Mount Sinai (Exod 18:1, 4, 8, 9, 10). After Jethro has heard of Yahweh's deliverance of Israel, initially from an unspecified report (Exod 18:1) but then directly from Moses' mouth (Exod 18:8), Jethro rejoices in Yahweh's deliverance of Israel, praises Yahweh, and confesses by acknowledging Yahweh who "is greater than all gods" (Exod 18:11).

The theme of Yahweh's self-revelation through his mighty acts of deliverance in Exod 18 answers the question of Pharaoh in Exod 5:2, as Thomas J. Egger observes, "In fact, Jethro's exclamation, 'Now I know that Yahweh is greater than all gods' (18:11), balances the Pharaoh's previous rebuff, 'Who is Yahweh, that I should obey his voice by letting Israel go? I do not know Yahweh, and I will not let Israel go' (5:2)."[40] Jaeyoung Jeon agrees:

---

38. Carpenter emphasizes one of "two ways of knowing Yahweh" which is "the knowledge of Yahweh available in and through the event of the exodus itself and its recitation (18.7–8)." Carpenter, "Exodus 18," 92. See also Carpenter, "Exodus 18," 98, 101, 108; Blackburn, *God Who Makes Himself Known*, 77–78. Furthermore, Rylaarsdam and Park, "Exodus," 1:965, note, "The meaning of Jethro's statement seems to be that this story of the insolence of Egypt against the Israelites and the deliverance of the latter had convinced him of the power of Israel's God." Noth, *Exodus*, 149, notes, "With respect to the content of this confession the recognition of a 'polytheistic-comparative' exaltation of Yahweh over 'all gods' such as still occurs occasionally in traditional language, especially in the Psalms, is here put in the mouth of a Midianite whom the divine acts have led to 'enlightenment.'"

39. Carpenter, *Exodus*, 1:613, notes, "The author-editor's use of יָדַעְתִּי ('I recognize') calls to mind his use of this verb (forty-five times in Exodus), often to indicate the purpose of Yahweh in the exodus (see 5:2; 33:5, 12, 13, 16, 17)." See also Blackburn, *God Who Makes Himself Known*, 76–77. Furthermore, Carpenter, *Exodus*, 1:602–3, notes, "The story of Yahweh's victories and the exodus are 'recounted' (ספר) for the first time by Moses, as Yahweh had announced it would be (9:16; 10:2), and a jurisprudence framework is put in place for the efficient functioning of the instructions Yahweh has already given to Israel and for the reception of the Torah at Sinai." See also Carpenter, *Exodus*, 1:612, 625; Carpenter, "Exodus 18," 103; Blackburn, *God Who Makes Himself Known*, 77.

40. Egger, "Visiting Iniquity," 453.

Exodus 18:11a contains Jethro's confession, 'Now I know that the Lord is greater than all gods' (עתה ידעתי כי גדול יהוה מכל האלהים). This passage has often been understood on a synchronic level in relation to the 'recognition formula' in the exodus story, especially beginning with Pharaoh's derogatory question in Exod 5:2, 'Who is the Lord, that I should heed his voice and let Israel go?' (מי יהוה אשר אשמע בקלו לשלח את־ישראל) and the consequent declaration, 'I do not know the Lord' (לא ידעתי את־יהוה).[41]

This theme also recalls the purpose of Yahweh's self-revelation through his mighty acts of deliverance to Pharaoh and all the nations in Exod 9:16, "But because of this, I have raised you [Pharaoh] up to show you [Pharaoh] my power and to recount my name in all the earth." William H. C. Propp notes, "For the first time ever, Moses fulfills the commandment to recount the Exodus story (9:16; 10:2)."[42] Daniel M. Gurtner, likewise, observes, "In verse 8 Mōusēs reports to Iothor all that the Lord (Κύριος) did both to Pharaō and to all the Egyptians. His report fulfills the command to recount the exodus story (9.16; 10.2)."[43]

Jethro's experience shows evidence that the knowledge of Yahweh comes through his mighty acts of deliverance. Having heard of Yahweh's mighty acts of deliverance from Moses' lips (Exod 18:8), Jethro acknowledges, "Now, I know (ידע) that Yahweh is greater than all gods" (Exod 18:11). Jethro's knowledge leads to a clear confession that there is no one like Yahweh, the greatest and incomparable God (cf. Exod 8:10; 9:14; 15:11).[44] As just noted, Jethro's acknowledgement of Yahweh re-

---

41. Jeon, "Visit of Jethro," 294. See also Fretheim, "Exodus, Book of," *DOTP* 253; Hughes, "Jethro," *DOTP* 468.

42. Propp, *Exodus*, 1:630.

43. Gurtner, *Exodus*, 363. Furthermore, Bruckner, *Exodus*, 165, notes, "As a descendant of Abraham, he [Jethro] may have known the promises given him and seen the beginning of God's work through Israel. What the Pharaoh and the Egyptians know (7:5; 14:4, 18) and the Israelites know firsthand (6:7; 10:2; 14:31), Jethro also claimed to know. The whole earth did not yet know but, with Jethro, the word had begun to spread (see comment at 9:14–16, 29)." Fretheim, "Exodus, Book of," *DOTP* 253, notes, "But the divine purpose with respect to the knowledge of God is expanded to embrace others, including Pharaoh and the Egyptians (Ex 7:5, 17; 8:10, 22 [MT 8:6, 18]; 9:14, 29; 11:7; 14:4, 18] and the Midianites (Jethro comes to know and confess, Ex 18:11; cf. 15:14–16 for still others). God's concern for self-disclosure is thus expanded to include the world (see Ex 9:16)."

44. Houtman, *Exodus*, 2:411, notes, "The text suggests the following scenario: YHWH's great deeds induce Jethro to praise and acknowledgement of YHWH as Lord of all (18:10, 11)." Further, he notes, "In short, 18:10–12 is to be understood as Jethro's

calls and diametrically opposes the earlier statement of Pharaoh, "Who is Yahweh that I should obey him by letting Israel go? I do not know (ידע) Yahweh, and also I will not let Israel go" (Exod 5:2). The sentence, "I do not know (ידע) Yahweh," reminds the initial announcement by the narrator, "Now, a new king arose over Egypt who did not know (ידע) Joseph [that is, Yahweh's people]" (Exod 1:8). Moreover, Jethro's acknowledgement of Yahweh in Exod 18:11 builds upon and resolves the earlier declaration of Yahweh, "I am Yahweh. I appeared to Abraham, to Isaac, and to Jacob as God Almighty, but my name, Yahweh, I did not make myself known (ידע) to them" (Exod 6:2–3).

Throughout the first narrative movement, the first half of the book of Exodus (Exod 1–17), Yahweh has made his sacred name known to Moses, the Israelites, Pharaoh, and the Egyptians at the mountain of God, in the land of Egypt, at the Red Sea, and on the wilderness journey to the mountain of God. When Yahweh first makes himself known to Moses at the burning bush at Mount Horeb, Yahweh reveals and introduces himself to Moses, "I am the God of your father, the God of Abraham, the God of Isaac, and the God of Jacob" (Exod 3:6; cf. 3:15, 16; 4:5), "I AM WHO I AM" (or literally "I WILL BE WHO I WILL BE") (Exod 3:14), and "Yahweh, the God of the Hebrews" (Exod 3:18; cf. 5:1 [of Israel], 3; 7:16; 9:1, 13; 10:3). After Pharaoh has said, "Who is Yahweh that I should obey him by letting Israel go? I do not know (ידע) Yahweh, and also I will not let Israel go" (Exod 5:2), Yahweh repeats, "I am Yahweh" (Exod 6:2; cf. 6:6, 8, 29; 15:26), "and you [Israel] shall know (ידע) that I am Yahweh, your [Israel's] God" (Exod 6:7; cf. 10:2; 16:12), and "Then the Egyptians shall know (ידע) that I am Yahweh" (Exod 7:5; cf. 7:17 [Pharaoh]; 8:22 [Pharaoh]; 14:4, 18).

Throughout the first narrative movement, the first half of the book of Exodus (Exod 1–17), Yahweh also revealed himself through his saving and mighty acts for the Israelites in Egypt, at the Red Sea, and in the wilderness. Yahweh brings salvation to the Israelites (Exod 14:13; 15:2)

---

acknowledgement of YHWH as Lord (cf. Introd. § 7.3.4)." Houtman, *Exodus*, 2:412. Meyers, *Exodus*, 136, notes, "Learning of God's saving power causes Jethro to acknowledge the sovereignty of Yahweh over all other deities. As in the Song of the Sea (15:11), the manifestation of divine power leads to an acknowledgment of Yahweh's uniqueness, which is not quite the same as acclaiming Yahweh as the only divine being (cf. 12:12)." Dozeman, *Exodus*, 405, notes, "The divine rescue of the Israelites confirms the incomparability of Yahweh over all other gods. Jethro's confession echoes the refrain in the Song of the Sea, where Yahweh's incomparability to the other gods was also confessed (15:11).... The point of the confession is that Jethro's knowledge of Yahweh is deepened by the events of the exodus."

and, thus, acts as the Savior of the Israelites (Exod 3:8; 6:6; 14:30; 15:13). While Yahweh is saving his people, the Israelites, with his mighty hand (Exod 3:19, 20; 6:1, 6 [arm]; 7:4, 5, 17; 8:19 [finger]; 9:3, 15; 13:3, 9, 14, 16; 15:6, 12, 16 [arm], 17; 16:3; 17:16), he brings judgment to Pharaoh and the Egyptians (Exod 6:6; 7:4; 12:12) and, thus, acts as the Judge of Pharaoh and the Egyptians (Exod 3:20; 4:23; 8:2; 9:14–15; 11:1, 4–8; 12:12–13, 23, 29; 13:15). These two distinct acts of Yahweh exhibit that Yahweh is "God Almighty" as stated in Exod 6:3. During the ten plagues in Egypt, Moses proclaims, "there is no one like Yahweh, our God" (Exod 8:10; cf. 9:14; 15:11). After the Israelites have left Egypt, Yahweh acts as the King of the Israelites (Exod 13:18, 21–22; 14:14, 19, 25; 15:1, 13–18, 21), as the Strength and Song of the Israelites (Exod 15:2), as the Warrior of the Israelites (Exod 15:3; 17:16), as the Healer of the Israelites (Exod 15:26), and as the Banner of the Israelites (Exod 17:15).

In the opening verses of Exod 18, Yahweh's mighty acts of deliverance are repeated (Exod 18:1, 4, 8, 9, 10). Jethro, a fellow Gentile, finally provides the clear answer to the question of Pharaoh, "Who is Yahweh that I should obey him by letting Israel go?" (Exod 5:2). Jethro confessed, "Yahweh is greater than all gods" (Exod 18:11; cf. 8:10; 9:14; 15:11).

In addition to providing the answer to Pharaoh's question in Exod 5:2, Exod 18 recalls the purpose of Yahweh's self-revelation through his mighty acts of deliverance to Pharaoh and all the nations in Exod 9:16, "But because of this, I have raised you [Pharaoh] up to show you [Pharaoh] my power and to recount (ספר) my name in all the earth." Yahweh's deliverance of the Israelites has been spread out by news (Exod 18:1) and first recounted (ספר)[45] by Moses (Exod 18:8). Jethro, a Midianite, represents all the nations who hear of Yahweh's deliverance of the Israelites

---

45. Fretheim, *Exodus*, 196, notes, "The word 'declare' (*sapar*) was used in 9:16 to refer to the basic divine purposes in these events [all that God has done on behalf of Israel]. This is the first reported instance of the carrying out of that purpose." Further, he notes, "The testimony of Moses to Jethro regarding all that God had done for Israel is central in the movement of this narrative. It issues in all of Jethro's subsequent words and actions. The verb *sapar* ('declare') is certainly intended to recall its use in 9:16 (cf. 10:2). Moses is the first of God's witnesses to another individual and another people. His witness serves to establish the exodus faith for the first time in a non-Israelite community. There is thus also an ancillary concern here for how an outsider becomes identified with his community. What Moses has done, Israel and all of God's people are also called upon to do (see Ps. 96:3–4, 10; 113:3; 57:9; 18:49; see 40:9–10; 67:4). Indeed, what Moses has done will be repeated 'throughout all the earth' (9:16) in the years to come." Fretheim, *Exodus*, 197.

(Exod 18:1, 8), and who properly respond to Yahweh with joy, praise, and confession (Exod 18:9-11).[46]

Pharaoh, the Egyptians, and even the Amalekites experience Yahweh by both hearing and seeing, but they neither turn to Yahweh nor confess Yahweh. The Israelites, who also experience Yahweh by both hearing and seeing, turn to Yahweh (cf. Exod 4:31; 14:31) and confess Yahweh (cf. Exod 15:1-18, 21). The Israelites have been inconstant, however, often thinking of the land of Egypt and longing to return to be slaves of Pharaoh during the difficult journey in the wilderness (cf. Exod 14:11-12; 16:3; 17:3).[47] In contrast with Pharaoh, the Egyptians, the Amalekites, and even the Israelites, Jethro, a Midianite, comes to know Yahweh only by way of hearing, yet he rejoices in, praises, and confesses Yahweh as the greatest and incomparable God (cf. Exod 18:8-11).[48] This foreigner becomes, as it

46. Murphy, *Exodus*, 120, notes, "Jethro gives expression to the joy he felt in the deliverance of Israel.... Jethro here explicitly acknowledges Jehovah as God. He was no doubt acquainted by the tradition of his Hebrew fathers with the being and the mercy of God, and he might have learned the significant name Jehovah from Moses, if not before." Furthermore, Enns, *Exodus*, 369, notes, "Midian is the one nation that gives a proper response to God's deliverance of his own people. God's dealings with Pharaoh were so that 'my name might be proclaimed in all the earth' (9:16)."

47. Egger, "Visiting Iniquity," 452, notes, "While the decimation of the Egyptian host at the sea in chs. 14-15 removes Pharaoh as a direct threat to the sons of Israel, a certain 'Egyptian orientation' carries on in the narrative through chs. 16-18. When the people grumble in the wilderness in 16:3 and 17:3, their complaints echo that of 14:11-12: they would have been better off if Moses had just left them alone in Egypt." See also Leveen, "Inside Out," 408-9; Reiss, "Jethro the Convert," 91.

48. Enns, *Exodus*, 369, notes, "Although neither the Egyptians nor the Amalekites get it, Jethro, the Midianite, has learned the lesson of the Exodus: 'The Lord is greater than all other gods.'" Carpenter, *Exodus*, 1:613, notes, "Although Jethro did not experience the exodus and oppression, the power of Yahweh's actions through Moses' report affects him and causes him to believe the report." Alexander, *Exodus*, 350, notes, "Whereas the Egyptians and the Israelites slowly came to a knowledge of YHWH through witnessing the events described in chs. 5-14, Jethro must rely upon the testimony of Moses, his son-in-law. Strikingly, his affirmation of YHWH's superiority over all gods is both swift and positive." Furthermore, Leveen, "Inside Out," 408, notes, "Jethro draws the implication of what he has realized in a clear and highly public manner: 'Now I know that YHWH is greater than all the gods...' (Exod. 18.11). This type of public acknowledgment of God's superior might is precisely what God sought in inflicting the ten plagues on Pharaoh and the Egyptians. Yet Pharaoh was disastrously slow in grasping the power of this Israelite God. In contrast, upon hearing the news, Jethro immediately recognizes and acknowledges God's superiority." See also Reiss, "Jethro the Convert," 92. Further, Leveen notes, "Perhaps ironically, as a Midianite, Jethro's praise of God is also contrasted to that of the insiders, the Israelites themselves, in a way that throws a negative light on the Israelite behavior since their departure from Egypt. Jethro celebrates God's liberation of Israel from Egypt in pointed contrast to the Israelite desires to return to Egypt, as noted already in Exod. 16.3 ('if only we had died in Egypt') and Exod. 17.3

were, a virtual Israelite by worshiping Yahweh (Exod 18:12) and faithfully speaking for Yahweh's purposes (Exod 18:19–23).[49] Jethro, thus, functions as an example that Yahweh has fulfilled the purpose of his self-revelation through his mighty acts of deliverance in Exod 9:16.[50]

Therefore, Exod 18 stands in strong retrospective relation with the chapters which precede it, answering Pharaoh's question in Exod 5:2 and also fulfilling Yahweh's purpose of deliverance explicitly declared in Exod 9:16. Yahweh has made himself known by means of his saving and mighty acts throughout the first narrative movement, the first half of the Exodus narrative (Exod 1–17). In fact, Yahweh has expressly indicated that such self-revelation-through-mighty-deeds has been his central purpose, along with actually saving his people, Israel, in these actions. Jethro's confession upon hearing of all Yahweh's saving and mighty acts for Israel—"now, I know that Yahweh is greater than all gods" (Exod 18:11)—brings this theme of the first half of the book of Exodus to its culmination and initial conclusion.

Moses as the Judge, Acting as "God" to Pharaoh and the Egyptians

In the first narrative movement of the Exodus narrative (Exod 1–17), Moses plays a massive role as a "judge," in that he is *the central agent of God's indictment and punishing judgments against Pharaoh and the Egyptians*. The prominent emphasis in the episode of Exod 18 upon Moses

---

('Why did you bring us up from Egypt. . .?'). Jethro sees clearly what Israel can only glimpse in fleeting moments punctuated by hunger, thirst, and complaint. Thus, as an outsider, a Midianite, Jethro stands in contrast with that other outsider, the Pharaoh, in acknowledging God. But it is also as an outsider that Jethro creates a shocking contrast with the Israelites. The contrast between his praise and their grumbling constitutes a withering critique of their complaints and preoccupations. This passage suggests a possible use of the figure of the outsider as one who heightens, by contrast, the failures of the Israelites." Leveen, "Inside Out," 408–9. See also Reiss, "Jethro the Convert," 91.

49. Murphy, *Exodus*, 120, notes, "Jethro gives a practical exhibition of his acknowledgment of the Lord by offering sacrifice. The burnt-offering is the completest symbol of the atonement for sin (Gen. 8:20). The sacrifice being eaten partly by the worshipper expresses communion with God as the result of atonement. The common participation *before God* of the sacrifice is the emblem of the communion of the worshippers in the blessings of the divine favor." Blackburn, *God Who Makes Himself Known*, 77, notes, "Unlike Pharaoh, Jethro's recognition of the Lord's incomparability leads appropriately to worship." See also Hughes, "Jethro," *DOTP* 468.

50. Propp, *Exodus*, 1:630, notes, "Israel, Egypt and now Jethro must know Yahweh's might, not just intellectually but experientially (*ydʿ*)."

as a "prince and judge" recalls this previous role, even as it sets the stage for a distinct but related role for Moses in the second half of the book of Exodus (Exod 19–40), as the "prince and judge" *for the Israelites*. In the first half of the book of Exodus (Exod 1–17), Moses acts as "God" over against Pharaoh and the Egyptians, judging Pharaoh and the Egyptians in the land of Egypt and at the Red Sea by all the wonders which Yahweh has sent and commanded Moses to perform. This Egyptian-oriented judicial theme is concluded in Exod 18.[51]

The prepositional phrase מִמָּחֳרָת, "on the next day," (Exod 18:13) divides Exod 18 into two days. On the first day, the brief conclusion of all Yahweh's deliverance of the Israelites is repeatedly expressed (Exod 18:1, 4, 8, 9, 10). In particular, Moses recounts to Jethro, "all which *Yahweh had done to Pharaoh and to the Egyptians* because of Israel, and all the hardship which had come upon them on the way; and Yahweh had delivered them!" (Exod 18:8). On the next day, Moses is sitting to judge the Israelites from morning until evening (Exod 18:13). Jethro then sees all and asks Moses why he is doing this all alone for the Israelites (Exod 18:14). Moses answers Jethro, "The people come to me to inquire of God. When they have a case, which comes to me, I judge between one and another, and I make known the statutes of God and his laws" (Exod 18:15–16). This is confirmation from Moses' lips that one of his roles is the judge for the Israelites. After that, Jethro advises Moses:

> Now, obey me; I will advise you, and may God be with you. You, be as the people in front of God, and, you, bring the cases to God. Then teach them the statutes and the laws, and make known to them the way in which they should walk and the work which they should do. Then, you, provide from all the people men of ability who fear God, men of faithfulness who hate unjust gain, and set over them chiefs of thousands, chiefs of hundreds, chiefs of fifties, and chiefs of tens. Then let them judge the people at all times, and it will be that, every great case, they can bring to you, but every small case, they can judge themselves, and thus lighten the load from upon you, and they will carry it with you. If you do this thing, and God commands you, then you will be able to endure, and also all this people will go to their place in peace (Exod 18:19–23).

---

51. Alexander, *Exodus*, 353, notes, "Earlier in the book of Exodus Moses was challenged by an Israelite regarding his authority to act as 'ruler and judge' (2:14); now he oversees the appointment of others to such positions."

This is the encouragement from Jethro's mouth that one of Moses' responsibilities which Moses should continue to do is the judge for the Israelites' great and hard cases. Finally, Moses does all which Jethro has advised, especially judging the Israelites' hard cases (Exod 18:25–26).

This judicial theme in Exod 18 recalls and brings to a deferred resolution of the earlier judicial event in Exod 2:11–14,[52] answering one of the two struggling Israelites' question, "Who made you [Moses] a prince and a judge over us?" (Exod 2:14).[53]

In Exod 18, on the first day, Yahweh is portrayed as the Savior to the Israelites (Exod 18:1, 4, 8, 9, 10) but as the Judge to Pharaoh and the Egyptians (Exod 18:8). On the next day, Moses is described as the judge to the Israelites (Exod 18:13, 16; cf. 18:22, 26).[54] This two-day division

---

52. As it comes to the suggestion of Exod 2:11–14 as "an example of literary prolepsis," Egger, "Visiting Iniquity," 460, notes, "The two days of Moses' first appearance thus anticipate the two great narrative arcs of Exodus: Yahweh's quest to deliver his people from the oppression of Egypt and from other threats (Exod 1–18) and Yahweh's quest to rule over and dwell in the midst of stiff-necked Israel (Exod 19–40)." Further, he notes, "Exod 2:11–14 functions as a proleptic paradigm for the overall Exodus narrative. The first day anticipates the first narrative arc, with Yahweh's *lex talionis* judgment upon Egypt to deliver his people. The second day anticipates the subsequent sin and rebellion of Israel against Moses and Yahweh." Egger, "Visiting Iniquity," 461.

53. Carpenter, *Exodus*, 1:616–17, notes, "That Moses sits 'to judge' the people indicates that God has indeed finally made him a judge (שׁוֹפֵט) and a prince (שַׂר) over the people. A fellow Heb. earlier (2:14) had mocked such a possibility. The answer to the Heb.'s question in that verse is that Yahweh has indeed made Moses both a prince and a judge in Israel, as he had done earlier before the Egyptians in Egypt (cf. 11:3)." See also Carpenter, "Exodus 18," 100–101; Mann, *Book of the Torah*, 97–98; Egger, "Visiting Iniquity," 455–57.

54. Murphy, *Exodus*, 120–21, notes, "Sitting is the posture of the judge, standing that of those who come to receive judgment." See also Erdman, *Exodus*, 84; Cassuto, *Exodus*, 218; Cole, *Exodus*, 140; Alexander, *Exodus*, 351; Carpenter, "Exodus 18," 100–101. Hamilton, *Exodus*, 285, notes, "The reason Moses is sitting and the people are standing is that during legal proceedings the judge sits while the litigants stand." Gurtner, *Exodus*, 364, notes, "Mōusēs, the subject, sits down (συνεκάθισεν) perhaps in a posture of judging (cf. 3 Kgdms 3.16; Mal 3.3; Ps 9.8; Prov 20.8)." Furthermore, by comparing Moses' role to sheik's role, Rylaarsdam and Park, "Exodus," 1:966, note, "The function of Moses was comparable to that of the Bedouin tribal sheik today. Each morning such a sheik 'sits' briefly as judge. As Israel gradually became an ever-greater aggregate of clan and tribal units such simple judicial administration by one man became impossible. Moses may here be considered as priest as well as tribal chief or judge." See also Hyatt, *Exodus*, 193. Some commentators think that there is a division between sacral and civil power. Rylaarsdam and Park, "Exodus," 1:966, note, "Originally there was no differentiation between sacral and civil power (cf. Bentzen, *Intro. to O.T.*, I, 215–16). This incident is part of a continual process of differentiation in which sacral and secular authorities become more separable. But they do not stand completely apart. The civil judges receive their authority from Moses, the sacral head. Besides, the oracular

recalls the earlier judicial event in Exod 2:11–14 which is also divided into two days by the prepositional phrase בַּיּוֹם הַשֵּׁנִי, "on the second day," (Exod 2:13). On the first day, Moses goes out to his brothers and sees an Egyptian beating a Hebrew, one of Moses' brothers. Moses delivers the Hebrew man by killing the guilty Egyptian, beating him and hiding him in the sand (Exod 2:11–12). On the second day, Moses sees two Hebrews struggling together. Moses asks a guilty man, "Why do you beat your friend?," and the guilty man answers Moses, "Who made you a prince and a judge over us? Do you intend to kill me as you killed the Egyptian?" (Exod 2:13–14).

---

decision, whether by sacred lot or prophetic inspiration, constitutes the 'precedents' on the basis of which the 'civil' magistrates work." See also Noth, *Exodus*, 150; Davies, *Exodus*, 150; Hyatt, *Exodus*, 192. In contrast, other commentators discern that there is no a distinction between sacred and civic cases but between difficult and simple cases. Cole, *Exodus*, 140, notes, "To see the anecdote as a separation of 'sacred' cases judged by Moses, and 'civic' cases judged by elders, seems mistaken: all justice was sacred to Israel. The administration of justice, of whatever kind, is here set in the context of sacrifice and sacred meal. The distinction is therefore not between sacred and secular but between difficult and simple matters, those already covered by tradition and revelation as against those requiring a fresh word from God, mediated through His agent, Moses." Houtman, *Exodus*, 2:420, notes, "It is not said which cases are the very difficult ones and which are only minor matters. It does not seem likely that the distinction between 'minor' and 'major' matters is that between sacral and civic matters (Greßmann*, 175; Noth; cf. Rylaarsdam; Fensham). Justice is wholly sacral. The entire social life of the community is to be regulated by God's demands. Both kinds of cases apparently deal with civic matters, and not with typical cultic problems." Furthermore, there is no evidence for a division between sacral and civil matters. Durham, *Exodus*, 251, notes, "There is no firm evidence, however, that there is in this passage any 'division between sacral and civic justice' such as Noth (150) and Knierim (163–67) suggest. Indeed, there is no division of civil from sacred, or profane from holy, in Israel's thought about and practice of laws of any kind." In addition, to know which matters are hard or small depends on hard or easy decision based on recent laws. Keil and Delitzsch, *Pentateuch*, 2:87–88, note, "The difference between the harder or greater matters and the smaller matters consisted in this: questions which there was no definite law to decide were great or hard; whereas, on the other hand, those which could easily be decided from existing laws or general principles of equity were simple or small." Houtman, *Exodus*, 2:420, notes, "The distinction concerns difficult matters (cf. Deut. 17:18; 2 Chr. 19:10) and simpler matters. Difficult matters are those in which hard evidence is lacking (cf. Num. 5:11ff.) or the guilt question is in dispute; simpler matters, in light of the above, on the one hand must have been especially those problems for which no (specific) regulations existed and which therefore required divine consultation, and problems that could be decided on the basis of existing rules and norms (cf. e.g. Calmet, Keil, Cole)." Finally, Gispen, *Exodus*, 176, notes, "The reason why the people came only to Moses and not to the elders may well be that the Israelites apparently never had the opportunity to consult the elders on a regular basis in Egypt. Moses was the leader now (cf. 14:31) and the elders did not as yet play an important role."

There is a proleptic dimention to Exod 2:11–14, with Moses playing a role as the judge over an Egyptian on the first day and over two Hebrews on the second day.[55] This prolepsis is developed throughout Exod 3–17 and is then bookended by Exod 18, which deals with Pharaoh and the Egyptians on the first day and with the Israelites on the second day. In the earlier scene of the call of Moses, Yahweh gave Moses the mission to bring the Israelites out of Egypt with the authority of Yahweh (Exod 3:7–4:23). Moses acts with such authority because Yahweh sent Moses to Pharaoh, so that Moses may deliver the Israelites from Egypt (Exod 3:10; cf. 3:12, 13, 14, 15; 4:28; 7:16). Thus, Yahweh will be with Moses (Exod 3:12; cf. 4:12, 15); Yahweh puts all the wonders in Moses' hand (Exod 4:21); and Yahweh, particularly, makes Moses as "God" to Aaron (Exod 4:16) and later to Pharaoh (Exod 7:1). This authority insists that Moses represents Yahweh, who brings "great judgments" to Pharaoh and the Egyptians (Exod 6:6; cf. 7:4; 12:12).

Throughout Exod 3–15, Yahweh declares to Moses all that he will do to Pharaoh and the Egyptians (Exod 3:19–22; 4:21, 23; 6:1, 6; 7:3–5, 17–19; 8:2–5, 16, 21–23; 9:3–5, 8–9 [with Aaron], 14–19, 22; 10:1–2, 12, 21; 11:1–2, 9; 12:12–13 [with Aaron]; 14:4, 17–18, 26).[56] Moses repeats Yahweh's words to Pharaoh (Exod 10:4–6 [with Aaron]; 11:4–8), to all the elders of Israel (Exod 12:23, 27), and to Israel (Exod 14:13–14). After Yahweh has revealed to Moses what he is going to do to Pharaoh and the Egyptians, Moses does what Yahweh said (Exod 7:20–21 [with Aaron], 24 [with Aaron]; 9:10–11 [with Aaron], 23; 10:13, 22–23; 11:10 [with Aaron]; 14:27); Aaron sometimes does what Yahweh has said (Exod 8:6–7, 17–18); and Yahweh himself explicitly does what he has said (Exod 7:13, 22, 25; 8:15, 19, 24; 9:6–7, 12, 23–26, 35; 10:13–15, 20, 27; 11:3, 10; 12:29–30, 35–36; 13:15; 14:24–25, 27–29). In praise and remembrance of Yahweh's deliverance of Israel at the Red Sea, Moses and Israel sing a song to Yahweh who acted as the Judge by punishing and destroying Pharaoh and the Egyptians (Exod 15:1, 4–10, 19, 21).

---

55. Cole, *Exodus*, 140, notes, "When Moses tried to act as a ruler or 'judge' they [the Israelites] resented it (Ex. 2:14)." Houtman, *Exodus*, 2:412, notes, "Moses functions in the role [to sit as judge] which, before his calling, had been denied him in Egypt; he looks after the well-being of the community."

56. In Exod 17:8–16, Yahweh is portrayed as the Judge who brings "judgment" to the Amalekites. After defeating the Amalekites and receiving Yahweh's command, Moses builds an altar and calls its name, "Yahweh is my sign," and he says, "A hand upon the throne of Yahweh, Yahweh will have war with the Amalekites from generation to generation" (Exod 17:15–16).

Yahweh, as the Judge of all, commissioned Moses to act as "God" with Yahweh's own authority at the burning bush. There, Yahweh declared to Moses, "Go and gather the elders of Israel and say to them, 'Yahweh, the God of your fathers, the God of Abraham, Isaac, and Jacob, has appeared to me, saying, "I have surely visited you and what has been done to you in Egypt"'" (Exod 3:16). Yahweh has observed his people, Israel, in Egypt and has seen the oppression which Pharaoh and the Egyptians have inflicted upon Israel.[57] In fact, during the ten plagues, especially in the seventh plague, Pharaoh says to Moses and Aaron, "This time, I have sinned (חטא); Yahweh is the righteous One (צַדִּיק), and I and my people are the wicked ones (רָשָׁע)" (Exod 9:27; cf. 9:34; 10:16–17). The two judicial words, צַדִּיק, "just, righteous," and רָשָׁע, "wicked, criminal," indicate that Yahweh has righteous authority to bring his judgment to the guilty, and that Pharaoh and the Egyptians deserve Yahweh's great punishment because of their wickedness.

Indeed, Pharaoh and the Egyptians have sinned against Yahweh by not letting Israel go out of Egypt to serve Yahweh. This sin causes Yahweh to bring "great judgments" to Pharaoh and the Egyptians. One of Yahweh's "great judgments" is to kill (הרג) Pharaoh's firstborn son (Exod 4:23) and all the firstborn of the people and the animals in Egypt (Exod 11:5; 12:12, 29; 13:15). This great punishment brings "a great cry (צְעָקָה) in all the land of Egypt" (Exod 11:6; 12:30). Yahweh's great punishment is portrayed as *lex talionis*. As narrated in Exod 1–6, Pharaoh and the Egyptians have oppressed Yahweh's firstborn son, Israel (Exod 4:22) with hard work as slaves (Exod 1:9–14; 5:5–21) and the death of every male child born to Israel (Exod 1:15–16, 22) and have caused them to cry (זעק/ צְעָקָה/שַׁוְעָה) and groan (אנח/נְאָקָה) (Exod 2:23, 24; 3:7, 9; 6:5). Thus, Yahweh pays back to Pharaoh and the Egyptians what they had done to Israel in Egypt with the "great judgments" (Exod 6:6; 7:4; 12:12).

In addition, Exod 18 recalls and settles the question from one of the two struggling Hebrews from the opening chapters of the narrative: "Who made you [Moses] a prince and a judge over us?" (Exod 2:14). After Moses fled from the land of Egypt to the land of Midian and lived there, Yahweh called Moses at the burning bush at Mount Horeb (Exod

---

57. In Gen 15, Yahweh had foretold all this to Abram in the vision, "Then he [Yahweh] said to Abram, 'Know for sure that your offspring will be sojourners in a land which does not belong to them, and they will serve them, and they will afflict them for four hundred years, but I am also going to judge the nation which they serve, and afterward they shall come out with great possessions'" (vv. 13–14).

3:1–4:17). While Yahweh is speaking to Moses to encourage Moses to obey and do what Yahweh has revealed and commanded, Yahweh commissions Moses to be as "God," that is, the representative of Yahweh with Yahweh's authority. As the representative of Yahweh, Moses brings judgment to Pharaoh and the Egyptians in the land of Egypt and at the Red Sea (Exod 7:20–21 [with Aaron], 24 [with Aaron]; 9:10–11 [with Aaron], 23; 10:4–6 [with Aaron]; 13, 22–23; 11:4–8, 10 [with Aaron]; 14:27). Thus, the answer to the question of one of the two struggling Hebrews asked in Exod 2:14 is answered definitively—Yahweh has indeed appointed Moses the prince and judge.

However, this answer is deferred in the narrative until the conversation between Jethro and Moses in Exod 18:13–27. Moses has been and will be the judge and prince for Israel. Indeed, this happens at Mount Sinai after Moses has brought Israel out of Egypt and through the Red Sea and the wilderness. With Yahweh's authority, Moses as the judge judges (שפט) Israel's cases (Exod 18:13, 16) and as the prince (or the chief judge, שַׂר) provides (or chooses) men of ability and faithfulness and sets (נתן/שׂים) them as heads over Israel, chiefs (שַׂר)[58] of thousands, chiefs (שַׂר) of hundreds, chiefs (שַׂר) of fifties, and chiefs (שַׂר) of tens (Exod 18:21, 25).[59]

Therefore, the theme of Moses as the judge also contributes to the retrospective function of Exod 18. This theme in Exod 18 forms an inclusio with the judicial event in Exod 2:11–14. Both events happen in two days. The first day deals with judgment against oppressive Egyptians: Moses kills an Egyptian (Exod 2:11–12), and Yahweh punishes and destroys Pharaoh and the Egyptians (Exod 18:8; cf. 18:1, 4, 8, 9, 10). The second day deals with the contentiousness of the Israelites themselves: Moses acts as the judge between the two disputing Israelites (Exod 2:13–14), and Moses officially assumes his role as the "prince and judge" between the Israelites (Exod 18:13, 16; cf. 18:22, 26). The extensive verbal relationships between Exod 18:13–27 and the Hebrew man's question in Exod 2:14 connect Exod 18 as the answer to the question of one of the two struggling Hebrews, thus bracketing the deliverance narrative in Exod 2–18 and further supporting

---

58. Propp, *Exodus*, 1:632, notes, "The term *śar* takes us back to 2:14 (J): 'Who set you [Moses] as a man, ruler (*śar*) and judge (*šōpēṭ*) over us?' Moses himself is now the one who appoints rulers and judges." Meyers, *Exodus*, 139, notes, "This Exodus description of judicial functions gives the title 'officer' (*śar*), not 'judge,' to the honest men who will adjudicate.... But it does recall the use in 2:14 of 'ruler and judge,' meaning a ruler who judges, in reference to Moses."

59. See Egger, "Visiting Iniquity," 456.

The Israelites as the Egyptian Slaves

The Israelites are depicted as the slaves of the Egyptians both physically and mentally. In the episode of Exod 18, Pharaoh, the Egyptians, and Egypt are mentioned in the reports of Yahweh's redemptive works:[60] "that Yahweh had brought Israel out of *Egypt*" (Exod 18:1), "and he [the God of my father] delivered me from the sword of *Pharaoh*" (Exod 18:4), "all which Yahweh had done to *Pharaoh* and to *the Egyptians* because of Israel" (Exod 18:8), "all the good which Yahweh had done for Israel, whom he had delivered from the hand of *the Egyptians*" (Exod 18:9), and "Yahweh who has delivered you from the hand of *the Egyptians* and from the hand of *Pharaoh*, and who has delivered the people from under the hand of *the Egyptians*" (Exod 18:10). Yahweh has delivered the Israelites from the burden and slavery in Egypt. These reports of Yahweh's saving and mighty acts summarize the theme of the Israelites as the Egyptian slaves. In other words, Exod 18 expresses the end of the Israelites as the Egyptian slaves.

These summarizing statements recall what Pharaoh and the Egyptians had done to the Israelites since a new Pharaoh who did not know Joseph arose over Egypt (Exod 1:8), oppressing them with hard work as slaves (Exod 1:9–14) and killing every male child born to the Israelites (Exod 1:15–16, 22). After Yahweh called Moses to go back to Egypt to deliver the Israelites from Egypt, Moses met Pharaoh and said to him to let the Israelites go as Yahweh commanded. However, Pharaoh did not obey (Exod 5:1–4) and burdened the Israelites with more hard work (Exod 5:5–21). Yahweh sent the ten plagues and brought the Israelites out of Egypt (Exod 7:14–12:36). At this point, it appears that the Israelites are no longer the Egyptian slaves.

However, during the crossing event at the Red Sea (Exod 14:1–31) and the wilderness journey—the lack of water at Marah (Exod 15:22–25), the lack of food (Exod 16:1–36), and the lack of water at Massah and Meribah (Exod 17:1–7)—the Israelites still think of Egypt and want to return to be the Egyptian slaves. The Israelites grumble against Moses,

---

60. Egger, "Visiting Iniquity," 453, notes, "While 112 of the 115 occurrences of 'Pharaoh' in Exodus are in chs. 1–15, the story's final three references to Pharaoh come in the Moses-Jethro discourse of ch. 18 (vv. 4, 8, 10)."

"Is it because there are no graves in Egypt, you have taken us away to die in the wilderness? What is this (that) you have done to us in bringing us out of Egypt? Is not this word which we spoke to you in Egypt, 'Let us alone, so that we may serve the Egyptians'? Because it would have been better for us to serve the Egyptians than to die in the wilderness" (Exod 14:11–12), "On that we had died by the hand of Yahweh in the land of Egypt when we sat by the pots of flesh (and) when we ate bread to satiety, because you have brought us out into this wilderness to kill this whole assembly with hunger" (Exod 16:3), and "Why did you bring us up out of Egypt to kill us and our sons and our cattle with thirst" (Exod 17:3).[61] These Israelite grumblings against Moses indicate that even though the Israelites are physically no longer under Pharaoh and the Egyptians, the Israelite mind still longs to return to Pharaoh and the Egyptians and to be the Egyptians' slaves.[62]

Throughout the first narrative movement, the first half of the book of Exodus (Exod 1–17), the Israelites have two possibilities: (1) to serve Pharaoh, the king of Egypt (Exod 1:8, 15, 17, 18; 2:23; 3:18, 19; 5:4; 6:11, 13, 27, 29; 14:5, 8), or (2) to serve Yahweh, the God of Abraham, Isaac, and Jacob (Exod 3:6, 13, 15, 16; 4:5; 18:4), the God of the Hebrews (Exod 3:18; 5:3; 7:16; 9:1, 13; 10:3), the God of Israel (Exod 5:1), their God (Exod 3:18; 5:3, 8; 6:7; 8:10, 25, 26, 27, 28; 10:7, 8, 16, 17, 25, 26; 15:26; 16:12).[63] Because of the multiplying population of the Israelites

---

61. Egger, "Visiting Iniquity," 452–53, notes, "While the decimation of the Egyptian host at the sea in chs. 14–15 removes Pharaoh as a direct threat to the sons of Israel, a certain 'Egyptian orientation' carries on in the narrative through chs. 16–18. When the people grumble in the wilderness in 16:3 and 17:3, their complaints echo that of 14:11–12: they would have been better off if Moses had just left them alone in Egypt. This undercurrent of ambivalence or even skepticism regarding the departure from Egypt is only removed in ch. 18, with Jethro's ringing approbation of Yahweh's work in bringing the people out from under the hand of the Egyptians."

62. Ber, "Moses and Jethro," 147, notes, "In the book of Exodus, there are passages in which the relationship between conflict and harmony is difficult to ascertain. The wilderness narrative in Exod. 15:22–18:27 exemplifies this situation. An important movement in the narrative occurs after Israel leaves the Sea of Reeds. At this point in the story, one has read about the conflict between the Lord and the pharaoh. Upon Israel's departure, the pharaoh and all of Egypt disappear and become nothing more than a memory of the Israelite. And whilst only God and his people are left on the scene, the pharaoh's disappearance does not resolve the conflict."

63. Fretheim, "Exodus, Book of," *DOTP* 250, notes, "The book moves from Israel's bondage to Pharaoh to its bonding with its ancestral God, from serving Pharaoh to serving Yahweh (the Hebrew root *ʿbd* ['to serve'] occurs ninety-seven times in Exodus). . . . More particularly, the book moves from the enforced construction of buildings for Pharaoh to the glad and obedient offering for a building for the worship of God

in the land of Egypt (Exod 1:7, 9–10, 12, 20; 5:5), and even more so after Moses and Aaron petition Pharaoh to let the Israelites go out of Egypt in order to serve Yahweh (Exod 5:1, 3; cf. 5:8, 17), the Israelites have to serve Pharaoh as slaves with burdens (Exod 1:11; 5:4, 5), harshness (Exod 1:13, 14), and hard service (Exod 1:14; 5:9, 11).[64] This causes the oppressed enslaved Israelites to cry out, suffer, and even die (Exod 1:11, 16, 22; 2:23; 5:19). Pharaoh is an unfortunate and illegitimate king for the Israelites, and they are serving the false king who gives them heavy burdens and even death.

In contrast, Yahweh has heard the Israelites' cry, remembered his covenant with Abraham, Isaac, and Jacob, seen the Israelites' affliction, and known the Israelites' suffering (Exod 2:24–25; 3:7, 9; 6:5). Yahweh also has come down to deliver them from the hand of Pharaoh and to bring them up from the slavery land to the Promised Land (Exod 3:8; 6:6, 8).[65] This will result in freedom from Egyptian slavery for the purpose of divine service—the Israelites will be free from the tyrant to serve Yahweh, their God (Exod 3:12, 18; 4:23; 5:3, 8, 17; 7:16; 8:1, 8, 20, 25, 26, 27, 28, 29; 9:1, 13; 10:3, 7, 8, 11, 24, 25, 26; 12:31). Yahweh is a just and rightful King for the Israelites, so now they may serve the true King who will give them peace and life.

To serve Yahweh recalls the promises of Yahweh with Moses at Mount Horeb, "I will be with you, and this is the sign for you that I have sent you: when you have brought the people out of Egypt, you shall serve God on this mountain" (Exod 3:12). In Exod 18, at the mountain of God, after Jethro has heard of Yahweh's deliverance, rejoiced in Yahweh's deliverance, praised Yahweh, and confessed about Yahweh, Jethro worships Yahweh by bringing a burnt offering and sacrifices to Yahweh and eating bread with Aaron and all the elders of the Israelites (and, presumably, Moses) in the presence of Yahweh (Exod 18:12). Thus, the sign promised

---

(see Fretheim 1991)."

64. Fretheim, "Exodus, Book of," *DOTP* 254, notes, "In Exodus 5:5–18 (and elsewhere) Pharaoh, upon hearing the cries of the people, is unmoved by their suffering, blames them for the problems they face and intensifies the oppression. In his exercise of sovereignty, Pharaoh holds absolute sway and remains unaffected by his subject; he is an unmoved mover."

65. Fretheim, "Exodus, Book of," *DOTP* 254, notes, "In contrast (Ex 3:7–10; cf. Ex 2:23–25) Israel's God hears the cries of the oppressed, 'knows' their suffering in such a way that their experience becomes his own and moves in powerful ways to remove them from the situation with the help of Moses (who can resist the call of God to do so)."

by Yahweh at Mount Horeb is first fulfilled in Jethro, Aaron, and all the elders of Israel's worship at Mount Sinai here in Exod 18.[66]

Therefore, Exod 18 functions retrospectively in this sense as well, that it concludes the theme of the Israelites as the Egyptian slaves, as narrated throughout Exod 1–17, and fulfills Yahweh's promise at Mount Sinai in Exod 3:12. Following Jethro's great confession in Exod 18 of Yahweh's deliverance of the Israelites from the hand of Pharaoh and the Egyptians, Pharaoh is never again mentioned in the Exodus narrative, and the Israelites never again utter their faithless refrain that they were better off in Egypt.

In conclusion, as discussed above, our examination of six themes—(1) the Jethro accounts, (2) Yahweh saving the Israelites from external threats through his mighty acts of deliverance, (3) the presence of Yahweh in various places, (4) the knowledge of Yahweh by Yahweh's self-revelation through his mighty acts of deliverance, (5) Moses as the judge, acting as "God" to Pharaoh and the Egyptians, and (6) the Israelites as the Egyptian slaves—supports and establishes that Exod 18 functions retrospectively as the key transitional midpoint of the Exodus narrative. With respect to these themes, Exod 18 brings the first narrative movement, the first half of the Exodus narrative (Exod 1–17) to dramatic summary and fulfillment. The following chapter will explore the strong prospective function of Exod 18, thus demonstrating that Exod 18 serves as the key transitional midpoint of the Exodus narrative.

---

66. Carpenter, "Exodus 18," 98, notes, "the true knowledge of Yahweh through the exodus event results in the worship of Yahweh, 'in the presence of God', in sacred time. This is clearly the purpose for which Yahweh called out his people and exercised judgment upon the Egyptians. Even Jethro worships Yahweh at the Mountain of God (cf. Exod. 3.12)." Further, he notes, "The purpose for the deliverance in chs. 2–4 is the worship of Yahweh (3.12; 4.23) and is paralleled in 18.11, 12, where Jethro, Moses, Aaron and the elders of Israel worship Yahweh in the vicinity of Sinai." Carpenter, "Exodus 18," 100. See also Carpenter, "Exodus 18," 101–3.

Chapter 6
The Prospective Function of Exodus 18

As discussed in the preceding chapter, Exod 18:1–27 carries out a distinct retrospective function within the flow of the Exodus narrative, connecting with and summarizing the key previous narrative elements and themes in Exod 1–17. In demonstrating Exod 18 as the key transitional midpoint of the Exodus narrative, this chapter will outline significant ways in which Exod 18 as a whole connects with and anticipates the following narratives in Exod 19–40. This anticipatory, prospective role of Exod 18 will be discussed under five themes: (1) the salvation of Yahweh from an internal threat through Yahweh's gracious forgiveness, (2) the presence of Yahweh in specific places in the midst of the Israelites, (3) the knowledge of Yahweh by Yahweh's self-revelation through his statutes and laws, covenant, and merciful forgiveness, (4) Moses as the judge to the Israelites, and (5) the Israelites as the chosen servant of Yahweh.

The Salvation of Yahweh from an Internal Threat through Yahweh's Gracious Forgiveness

We have discussed above the retrospective summary in Exod 18 of Yahweh's salvation of the Israelites from external threats in the first narrative movement, the first half of the book of Exodus (Exod 1–17)—Pharaoh and the Egyptians, thirst, hunger, thirst, and the Amalekites—through his mighty acts of deliverance. In the second narrative movement, the second half of the book of Exodus (Exod 19–40), a different threat will come to the fore which endangers the Israelites' existence and future, an internal threat—their own sin and stiff-necked idolatry. For this, the great remedy and rescue will come from Yahweh's great compassion and forgiveness (Exod 34:6–10).[1] Within the flow of the Exodus narrative, Exod 18 contributes prospectively to the development of this theme by anticipating the central place of justice, statutes and laws, and obedience in the relationship between Yahweh and his people, the Israelites. While Yahweh's later forgiveness is not directly foreshadowed in Exod 18, this key transitional chapter does serve in important ways to set the stage for the narrative conflict of the second half of the book of Exodus, a conflict which Yahweh's mercy will resolve. Exodus 18 also establishes the key role of Moses in defining and navigating Yahweh's justice with regard to the Israelites.

The salvation of Yahweh through his powerful deeds is concluded in the episode of Exod 18, especially in the first scene (Exod 18:1–12), with the all-encompassing clauses: "all which God had done for Moses and for Israel, his people" (Exod 18:1; cf. 18:8, 9) and "all the hardship which had come upon them [Israel] on the way" (Exod 18:8). These two all-encompassing clauses refer to Yahweh's deliverance of Israel from Egypt and through the Red Sea and the wilderness, as narrated in Exod 1–17. Now, Israel is no longer the slave of Pharaoh and the Egyptians. There is no more affliction, oppression, and suffering from Pharaoh and the Egyptians, or from any other external threats, such as thirst, hunger, or enemy armies. In other words, Israel has been delivered from their burdens but is now under Yahweh, who has redeemed Israel and brought them to himself. In the narrative which will follow in Exod 19–40, a different kind of salvation will take place at the mountain of God/Mount Horeb or Sinai.[2]

---

1. Geisler, *Popular Survey*, 55, notes, "The overall theme of Exodus is redemption. It tells how God buys back His people from the slavery of sin and brings them into His presence. This redemption is revealed in two ways in Exodus: first, by deliverance from Egypt (1–18) and then by the duties enjoined upon God's people as His redeemed people (19–40)." For summary details on the redemptive theme in the book of Exodus, see Geisler, *Popular Survey*, 56–62. Nevertheless, some scholars only focus on the theme of the deliverance of Yahweh in their first part (Exod 1–18) rather than the entire Exodus narrative as presented in the book (see Erdman, *Exodus*, 7; LaSor, Hubbard, and Bush, *Old Testament Survey*, 131; Longman and Dillard, *Introduction to the Old Testament*, 70–71; Arnold and Beyer, *Encountering the Old Testament*, 86; Wells, "Exodus," 56.

2. Stuart, *Exodus*, 411, notes, "'How the Lord had saved them' does not therefore refer specifically to salvation from sin in the present context but does help establish the

In the second scene of Exod 18 (vv. 13–27), the narrator portrays Moses as one who readily heeds the counsel of Jethro, his father-in-law. Jethro advises Moses, "Now, obey me; I will advise you, and may God be with you.... If you do this thing, and God commands you, then you will be able to endure, and also all this people will go to their place in peace" (Exod 18:19, 23). After that, Moses obeys Jethro by doing all which Jethro has advised Moses (Exod 18:24). The narrator also explains one of Moses' three sole responsibilities,[3] an instructor. As such, Moses instructs Israel regarding Yahweh's statutes and laws (Exod 18:16, 20), so that Israel may properly learn and know Yahweh's will for his people.

These two elements in Exod 18:13–27—Moses' compliance and Yahweh's statutes and laws—set the stage for and provide a contrast to the Israelites' transgression and rebellion against Yahweh's statutes and laws in the golden calf event at Mount Sinai (Exod 32–34). Terence E. Fretheim observes, "In these texts [Ex 3:8; 6:6; 14:13; 15:2, 13; 18:4–11] salvation is understood as deliverance from the *sins of other people* (the Egyptians) and their devastating effects. Later in Exodus salvation is understood as deliverance from *their own sins* and their effects."[4] Regarding the redemptive theme of the two-part narrative (Exod 1–18 and 19–40), Thomas J. Egger also recognizes:

> Third, and closely related, the deliverance characterizing the Exod 1–18 narrative arc takes place in the face of *external* threats: bitter slavery and oppression, infanticide, military foes (Egypt and later Amalek), and life-threatening hunger and thirst in the wilderness. In contrast, the tension which drives the plot in the Exod 19–40 narrative arises from an *internal* threat: the

---

character of Yahweh as a saving, rescuing God who acts to keep his people from being destroyed. Later in Exodus the focus will shift from God's saving his people from physical danger to his saving them from sin by teaching them how to be holy and preserve his holiness, but that is not yet the topic here."

3. As narrated in Exod 18:13–27, Moses alone plays three narrative roles—a mediator, a judge, and an instructor—which will be prominent throughout Exod 19–40. First, Moses acts as the mediator between Yahweh and Israel by being as Israel in the presence of Yahweh to inquire of Yahweh (Exod 18:15, 19). Second, Moses plays a sole responsibility as the instructor for Israel by making known and teaching Yahweh's statutes and laws (Exod 18:16, 20). Finally, Moses sits as the judge by judging Israel's cases and setting lesser chiefs (or judges) over Israel (Exod 18:13, 16, 21–22, 25–26).

4. Fretheim, "Exodus, Book of," *DOTP* 254. Nevertheless, Birch, Brueggemann, Fretheim, and Petersen, *Theological Introduction to Old Testament*, 115, note, "God's salvation in Exodus does not focus on saving Israel from sin but is experienced as liberation of Israel from the oppression of a tyrant. Thus, the Exodus story is a major biblical corrective to a spiritualized notion of God's salvation."

rebellious, stiff-necked character of the sons of Israel, requiring a "deeper liberation and renewal."[5]

Thus, the golden calf event at Mount Sinai, and Yahweh's gracious response, establishes the theme of Yahweh's deliverance of the Israelites from an internal threat—their own sin and stiff-necked idolatry—through his gracious forgiveness.

The Exodus narrative's interest in the Israelites' obedience to Yahweh begins early in the second narrative movement, the second half of the Exodus narrative (Exod 19–40), before the great self-revelation of Yahweh at Mount Sinai. On Mount Sinai, Yahweh calls Moses to say to the Israelites, "Then, now, if you will surely obey me, and you will keep my covenant, then you shall be to me a treasured possession from all the peoples because all the earth belongs to me, and you shall be to me a kingdom of priests and a holy nation" (Exod 19:5–6). These words are spoken to the Israelites as the delivered people of Yahweh, so that the Israelites may realize that they should obey Yahweh, who delivered them from the land of Egypt and throughout the Red Sea and the wilderness journey to Mount Sinai, and keep his covenant, including his statutes and laws to come. When Moses relates to the Israelites all which Yahweh has said, they listen to Moses and promise to obey by saying, "All which Yahweh has spoken we will do" (Exod 19:8). Later, after Moses has received Yahweh's statutes, laws, and covenant on Mount Sinai, Moses recounts to the Israelites all which Yahweh has spoken, and they again promise to obey by saying, "All the words which Yahweh has spoken we will do" (Exod 24:3). After Moses has written down all the words of Yahweh, Moses reads the Book of the Covenant to the Israelites, and, finally, they promise to obey by responding, "All which Yahweh has spoken we will do, and we will be obedient" (Exod 24:7; cf. 20:19). These direct responses from the Israelites express their obedience to Yahweh, especially to all his commandments, consisting of his statutes, laws, and covenant which are spoken through Moses on Mount Sinai (Exod 20–23).

In addition, the Israelites' obedience to Yahweh is demanded pre-eminently in the first commandment. Yahweh stresses, "You shall have no other gods before me" (Exod 20:3), and he continues to emphasize, "You shall not make for yourself an idol or any likeness which is in heaven above, or which is in the earth beneath, or which is in the water

---

5. Egger, "Visiting Iniquity," 450. On this point, Egger cites Larsson, *Bound for Freedom*, 85.

under the earth. You shall not bow down to them, and you shall not serve them" (Exod 20:4–5). Here Yahweh makes explicit as a matter of the first importance that the Israelites must bow down and serve Yahweh, their only God (cf. Exod 23:25). In other words, the Israelites should fear, love, and trust in Yahweh above all heavenly, earthly, and watery things. Then Yahweh reveals his sacred name, "because I, Yahweh your God, am a jealous God, visiting iniquity of fathers on sons to the third generation and to the fourth generation of those who hate me, but showing steadfast love to thousands of those who love me and of those who keep my commandments" (Exod 20:5–6). Yahweh's holy name illustrates his own characteristics: (1) Yahweh will bring his punishment to those who hate him, but (2) he will show his steadfast love to those who love him and keep his commandments. In other words, whereas Yahweh's wrath and judgment will come upon those who have sinned and rebelled against him, his steadfast love will come upon those who have loved him and kept his statutes, laws, and covenant. This, thus, explains the contrasting character between those who receive Yahweh's acts: (1) the disobedient ones who will receive Yahweh's wrath and judgment and (2) the obedient ones who will receive his steadfast love.

After Yahweh has given the statutes and laws, the obedience of the Israelites is an essential response to Yahweh's promises regarding the conquest of the Promised Land, the land of Canaan: "Behold, I am sending an angel before you to guard you on the way and to bring you to the place which I have prepared. Take heed of him and obey him; do not make bitter against him, because he will not forgive your transgression; because my name is in the midst of him; but if you will surely obey him, and you will do all which I speak, then I will be hostile to your enemies, and I will show hostility to your foes" (Exod 23:20–22). Yahweh, thus, makes clear that obedience to his angel and the keeping of his commandments are necessary for the Israelites to live as Yahweh's delivered people not only initially at Mount Sinai but also later in the Promised Land, the land of Canaan.

Yahweh, likewise, forbids the Israelites from entangling themselves with the gods of the Canaanites. Yahweh emphasizes, "You shall not bow down to their [the Canaanites'] gods, and you shall not serve them, and you shall not do as their works; but you shall surely overthrow them, and you shall surely break their pillars. Then you shall serve Yahweh, your God, and he [an angel] will bless your bread and your water; and I will take sickness away from the midst of you" (Exod 23:24–25). Lastly,

Yahweh stresses, "You shall not make any covenant with them and their gods. They shall not dwell in your land, lest they will cause you to sin against me; because you will serve their gods which will be a snare to you" (Exod 23:32–33). This points out that the inhabitants in the land of Canaan have their own gods who act as an idolatrous foil to the relationship which the Israelites have with Yahweh. When the Israelites come to the land of Canaan, they should only serve and worship Yahweh, that is, they should only obey Yahweh (or his angel). Turning aside to worship gods in the land of Canaan would constitute sin and rebellion against Yahweh, and Yahweh's wrath and judgment will come upon those who have sinned and rebelled against him through his angel.

In spite of Yahweh's many exhortations, admonitions, and warnings to obey, the Israelites quickly abandon their obedience to Yahweh, which they had pledged three times to Moses (Exod 19:8; 24:3, 7; cf. 20:19). While Moses is on Mount Sinai, the Israelites sin against Yahweh by making a golden calf (Exod 32:1–4) and worshiping it (Exod 32:5–6). The Israelites, thus, disobey Yahweh and break Yahweh's commandments (Exod 32:7–8). Yahweh then calls the Israelites "a stiff-necked people" (Exod 32:9; cf. 33:3, 5; 34:9) because of their faithless actions.[6] Yahweh's wrath burns hot against the Israelites (Exod 32:9–10), but Moses implores Yahweh to recall his promises with Abraham, Isaac, and Jacob (the Israelites) (Exod 32:11–13). Yahweh ultimately has compassion on the Israelites and relents from the disaster which he had threatened (Exod 32:14). Yahweh takes full notice of the Israelites' disobedience against him and resolves to punish them because of their sin. While Yahweh ultimately extends mercy and forgives the Israelites, the danger of divine wrath, destruction, and abandonment for their disobedience is real. Yahweh's mercy, forgiveness, and continued presence are not simply taken for granted.

The fallout for Israel's disobedience comes almost immediately. After Moses has come down from Mount Sinai and seen the golden calf, his anger burns hot against Israel, and he breaks the two tablets of the testimony (Exod 32:15–19). Moses also declares that the golden calf is "a great sin" of Israel against Yahweh (cf. Exod 32:21, 30, 31). Then Moses takes the golden calf, burns it, grinds it to powder, scatters it on the water, and makes

---

6. Yahweh recognizes and proclaims that the Israelites are "a stiff-necked people" (Exod 32:9; 33:3, 5). Furthermore, in Moses' prayer, it is indicated that the Israelites will continue to be "a stiff-necked people" (Exod 34:9). "A stiff-necked people" establishes the overall theme of the second half of the Exodus narrative (Exod 19–40), that is, Yahweh's merciful deliverance of the Israelites from an internal threat—their own sin and stiff-necked idolatry—through the forgiveness of sins.

Israel drink it (Exod 32:20). Consequently, Moses as the judge punishes Israel by ordering the execution of about three thousand men of Israel (Exod 32:21-28). Moses pleads to Yahweh for the forgiveness of such a great sin (Exod 32:30-32), but Yahweh announces that he will blot those who have sinned and rebelled against him out of his book (Exod 32:33) and visit Israel's sin by sending a plague (Exod 32:34-35). This demonstrates that because of Israel's disobedience to Yahweh's commandments, Yahweh's punishment, that is, death, should come upon Israel.

The depth of Israel's disobedience is only matched by the astonishing mercy of Yahweh. While Moses is talking to Yahweh, is known by name, and finds favor in Yahweh's eyes (Exod 33:12; cf. 33:13, 16, 17; 34:9), Yahweh is pleased to say, "I will be gracious to whom I will be gracious, and I will have compassion on whom I will have compassion" (Exod 33:19). Ultimately, Yahweh has compassion on and saves Israel, a stiff-necked people, from his wrath and judgment by giving a merciful word of self-revelation:

> Yahweh, Yahweh, a God, merciful and gracious, slow to anger, and abounding in steadfast love and faithfulness, keeping steadfast love for thousands, forgiving iniquity and transgression and sin, but he will surely not leave unpunished, visiting iniquity of fathers on sons and on sons of sons to the third generation and to the fourth generation (Exod 34:6-7).

This illustrates how gracious Yahweh is and how much he loves Israel, his own people.[7]

As the mediator, Moses speaks to Yahweh for Israel, "If now I have found favor in your eyes, O Lord, please let the Lord go in the midst of us because it is a stiff-necked people, and forgive our iniquity and our sin, and take us as his private property" (Exod 34:9). Even though Yahweh hates those who disobey him and do not keep his commandments, that is, Israel, a stiff-necked people, he, out of the depth of his own person and character, has mercy on them, shows steadfast love to them, and graciously forgives their great sin. This is made evident in

---

7. Fretheim, "Exodus, Book of," *DOTP* 254-55, notes, "Moses prays that God deliver the people from the effects of their sins (Ex 32:7-14) and forgive the sin of the people (Ex 32:32; 34:9); the identity of God is marked by the forgiveness of iniquity, transgression and sin (Ex 34:7).... In these varying contexts it is shown that God's salvation has to do with both internal and external dimensions of life, with both sin and hurt (and all their effects), whether self inflicted, imposed by others or due to causes unknown."

Yahweh's continued care for and shepherding of Israel throughout the rest of the book of Exodus.

As discussed in chapter 4 concerning the rhetorical uses of Jethro in the Exodus narrative as a whole, Jethro is rhetorically used by the narrator as a model to contrast with all the faithless Israelites in Exod 18-40, especially in the golden calf episode at Mount Sinai (Exod 32-34). In Exod 18, the narrator prospectively portrays Jethro as a model to contrast with all the faithless Israelites. After all Jethro rejoices in, praises, and confesses Yahweh as the greatest and incomparable God (Exod 18:9-11), and he worships Yahweh by bringing a burnt offering and sacrifices to Yahweh, and eating bread with Aaron and all the elders of the Israelites in the presence of Yahweh (Exod 18:12). After that, Jethro advises Moses with fatherly and godly words (Exod 18:19-23). It is apparent that Jethro is faithful and obedient to Yahweh. However, even though the Israelites have previously affirmed that they will obey and do all which Yahweh has spoken (Exod 19:8; 20:19; 24:3, 7), in the golden calf episode at Mount Sinai, they are faithless and disobedient to Yahweh. Three time, Yahweh calls them "a stiff-necked people" (Exod 32:9; 33:3, 5; cf. 34:9). Thus, here the Israelites' faithless acts of making a golden calf and worshiping it (Exod 32:1-6) stand in contrast with Jethro's faithful acts of rejoicing in, praising, and confessing Yahweh as the greatest and incomparable God and, of course, worshiping Yahweh (Exod 18:9-12).

Therefore, Exod 18, functioning prospectively, with its emphasis upon Moses as the chief mediator of Yahweh's obligatory statutes and laws, sets the stage for the conflict and climax of the second narrative movement, the second half of the book of Exodus (Exod 19-40). While Exod 18, functioning retrospectively, concludes the theme of Yahweh's salvation of the Israelites from external threats—Pharaoh and the Egyptians, thirst, hunger, thirst, and the Amalekites—through Yahweh's mighty acts of deliverance and judgment, as narrated in Exod 1-17, its strong note of "deliverance" also sets the stage for and anticipates a new aspect of Yahweh's salvation—salvation from the Israelites' own sin, iniquity, and rebellion by Yahweh's loving-kindness and gracious forgiveness. This salvation is narrated and revealed in Exod 19-40, especially in the golden calf episode at Mount Sinai (Exod 32-34), a narrative episode which will express Yahweh's salvation of the Israelites who quickly turn away from Yahweh and disobey his statutes and laws, a salvation and rescue grounded not in Yahweh's acts of power but in his mercy and forgiveness. Indeed, Yahweh will have compassion on and save the Israelites from their golden calf apostasy, which is the Israelites' first great sin. Exodus 18, thus, serves to set the stage for the narrative conflict in the second narrative movement, the second half of the Exodus narrative (Exod 19–40) by highlighting the themes of commandments, judgment, and obedience.

The Presence of Yahweh in Specific Places in the Midst of the Israelites

We have noted that, in the first narrative movement, the first half of the Exodus narrative, the presence of Yahweh is manifested in varied places, beginning and ending at the mountain of God/Mount Horeb or Sinai. In this regard, at the same time which Exod 18 brings this theme a full circle for the first narrative movement, the first half of the Exodus narrative, it emphasizes that Yahweh's presence is now with the Israelites, at the mountain and at the tent. This theme of Yahweh's presence in the midst of the Israelites at the mountain and in a tent/tabernacle[8] will dominate the second narrative movement, the second half of the Exodus narrative, and even the meal shared "in the presence of God" in Exod 18 will be echoed by the covenant meal in Exod 24. This shift from the presence of Yahweh being manifested in various places to his being present in specific places in the midst of the Israelites provides another indication of the function of Exod 18 as the key transitional midpoint of the Exodus narrative.

The episode of Exod 18 completes a full circle around the theme of the presence of Yahweh in various places by beginning and ending with the same place, the mountain of God, and with the same person, Moses (cf. Exod 3:1; 18:5). In Exod 18, Moses returns to the mountain of God to fulfill Yahweh's declaration of the sign of bringing the Israelites out of the land of Egypt, so that the Israelites will serve (or worship) Yahweh "on this mountain" (Exod 3:12). However, a distinct aspect of presence will take place in Exod 19–40 as Yahweh will come down from heaven to reveal himself to his people, the Israelites, to meet with them, and to dwell

---

8. Arnold and Beyer, *Encountering the Old Testament*, 87, notes, "Deliverance and covenant—these are the themes of the two main sections of Exodus (chapters 1–18 and 19–40, respectively). Moreover, an emphasis on the presence of God runs throughout the whole book. The purpose of the exodus from Egypt and the covenant at Sinai, with its Law and tabernacle, can be summarized in this way: God was preparing Israel for his arrival in its midst."

among them on the mountain of God. Later, Yahweh will be present and dwell in the midst of the Israelites in the tent of meeting and, finally, in the tabernacle to meet with them.[9]

In Exod 18, the narrator expresses Yahweh's presence in specific places: Jethro comes to meet Moses *at the mountain of God* (Exod 18:5) where Yahweh makes himself known to Moses and his people, Israel, and dwells among them. Moses and Jethro go *into the tent* (Exod 18:7) where Jethro, Aaron, and all the elders of Israel (and, presumably, Moses) eat bread *in the presence of Yahweh* (Exod 18:12). This suggests that the mountain of God and, perhaps, the tent are Yahweh's revelatory places. The revelatory acts of Yahweh are also recounted through Moses and Jethro's speeches: Israel comes to Moses *to inquire of Yahweh* (Exod 18:15). After confessing Yahweh, Jethro says, "may God be with you" (Exod 18:19) and "God commands you" (Exod 18:23) and advises Moses, "You, be as the people" *in front of Yahweh* (Exod 18:19). This makes it obvious that Yahweh is with Moses and his people, Israel.

These revelatory elements in Exod 18—the specific places of the presence of Yahweh and the ongoing presence of Yahweh—directly anticipate Yahweh's presence in specific places in the midst of the Israelites, specifically, Mount Sinai, the tent of meeting, and the tabernacle, as narrated throughout Exod 19–40.

Throughout Exod 19–40, the three specific places where Yahweh is present in the midst of the Israelites are (1) Mount Sinai, (2) the tent of meeting, and (3) the tabernacle. First, at Mount Sinai, Yahweh is going to reveal himself in the eyes of the Israelites and speak to Moses alone as the mediator between Yahweh and the Israelites. From Mount Sinai, Yahweh calls Moses to remind the Israelites of Yahweh's delivering and powerful deeds and to confirm the Israelites in their identity as Yahweh's "treasured possession from all the peoples," "kingdom of priests," and "holy nation" (Exod 19:3–6). Yahweh also instructs Moses to say to the Israelites that, on the third day, Yahweh will come down to be present on Mount Sinai (Exod 19:9–13). This portrays the beginning of the great self-revelation of Yahweh in a specific place, on Mount Sinai, in the midst of his people, the

---

9. Propp, *Exodus*, 1:634, notes, "We could also call Horeb a 'mountain of meeting.' There Moses encounters Yahweh, Aaron and Jethro; Israel meets God, and, centuries later, Elijah hears the small, still voice (1 Kgs 19:8–18). Exodus 18:12; 24:5, 9–11, moreover, describe banquets on Horeb. And from Horeb, Israel bears the *ōhel môʿēd* 'Meeting Tent,' where humans can commune with the divine."

Israelites.[10] Finally, on the third day, Yahweh comes down and is present to meet with Moses and the Israelites on Mount Sinai (Exod 19:16–20).

Since Mount Sinai is the location for the great self-revelation of Yahweh and his dwelling place, Mount Sinai is holy (cf. Exod 3:5). Thus, Yahweh commands Moses to consecrate Israel and their garments before meeting with Yahweh (Exod 19:10, 14, 22) and to let them neither go up into it nor touch it (Exod 19:12–13, 23). Even though Yahweh reveals himself in the eyes of Israel on Mount Sinai, neither Moses nor Israel can see the appearance of Yahweh, since Yahweh reveals himself and appears to Moses and Israel in a thick cloud (Exod 19:9, 16; 20:21; 24:15, 16, 18; 34:5), in smoke (Exod 19:18; 20:18), and in fire (Exod 19:18; 24:17); and with the sound of the trumpet (Exod 19:13, 16, 19; 20:18), with thunder (Exod 19:16, 19; 20:18), with lightning (Exod 19:16; 20:18), and with the glory of Yahweh (Exod 24:16, 17). This theophany[11] manifests that Yahweh, the holy God, dwells among his holy people, Israel, on Mount Sinai (cf. Exod 24:16).

After Yahweh has come down and appeared on Mount Sinai, he gives Israel his statutes, laws, and covenant by speaking directly to Moses who speaks to Israel (Exod 20–23).[12] Yahweh also makes a covenant with them through the words of the covenant, the Book of the Covenant, and the blood of the covenant (Exod 24:3–8). Then Moses, Aaron, Nadab, Abihu, and the elders of Israel go up to eat and drink in the presence of Yahweh (Exod 24:9–11). Significantly, Yahweh gives Moses instructions

---

10. Durham, *Exodus*, 243, notes, "'The mountain of God' at which Moses and Israel are camped and to which Jethro comes with Moses' wife and sons is Sinai/Horeb, as the use of the same phrase at 3:1; 4:27; and 24:13 makes clear. Whatever the time of Jethro's rendezvous, the place quite appropriately is the mountain of the supreme revelation of Yahweh's Presence."

11. Furthermore, the theophany is the manifest advent of Yahweh, coming down from heaven to dwell with his people, Israel, on the earth (Exod 24:16; 25:8; 29:45, 46). Yahweh has come to stay, to remain, and to dwell with his people in an ongoing way (Exod 40:38). Actually, Exod 19–40 involves the transfer of the holy presence of Yahweh in the midst of his people from Mount Sinai to the tent of meeting and the tabernacle, so that he may dwell in the midst of his people throughout their journeys and, eventually, in the Promised Land.

12. Murphy, *Exodus*, 120, notes, "'The mount of God' is that mount in Horeb on which the law was delivered." Enns, *Exodus*, 369, notes, "The reference to 'the mountain of God' in Exodus 18:5 both describes the Israelites' relative location and foreshadows what is now about to command our full attention: the revelation at Sinai of God's law and the tabernacle." See also Carpenter, "Exodus 18," 93.

for constructing the tabernacle (Exod 25:1–31:17), where Yahweh will dwell in the midst of Israel (Exod 25:8; cf. 29:45, 46).[13]

In contrast, after Israel has sinned against Yahweh (Exod 32:1–6), Yahweh commands Moses to bring Israel, a stiff-necked people, away from Mount Sinai (Exod 33:1). Yahweh says to Moses that Yahweh will not go with Israel but, instead, will send an angel before them because, should Yahweh himself go in the midst, he would consume them on the way (Exod 33:2–3). However, Moses mediates between Yahweh and Israel and finds favor in the eyes of Yahweh (Exod 34:8–9). Yahweh, therefore, has compassion on Israel and forgives their great sin by renewing his covenant with them (Exod 34:10–28).[14] Yahweh, thus, graciously continues and manifests his dwelling among Israel (cf. Exod 40:34–38).

After Yahweh has renewed his covenant with the Israelites, a stiff-necked people, and spoken to Moses on Mount Sinai, Moses comes down from Mount Sinai with the two new tablets of the testimony. Moses does not know that his face is shining from talking with Yahweh (Exod 34:29). Moses' shining face causes Aaron and the Israelites to be afraid of coming near Moses (Exod 34:30). While Moses is speaking to Aaron and the Israelites, Moses has to put a veil on his shining face (Exod 34:31–33). Whenever Moses would go up to Mount Sinai to talk with Yahweh, Moses would remove the veil (Exod 34:34–35). Moses' shining face represents the glory of Yahweh, because Moses talks with Yahweh and receives his commandments on Mount Sinai.

Second, besides Mount Sinai, in Exod 18:7, the narrator mentions "the tent"[15] where Jethro, Aaron, and all the elders of Israel (and,

---

13. Egger, "Visiting Iniquity," 455, notes, "Eleventh, just as chs. 1–18 share a narrative coherence around the theme of deliverance (the second point above), so also chs. 19–40 cohere around the theme *Yahweh's covenant and presence with his people*. The theophanic appearance to Israel in Exod 19–24, with words of the covenant, book of the covenant, and blood of the covenant, remains incomplete without the tabernacle instructions and constructions, the tension between divine presence and the people's sin, and the theophanic transfer from mountain to tabernacle in chs. 25–40."

14. Nevertheless, Moses' prayer in Exod 34:9 is not simply that Yahweh would forgive his people and renew his covenant. Moses' very first request—which Yahweh does not directly answer verbally, but which the rest of the Exodus narrative makes clear that Yahweh grants—is that Yahweh would "go in the midst of us."

15. Enns, *Exodus*, 370, notes, "We should also note that this sacrifice presumably takes place in 'the tent' (v. 7, likely Moses' tent), and that a show of hospitality is to be expected. Yet some have remarked that this may be a portable sanctuary of some sort. In fact, the ambiguity of the phrase 'the tent' may be purposeful so as to suggest either option. In any case, that a sacrifice occurs is significant. It is clearly another forward look to the supreme cultic site, the tabernacle of chapters 25–40." Stuart, *Exodus*, 410, notes, "The Israelites were at that time, of course, living in tents, making appropriate comparable but symbolic dwelling of God in a tent—the tabernacle—as specified later

presumably, Moses) eat bread in the presence of Yahweh (Exod 18:12). In connection with this tent, the acts of taking a burnt offering and sacrifices to Yahweh and of eating bread in the presence of Yahweh in Exod 18:12[16] invite two observations: (1) The tent is "the holy place"[17] because Yahweh is present. And (2) the acts of taking a burnt offering and sacrifices to Yahweh and of eating bread in the presence of Yahweh in the tent in Exod 18:12 anticipate the acts of eating and drinking in the presence of Yahweh on Mount Sinai in Exod 24:9–11.[18] This tent refers to

---

in the book [the Book of Exodus] in great detail." Carpenter, *Exodus*, 1:609–10, notes, "'The tent' (הָאֹהֱלָה) means Moses' tent, but it is striking that the definite article is used. This indicates a tent previously mentioned or recognized by the reader, but no tent has yet been mentioned. If the events in Exod 18 took place after Sinai, this could possibly refer to the temporary tent of meeting, for Moses used the tent of meeting then (אֹהֶל מוֹעֵד, Exod 33:7). It is just as likely that he had used the temporary tent before Sinai as a place to confer with Yahweh, although it is not otherwise clear that he had met 'face to face' with Yahweh before Sinai in this capacity. It is in his tent, serving as a concentrated *holy place and space*, that Moses reports the exodus events to his father-in-law. Telling the story in that tent anticipated its telling in the tabernacle and later in the temple when Israel worshiped."

16. Enns, *Exodus*, 369, notes, "The reference to 'a burnt offering and other sacrifices' (v. 12) should not be passed over too quickly. This is the first 'sacrifice in the desert' to which Moses referred in his earlier audience with Pharaoh (3:18; 5:3; 8:27). Exodus 10:25 is especially relevant, since there burnt offerings and sacrifices are mentioned together: 'You must allow us to have sacrifices and burnt offerings to present to the Lord our God.' This is what begins to happen in 18:12. Of course, this is not the last sacrifice. In 20:24 and throughout the remainder of the book [the Book of Exodus], we have many references to sacrifices. Moreover, 18:12 should not be thought of as the fulfillment of 10:25, but perhaps as a first installment on the importance placed on sacrifice in subsequent chapters."

17. Noth argues that a place where "the communal sacrificial meal" happens "before God" is "the holy place." Noth, *Exodus*, 149. Keil and Delitzsch, *Pentateuch*, 2:85–86, notes, "The sacrifices, which Jethro offered to God, were applied to a sacrificial meal, in which Moses joined, as well as Aaron and all the elders. Eating bread before God signified the holding of a sacrificial meal, which was eating before God, because it was celebrated in a holy place of sacrifice, where God was supposed to be present." See also Houtman, *Exodus*, 2:394, 409–10, 412. Carpenter, *Exodus*, 1:609–10, notes, "It is in his tent, serving as a concentrated *holy place and space*, that Moses reports the exodus events to his father-in-law." See also Carpenter, "Exodus 18," 99, 107, 108.

18. Rylaarsdam and Park, "Exodus," 1:965, notes, "The chief part of the sacrifice is a sacred meal consumed by the group *before God* (cf. 24:9–11)." See also Hyatt, *Exodus*, 190. Cole, *Exodus*, 139, notes, "The general term *sacrifices* would cover the 'communion meal', feasting in the presence of God, as here [Exod 18:12] and in Exodus 24:11, where the 'elders' again appear, possibly in a primitive priestly capacity." Enns, *Exodus*, 370–71, notes, "The fact that they [Jethro, Moses, Aaron, and the elders] partake of a meal together is certainly theologically significant in that it provides a further hint of what is to come in 24:11, and this is true whether or not this particular meal with Jethro is actually covenantal. The events recorded in 18:9–12 unmistakably echo things that came before and that will come later." Janzen, *Exodus*, 227, notes, "A burnt offering (*'olah*) was burnt completely; only parts of the sacrifices (*zebaḥim*) were burnt, and

"Moses' tent"[19] and foreshadows both the tent of meeting (Exod 33:7–11) and the tabernacle (Exod 40:34–38).[20] Even though the tent of

---

the remainder was eaten in a communal meal. This practice is underscored here by the reference to eating *bread* (which can also mean *food*; cf. 24:11)." Bruckner, *Exodus*, 165–66, notes, "Jethro offered the two general types of sacrifices common of the OT: 'burnt offering' (*'olah*) and 'sacrifices' (*zebakh*). The former were wholly consumed by the first in tribute to God. The latter were sacrificed with the blood and fat offered to God and the meat eaten by the people in a fellowship (*shalom*) or thanksgiving (*todah*) meal (24:5, 9–11; 32:6; Deut. 12:27; 27:7; Lev. 3:1)." Further, he notes, "The meal is a part of the formal acceptance of the Sinai covenant in Exod. 24 (see comment at 24:11)." Bruckner, *Exodus*, 169. Johnstone, *Exodus*, 1:377, notes, "It [the meal in Exod 18:12] corresponds to the meal at Sinai that will express, with similar participants and in similar harmony, Israel's response to YHWH's theophany (24:9–11[P])." Carpenter, *Exodus*, 1:614, notes, "A 'sacred meal' is indicated by the context, for 'before Yahweh' describes the context of a holy religious celebration held in an area recognized to be a place where Yahweh would meet with them (cf. Exod 24:9–11)." See also Blenkinsopp, "Structure and Meaning," 117–18. In contrast, Gispen, *Exodus*, 175, notes, "'In the presence of God' (lit.: 'before God') probably refers to the nearness of the pillar of cloud and fire, rather than to the thought expressed in 16:33; it seems incorrect to make 'in the presence of God' refer to the altar or to the place where the sacrifices were brought." Jacob, *Exodus*, 498, notes, "This sacrifice did not presuppose the altar of the Tent of Meeting (Ibn Ezra) any more than that of 24:5; an ad hoc altar was erected, as implied in *lif-nei ha-e-lo-him*." Stuart, *Exodus*, 413, notes, "The religious leader of the nation, Aaron, and all the other leaders ('the elders') had a meal with him [Moses' father-in-law] 'in the presence of God,' which can only mean before the altar that at that point most symbolized God's presence, that is, that altar that Moses had publicly built at Rephidim/Sinai (17:15–16)—inasmuch as the tabernacle/tent of meeting had not yet been constructed."

19. Hyatt, *Exodus*, 188, notes, "Some have suggested that this [the tent] was the tent of meeting described in 33:7–11. However, that tent was a place where oracles were received, where Yahweh spoke to Moses. The tent here is probably Moses' own tent." See also Childs, *Exodus*, 328; Alexander, *Exodus*, 343–44, 349. Osborn and Hatton, *Exodus*, 431, note, "*And went into the tent* uses the definite article, but without a possessive pronoun. This may be understood as 'Moses' tent' (TEV), since each family had their own tents. This should not be understood as the 'tent of meeting' in 33.7." Dozeman, *Exodus*, 403, notes, "The family setting of the encounter in Exod 18:1–5, the lack of a more specific identification of 'the tent,' and the initial appearance of the tent of meeting in 33:7–11 favor a domestic rather than a cultic interpretation. But the reference to the mountain of God and the concluding worship do not exclude a cultic interpretation."

20. Cassuto, *Exodus*, 217, notes, "*And there came*, apart from Moses, also *Aaron and all the elders of Israel to eat bread*—that is, to partake of the holy meal and to eat of the flesh of the peace-offerings—*with Moses' father-in-law before God*, to wit, at the entrance of the Tent of Meeting, which had already been erected before Jethro's visit (on the arrangement of the sections, which is not in accord with the chronological order, see the introductory notes to this section)." Fretheim, *Exodus*, 196, notes, "They [Moses and Jethro] *go into the tent (sanctuary)*. This seemingly innocuous reference is important because of what happens in verse 12, apparently the same place. It may well be a reference to a traveling sanctuary (see 16:34; 33:7–11)." Further, he notes, "Jethro *presents an offering* to God and in the portable sanctuary ('before God') worships with the leaders of Israel (Moses is assumed to be present in the sanctuary from v.

meeting was outside the camp of Israel, Israel could either go out to the tent of meeting to seek Yahweh or see from afar at the entrance of their tents to rise up and bow down when the pillar of cloud came down and stood at the entrance of the tent of meeting (Exod 33:7–9). However, Moses alone could enter the tent of meeting (Exod 33:8–9). Yahweh spoke to Moses face to face (Exod 33:9–11). Here the pillar of cloud, as seen in the eyes of Israel, signifies that Yahweh appeared to Moses with conversations in the tent of meeting (Exod 33:9, 10).[21]

Finally, in the tabernacle, Yahweh dwelt in the midst of his people, Israel, during their journeys in an ongoing way (Exod 40:38). Yahweh dwelt in the midst of Israel (Exod 25:8; 29:45, 46) in the tabernacle, which was "a sacred place" or "a sanctuary" (Exod 25:8; 36:1, 3, 4, 6; 38:24). Yahweh was present in "the Most Holy Place" inside of "the Holy Place" in the tabernacle (Exod 26:33–34).

Therefore, Exod 18 retrospectively brings the theme of Yahweh's presence in the first narrative movement, the first half of the Exodus narrative to a full circle: Yahweh has come down and revealed himself at the burning bush at the mountain of God, in the land of Midian, in the land of Egypt, in the pillars of cloud and fire, at the Red Sea, in the wilderness, and again at the mountain of God. Anticipating the second narrative movement, the second half of the Exodus narrative, Exod 18 prospectively ties the presence of Yahweh in specific places in the midst of his people, the Israelites, to Mount Sinai, to the person of Moses, and even to the tent, foreshadowing the tent of meeting and the tabernacle where Yahweh will dwell among the Israelites (Exod 25:8; cf. 29:45, 46).

---

7)." Fretheim, *Exodus*, 196. Carpenter, "Exodus 18," 99, notes, "In vv. 1–12, Israel moves into the sacred space, 'the vicinity of the Mountain of God', then the sacred story is told, not merely in the sacred space of the Mountain of God, but even in the Tent (האהלה), a concentrated 'holy space' that points forward to the tabernacle (Exod. 25.8) and the portable personal tent of Moses (Exod. 33.1–7)." See also Carpenter, "Exodus 18," 105.

21. Hyatt, *Exodus*, 193, notes, "According to Exod. 33:7–11, Moses would enter the tent of meeting and there 'the Lord would speak with Moses.' This may have been the method by which Moses inquired of Yahweh in judicial cases, but we cannot be certain." Childs, *Exodus*, 330, notes, "Ex. 33:7ff. mentions Moses' role in connection with the tent of meeting when it served as a sacred place outside the camp to which people went 'to seek Yahweh.'"

The Knowledge of Yahweh by Yahweh's Self-revelation through His Statutes and Laws, Covenant, and Merciful Forgiveness

As the key midpoint in the two-part Exodus narrative, Exod 18 also stands at a transitional point, and participates in that transition, between different means of Yahweh's making himself known. In the first narrative movement, the first half of the Exodus narrative (Exod 1–17), Yahweh reveals himself primarily through his mighty acts of deliverance and judgment. The retrospective function of Exod 18 in summarizing and concluding this theme has been discussed above. However, Exod 18 also anticipates prospectively the transition to a different means of Yahweh's self-revelation in the chapters which follow. Throughout the second narrative movement, the second half of the Exodus narrative (Exod 19–40), Yahweh makes himself known primarily through his statutes and laws,[22] covenant,[23] and merciful forgiveness.

The first half of the episode of Exod 18 (vv. 1–12) concludes the theme of the knowledge of Yahweh through his delivering and powerful acts with the concise summary clauses of all of Yahweh's deliverance of the Israelites in the land of Egypt, at the Red Sea, and on the wilderness journey to Mount Sinai (Exod 18:1, 4, 8, 9, 10). By hearing of the salvation of Yahweh, initially from a report (Exod 18:1) but then directly from Moses' lips (Exod 18:8), Jethro knows and acknowledges Yahweh as the greatest and incomparable God (Exod 18:11). Here Moses has led the delivered people, the Israelites, to Mount Sinai where Yahweh has promised Moses to bring the Israelites out of Egypt, so that the Israelites will serve (or worship) Yahweh (Exod 3:12; 18:12).

In the second half of Exod 18 (vv. 13–27), the narrator presents Moses carrying out three exclusive responsibilities: (1) Moses judges Israel (Exod 18:13, 16). (2) Moses inquires of Yahweh for Israel (Exod 18:15).

---

22. Carpenter emphasizes one of "two ways of knowing Yahweh" which is "the knowledge of Yahweh found in the way (דרך) of Yahweh—his Torah." Carpenter, "Exodus 18," 92, 108.

23. Wendland, *Exodus*, 121, notes, "With this chapter [Exod 18] we bring Part I [Exod 1–18] of the book of Exodus to a close. The theme of the entire book, we recall, is 'Jehovah's Covenant with the People of Israel.' The first eighteen chapters have presented 'the deliverance of the covenant people out of Egypt.' What we have considered thus far—the birth and call of Moses, the negotiations between Moses and Pharaoh concerning Israel's release from bondage, the plagues, the Passover, the departure out of Egypt, the crossing of the Red Sea and Israel's early experiences in the desert on their journey to Mount Sinai—all this has been preparatory to 'the establishment of Jehovah's covenant with Israel' (Part II) [Exod 19–24]."

And (3) Moses makes known to Israel Yahweh's statutes and laws (Exod 18:16). Later, the narrator gives Jethro's advice for Moses which depicts Moses fulfilling three lone responsibilities: (1) Moses is the mediator[24] between Yahweh and Israel by representing Israel in the presence of Yahweh and representing Yahweh before Israel (Exod 18:19). (2) Moses is the instructor[25] for Israel by making known and teaching Yahweh's statutes and laws (Exod 18:20). And (3) Moses is the judge[26] by judging Israel's cases and setting lesser chiefs (or judges) over Israel (Exod 18:21–22, 25–26). Significantly, since Israel was enslaved in the land of Egypt for four hundred and thirty years (Exod 12:40), they needed to learn and

---

24. Sarna, *Exodus*, 100, notes, "Moses, who acts as the supreme judicial authority, functions as the mediator of divine will, but not as lawmaker or as one who dispenses justice by virtue of superior wisdom." See also Dozeman, *Exodus*, 408. Stuart, *Exodus*, 416, notes, "A better translation would be 'the people come to me to inquire of God,' which connotes better Moses' intermediary role." In contrast, Houtman, *Exodus*, 2:401, notes, "As the highest judge, he [Moses] is the mediator between God and man and the lawgiver (18:15–16, 19–20). In short, Moses is given the role he will occupy in Exod 19ff. The new structure legitimizes his position as mediator and lawgiver, and enables him to devote himself completely to the tasks which, according to Exod. 19ff., will take up all his time." See also Houtman, *Exodus*, 2:415.

25. Murphy, *Exodus*, 121, notes, "Moses is thus to be, under God, the great teacher of the people, the promulgator of law, and the director of its administration." Sarna, *Exploring Exodus*, 126, notes, "First, it is necessary to have an informed citizenry knowledgeable in the law, and Moses is to act as teacher to the people." Fretheim, *Exodus*, 199, notes, "Moreover, he [Moses] is to be the teacher of the community in the ways in which God would have the people to walk." See also Zweck, *Freed to Follow*, 165. Larsson, *Bound for Freedom*, 124, notes, "He [Moses] will not only receive God's law as the great teacher, but will also have to see to it that the people understand, accept, and apply God's word in their lives." Bruckner, *Exodus*, 167, notes, "Here Jethro describes a general teaching role, with Moses as the first law-school professor. His legacy in bringing the commandments to the people from Sinai quintessentially fulfilled this role. The first two foundation stones of justice were rule by law that was centered in God's instruction."

26. Murphy, *Exodus*, 120–21, notes, "Sitting is the posture of the judge, standing that of those who come to receive judgment." See also Erdman, *Exodus*, 84; Cassuto, *Exodus*, 218; Cole, *Exodus*, 140; Alexander, *Exodus*, 351; Carpenter, "Exodus 18," 100–101. Hamilton, *Exodus*, 285, notes, "The reason Moses is sitting and the people are standing is that during legal proceedings the judge sits while the litigants stand." Gurtner, *Exodus*, 364, notes, "Mōusēs, the subject, sits down (συνεκάθισεν) perhaps in a posture of judging (cf. 3 Kgdms 3.16; Mal 3.3; Ps 9.8; Prov 20.8)." Furthermore, by comparing Moses' role to sheik's role, Rylaarsdam and Park, "Exodus," 1:966, note, "The function of Moses was comparable to that of the Bedouin tribal sheik today. Each morning such a sheik 'sits' briefly as judge. As Israel gradually became an ever-greater aggregate of clan and tribal units such simple judicial administration by one man became impossible. Moses may here be considered as priest as well as tribal chief or judge." See also Hyatt, *Exodus*, 193.

know more about Yahweh who delivered them from the slavery, that is, an old dead life under Pharaoh and the Egyptians, and who brought them to the freedom, that is, a new fullness of life under Yahweh. Moses' three responsibilities highlight that even after Israel's deliverance from Egypt, the Red Sea, and the wilderness, they still needed help from Yahweh through Moses. Specifically, Israel needed to learn to know who Yahweh is and how to live as his people, so that they might walk in his way and do his work (Exod 18:20). Through Moses alone as Yahweh's mediator, Yahweh revealed his way and work through his commandments, that is, his statutes, laws, and covenant. Yahweh was the source of instruction and knowledge.[27] Thus, in Exod 18:13-27, mediation, instruction, and judgment anticipate the knowledge of Yahweh by Yahweh's self-revelation through his statutes and laws, covenant, and merciful forgiveness through Moses alone throughout Exod 19-40.[28]

27. Durham, *Exodus*, 250, notes, "God is the origin of the requirements and instructions, so God must give the explanatory application of them, and Moses is the medium of access by whom the people may approach God with problems of this kind. Since 'the requirements of God and his instructions' are what Moses must 'make understandable' to the people, God is the authority of each explanation and may need to be consulted." Further, he notes, "The essential point of the second of these two narratives [the beginning of Israel's legal system] is that Israel's covenant law has its source in God. He gives it, he provides its authority, and to him therefore Israel must turn to have it interpreted and applied at any point of potential misunderstanding. Moses is an intermediary in this process, and he is instructed to select with great care men who can assist him in this work, a task too heavy for any one man. But the source of information about God's requirements and instructions remains God who issued the requirements and instructions." Durham, *Exodus*, 252.

28. Cassuto, *Exodus*, 211, notes, "With fine artistic understanding, the Torah prefaces the account of the central theme of this part of the Book of Exodus [Exod 18-24] with a prologue, the purpose of which is to prepare the reader's mind for the narrative that follows." Further, he refers Yahweh's statutes and laws (Exod 18:16) to the preparation of the reader "for what will subsequently be related regarding the giving of the Torah to the people of Israel." Cassuto, *Exodus*, 211. Sarna, *Exploring Exodus*, 129, notes, "The second part of the chapter [Exod 18:13-27], the establishment of Israel's system of judicial administration, acts, of course, to focus attention upon 'God's laws and teachings.' In this way, the narrative serves as a kind of prologue to the ensuing revelation of the Torah, preparing the reader for that climactic event." See also Carpenter, "Exodus 18," 91, 92, 107. Fox, *Now These Are the Names*, 99-101, notes, "The real concern of the story, however, is Moshe's early attempt to set up a functioning judicial system in Israel (hence the key word *davar*, ten times, translated here [Exod 18] as 'matter' in the sense of 'legal matter'). The chapter [Exod 18] thus serves a good prelude to Sinai, which will include far-ranging legal material (despite the fact that some scholars see it as an insertion from a later period—cf. verse 16, 'God's laws and his instructions')." Sarna, *Exodus*, 98, notes, "At the same time, the second part of this chapter, verses 13-26, focuses on God's 'laws and teachings' and deals with the administrative arrangements for their implementation in the daily life of the people,

At Mount Sinai, Yahweh called Moses and identified the delivered people, the Israelites, as Yahweh's "treasured possession from all the peoples," "kingdom of priests," and "holy nation" (Exod 19:5-6). Then Yahweh was present and revealed himself to Moses and the Israelites in a thick cloud on Mount Sinai (Exod 19:16-20). As Yahweh's own people whom Yahweh had delivered from the slavery of Egypt, the Israelites, of course, have to learn and know who Yahweh is and what his purpose for his own people is, so that they may walk in his way and do his work. Thus, Yahweh gives his statutes, laws, and covenant to the Israelites through Moses' mouth (Exod 20-23),[29] and then Yahweh makes a covenant with them with the words of the covenant, the Book of the Covenant, and the blood of the covenant (Exod 24:3-8). This demonstrates explicitly that the statutes, laws, and covenant of Yahweh are given to the Israelites through Moses, so that they may properly learn and know the way to live as Yahweh's own people.[30] After Yahweh has made the covenant with the Israelites, Yahweh continues to give Moses instructions for constructing the tabernacle where Yahweh will dwell among his own people (Exod 25:1-31:17). This is the proper work of Yahweh (cf. Exod 35-40) which the Israelites should do as their service to Yahweh, their God (Exod 29:45; cf. 20:2, 5, 7, 10, 12; 23:19, 25; 29:46; 34:24, 26).

However, in the golden calf event (Exod 32-34), the Israelites sinned against Yahweh by making and worshiping a golden calf (Exod 32:1-6). The Israelites received Yahweh's punishment through Moses

---

thereby smoothing the transition to the theme of the succeeding chapters: the giving of the law." Larsson, *Bound for Freedom*, 124, notes, "Mount Sinai, the mountain of the Torah, stands out against the horizon. Now the preparations begin for the great task still ahead of Moses." Further, he notes, "Great persons are often reluctant to share power. Humble as he is (Num. 12:3), Moses, however, has no difficulty in listening and accepting Jethro's good advice (18:24ff.; cf. Deut. 1:9-18). With that, Israel is prepared not only to receive the Torah at Sinai, but the preconditions are also set down for a new, responsible leadership to step forward after Moses fulfills his great mission." Larsson, *Bound for Freedom*, 125. Enns, *Exodus*, 373, notes, "As we come to the close of this chapter [Exod 18], we, like the Israelites, are prepared to approach God at Mount Sinai. A number of elements of chapter 18 have provided further hints of this climactic event, as have other passages since the beginning of the book [the Book of Exodus]." Meyers, *Exodus*, 136, notes, "[T]he second part (vv. 13-27), which explains how social order is established with Jethro's guidance, anticipating the guidelines for social order to be revealed in the theophany at the mountain of God."

29. Carpenter, *Exodus*, 1:617, notes, "The laws came from God, were communicated by Moses, and given in direct response to real cases presented by the people."

30. Carpenter, *Exodus*, 1:622, notes, "This term ['the way' (הַדֶּרֶךְ)] becomes the 'way of Yahweh' (cf. Exod 32:8; 33:13; Deut 5:33; 8:2; 10:12; 11:22; 32:4) and indicates life lived according to Yahweh's instructions, his words, his acts."

(Exod 32:20, 25–28, 33–35). The Israelites departed from the way of Yahweh as directed and commanded in his statutes, laws, and covenant, and they were, thus, punished justly because of their great sin.[31] Moses inquired of Yahweh for the Israelites and found favor in Yahweh's sight, so that Yahweh extended his mercy to the Israelites and forgave their great sin (Exod 34:8–9). Yahweh's mercy and forgiveness were so great that he also renewed his covenant with the Israelites (Exod 34:10–28). Through these episodes, Yahweh makes himself known to the Israelites through his statutes and laws, covenant, and merciful forgiveness, so that they may know who he is and what his will for his own people is. Therefore, the Israelites walk in his right way and do his proper work. The Israelites also come to know that Yahweh is rich in mercy and forgiveness, so that they may turn to him for mercy and continue to rely on his longstanding promises to them (Exod 34:9).

In addition to the other characteristics of Yahweh in Exod 19–40, to know Yahweh is to know him as *the holy God* through his statutes and laws, instructions regarding the Sabbath, and instructions for constructing the tabernacle. The importance of Yahweh's statutes and laws is noticeable in Exod 18, when Israel comes to Moses, and Moses makes known to Israel the statutes (חֹק) and laws (תּוֹרָה) of Yahweh (Exod 18:16, 20).[32] Yahweh's statutes and laws mentioned in Exod 18:16 and 18:20 recall a statute (חֹק/חֻקָּה) about the Passover (Exod 12:14, 17, 24, 43; 13:10), a law (תּוֹרָה) about the Passover (Exod 12:49; 13:9), a statute (חֹק) in the wilderness (Exod 15:25, 26), and a law (תּוֹרָה) about the Sabbath (Exod 16:4, 28). They also anticipate specific statutes and laws in Yahweh's great self-revelation event at Mount Sinai.[33] It appears that

---

31. Carpenter, *Exodus*, 1:617, notes, "Israel's law was living and growing, given to guide a people in the realities of historical life."

32. Murphy, *Exodus*, 121, notes, "This [*and I make known*] was a process of instruction especially necessary for a new nation for which a code of jurisprudence had not yet been provided."

33. Blackburn, *God Who Makes Himself Known*, 77, notes, "Jethro's solution, for Moses to share the burden with God-fearing men in positions of authority, allows the resolution of disputes and the teaching of the Lord's statutes to be carried out among the people. In other words it is a practical measure that enables Israel to be governed under the law of the Lord. As such, it anticipates the coming legal material of 19–24." Further, he notes, "In addition, Moses' language of 18:16 concerning 'the statutes of God and his laws' looks back to language already encountered in the wilderness section ('statutes' in 15:25–26 and 'law' in 16:4). As with the earlier wilderness material, 18:13–27 anticipates the giving of the law." Blackburn, *God Who Makes Himself Known*, 77. As approaching Exod 15–18 as "a continuation and conclusion of the deliverance movement," Egger, "Visiting Iniquity," 462, notes, "Reference to keeping Yahweh's 'statutes'

some statutes and laws had already been given to Israel before Yahweh's great self-revelation event at Mount Sinai, but a distinction can be made. Whereas the previous statutes and laws in Exod 12, 13, 15, 16, and 18 are articulated in connection with the ad hoc situations to which they relate, the statutes and laws to come in Exod 20–23 are organized and formally announced at Mount Sinai.[34] Moreover, Yahweh's statutes and laws portraying Yahweh as the holy God can be discerned in several ways. Having arrived at Mount Sinai, Israel is identified as "a holy nation" (Exod 19:6). Before meeting with Yahweh, Moses is commanded to consecrate

---

(חקים, 15:25–26; 18:16, 20), 'laws' (תורות, 16:4, 28; 18:16, 20), 'commandments' (מצות, 15:26; 16:28), and 'ordinances' (משפטים, 15:25) point ahead to the giving of the law at Sinai in Exod 19–40."

34. Kaiser, "Exodus," 2:411, notes, "In fact, we have already seen that portions of the law were already known before they were formalized at Sinai." Enns, *Exodus*, 371, notes, "We have here another transparent hint of the more detailed legal administration of Sinai. One may well ask how they could have known God's laws and decrees before Sinai, but we have seen this problem earlier with respect to the 'commands and decrees' of 15:26 and the Sabbath law of 16:5, 23, 25–26, 29–30, which as we argued, must have been common knowledge at the time. The 'giving' of the law at Sinai is not the first time Israel hears of God's laws, but is the codification and explicit promulgation of those laws (allowing, of course, for the imposition of additional laws at Sinai)." See also Janzen, *Exodus*, 228. Furthermore, Stuart, *Exodus*, 416, notes, "But do not 'God's decrees and laws' come only later, in chap. 20 and following, with the formal revelation of the covenant? The answer must be no; some of the decrees and laws of God were being proleptically revealed to the people for their benefit even before the unveiling of the Sinai covenant because answers were needed to important questions during the three months while the people were on their way to Sinai/Horeb and also because by dispensing decrees and laws in advance of Sinai, God was able to continue shaping his people's thinking in the direction of his eventual covenant relationship with them. Good education involves preparatory (propaedeutic) instruction as well as concomitant instruction and follow-up instruction." Sailhamer, *Pentateuch as Narrative*, 281, notes, "As far as the mention of other 'laws' is concerned, the Lord had already given them 'commandments and statutes' at Marah (Ex 15:25–26); hence the mention of the 'statutes and laws' is not inappropriate here." Bruckner, *Exodus*, 167, notes, "The terms 'decrees' (*khoq*) and 'laws' (*torah*) previously occurred in Exodus to refer to the observance of festivals (12:24, 49; 13:9) and the Sabbath (16:4, 28). Moses' reference, however, now includes the settlement of civil disputes, generally known as OT case (casuistic) law (see additional notes)." See also Alexander, *Exodus*, 351. Carpenter, *Exodus*, 1:617, notes, "God began to deliver his laws at Marah (15:25) and continued throughout the desert wanderings. Here they begin to be consolidated, and provision is made for preserving and adding to them. . . . From the time of God's testing and Israel's murmuring at Marah (15:25), Yahweh had given them his instructions and guidance in words, statutes, ordinances, laws, teachings, and instructions. This chapter [Exod 18] recognizes that fact. Moses had practically been God's sole instrument of communication for his living Torah to his people during this time. Now a more appropriate and efficient system is established to continue to disseminate Yahweh's holy instructions to his people." See also Carpenter, "Exodus 18," 106.

Israel and to instruct them wash their garments (Exod 19:10, 14, 22; cf. 22:31). When Yahweh comes down on Mount Sinai, Israel cannot go up upon Mount Sinai or touch it (Exod 19:12–13). Whoever does not obey Yahweh's command is subject to death (Exod 19:12–13, 21). Later, after the golden calf event, when Yahweh calls Moses to go up to Mount Sinai, Yahweh commands Moses, "Then no one shall go up with you, and also let no one be seen on all the mountain; let neither flock nor herd also pasture in front of that mountain" (Exod 34:3).

Likewise, Yahweh's holiness is discernible in his instructions regarding the Sabbath. Since Yahweh blesses the Sabbath day and makes it holy (Exod 20:11), Israel must remember it and keep it holy (Exod 20:8; cf. 31:12–17). The Sabbath day is the seventh day, which is for Yahweh and his people, a day to rest from work (Exod 20:8–11; 23:10–12; 31:12–17; 34:21; 35:1–3). Since this rest day is holy to Yahweh (Exod 31:15; 35:2), his people should obey as he has commanded. As with Mount Sinai, the seriousness of this point is emphasized by the fact that whoever does not obey Yahweh's command shall be put to death (Exod 31:14, 15; 35:2).

The revelation of Yahweh's holiness is probably most keenly displayed in his instructions for constructing the tabernacle. In the tabernacle, Yahweh will be present at "the Most Holy Place" where Moses put the mercy seat on the ark of the testimony (Exod 26:33–34). "The Holy Place" was the area outside of the Most Holy place where only Aaron and his sons served Yahweh as priests in his presence (Exod 28:29, 35, 43; 29:29–30; 31:10–11; 35:19; 39:1, 41). Moses shall make the garments for Aaron holy to Yahweh (Exod 28:3, 36, 38, 41; 29:21; 39:30), and they shall be holy garments for Aaron (Exod 28:2, 4; 29:29; 31:10; 35:19, 21; 39:1, 41; 40:13). Moses shall consecrate Aaron and his sons to serve Yahweh as priests (Exod 28:41; 29:1, 4, 21, 44; 30:17–21, 30; 40:12–15, 30–32). The altar of incense shall be holy to Yahweh (Exod 30:10). The anointing oil and incense shall be holy to Yahweh (Exod 30:25, 31–32, 36, 37; 37:29; 40:9), but whoever does not obey his command shall be cut off from his people (Exod 30:33, 38). With the anointing oil, Moses shall consecrate the tabernacle and all its furniture (Exod 30:26–29; 40:9–11). Thus, according to his statutes and laws, instructions regarding the Sabbath, and instructions for constructing the tabernacle, Yahweh is known as the holy God, and his holiness will cause those who disobey his commandments to be put to death or be cut off from his people.

At Mount Sinai, there is a particular emphasis on Yahweh's lawgiving through Moses and also on his people, the Israelites, coming to learn and know the will of God who has delivered them, so that they may learn and know him more fully as *their own God* and also live in accord with his will, in his presence. In Yahweh's covenant, since Yahweh as the Savior had delivered the Israelites from the land of Egypt, he calls his delivered people his "treasured possession from all the peoples," "kingdom of priests," and "holy nation" (Exod 19:5–6). Yahweh addresses himself to the Israelites, "I am Yahweh, your God" (Exod 20:2; cf. 29:46) and "Yahweh, your God" (Exod 20:5, 7, 10, 12; 23:19, 25; 34:24, 26; cf. 29:45). Yahweh is sometimes addressed, "the God of Israel" (Exod 24:10; 32:27; 34:23). At Mount Sinai, after Yahweh gave his commandments to the Israelites through Moses alone, Yahweh made a covenant with them with the words of the covenant, the Book of the Covenant, and the blood of the covenant (Exod 24:3–8; cf. 24:12; 31:16, 18; 34:1, 10–28). Yahweh declared, "Then I will dwell in the midst of the sons of Israel, and I will be their God; and they shall know that I am Yahweh, their God, who brought them out of the land of Egypt, so that I might dwell in the midst of them. I am Yahweh, their God" (Exod 29:45–46). Thus, this covenant language expresses that Yahweh is truly known as the God of the Israelites because they are his "firstborn son" (Exod 4:22) and, specifically, his "treasured possession" (Exod 19:5) whom he delivered from the slavery of Egypt.

Besides Yahweh's making himself known as the holy God and the Israelites' own God, the golden calf event at Mount Sinai (Exod 32–34) not only expresses the Israelites' great sin but also Yahweh's merciful forgiveness. Yahweh's merciful forgiveness portrays Yahweh as *the merciful and gracious God*. In laws about social justice, Yahweh says, "And it shall come to pass, when he cries to me, I will hear; because I am gracious" (Exod 22:27). In the golden calf event, Yahweh initially knows that the Israelites have turned quickly away from his commandments by making and worshiping a golden calf (Exod 32:7–8). Yahweh at first threatens to pour out his wrath and judgment upon the Israelites (Exod 32:9–10), but Moses prays to Yahweh to relent from his punishment against the Israelites and causes Yahweh to remember his promises with Abraham, Isaac, and Jacob (Exod 32:11–13). Yahweh, therefore, relents from his wrath and judgment against the Israelites (Exod 32:14). On Mount Sinai, Yahweh had addressed himself to the Israelites as "a jealous God" (Exod 20:5; cf. 34:14), "visiting iniquity of fathers on sons to the third generation and to the fourth generation of those who hate me, but showing steadfast love to thousands of those who love me and of those who keep my commandments" (Exod 20:5–6). The Israelites have sinned greatly by forming and bowing down to a golden calf as their deliverer (Exod 32:1-6) and, thus, face Yahweh's wrath and judgment through Moses (Exod 32:20, 25-28, 33-35). After the great sin of the Israelites, however, Moses finds favor in Yahweh's sight, and Yahweh reveals a deeper aspect of his character to Moses, "I will be gracious to whom I will be gracious, and I will have compassion on whom I will have compassion" (Exod 33:19). Finally, Yahweh grants a new and fullest revelation of his mercy and grace to Moses by passing by and proclaiming:

> Yahweh, Yahweh, a God, merciful and gracious, slow to anger, and abounding in steadfast love and faithfulness, keeping steadfast love for thousands, forgiving iniquity and transgression and sin, but he will surely not leave unpunished, visiting iniquity of fathers on sons and on sons of sons to the third generation and to the fourth generation (Exod 34:6-7).

Yahweh has compassion on the Israelites and pardons their great sin (Exod 34:9), restores his covenant with them (Exod 34:10-28), and goes in the midst of them on all their journeys (Exod 40:38). Thus, these emphasize that both in exalted rhetoric (Exod 34:6-7) and in actually forgiving the sin (Exod 34:9), renewing the covenant (Exod 34:10-28), and going among the Israelites (Exod 40:38) in the narratives, Yahweh makes himself known as the merciful and gracious God in the golden calf event and the following chapters.

When it comes to Yahweh's making himself known to Moses and the Israelites throughout Exod 19-40, Moses alone plays a role as Yahweh's representative in the second half of the Exodus narrative (Exod 19-40) which differs from the first half of the Exodus narrative (Exod 1-17). Throughout Exod 1-17, Yahweh directed and commanded the Israelites, Pharaoh, and the Egyptians through Moses *and Aaron* as Yahweh's representatives (cf. Exod 4:15-16; 7:1-2). After Yahweh had spoken to Moses, Moses repeated to Aaron all the words which Yahweh had said to him. Aaron then spoke to the Israelites all the words which Yahweh had said to Moses (Exod 4:30; 16:6, 9-10). When Moses and Aaron stood in front of Pharaoh, Moses and Aaron spoke to Pharaoh all the words which Yahweh had said to Moses (Exod 5:1, 3; 10:3). Throughout the ten plagues, after Yahweh commanded Moses, and sometimes Aaron, to deal with Pharaoh, Moses and Aaron did everything which Yahweh commanded before Pharaoh (Exod 7:6, 10, 20; 8:17; 9:10; 11:10). After Yahweh spoke to Moses, Moses spoke to Aaron all the words which Yahweh had spoken to Moses, and then Aaron obeyed all which Yahweh had spoken to Moses (Exod 7:10, 20; 8:6, 17; 16:10, 34).

In addition, Yahweh's statutes and laws were initially conveyed to Israel through Moses *and Aaron* about the Passover (Exod 12:1–28, 43–50) and the appearance of the glory of Yahweh (Exod 16:6–10). Concerning the Passover, Yahweh directed both Moses and Aaron to "speak to all the congregation of Israel . . ." (Exod 12:3). After Moses and Aaron had spoken to Israel all of Yahweh's words, "the sons of Israel went and did as Yahweh had commanded Moses and Aaron . . ." (Exod 12:28; cf. 12:50). When Israel faced hunger in the wilderness, Moses and Aaron spoke "to all the sons of Israel" concerning the appearance of the glory of Yahweh (Exod 16:6–7). Then, after Yahweh had spoken to Moses, Moses directed Aaron, "say to all the congregation of the sons of Israel . . ." (Exod 16:9), and then Aaron "spoke to all the congregation of the sons of Israel . . ." (Exod 16:10).

Throughout Exod 1–17, Moses *along with Aaron* communicated Yahweh's directions and commands to Israel, Pharaoh, and the Egyptians. In Exod 18, a shift takes place to Moses' exclusive responsibility for the authoritative proclamation and promulgation of Yahweh's words. Moses alone recounts to Jethro all of Yahweh's deliverance of Israel (Exod 18:8), judges Israel's cases (Exod 18:13, 16, 22, 26), inquires of Yahweh for Israel (Exod 18:15, 19), teaches Israel Yahweh's statutes and laws (Exod 18:16, 20), and chooses chiefs (or judges) over Israel (Exod 18:21, 25). Henceforth, Moses serves as the sole mediator of Yahweh to whom Yahweh will speak, and who will bring Yahweh's directions and commands to the people of Yahweh, Israel (cf. Exod 18:14, 18; 24:2).

Moses' unique responsibility as Yahweh's mediator throughout Exod 19–40 is demonstrated by Moses' going up to Mount Sinai alone to talk with Yahweh (Exod 19:3, 20; 24:1–2, 13, 15, 18; 32:30; 34:1–3, 4) and coming down from Mount Sinai to bring Yahweh's commands and instructions to the Israelites (Exod 19:14, 21, 25; 32:15; 34:29). On Mount Sinai, Yahweh calls Moses to speak to the Israelites, and then Moses relays to them Yahweh's call to be Yahweh's "treasured possession from all the peoples," "kingdom of priests," and "holy nation" (Exod 19:5–6). Yahweh instructs Moses that the Israelites must be set apart and holy in the presence of Yahweh. Before Yahweh comes down in a thick cloud on Mount Sinai, Yahweh says to Moses to consecrate the Israelites and wash their garments (Exod 19:10–15). Other commands and instructions of Yahweh for the Israelites follow. After Yahweh has appeared to Moses and the Israelites in a thick cloud on Mount Sinai, the Israelites learn and know the statutes and laws of Yahweh, for example, the Ten Commandments (Exod 20:1–17) and the laws about altars (Exod 20:22–26), slaves (Exod 21:1–32), restitution (Exod 21:33–22:15), social justice (Exod 22:16–23:9), and the Sabbath and festivals (Exod 23:10–19). Through Moses alone, Yahweh instructs the Israelites concerning the construction of the tabernacle and all its furnishings, concerning priestly garments and consecration, and again concerning the Sabbath (Exod 25–31). Finally, when all the work has been done as Yahweh had commanded Moses (Exod 39:42–43; cf. 39:1, 5, 7, 21, 26, 29, 31, 32; 40:16, 19, 21, 23, 25, 27, 29, 32), Yahweh instructs Moses to erect the tabernacle, so that Yahweh may dwell among his people, the Israelites, in the cloud and with his glory at the tabernacle (Exod 40:1–38).

In addition, in the golden calf event at Mount Sinai (Exod 32–34), after the Israelites have asked Aaron to make them "gods" (Exod 32:1), Aaron says, "Take off the rings of gold which are on the ears of your wives, your sons, and your daughters, and bring [them] to me" (Exod 32:2) to make a golden calf (Exod 32:3–4). Aaron commands and instructs the Israelites, but they are certainly not true commands and instructions from Yahweh. However, Moses intercedes with Yahweh by imploring favor upon the Israelites in the light of Yahweh's promises to Abraham, Isaac, and Jacob (Exod 32:11–13). After coming down from Mount Sinai and seeing the Israelites' great sin, Moses instructs the sons of Levi to kill the Israelites throughout the camp with the sword (Exod 32:27), and later, he conveys Yahweh's command and instruction to the Israelites to take off their ornaments (Exod 33:5). In Exod 33:7–11, the narrator interrupts and pauses the golden calf narrative at a moment of great tension to depict Moses' regular meeting with Yahweh at the tent of meeting in the sight of the Israelites. After that, in Exod 34:29–35, when Moses comes down from Mount Sinai with the two new tablets of the testimony, his face shines because of talking with Yahweh (Exod 34:29). Moses calls Aaron and the Israelites and talks with them, after putting a veil over his shining face (Exod 34:31–33). This scene concludes by emphasizing that Moses keeps going in "before Yahweh" to speak with Yahweh and going out to speak to the Israelites "what he was commanded" with his shining face (Exod 34:34–35). The golden calf narrative reaches its climax in Yahweh's profound self-revelation of the divine name and of divine merciful forgiveness in the theophany of Exod 34:5–7. This proclamation of Yahweh's character and ways was made only to Moses, but, through

Moses alone as the mediator of Yahweh's commands and instructions, also to the Israelites throughout their generations.

Therefore, Exod 18, serving as the retrospective function, not only summarizes the theme of the knowledge of Yahweh in his self-revelation primarily through his mighty deeds of deliverance in the first half of the book of Exodus (Exod 1–17), but also it, serving as the prospective function, anticipates the theme of the knowledge of Yahweh at Mount Sinai in his self-revelation primarily through his statutes and laws, covenant, and merciful forgiveness in the second half of the book of Exodus (Exod 19–40). Moreover, the knowledge of Yahweh is tied directly to the person of Moses. Throughout the first half of the Exodus narrative (Exod 1–17), Yahweh directs and commands Israel, Pharaoh, and the Egyptians through both Moses *and Aaron* as Yahweh's representatives. Exodus 18, on the other hand, draws this paired role to an emphatic close with its strong depiction of Moses alone as the narrator of Yahweh's deeds and as the mediator of Yahweh's statutes, laws, and covenant, setting the stage for Moses' lone and towering role in this regard in Exod 19–40. Exodus 18 also anticipates the shifting role of Aaron in the second half of the Exodus narrative (Exod 19–40). Aaron will no longer function as a divine mouthpiece alongside Moses but rather as the primary priest of Israel (Exod 31:10; 35:19; 38:21; 39:41; 40:13; cf. 28:1, 4, 41; 29:1, 44; 30:30), a role exhibited in Exod 18, where Aaron comes along with all the elders of Israel to eat bread with Jethro in the presence of Yahweh (Exod 18:12).

Moses as the Judge to the Israelites

Exodus 1–18 emphasizes that Moses acted as "God" and, thus, a judge *to Pharaoh and the Egyptians* in the land of Egypt and at the Red Sea through all the wonders as Yahweh has revealed to and commanded Moses. As Exod 18 looks forward, the theme of Moses as the judge will shift from his role as an agent of God's justice upon Pharaoh and the Egyptians to his role as an agent of God's just lawgiving and chastening, and, ultimately, of God's pardon *for the Israelites* in the second half of the Exodus narrative. This latter emphasis finds its greatest illustrative moment in the golden calf event by the revelation and command of Yahweh through Moses.

This theme of Moses as the judge is highlighted in the episode of Exod 18 by paralleling the earlier judicial event in Exod 2:11–14, the two-day event of "judging" an Egyptian on the first day (Exod 2:11–12) and two struggling Israelites on the second day (Exod 2:13–14). This two-day quasi-judicial event in Exod 2:11–14 proleptically anticipates the two-day judicial event in Exod 18.[35]

The first scene of Exod 18 (vv. 1–12) corresponds with the first proleptic day of Exod 2:11–12 by recounting all of Yahweh's *deliverance of the Israelites* in Egypt, at the Red Sea, and in the wilderness (Exod 18:1, 4, 8, 9, 10). In particular, the delivering and powerful acts in Egypt and at the Red Sea were originated by Yahweh through Moses whom Yahweh authorized to judge Pharaoh and the Egyptians by bringing "great judgments" to them (Exod 6:6; 7:4; 12:12). In other words, Moses as Yahweh or the representative of Yahweh (cf. Exod 4:16; 7:1) judged Pharaoh and the Egyptians. Whereas the first day ends with the act of judgment upon Pharaoh and the Egyptians through Moses, the second day begins with the act of judgment over the Israelites through Moses alone with the authority of Yahweh. Now, a distinct aspect of judgment will take place at Mount Sinai in Exod 19–40.

The second scene of Exod 18 (vv. 13–27) corresponds with the second proleptic day of Exod 2:13–14 by narrating Moses' act of sitting alone as the judge over Israel all day (Exod 18:13).[36] Jethro sees all which Moses is doing by himself for Israel (Exod 18:14) and advises Moses to continue his responsibilities for Israel. Here Moses is portrayed as the

---

35. As considering Exod 2:11–14 as "an example of literary prolepsis," Egger, "Visiting Iniquity," 460, notes, "The two days of Moses' first appearance thus anticipate the two great narrative arcs of Exodus: Yahweh's quest to deliver his people from the oppression of Egypt and from other threats (Exod 1–18) and Yahweh's quest to rule over and dwell in the midst of stiff-necked Israel (Exod 19–40)." Further, he notes, "Exod 2:11–14 functions as a proleptic paradigm for the overall Exodus narrative. The first day anticipates the first narrative arc, with Yahweh's *lex talionis* judgment upon Egypt to deliver his people. The second day anticipates the subsequent sin and rebellion of Israel against Moses and Yahweh." Egger, "Visiting Iniquity," 461.

36. Murphy, *Exodus*, 120–21, notes, "Sitting is the posture of the judge, standing that of those who come to receive judgment." See also Cole, *Exodus*, 140; Houtman, *Exodus*, 2:395, 412, 414, 415; Hamilton, *Exodus*, 285; Gurtner, *Exodus*, 364; Alexander, *Exodus*, 351. Furthermore, Erdman observes that Moses does his lone responsibility as "the sole judge" to the Israelites from morning until evening (see Erdman, *Exodus*, 84). See also Sarna, *Exploring Exodus*, 126; Garrett, *Exodus*, 449. Stuart, *Exodus*, 416, notes, "Through him [Moses] the people asked God for answers to their disputes, and thus Moses asserted that he did not really judge on his own but 'decides between the parties and informs them of God's decrees and laws.' In other words, the legal process involved the revelatory process in this case. That was almost certainly the reason Moses had felt obligated to do all the judging himself: the answers involved God's own decisions, and Moses understood himself to be the sole conduit for those to the people."

mediator between Yahweh and Israel, the instructor for Israel, and even the "chief" judge over Israel and later chosen judges (Exod 18:15–16, 19–23).[37] Moses alone judges Israel with the authority of Yahweh who sent Moses to Pharaoh to bring Israel out of Egypt (Exod 3:10; 3:12, 13, 14, 15; 4:28; 7:16), was with Moses (Exod 3:12; 4:12, 15), put all the wonders in Moses' hand (Exod 4:21), and, particularly, made Moses as "God" to Aaron (Exod 4:16) and later to Pharaoh (Exod 7:1).[38]

The prominent judicial responsibility of Moses to bring Yahweh's justice to the Israelites in Exod 18:13–27 anticipates Moses' judging of the Israelites in the second half of the Exodus narrative (Exod 19–40), especially in the golden calf episode at Mount Sinai (Exod 32–34).[39]

At Mount Sinai, Yahweh calls Moses and directs Moses to say to the Israelites, "Then, now, if you will surely obey me, and you will keep my covenant, then you shall be to me a treasured possession from all the peoples because all the earth belongs to me, and you shall be to me a kingdom of priests and a holy nation" (Exod 19:5–6). To be Yahweh's own people as a priestly and holy nation among all the nations is to obey him and keep his commandments. Yahweh's delivered people, the Israelites, respond, "All which Yahweh has spoken we will do" (Exod 19:8). When Moses has received Yahweh's statutes, laws, and covenant from Yahweh on Mount Sinai (Exod 20–23), Moses tells the Israelites all which Yahweh had spoken,[40] and they respond, "All the words which Yahweh has

37. Mann, *Book of the Torah*, 98, notes, "The point of Jethro's advice, of course, is to designate Moses as the 'chief justice' and thus to spare him all of the relatively petty legal cases, which his newly appointed assistant judges will decide." See also Houtman, *Exodus*, 2:401, 415.

38. Carpenter, "Exodus 18," 100–101, notes, "However, the reference to Moses as a judge (שׁוֹפט) is especially noticeable in Exod. 2.14. Moses' right to act as a judge of cases among Israelites is challenged by the Israelites. In 18.13, Moses indeed does sit and judge as a prince! Yahweh has made him a judge over all Israel." Mann, *Book of the Torah*, 98, notes, "However, the context of the story points again to what will happen at Sinai, for only there will Moses' new role as legislator be publicly confirmed by Yahweh and formally accepted by the people."

39. Carpenter, "Exodus 18," 93, notes, "The second half of the chapter (vv. 13–27) points forward to the dissemination of *mišpaṭ* (משׁפט) and therefore, to Sinai." See also Carpenter, "Exodus 18," 97, 99, 104–5. Bacon, "JE in the Middle Books," 29, notes, "The *Mishpatim* of chapters xxi., xxii., as they are most appropriately called, are the directions which the *judges* of xviii. 21 ff. will require for the decision of causes. It is what Moses is instructed in in xxiv. 12, that he may teach it; what we find him putting in practice in xviii. 16; what we expect from xxiv. 12 that he will at his death, if not sooner, transmit as the authoritative common-law of Israel; . . ."

40. Cassuto, *Exodus*, 218, notes, "Moses was sitting as judge and teacher, and whoever had a dispute with his fellow, or wished to receive instruction from Moses, came

spoken we will do" (Exod 24:3). Finally, after Moses has written down all the words of Yahweh, he reads the Book of the Covenant to the Israelites, and, again, they respond, "All which Yahweh has spoken we will do, and we will be obedient" (Exod 24:7; cf. 20:19). These direct responses of the Israelites demonstrate their explicit, emphatic commitment to obey Yahweh and keep his commandments.

However, when Moses tarries on Mount Sinai as he receives instructions for constructing the tabernacle from Yahweh, the Israelites turn aside quickly from Yahweh (Exod 32:7-8) and ignore their repeated promise to do all which Yahweh has spoken through Moses (cf. Exod 19:8; 20:19; 24:3, 7). The Israelites cannot wait for Moses, so they ask Aaron to make a golden calf (Exod 32:1-4) and then worship it (Exod 32:5-6). The Israelites, thus, disobey Yahweh and break the first commandment: "You shall have no other gods before me" (Exod 20:3). That commandment continues, "You shall not make for yourself an idol or any likeness which is in heaven above, or which is in the earth beneath, or which is in the water under the earth. You shall not bow down to them, and you shall not serve them" (Exod 20:4-5). To form the golden calf and bow down to it is "a great sin" against Yahweh (Exod 32:21, 30, 31), which provokes Yahweh's wrath (Exod 32:10, 11) and brings his judgment to the Israelites (Exod 32:10, 12, 14, 35; 33:3, 5).

In the golden calf event at Mount Sinai, Moses functions as the lone human judge over Israel by taking the golden calf, burning it with fire, grinding it to powder, scattering it on the water, and making Israel drink it (Exod 32:20). As the judge, Moses asks Aaron, "What did this people do to you [Aaron] that you [Aaron] have brought a great sin upon them?" (Exod 32:21), and as a defendant, Aaron tells Moses all which had happened (Exod 32:22-24). After that, Moses pronounces Yahweh's judicial decree to the sons of Levi: "Put, each of you, your sword on your side! Go to and fro from a gate to another gate in the camp, and kill, each of you, your brother, and each of you, your friend, and each of you,

---

to him." Further, he notes, "I act thus, *Because the people come to me to inquire of God,* and this inquiry can take one of two forms: first, a judicial form: *when they have a matter*—that is, a judgment, a dispute—the matter *comes to me, and I judge between a man and his neighbor.* Secondly, when they come to ask for instruction and guidance, and I answer in God's name, *and I make them know the statutes of God and His direction.*" Cassuto, *Exodus*, 219. Cole, *Exodus*, 141, notes, "Moses obviously regarded his judicial task as a teaching ministry, telling the Israelites of God's 'statutes', 'set laws', and 'decisions' or 'instructions', given on specific occasions to deal with particular cases. Perhaps we have here the method by which the law of Moses came into being, a combination of great principles of revelation and their application to day-by-day living in the desert."

your neighbor," and they kill about three thousand men of Israel (Exod 32:27–28). Through Moses as the judge, Yahweh's punishment has come upon Israel, "a stiff-necked people" (Exod 32:9; cf. 33:3, 5; 34:9).

Finally, after Moses has judged the Israelites, he goes up to Yahweh on Mount Sinai to "make propitiation" for their great sin (Exod 32:30). Moses asks Yahweh to forgive the Israelites' great sin (Exod 32:31–32), but Yahweh insists, "Whoever has sinned against me, I will blot out of my book; and now, go, lead the people to [the place] where I have spoken to you; behold, my angel shall go before you, but in the day, when I visit, I will visit their sin upon them" (Exod 32:33–34). Yahweh then punished the Israelites because they made the golden calf and bowed down to it (Exod 32:35). Yet the story does end here, and as Moses continues to intercede for the Israelites, Yahweh tempers his justice with his abundant lovingkindness, mercy, and forgiveness. In eliciting and conveying clemency from Yahweh to his people, Moses remains the only human figure functioning as the "judge" in Yahweh's stead among them.

Therefore, the shift to a focus on Moses' role as Yahweh's authorized judge *over the Israelites* is another element in Exod 18's strong prospective concern, another indication that Exod 18 functions as the key transitional midpoint of the Exodus narrative. Through the first half of the Exodus narrative (Exod 1–17), Moses acts as the judge along with Yahweh, the ultimate Judge, especially with respect to Pharaoh and the Egyptians (cf. Exod 2:11–12; 7:14–12:36; 14:1–31). Through the second half of the Exodus narrative (Exod 19–40), especially through the golden calf event at Mount Sinai in Exod 32–34, Moses acts as the judge over the Israelites (cf. Exod 2:13–14).

The Israelites as the Chosen Servant of Yahweh

Finally, Exod 18 signals a transition with respect to the theme of slavery and service. The first narrative movement (Exod 1–17) portrays the Israelites as the slaves of the Egyptians, for a long while physically, and for some time after that, still, mentally. Exodus 18 both draws this theme to its conclusion and also shifts the narrative focus to a new role which the Israelites will play through the remainder of the book of Exodus (Exod 19–40): the chosen servant of Yahweh.

The first scene of the episode of Exod 18 (vv. 1–12) repeatedly mentions Yahweh's deliverance of the Israelites from the hand of Pharaoh and the Egyptians (vv. 1, 4, 8, 9, 10). The Israelites are no longer the slaves of Pharaoh and the Egyptians. Instead, having arrived at Mount Sinai, the Israelites are living under the commands and instructions of Yahweh. A different kind of Israelite identity will take place at Mount Sinai in Exod 19-40.

In the second scene of Exod 18 (vv. 13-27), through Moses, Israel inquires of Yahweh (Exod 18:15, 19), and Moses embodies the instruction and judgment of Yahweh in their midst (Exod 18:16, 20-22). After Israel has been brought out of Egypt and led through the Red Sea and the wilderness, through Moses, they as the delivered people need to learn and know more about Yahweh who delivered them from Egypt and will reveal himself to them on Mount Sinai.[41] Through Moses, Yahweh will help the delivered people, Israel, learn and know who he is and how to live as his people, so that they may properly walk in his way and do his work (Exod 18:20).[42]

The identity of the Israelites as the chosen servant of Yahweh in Exod 18:13-27 anticipates Yahweh's self-revelation to his own people, the Israelites, at Mount Sinai throughout Exod 19-40.

In Exod 18, Jethro's appeal to Moses to "obey me" (Exod 18:19), along with the narrator's report that Moses did so (Exod 18:24), anticipates language of Yahweh's special summons to the Israelites in the coming chapter to be his chosen servant. On Mount Sinai, Yahweh calls Moses to say to the Israelites, "Then, now, if you will surely obey me, and you will keep my covenant, then you shall be to me a treasured possession from all the peoples because all the earth belongs to me, and you shall be to me a kingdom of priests and a holy nation" (Exod 19:5-6).[43] This is Yahweh's

41. Osborn and Hatton, *Exodus*, 426, note, "Even with these technical problems, however, the chapter [Exod 18] serves a special function in the structure of the book [the Book of Exodus]. First of all, it shows how a working relationship between Moses and the people had to be reached before an effective relationship between the people and Yahweh could be achieved."

42. Fretheim, *Exodus*, 197-98, notes, "God's redemptive activity does not respond to Israel's every need. Those who have experienced the salvation of God are not thereby given an answer to all the issues or problems faced by their community. They are indeed freed from bondage, but freedom brings with it new opportunities and responsibilities. However much redemption may bring with it new perspectives and energies for such tasks, those who are redeemed are in need of other resources for life beyond the salvific experience."

43. Fretheim, "Exodus, Book of," *DOTP* 255, notes, "The vocational covenant is defined in Exodus 19:5-6: Israel is to be a priestly kingdom and a holy nation. Israel is to function among the nations as a priest functions at the tabernacle. Israel is set apart not only *from* other peoples but *for* a specific purpose in relation to those

command for the Israelites to obey Yahweh and keep his covenant, so that they may properly be his chosen servant as he has commanded. In other words, Yahweh's chosen people, the Israelites, are called to be his own people as a priestly and holy nation in the midst of all the nations by the acts of obeying Yahweh and keeping his commandments.[44] Before Yahweh's descent in a thick cloud on Mount Sinai, Yahweh instructs Moses to consecrate the Israelites and let them wash their garments (Exod 19:10–15). Since Yahweh is holy, his people as "a holy nation" must be set apart and holy in his presence (cf. Exod 3:5).

The verb עבד, "to work, to serve,"[45] occurs thirty-one times in the book of Exodus. Throughout Exod 1–17, this verb is used in two ways: (1) In Egypt, the Israelites work (עבד) hard for Pharaoh and the Egyptians (Exod 1:14; 5:18; 14:5, 12 [twice]), or Pharaoh and the Egyptians cause the Israelites to work (עבד) hard (Exod 1:13; 6:5). And (2) the Israelites will be let go out of Egypt to serve (עבד) Yahweh at Mount Sinai (Exod 3:12; 4:23; 7:16; 8:1, 20; 9:1, 13; 10:3, 7, 8, 11, 24, 26 [twice]; 12:31).

Throughout Exod 19–40, Yahweh demands his chosen servant, the Israelites, to serve (עבד) him alone (Exod 23:25).[46] To obey Yahweh and keep his commandments mean to serve only Yahweh, the jealous God (Exod 20:5; 34:14), the God of Israel (Exod 24:10; 32:27; 34:23), the merciful and gracious God (Exod 34:6), their God (Exod 20:2, 5, 7, 10, 12; 23:19, 25; 29:45, 46; 34:24, 26), and not to serve (עבד) other gods (Exod 20:5; cf. 23:24, 33), whether a golden calf (Exod 32:1, 4, 8, 23, 31) or gods of the inhabitants in the Promised Land, the land of Canaan (Exod 23:23–33; 34:12–16). Yahweh delivered the Israelites from Egyptian slavery to divine service and has called them to be to him "a treasured possession from all the peoples," "a kingdom of priests," and "a holy nation" (Exod 19:5–6), so that as his people, they may serve (עבד) him alone (Exod 23:25). When the Israelites show themselves to be "a stiff-necked people" (Exod 32:9; 33:3, 5; 34:9), worshiping and

---

nations, for, as God says, 'the whole earth is mine' (see Ex 9:29; 1 Pet 2:9 picks up on this understanding)."

44. Fretheim, "Exodus, Book of," *DOTP* 255, notes, "Israel's obedience of the law, while certainly in the best interests of its own life as a community, is finally in service of the vocation to which it has been called by God (Ex 19:5–6; cf. Deut 4:6)."

45. BDB, s.v. עָבַד, 712–13.

46. Fretheim, *Exodus*, 200, notes, "Rather, the people of God, both as individuals and as community, should accept its common dependence upon general human experience in the world for much of what they do, recognizing that God the Creator has been powerfully at work in that sphere in the interests of the well-being of all."

sacrificing to a golden calf idol, a great sin and rebellion against Yahweh, the Lord shows himself to be:

> A God, merciful and gracious, slow to anger, and abounding in steadfast love and faithfulness, keeping steadfast love for thousands, forgiving iniquity and transgression and sin, but he will surely not leave unpunished, visiting iniquity of fathers on sons and on sons of sons to the third generation and to the fourth generation (Exod 34:6–7).

Indeed, Yahweh is the God whom the stiff-necked people, the Israelites, need, the One who forgives their sins and gives them peace and even life.[47]

As the chosen servant of Yahweh, the Israelites receive through Moses all of Yahweh's statutes, laws, and covenant (Exod 20–23; 31:12–17; 34:10–28; 35:1–3) and Yahweh's instructions for the tabernacle and all its furniture and priesthood (Exod 25:1–31:11; 35:4–19, 30–36:1; 40:1–15). All of these will shape the Israelites to be Yahweh's people whom Yahweh delivered from the land of Egypt, the house of slavery (Exod 19:4; 20:2; 29:46; 32:11; cf. 32:1, 7, 23; 33:1). Through Moses, Yahweh's mediator, the Israelites learn and know who Yahweh is and how to live as his people, so that they may properly walk in his right way, that is, the way through Yahweh's statutes, laws, and covenant (Exod 20–23), and do his proper work, that is, the work through Yahweh's instructions for the tabernacle (Exod 25:1–31:17). Whereas Yahweh warned the Israelites *not* to serve (עָבַד) other gods (Exod 20:5; 23:24, 33), the Israelites failed to heed Yahweh's warnings and chose to disobey him by serving (or worshiping) a golden calf (Exod 32:1, 4, 8, 23, 31). Indeed, the Israelites received Yahweh's punishment (Exod 32:20, 25–28, 33–35). After that, Yahweh showed his merciful forgiveness (Exod 34:9) to the Israelites, including his presence in their midst (Exod 40:38). The chosen servant of Yahweh, the Israelites, must serve Yahweh as their only God.

Therefore, Exod 18 serves a transitional function by bringing closure to the theme of the Israelites serving Pharaoh and the Egyptians with heavy and bitter work in the land of Egypt in the first half

---

47. Lawlor, "'At-Sinai Narrative,'" 32, notes, "The juxtaposition of these two bodies of legal expression [the Decalogue and the Book of Covenant] at this point in the at-Sinai narrative signals a dramatic change of status for these recently released 'servants of Pharaoh and Egypt' (Exod 5:15; 14:12). YHWH initiates a covenant relationship with them and takes them as his people (Exod 6:7), presenting himself to them as their great king."

of the book of Exodus (Exod 1–17). The Israelites are free from being the Egyptian slaves through Yahweh's mighty acts of deliverance and now, as the chosen servant of Yahweh, live under Yahweh's commands and instructions. By serving as the prospective function, Exod 18 also anticipates the second half of the book of Exodus (Exod 19–40) and exhibits the Israelites as the divinely-chosen servant serving Yahweh as their sole God at Mount Sinai.

In conclusion, as discussed above, these five themes—(1) the salvation of Yahweh from an internal threat through Yahweh's gracious forgiveness, (2) the presence of Yahweh in specific places in the midst of the Israelites, (3) the knowledge of Yahweh by Yahweh's self-revelation through his statutes and laws, covenant, and merciful forgiveness, (4) Moses as the judge to the Israelites, and (5) the Israelites as the chosen servant of Yahweh—receive transitional impetus and are prospectively anticipated by Exod 18, further suggesting Exod 18 as the key transitional midpoint of the Exodus narrative.

– Chapter 7 –
Conclusion

IN SUMMARY, THIS STUDY has argued that Exod 18:1–27 functions literarily and theologically as the key transitional midpoint in the Exodus narrative.

Our literary-narrative analysis of Exod 18 has presented a strong case for the literary unity and coherence of this chapter, with key words and repeated phrases unifying both of its two halves (vv. 1–12 and 13–27) and the chapter as a whole. The consistent setting at Mount Sinai and the two-day sequence of time, along with the prominence of the characters of Jethro and Moses, also serve to unify this chapter. The chapter is further structured as a unit by the inclusio of Jethro's arrival (v. 5) and departure (v. 27b).

The exploration of the strong transitional nature of Exod 18 provided in this study strengthens the argument that, while the episode may be presented out of its strict chronological sequence within the Exodus narrative, it is not situated by the narrator haphazardly. Instead, narrated prior to the Sinai theophany, lawgiving, and covenant of the succeeding chapters, it serves to draw the first narrative movement of mighty deliverance to its close and to anticipate the life of the Israelites under Yahweh's law and justice through Moses' mediation in the chapters to come. This sets the stage for and necessitates the climactic revelation of Yahweh's rescuing forgiveness in the second half of the Exodus narrative.

The placement of Exod 18 also highlights and utilizes the character of Jethro for literary and thematic purposes. In particular, the re-appearance of Jethro in Exod 18 creates an inclusio around the first narrative

CONCLUSION

movement of deliverance. Jethro's re-appearance here, as he hears of Yahweh's great deeds for the Israelites and acknowledges Yahweh's incomparability among all gods, stands in stark contrast not only with the stubborn refusal of Pharaoh to acknowledge Yahweh but also with the hostility of the Amalekites in the preceding chapter (Exod 17:8–16). Jethro is presented as the ideal Gentile, who faithfully acknowledges, worships, and trusts in Yahweh throughout Exod 18. He is also set up as a foil to the Israelites' own mistrust and disobedience in the chapters which follow. Thus, Jethro plays an essential role in Exod 18's function both retrospectively and prospectively as the key transitional midpoint of the Exodus narrative, drawing to a close the contrasting Gentile responses to Yahweh in Exod 1–17 and anticipating the Israelites' often contrasting response to Yahweh in Exod 19–40.

It is significant that Jethro's arrival in Exod 18 is a *re-appearance* within the Exodus narrative. Exodus 18 functions retrospectively as the key transitional midpoint of the Exodus narrative, by pairing with Exod 2:16–4:26, the only other previous Jethro scene, as an inclusio through key literary and theological elements: (1) the characters of Moses, Jethro, Zipporah, and son(s); (2) the actions of (a) saving (ישע)/delivering (נצל) Jethro's seven daughters from the hand of shepherds (מִיַּד הָרֹעִים) (Exod 2:17, 19) and delivering (נצל) Moses from the sword of Pharaoh (מֵחֶרֶב פַּרְעֹה) (Exod 18:4)/delivering (נצל) Israel from the hand of Pharaoh and the Egyptians (מִיַּד פַּרְעֹה/מִצְרָיִם) (Exod 18:8, 9, 10) and (b) eating (אכל) bread (לֶחֶם) (Exod 2:20; 18:12); and (3) Jethro's concern regarding Moses' peace/welfare, indicated by his repetition of the word שָׁלוֹם (Exod 4:18; 18:7, 23).

This book has especially examined the transitional function of Exod 18 by considering certain literary themes and their development within the Exodus narrative: (1) the salvation of Yahweh, (2) the presence of Yahweh, (3) the knowledge of Yahweh, (4) the role of Moses as the judge, and (5) the identity of the Israelites.

With respect to the theme of Yahweh's salvation (and the nature of Yahweh's salvation), Exod 18 functions both retrospectively and prospectively as the key transitional midpoint of the Exodus narrative, turning from *Yahweh's deliverance of the Israelites from external threats—Pharaoh and the Egyptians, thirst, hunger, thirst, and the Amalekites—through Yahweh's mighty acts of deliverance*, as narrated in Exod 1–17 to *Yahweh's deliverance of the Israelites from an internal threat—the Israelites' own sin and stiff-necked idolatry—through Yahweh's gracious forgiveness,* as narrated in Exod 19–40. Exodus 18's summative, emphatic focus on Yahweh's accomplished salvation of the Israelites concludes the preceding narrative of Yahweh's mighty deliverance from powers and dangers which threatened the Israelites in the land of Egypt, at the Red Sea, and on the wilderness journey to Mount Sinai throughout Exod 1–17, thus fulfilling the original declaration of Yahweh to Moses at Mount Horeb, "and I have come down to deliver them [the Israelites] from the hand of the Egyptians" (Exod 3:8; cf. 3:10, 17; 6:6). Exodus 18 also serves to anticipate a situation—the Israelites under Yahweh's commandments and justice—in which a new kind of deliverance will be required: Yahweh's gracious forgiveness toward the Israelites in the face of their great sin and rebellion against his commandments (Exod 20–23) in the golden calf event at Mount Sinai (Exod 32–34). The role of Moses within the Exodus narrative also undergoes a definite shift—certainly a shift in emphasis, at least—here at Exod 18. In the preceding chapters, Moses is the agent of Yahweh's mighty deliverance: from Egypt, thirst, hunger, thirst, and Amalek. In the succeeding chapters, Moses will be primarily the agent of Yahweh's lawgiving and justice, as well as the intercessor on behalf of the Israelites, pleading for and securing Yahweh's mercy.

With respect to the theme of Yahweh's presence, Exod 18 functions both retrospectively and prospectively as the key transitional midpoint of the Exodus narrative, turning from *Yahweh's presence in various places, such as the mountain of God/Mount Horeb, the burning bush, the land of Midian, the land of Egypt, the pillars of cloud and fire, the Red Sea, the wilderness, and the mountain of God/Mount Sinai*, as presented in Exod 1–17 to *Yahweh's presence in specific places in the midst of the Israelites, such as the mountain of God/Mount Horeb or Sinai, the tent of meeting, and the tabernacle*, as presented in Exod 19–40. Retrospectively, Exod 18 serves to conclude the preceding narratives (Exod 3–17) with Yahweh's presence in various locations as a full circle by beginning and ending with the same location, that is, the mountain of God/Mount Horeb or Sinai (Exod 3:1; 18:5) and serves to fulfill the original declaration of Yahweh to Moses at the mountain of God, "I will be with you, and this is the sign for you that I have sent you: when you have brought the people out of Egypt, you shall serve God on this mountain" (Exod 3:12; cf. 3:18; 4:23; 5:1, 3; 7:16; 8:1, 20, 27; 9:1, 13; 10:3). Prospectively, Exod 18 signals the narrative transition to a strongly located divine presence in the midst of the Israelite camp throughout the second half of the book of Exodus: in theophany at the mountain of God and, ultimately, in the glory-presence of Yahweh in the tabernacle (Exod 19–40).

With respect to the theme of the knowledge of Yahweh, Exod 18 again functions both retrospectively and prospectively as the key transitional midpoint of the Exodus narrative, turning from *the knowledge of Yahweh by Yahweh's self-revelation through his mighty acts of deliverance*, as recorded in Exod 1–17 to *the knowledge of Yahweh by Yahweh's self-revelation through his statutes and laws, covenant, and merciful forgiveness*, as recorded in Exod 19–40. Much of the first half of the book of Exodus is fueled by the defiance of Pharaoh in Exod 5:2, "Who is Yahweh that I should obey him by letting Israel go? I do not know Yahweh, and also I will not let Israel go." Yahweh has declared that a central purpose of his mighty acts of deliverance is to make himself known to Pharaoh, to the Egyptians, and to all the nations, "But because of this, I have raised you [Pharaoh] up to show you [Pharaoh] my power and to recount my name in all the earth" (Exod 9:16). Exodus 18 draws this first narrative movement to a close by describing the attainment of Yahweh's purpose: both the general recounting of the deeds of Yahweh as far as the land of Midian (Exod 18:1) and the specific acknowledgement of Yahweh by Jethro: "Now, I know that Yahweh is greater than all gods" (Exod 18:11). At the same time, this transitional chapter serves to anticipate a new self-revelation of Yahweh through his statutes and laws, covenant, and merciful forgiveness through Moses alone as the mediator of Yahweh throughout the second half of the Exodus narrative (Exod 19–40). The theme of the knowledge of Yahweh serves as a narrative pivot in terms of character roles as well, since, throughout Exod 4–17, Yahweh directs and commands the Israelites, Pharaoh, and the Egyptians through both Moses and Aaron as Yahweh's representatives, but Exod 18 emphasizes that henceforth Moses alone will direct and command the Israelites as Yahweh's mediator at Mount Sinai throughout Exod 19–40.

With respect to the theme of Moses' role as the judge, that is, as the executor of judgment, Exod 18 again functions both retrospectively and prospectively as the key transitional midpoint of the Exodus narrative, turning from *Moses' role as the judge, acting as "God" to Pharaoh and the Egyptians*, as recounted in Exod 1–17 to *Moses' role as the judge to the Israelites*, as recounted in Exod 19–40. The judicial scene in Exod 18 forms an inclusio with the earlier judicial scene in Exod 2:11–14 by providing the answer to the struggling Israelite's question, "Who made you [Moses] a prince and a judge over us?" (Exod 2:14). Exodus 18 also concludes the preceding account of judgment toward Pharaoh and the Egyptians by all the wonders which Yahweh revealed to Moses and commanded Moses to perform in the land of Egypt and at the Red Sea (Exod 7:14–12:36; 14:1–31). At the same time, the emphatic role of Moses as the judge *over the Israelites* in Exod 18 also anticipates a new aspect of Yahweh's justice executed through Moses against the Israelites, in a restrained and preliminary way, in the climactic scene of the second half of the Exodus narrative, the episode of the golden calf at Mount Sinai (Exod 32:20, 25–28).

Finally, with respect to the theme of the Israelites' identity, Exod 18 has a clear transitional sense, turning from *the Israelite identity as the slaves of Egypt/Pharaoh*, as reported in Exod 1–17 (persisting in the minds and hearts of the Israelites even into the wilderness chapters) to *the Israelite identity as the chosen servant of Yahweh*, as reported in Exod 19–40. Whereas Exod 18 serves to conclude the Israelite identity as the physical and mental slaves of Egypt throughout Exod 1–17, it serves to anticipate a new kind of the Israelite identity as the divinely-chosen servant in the second half of the book of Exodus, dramatically articulated by Yahweh in Exod 19:5–6 and embodied by the Israelites' willing and obedient construction of the tabernacle in Exod 35–40.

In conclusion, Exod 18:1–27 (rather than other options which have been proposed) functions literarily and theologically as the key transitional midpoint in the Exodus narrative by means of the characterization of the most prominent figure of Exod 18—Jethro, the priest of Midian, the father-in-law of Moses—who comes to praise Yahweh and acknowledges Yahweh in contrast to all the nations in Exod 1–17, and who worships Yahweh and lives as a faithful and obedient person to Yahweh in contrast to all the faithless Israelites in Exod 19–40, and by means of the transitional (summative and anticipatory) functions of Exod 18 within the Exodus narrative's development of several major themes.

Bibliography

Ackerman, James S. "The Literary Context of the Moses Birth Story (Exodus 1–2)." In *Literary Interpretations of Biblical Narratives,* edited by Kenneth R. R. Gros Louis, James S. Ackerman, and Thayer S. Warshaw, 1:74–119. BLC. Nashville: Abingdon, 1974.
Albright, William Foxwell. "Jethro, Hobab and Reuel in Early Hebrew Tradition." *CBQ* 25.1 (1963) 1–11.
Alexander, T. Desmond. *Exodus.* ApOTC 2. Downers Grove, IL: InterVarsity, 2017.
Alexander, T. Desmond, and David W. Baker, eds. *Dictionary of the Old Testament: Pentateuch.* Downers Grove, IL: InterVarsity, 2003.
Alter, Robert. *The Art of Biblical Narrative.* Rev. ed. New York: Basic, 2011.
Andersen, Francis I., and A. Dean Forbes. *The Vocabulary of the Old Testament.* Rome: Pontifical Biblical Institute, 1989.
Anderson, Bernhard W. *Contours of Old Testament Theology.* Minneapolis: Fortress, 1999.
Anderson, George W. *A Critical Introduction to the Old Testament.* London: Gerald Duckworth, 1959.
Archer, Gleason L., Jr. *A Survey of Old Testament Introduction.* Rev. ed. Chicago: Moody, 1974.
Arnold, Bill T., and Bryan E. Beyer. *Encountering the Old Testament: A Christian Survey.* Edited by Eugene H. Merrill. 3rd ed. EBS. Grand Rapids: Baker Academic, 2015.
Arnold, Bill T., and John H. Choi. *A Guide to Biblical Hebrew Syntax.* 2nd ed. Cambridge: Cambridge University Press, 2018.
Ashby, Godfrey. *Go Out and Meet God: A Commentary on the Book of Exodus.* ITC. Grand Rapids: Eerdmans, 1998.
Auffret, Pierre. "The Literary Structure of Exodus 6.2–8." *JSOT* 8.27 (1983) 46–54.
———. "Remarks on J. Magonet's Interpretation of Exodus 6.2–8." *JSOT* 8.27 (1983) 69–71.
Avishur, Yitzhak. *Studies in Biblical Narrative: Style, Structure, and the Ancient Near Eastern Literary Background.* Tel Aviv: Archaeological Center, 1999.
Bacon, Benjamin Wisner. "JE in the Middle Books of the Pentateuch." *JBL* 12.1 (1893) 23–46.
Baden, Joel S. *The Composition of the Pentateuch: Renewing the Documentary Hypothesis.* Edited by John J. Collins. AYBRL. New Haven: Yale University Press, 2012.

Bailey, Randall C. *Exodus*. CPNIVC. Joplin, MO: College, 2007.
Bar-Efrat, Shimon. *Narrative Art in the Bible*. Edited by David M. Gunn. BLS 17; Edited by David J. A. Clines and Philip R. Davies. Translated by Dorothea Shefer-Vanson. JSOTSup 70. Sheffield: Almond, 1989.
Barr, James. *The Concept of Biblical Theology: An Old Testament Perspective*. Minneapolis: Fortress, 1999.
Barthélemy, Dominique. *Studies in the Text of the Old Testament: An Introduction to the Hebrew Old Testament Text Project*. Edited by Roger L. Omanson. Translated by Stephen Pisano, Peter A. Pettit, Joan E. Cook, and Sarah Lind. TCT 3. Winona Lake, IN: Eisenbrauns, 2012.
Barton, John. *Reading the Old Testament: Method in Biblical Study*. Rev. ed. Louisville: Westminster John Knox, 1996.
Ben-David, Eliezer. *Out of the Iron Furnace: The Jewish Redemption from Ancient Egypt and the Delivery from Spiritual Bondage*. Translated and adapted by Yaakov Feitman. New York: Shengold, 1975.
Ber, Viktor. "Moses and Jethro: Harmony and Conflict in the Interpretation of Exodus 18." *CV* 50.2 (2008) 147–70.
Berge, Kåre. *Reading Sources in a Text: Coherence and Literary Criticism in the Call of Moses; Models – Methods – Micro-Analysis*. Edited by Walter Groß, Hubert Irsigler, and Theodor Seidl. ATSAT 54. St. Ottilien: EOS Verlag, 1997.
Birch, Bruce C., Walter Brueggemann, Terence E. Fretheim, and David L. Petersen. *A Theological Introduction to the Old Testament*. Nashville: Abingdon, 1999.
Blackburn, W. Ross. *The God Who Makes Himself Known: The Missionary Heart of the Book of Exodus*. Edited by D. A. Carson. NSBT 28. Downers Grove, IL: InterVarsity, 2012.
Blenkinsopp, Joseph. *The Pentateuch: An Introduction to the First Five Books of the Bible*. Edited by David Noel Freedman. ABRL. New York: Doubleday, 1992.
———. "Structure and Meaning in the Sinai–Horeb Narrative (Exodus 19–34)." In *A Biblical Itinerary: In Search of Method, Form and Content: Essays in Honor of George W. Coats*, edited by Eugene E. Carpenter, 109–25. JSOTSup 240. Sheffield: Sheffield Academic, 1997.
Boadt, Lawrence. *Reading the Old Testament: An Introduction*. New York: Paulist, 1984.
Boda, Mark J. *The Heartbeat of Old Testament Theology: Three Creedal Expressions*. Edited by Craig A. Evans. ASBT. Grand Rapids: Baker Academic, 2017.
Bodner, Keith. *An Ark on the Nile: The Beginning of the Book of Exodus*. Oxford: Oxford University Press, 2016.
Botterweck, G. Johannes, Helmer Ringgren, and Heinz-Josef Fabry, eds. *Theological Dictionary of the Old Testament*. Translated by John T. Willis, Geoffrey W. Bromiley, David E. Green, and Douglas W. Stott. 15 vols. Grand Rapids: Eerdmans, 1974–2006.
Brotzman, Ellis R. *Old Testament Textual Criticism: A Practical Introduction*. Grand Rapids: Baker, 1994.
Brown, Francis, S. R. Driver, and Charles A. Briggs. *The Brown-Driver-Briggs Hebrew and English Lexicon: With an Appendix Containing the Biblical Aramaic*. Boston, MA: Houghton, Mifflin and Company, 1906. Repr., Peabody, MA: Hendrickson, 2005.
Bruckner, James K. *Exodus*. NIBCOT 2. Peabody, MA: Hendrickson, 2008.

Brueggemann, Walter. "The Book of Exodus." In *The New Interpreter's Bible: General Articles on the Bible; General Articles on the Old Testament; The Book of Genesis; The Book of Exodus; The Book of Leviticus*, edited by Leander E. Keck, 1:675–981. Nashville: Abingdon, 1994.

———. *An Introduction to the Old Testament: The Canon and Christian Imagination*. Louisville: Westminster John Knox, 2003.

———. *Theology of the Old Testament: Testimony, Dispute, Advocacy*. Minneapolis: Fortress, 1997.

Burden, Terry L. *The Kerygma of the Wilderness Traditions in the Hebrew Bible*. AUSTR 163. New York: Peter Lang, 1994.

Burns, Rita J. *Exodus, Leviticus, Numbers: With Excursuses on Feasts/Ritual and Typology*. OTM 3. Wilmington, DE: Michael Glazier, 1983.

Carmichael, Calum M. *The Origins of Biblical Law: The Decalogues and the Book of the Covenant*. Ithaca, NY: Cornell University Press, 1992.

Carpenter, Eugene. *Exodus*. 2 vols. EEC. Bellingham, WA: Lexham, 2016.

———. "Exodus 18: Its Structure, Style, Motifs and Function in the Book of Exodus." In *A Biblical Itinerary: In Search of Method, Form and Content: Essays in Honor of George W. Coats*, edited by Eugene E. Carpenter, 91–108. JSOTSup 240. Sheffield: Sheffield Academic, 1997.

Cassuto, Umberto. *A Commentary on the Book of Exodus*. Translated by Israel Abrahams. Jerusalem: Magnes, 1967.

Chen, Kevin. *Eschatological Sanctuary in Exodus 15:17 and Related Texts*. Edited by Hemchand Gossai. StBibLit 154. New York: Peter Lang, 2013.

Childs, Brevard S. *The Book of Exodus: A Critical, Theological Commentary*. OTL. Louisville: Westminster John Knox, 1974.

———. *Introduction to the Old Testament as Scripture*. Philadelphia: Fortress, 1979.

———. *Old Testament Theology in a Canonical Context*. Philadelphia: Fortress, 1986.

Chung, Youn Ho. *The Sin of the Calf: The Rise of the Bible's Negative Attitude toward the Golden Calf*. Edited by Claudia V. Camp and Andrew Mein. LHBOTS 523. New York: T&T Clark, 2010.

Clements, Ronald E. *Old Testament Theology: A Fresh Approach*. Edited by Peter Toon. MTL. London: Marshall, Morgan & Scott, 1978.

Clines, David J. A., ed. *The Dictionary of Classical Hebrew*. 8 vols. Sheffield: Sheffield Academic, 1993–2001; Sheffield: Sheffield Phoenix, 2007–2011.

Coats, George W. *Exodus 1–18*. FOTL 2A. Grand Rapids: Eerdmans, 1999.

———. "Moses as a Model for Ministry: An Exegesis of Exodus 2:11–22." *FM* 3.2 (1986) 49–57.

———. "Moses in Midian." *JBL* 92.1 (1973) 3–10.

———. *Rebellion in the Wilderness: The Murmuring Motif in the Wilderness Traditions of the Old Testament*. Nashville: Abingdon, 1968.

———. "The Song of the Sea." *CBQ* 31.1 (1969) 1–17.

———. "A Structural Transition in Exodus." *VT* 22.2 (1972) 129–42.

Cody, Aelred. "Exodus 18,12: Jethro Accepts a Covenant with the Israelites." *Bib* 49.2 (1968) 153–66.

Coggins, Richard. *Introducing the Old Testament*. Edited by P. R. Ackroyd and G. N. Stanton. 2nd ed. OBS. Oxford: Oxford University Press, 2001.

Cohen, Jeffrey M. "Jethro/Hobab's Detainment." *JBQ* 32.2 (2004) 115–21.

Cole, R. Alan. *Exodus: An Introduction and Commentary*. TOTC 2. Leicester: InterVarsity, 1973.

Collins, John J. *Introduction to the Hebrew Bible*. Minneapolis: Fortress, 2004.

Crenshaw, James L. *Old Testament Story and Faith: A Literary and Theological Introduction*. Peabody, MA: Hendrickson, 1992.

Dalglish, Edward R. *The Great Deliverance: Studies in the Book of Exodus*. Nashville: Broadman, 1977.

Dalman, Rodger. *A People Come out of Egypt: Studies in the Books of Exodus, Deuteronomy and Judges*. Conrad, MT: Send the Light Press, 2002.

Daube, David. *The Exodus Pattern in the Bible*. Westport, CT: Greenwood, 1963.

Davidson, A. B. *Hebrew Syntax*. 3rd ed. Edinburgh: T&T Clark, 1901.

———. *The Theology of the Old Testament*. Edited by S. D. F. Salmond. New York: Scribner's Sons, 1914.

Davies, G. Henton. *Exodus*. TBC. London: SCM, 1967.

Davies, Gordon F. *Israel in Egypt: Reading Exodus 1–2*. Edited by David J. A. Clines and Philip R. Davies. JSOTSup 135. Sheffield: JSOT, 1992.

Davies, John A. *A Royal Priesthood: Literary and Intertextual Perspectives on an Image of Israel in Exodus 19.6*. Edited by Claudia V. Camp and Andrew Mein. JSOTSup 395. London: T&T Clark, 2004.

Davis, John J. *Moses and the Gods of Egypt: Studies in Exodus*. 2nd ed. Winona Lake, IN: BHM, 1986.

DeLapp, Nevada Levi. *Theophanic "Type-Scenes" in the Pentateuch: Visions of YHWH*. Edited by Claudia V. Camp and Andrew Mein. LHBOTS 660. London: Bloomsbury, 2018.

Dempster, Stephen G. *Dominion and Dynasty: A Biblical Theology of the Hebrew Bible*. Edited by D. A. Carson. NSBT 15. Downers Grove, IL: InterVarsity, 2003.

Dobson, John H. *A Guide to the Book of Exodus*. Valley Forge, PA: Judson, 1977.

Dorsey, David A. *The Literary Structure of the Old Testament: A Commentary on Genesis–Malachi*. Grand Rapids: Baker, 1999.

Dozeman, Thomas B. *Exodus*. ECC. Grand Rapids: Eerdmans, 2009.

———. *God at War: Power in the Exodus Tradition*. Oxford: Oxford University Press, 1996.

———. *God on the Mountain: A Study of Redaction, Theology and Canon in Exodus 19–24*. Edited by Adela Yarbro Collins. SBLMS 37. Atlanta: Scholars, 1989.

———. *The Pentateuch: Introducing the Torah*. Minneapolis: Fortress, 2017.

Driver, S. R. *An Introduction to the Literature of the Old Testament*. ML 3. New York: Meridian Books, 1956.

Dumbrell, William J. *The Faith of Israel: A Theological Survey of the Old Testament*. 2nd ed. Grand Rapids: Baker Academic, 2002.

Durham, John I. *Exodus*. WBC 3. Waco, TX: Word, 1987.

Dyrness, William. *Themes in Old Testament Theology*. Downers Grove, IL: InterVarsity, 1979.

Egger, Thomas J. "'Visiting Iniquity of Fathers against Sons' in Exodus." PhD diss., Concordia Seminary, 2019.

Eichrodt, Walther. *Theology of the Old Testament*. Edited by G. Ernest Wright, John Bright, James Barr, and Peter Ackroyd. Translated by J. A. Baker. 2 vols. OTL. London: SCM, 1961; Louisville: Westminster John Knox, 1967.

Eissfeldt, Otto. *The Old Testament: An Introduction*. Translated by Peter R. Ackroyd. New York: Harper & Row, 1965.
Ellis, Peter F. *The Men and the Message of the Old Testament*. Collegeville, MN: Liturgical, 1963.
Ellison, H. L. *Exodus*. DSB. Louisville: Westminster John Knox, 1982.
Enns, Peter. *Exodus*. NIVAC. Grand Rapids: Zondervan, 2000.
Erdman, Charles R. *The Book of Exodus*. Grand Rapids: Baker, 1949.
Eslinger, Lyle. "Freedom or Knowledge? Perspective and Purpose in the Exodus Narrative (Exodus 1–15)." In *The Pentateuch: A Sheffield Reader*, edited by John W. Rogerson, 186–202. BibSem 39. Sheffield: Sheffield Academic, 1996.
———. "Knowing Yahweh: Exod 6:3 in the Context of Genesis 1–Exodus 15." In *Literary Structure and Rhetorical Strategies in the Hebrew Bible*, edited by L. J. de Regt, J. de Waard, and J. P. Fokkelman, 188–98. Winona Lake, IN: Eisenbrauns, 1996.
Esses, Michael. *Jesus in Exodus*. Plainfield, NJ: Logos, 1977.
Even-Shoshan, Abraham, ed. *A New Concordance of the Bible: Thesaurus of the Language of the Bible Hebrew and Aramaic Roots, Words, Proper Names, Phrases, and Synonyms*. Jerusalem: Kiryat Sefer, 1990.
Finegan, Jack. *Let My People Go: A Journey through Exodus*. New York: Harper & Row, 1963.
Fokkelman, J. P. "Exodus." In *The Literary Guide to the Bible*, edited by Robert Alter and Frank Kermode, 56–65. Cambridge: Harvard University Press, 1987.
———. *Narrative Art in Genesis: Specimens of Stylistic and Structural Analysis*. Edited by M. A. Beek, J. H. Hospers, Th. C. Vriezen, and R. Frankena. SSN 17. Assen: Van Gorcum, 1975.
———. *Reading Biblical Narrative: An Introductory Guide*. Translated by Ineke Smit. Leiderdorp: Deo, 1999.
Ford, William A. *God, Pharaoh and Moses: Explaining the Lord's Actions in the Exodus Plagues Narrative*. Edited by I. Howard Marshall, Richard J. Bauckham, Craig Blomberg, Robert P. Gordon, and Tremper Longman III. PBM. Eugene, OR: Wipf & Stock, 2006.
Fox, Everett. *Now These Are the Names: A New English Rendition of the Book of Exodus*. New York: Schocken, 1986.
Freedman, Amelia Devin. *God as an Absent Character in Biblical Hebrew Narrative: A Literary-Theoretical Study*. Edited by Hemchand Gossai. StBibLit 82. New York: Peter Lang, 2005.
Freedman, David Noel, ed. *The Anchor Bible Dictionary*. 6 vols. New York: Doubleday, 1992.
Fretheim, Terence E. *Exodus*. Int. Louisville: Westminster John Knox, 1991.
———. *The Pentateuch*. Edited by Gene M. Tucker. IBT. Nashville: Abingdon, 1996.
Garrett, Duane A. *A Commentary on Exodus*. KEL. Grand Rapids: Kregel, 2014.
Gavigan, James, Brian McCarthy, and Thomas McGovern, eds. *The Navarre Bible: The Pentateuch*. Princeton, NJ: Scepter, 1999.
Geisler, Norman L. *A Popular Survey of the Old Testament*. Grand Rapids: Baker, 1977.
Gibson, J. C. L. *Davidson's Introductory Hebrew Grammar-Syntax*. 4th ed. Edinburgh: T&T Clark, 1994.
Gignilliat, Mark S. *A Brief History of Old Testament Criticism: From Benedict Spinoza to Brevard Childs*. Grand Rapids: Zondervan, 2012.

Gispen, W. H. *Exodus*. Translated by Ed van der Maas. BSC. Grand Rapids: Zondervan, 1982.
Goldberg, Michael. *Jews and Christians, Getting Our Stories Straight: The Exodus and the Passion-Resurrection*. Nashville: Abingdon, 1985.
Goldingay, John. *Old Testament Theology*. 3 vols. Downers Grove, IL: InterVarsity, 2003–2009.
Gorospe, Athena E. *Narrative and Identity: An Ethical Reading of Exodus 4*. Edited by R. Alan Culpepper and Ellen van Wolde. BibInt 86. Leiden: Brill, 2007.
Gowan, Donald E. *Theology in Exodus: Biblical Theology in the Form of a Commentary*. Louisville: Westminster John Knox, 1994.
Greenberg, Moshe. *Understanding Exodus: The Heritage of Biblical Israel*. MRCS 2.1. New York: Behrman House, 1969.
Greifenhagen, F. V. *Egypt on the Pentateuch's Ideological Map: Constructing Biblical Israel's Identity*. Edited by David J. A. Clines and Philip R. Davies. JSOTSup 361. Sheffield: Sheffield Academic, 2002.
Gunn, David M., and Danna Nolan Fewell. *Narrative in the Hebrew Bible*. Edited by P. R. Ackroyd and G. N. Stanton. OBS. Oxford: Oxford University Press, 1993.
Gurtner, Daniel M. *Exodus: A Commentary on the Greek Text of Codex Vaticanus*. SEPT. Leiden: Brill, 2013.
Gutzke, Manford George. *Plain Talk on Exodus*. Grand Rapids: Zondervan, 1974.
Hamilton, Victor P. *Exodus: An Exegetical Commentary*. Grand Rapids: Baker Academic, 2011.
———. *Handbook on the Pentateuch: Genesis, Exodus, Leviticus, Numbers, Deuteronomy*. 2nd ed. Grand Rapids: Baker Academic, 2005.
Harrelson, Walter. *Interpreting the Old Testament*. New York: Holt, Rinehart & Winston, 1964.
Harrington, Daniel J., S.J. *Interpreting the Old Testament: A Practical Guide*. Edited by Carroll Stuhlmueller and Martin McNamara. OTM 1. Wilmington, DE: Michael Glazier, 1982.
Harris, R. Laird, Gleason L. Archer, Jr., and Bruce K. Waltke, eds. *Theological Wordbook of the Old Testament*. 2 vols. Chicago: Moody, 1980.
Harrison, R. K. *Introduction to the Old Testament: With a Comprehensive Review of Old Testament Studies and a Special Supplement on the Apocrypha*. Grand Rapids: Eerdmans, 1969.
Hauge, Martin Ravndal. *The Descent from the Mountain: Narrative Patterns in Exodus 19–40*. Edited by David J. A. Clines and Philip R. Davies. JSOTSup 323. Sheffield: Sheffield Academic, 2001.
Hayes, John H., and Frederick C. Prussner. *Old Testament Theology: Its History and Development*. Louisville: Westminster John Knox, 1985.
Hebert, Gabriel. *When Israel Came out of Egypt*. SCMBC 143. London: SCM, 1961.
Heinisch, Paul. *Theology of the Old Testament*. Translated by William Heidt. Collegeville, MN: Liturgical, 1950.
House, Paul R., ed. *Beyond Form Criticism: Essays in Old Testament Literary Criticism*. Edited by David W. Baker. SBTS 2. Winona Lake, IN: Eisenbrauns, 1992.
———. *Old Testament Theology*. Downers Grove, IL: InterVarsity, 1998.
Houtman, Cornelis. *Exodus*. Translated by Johan Rebel and Sierd Woudstra. 4 vols. HCOT. Kampen: Kok, 1993–1996; Leuven: Peeters, 2000–2002.
Huey, F. B., Jr. *Exodus*. BiStC. Grand Rapids: Zondervan, 1977.

Hummel, Horace D. *The Word Becoming Flesh: An Introduction to the Origin, Purpose, and Meaning of the Old Testament*. St. Louis: Concordia, 1979.
Hyatt, J. Philip. *Exodus*. NCB. London: Oliphants, 1971.
Isbell, Charles. "Exodus 1–2 in the Context of Exodus 1–14: Story Lines and Key Words." In *Art and Meaning: Rhetoric in Biblical Literature*, edited by David J. A. Clines, David M. Gunn, and Alan J. Hauser, 37–61. JSOTSup 19. Sheffield: JSOT, 1982.
———. *The Function of Exodus Motifs in Biblical Narratives: Theological Didactic Drama*. SBEC 52. Lewiston, NY: Mellen, 2002.
Jacob, Benno. *The Second Book of the Bible: Exodus*. Translated by Walter Jacob. New Jersey: Ktav, 1992.
Jacob, Edmond. *Theology of the Old Testament*. Translated by Arthur W. Heathcote and Philip J. Allcock. New York: Harper & Row, 1958.
Janzen, Waldemar. *Exodus*. BCBC. Waterloo, ON: Herald, 2000.
———. "Jethro in the Structure of the Book of Exodus." In *The Old Testament in the Life of God's People: Essays in Honor of Elmer A. Martens*, edited by Jon Isaak, 159–72. Winona Lake, IN: Eisenbrauns, 2009.
Jenni, Ernst, and Claus Westermann. *Theological Lexicon of the Old Testament*. Translated by Mark E. Biddle. 3 vols. Peabody, MA: Hendrickson, 1997.
Jensen, Joseph. *God's Word to Israel*. Rev. ed. Wilmington, DE: Glazier, 1982.
Jeon, Jaeyoung. "The Visit of Jethro (Exodus 18): Its Composition and Levitical Reworking." *JBL* 136.2 (2017) 289–306.
Johnstone, William. *Chronicles and Exodus: An Analogy and Its Application*. Edited by David J. A. Clines and Philip R. Davies. JSOTSup 275. Sheffield: Sheffield Academic, 1998.
———. *Exodus*. 2 vols. SHBC 2a–2b. Macon, GA: Smyth & Helwys, 2014.
———. *Exodus*. Edited by R. N. Whybray. OTG. Sheffield: JSOT, 1990.
Jordan, James B. *The Law of the Covenant: An Exposition of Exodus 21–23*. Tyler, TX: Institute for Christian Economics, 1984.
Joüon, Paul, S.J. *A Grammar of Biblical Hebrew*. Translated and revised by T. Muraoka. 2 vols. SubBi 14/1–14/2. Rome: Pontifical Biblical Institute, 1991.
Kaiser, Otto. *Introduction to the Old Testament: A Presentation of Its Results and Problems*. Translated by John Sturdy. Minneapolis: Augsburg, 1975.
Kaiser, Walter C., Jr. *The Christian and the "Old" Testament*. Pasadena, CA: William Carey Library, 1998.
———. "Exodus." In *The Expositor's Bible Commentary: Genesis–Numbers*, edited by Frank E. Gaebelein, 2:285–497. Grand Rapids: Zondervan, 1990.
Kautzsch, E., ed. *Gesenius' Hebrew Grammar*. Translated by A. E. Cowley. 2nd ed. Oxford: Clarendon, 1910.
Keil, C. F., and F. Delitzsch. *The Pentateuch*. Vol. 1 of *Commentary on the Old Testament*. Translated by James Martin. Grand Rapids: Eerdmans, 1975.
Kelle, Brad E. *Telling the Old Testament Story: God's Mission and God's People*. Nashville: Abingdon, 2017.
Kessler, John. *Old Testament Theology: Divine Call and Human Response*. Waco, TX: Baylor University Press, 2013.
Klein, Ralph W. *Textual Criticism of the Old Testament: The Septuagint after Qumran*. Edited by Gene M. Tucker. GBS. Philadelphia: Fortress, 1974.
Knight, George A. F. *A Christian Theology of the Old Testament*. London: SCM, 1959.

———. *Theology as Narration: A Commentary on the Book of Exodus*. Grand Rapids: Eerdmans, 1976.

Koehler, Ludwig, and Walter Baumgartner. *The Hebrew and Aramaic Lexicon of the Old Testament*. Translated and edited by M. E. J. Richardson. 2 vols. Leiden: Brill, 2001.

Kok, Johnson Lim Teng. *The Sin of Moses and the Staff of God: A Narrative Approach*. Edited by W. J. van Bekkum, W. A. M. Beuken, H. Daiber, C. H. J. de Geus, J. Hoftijzer, T. Muraoka, W. S. Prinsloo, K. A. D. Smelik, K. van der Toorn, and K. R. Veenhof. SSN 35. Assen: Van Gorcum, 1997.

Kuhl, Curt. *The Old Testament: Its Origins and Composition*. Translated by C. T. M. Herriott. Edinburgh: Oliver & Boyd, 1961.

Kuntz, J. Kenneth. *The People of Ancient Israel: An Introduction to Old Testament Literature, History, and Thought*. New York: Harper & Row, 1974.

Kürle, Stefan. *The Appeal of Exodus: The Characters God, Moses and Israel in the Rhetoric of the Book of Exodus*. Edited by I. Howard Marshall, Richard J. Bauckham, Craig Blomberg, Robert P. Gordon, Tremper Longman III, and Stanley E. Porter. PBM. Milton Keynes: Paternoster, 2013.

Lamsa, George M. *Old Testament Light: A Scriptural Commentary Based on the Aramaic of the Ancient Peshitta Text*. Englewood Cliffs, NJ: Prentice Hall, 1964.

Lane, Nathan C. *The Compassionate, but Punishing God: A Canonical Analysis of Exodus 34:6–7*. Eugene, OR: Pickwick, 2010.

Langston, Scott M. *Exodus through the Centuries*. BBC. Malden, MA: Blackwell, 2006.

Larsson, Göran. *Bound for Freedom: The Book of Exodus in Jewish and Christian Traditions*. Peabody, MA: Hendrickson, 1999.

LaSor, William Sanford, David Allan Hubbard, and Frederic Wm. Bush. *Old Testament Survey: The Message, Form, and Background of the Old Testament*. Grand Rapids: Eerdmans, 1982.

Law, Henry. *The Gospel in Exodus*. Memphis, TN: Bottom of the Hill, 2013.

Lawlor, John I. "The 'At-Sinai Narrative': Exodus 18–Numbers 10." *BBR* 21.1 (2011) 23–42.

Lemche, Niels Peter. *The Old Testament between Theology and History: A Critical Survey*. Louisville: Westminster John Knox, 2008.

Lerner, Phillip. "Redefining התלאה: An Assurance of Israel's Return to the Land in Jethro's Covenant." *Bib* 87.3 (2006) 402–11.

Lessing, R. Reed, and Andrew E. Steinmann. *Prepare the Way of the Lord: An Introduction to the Old Testament*. St. Louis: Concordia, 2014.

Leveen, Adriane. "Inside Out: Jethro, the Midianites and a Biblical Construction of the Outsider." *JSOT* 34.4 (2010) 395–417.

Lienhard, Joseph T., S.J., ed. *Exodus, Leviticus, Numbers, Deuteronomy*. ACCSOT 3. Downers Grove, IL: InterVarsity, 2001.

Lindqvist, Pekka. *Sin at Sinai: Early Judaism Encounters Exodus 32*. Edited by Antti Laato. SRB 2. Åbo: Åbo Akademi University, 2008.

Longman, Tremper, III. *How to Read Exodus*. Downers Grove, IL: InterVarsity, 2009.

Longman, Tremper, III, and Raymond B. Dillard. *An Introduction to the Old Testament*. 2nd ed. Grand Rapids: Zondervan, 2006.

Magonet, Jonathan. "A Response to 'The Literary Structure of Exodus 6.2–8' by Pierre Auffret." *JSOT* 8.27 (1983) 73–74.

———. "The Rhetoric of God: Exodus 6.2–8." *JSOT* 8.27 (1983) 56–67.

Malina, Bruce J. *The Palestinian Manna Tradition: The Manna Tradition in the Palestinian Targums and Its Relationship to the New Testament Writings*. Edited by Otto Michel. AGSJU 7. Leiden: Brill, 1968.
Mangano, Mark, ed. *Old Testament Introduction*. CPNIVC. Joplin, MO: College, 2005.
Mann, Thomas W. *The Book of the Torah: The Narrative Integrity of the Pentateuch*. Louisville: Westminster John Knox, 1988.
Marshall, Jay W. *Israel and the Book of the Covenant: An Anthropological Approach to Biblical Law*. Edited by David L. Petersen. SBLDS 140. Atlanta: Scholars, 1993.
Martens, Elmer A. *God's Design: A Focus on Old Testament Theology*. 3rd ed. N. Richland Hills, TX: Bibal, 1998.
Mathews, Danny. *Royal Motifs in the Pentateuchal Portrayal of Moses*. Edited by Claudia V. Camp and Andrew Mein. LHBOTS 571. New York: T&T Clark, 2012.
McCarter, P. Kyle, Jr. *Textual Criticism: Recovering the Text of the Hebrew Bible*. Edited by Gene M. Tucker. GBS. Philadelphia: Fortress, 1986.
McEntire, Mark. *Struggling with God: An Introduction to the Pentateuch*. Macon, GA: Mercer University Press, 2008.
Mellor, Enid B., ed. *The Making of the Old Testament*. Edited by P. R. Ackroyd, A. R. C. Leaney, and J. W. Packer. CBC. Cambridge: Cambridge University Press, 1972.
Menezes, Rui de, S.J. *God of Israel or God of All? Goal and Function of the Pentateuch*. Mumbai: Bombay Saint Paul Society, 2010.
Meyer, F. B. *Devotional Commentary on Exodus*. Grand Rapids: Kregel, 1978.
Meyer, Lester. *The Message of Exodus: A Theological Commentary*. Minneapolis: Augsburg, 1983.
Meyers, Carol. *Exodus*. NCBC. Cambridge: Cambridge University Press, 2005.
Mitchell, Christopher Wright. *The Meaning of BRK "to Bless" in the Old Testament*. Edited by J. J. M. Roberts. SBLDS 95. Atlanta: Scholars, 1987.
Moberly, R. W. L. *At the Mountain of God: Story and Theology in Exodus 32–34*. Edited by David J. A. Clines, Philip R. Davies, and David M. Gunn. JSOTSup 22. Sheffield: JSOT, 1983.
Motyer, Alec. *The Message of Exodus: The Days of Our Pilgrimage*. BST. Downers Grove, IL: InterVarsity, 2005.
Murphy, James G. *A Critical and Exegetical Commentary on the Book of Exodus, with a New Translation*. New York: I. K. Funk, 1881.
Noth, Martin. *Exodus: A Commentary*. Translated by J. S. Bowden. OTL. London: SCM, 1962.
Ollenburger, Ben C., ed. *Old Testament Theology: Flowering and Future*. Edited by David W. Baker. Rev. ed. SBTS 1. Winona Lake, IN: Eisenbrauns, 2004.
Ollenburger, Ben C., Elmer A. Martens, and Gerhard F. Hasel, eds. *The Flowering of Old Testament Theology: A Reader in Twentieth-century Old Testament Theology, 1930–1990*. Edited by David W. Baker. SBTS 1. Winona Lake, IN: Eisenbrauns, 1992.
Olson, Dennis T. "Literary and Rhetorical Criticism." In *Methods for Exodus*, edited by Thomas B. Dozeman, 13–54. MBI. Cambridge: Cambridge University Press, 2010.
Osborn, Noel D., and Howard A. Hatton. *A Handbook on Exodus*. UBSHS. New York: United Bible Societies, 1999.
Oswald, Wolfgang. "Early Democracy in Ancient Judah: Considerations on Ex 18–24 with an Outlook on Dtn 16–18." *CV* 52.2 (2010) 121–35.
Patrick, Dale. "The Covenant Code Source." *VT* 27.2 (1977) 145–57.

———. "The First Commandment in the Structure of the Pentateuch." *VT* 45.1 (1995) 107–18.

———. "God's Commandment." In *God in the Fray: A Tribute to Walter Brueggemann*, edited by Tod Linafelt and Timothy K. Beal, 93–111. Minneapolis: Fortress, 1998.

———. *Old Testament Law*. Louisville: Westminster John Knox, 1985.

Perdue, Leo G., Joseph Blenkinsopp, John J. Collins, and Carol Meyers. *Families in Ancient Israel*. Edited by Don S. Browning and Ian S. Evison. FRC. Louisville: Westminster John Knox, 1997.

Pixley, George V. *On Exodus: A Liberation Perspective*. Translated by Robert R. Barr. Maryknoll, NY: Orbis, 1987.

Plastaras, James. *The God of Exodus: The Theology of the Exodus Narrative*. Milwaukee: Bruce, 1966.

Postell, Seth D. "Abram as Israel, Israel as Abram: Literary Analogy as Macro-Structural Strategy in the Torah." *TynBul* 67.2 (2016) 161–82.

Powell, Mark Allan. *What Is Narrative Criticism?* Edited by Dan O. Via, Jr. GBS. Minneapolis: Fortress, 1990.

Pratico, Gary D., and Miles V. Van Pelt. *Basics of Biblical Hebrew Grammar*. 3rd ed. Grand Rapids: Zondervan, 2019.

Preuss, Horst Dietrich. *Old Testament Theology*. Edited by James L. Mays, Carol A. Newsom, and David L. Petersen. Translated by Leo G. Perdue. 2 vols. OTL. Louisville: Westminster John Knox, 1995–1996.

Propp, William H. C. *Exodus: A New Translation with Introduction and Commentary*. 2 vols. AB 2–2A. New York: Doubleday, 1999–2006.

Rad, Gerhard von. *Old Testament Theology*. Translated by D. M. G. Stalker. 2 vols. New York: Harper & Row, 1962–1965.

Reiss, Moshe. "Jethro the Convert." *JBQ* 41.2 (2013) 89–94.

Rendtorff, Rolf. *The Canonical Hebrew Bible: A Theology of the Old Testament*. Translated by David E. Orton. Leiden: Deo, 2005.

———. *The Old Testament: An Introduction*. Translated by John Bowden. Philadelphia: Fortress, 1985.

Rhodes, Daniel D. *A Covenant Community: A Study of the Book of Exodus*. Louisville: Westminster John Knox, 1964.

Robinson, Bernard P. "Acknowledging One's Dependence: The Jethro Story of Exodus 18." *NBf* 69.814 (1988) 139–42.

———. "Israel and Amalek: The Context of Exodus 17:8–16." *JSOT* 10.32 (1985) 15–22.

Roth, Federico Alfredo. *Hyphenating Moses: A Postcolonial Exegesis of Identity in Exodus 1:1–3:15*. Edited by Paul Anderson and Jennifer Koosed. BibInt 154. Leiden: Brill, 2017.

Rozelaar, Marc. "The Song of the Sea (Exodus XV, 1b–18)." *VT* 2.3 (1952) 221–28.

Russell, Brian D. *The Song of the Sea: The Date of Composition and Influence of Exodus 15:1–21*. Edited by Hemchand Gossai. StBibLit 101. New York: Peter Lang, 2007.

Ryken, Leland. *How Bible Stories Work: A Guided Study of Biblical Narrative*. Wooster, OH: Weaver, 2015.

Rylaarsdam, J. Coert, and J. Edgar Park. "The Book of Exodus." In *The Interpreter's Bible: General Articles on the Bible; General Articles on the Old Testament; The Book of Genesis; The Book of Exodus*, edited by George Arthur Buttrick, 1:831–1099. Nashville: Abingdon, 1952.

Sailhamer, John H. *The Pentateuch as Narrative: A Biblical-Theological Commentary*. Grand Rapids: Zondervan, 1992.

Sarna, Nahum M. *Exodus* שמות: *The Traditional Hebrew Text with the New JPS Translation*. JPSTC. Philadelphia: Jewish Publication Society, 1991.

———. *Exploring Exodus: The Heritage of Biblical Israel*. New York: Schocken, 1986.

Scharfstein, Sol. *Torah and Commentary:* חֲמִשָּׁה חֻמְשֵׁי תּוֹרָה *The Five Books of Moses*. Jersey City, NJ: Ktav, 2008.

Schmidt, Werner H. *Old Testament Introduction*. Translated by Matthew J. O'Connell. 2nd ed. Louisville: Westminster John Knox, 1999.

Scott, William R. *A Simplified Guide to BHS: Critical Apparatus, Masora, Accents, Unusual Letters & Other Markings*. 3rd ed. N. Richland Hills, TX: Bibal, 1995.

Shankman, Ray. "The Cut That Unites: Word as Covenant in Exodus 4:24–26." CC 41.2 (1991) 168–78.

Shreckhise, Robert L. "'I Will Sing unto the Lord': A Rhetorical-Narrative Analysis of the Poem in Exodus 15:1–21." PhD diss., Concordia Seminary, 2006.

Siebert-Hommes, Jopie. *Let the Daughters Live! The Literary Architecture of Exodus 1–2 as a Key for Interpretation*. Edited by R. Alan Culpepper and Rolf Rendtorff. Translated by Janet W. Dyk. BibInt 37. Leiden: Brill, 1998.

Silver, Daniel Jeremy. *The Story of Scripture: From Oral Tradition to the Written Word*. New York: Basic Books, 1990.

Ska, Jean-Louis. *Introduction to Reading the Pentateuch*. Translated by Sr. Pascale Dominique. Winona Lake, IN: Eisenbrauns, 2006.

Smith, James E. *The Pentateuch*. 2nd ed. OTSS. Joplin, MO: College, 1993.

Smith, Mark S. *The Pilgrimage Pattern in Exodus*. Edited by David J. A. Clines and Philip R. Davies. JSOTSup 239. Sheffield: Sheffield Academic, 1997.

Soggin, J. Alberto. *Introduction to the Old Testament: From Its Origins to the Closing of the Alexandrian Canon*. Edited by Peter Ackroyd, James Barr, Bernhard W. Anderson, and John Bright. Translated by John Bowden. Rev. ed. OTL. Louisville: Westminster John Knox, 1980.

Sprinkle, Joe M. *'The Book of the Covenant': A Literary Approach*. Edited by David J. A. Clines and Philip R. Davies. JSOTSup 174. Sheffield: JSOT, 1994.

Steck, Odil Hannes. *Old Testament Exegesis: A Guide to the Methodology*. Edited by Marvin A. Sweeney. Translated by James D. Nogalski. 2nd ed. RBS 39. Atlanta: Scholars, 1998.

Steinmann, Andrew E. *Called to Be God's People: An Introduction to the Old Testament*. Eugene, OR: Wipf & Stock, 2006.

———. *The Oracles of God: The Old Testament Canon*. St. Louis: Concordia Academic Press, 1999.

Sternberg, Meir. *The Poetics of Biblical Narrative: Ideological Literature and the Drama of Reading*. Edited by Robert M. Polzin. ILBS. Bloomington: Indiana University Press, 1985.

Stuart, Douglas K. *Exodus*. NAC 2. Nashville: Broadman & Holman, 2006.

Suh, Myung Soo. *The Tabernacle in the Narrative History of Israel from the Exodus to the Conquest*. Edited by Hemchand Gossai. StBibLit 50. New York: Peter Lang, 2003.

Suomala, Karla R. *Moses and God in Dialogue: Exodus 32–34 in Postbiblical Literature*. Edited by Hemchand Gossai. StBibLit 61. New York: Peter Lang, 2004.

Sweeney, Marvin A. *TANAK: A Theological and Critical Introduction to the Jewish Bible*. Minneapolis: Fortress, 2012.

Talmon, Shemaryahu. *Text and Canon of the Hebrew Bible: Collected Studies*. Winona Lake, IN: Eisenbrauns, 2010.

Thomas, W. H. Griffith. *Through the Pentateuch Chapter by Chapter*. Edited by Winifred G. T. Gillespie. Grand Rapids: Eerdmans, 1957.

Thompson, Thomas L. *The Origin Tradition of Ancient Israel: I. The Literary Formation of Genesis and Exodus 1–23*. Edited by David J. A. Clines and Philip R. Davies. JSOTSup 55. Sheffield: JSOT, 1987.

Tov, Emanuel. *Textual Criticism of the Hebrew Bible*. 3rd ed. Minneapolis: Fortress, 2012.

Trimm, Charlie. *"YHWH Fights for Them!": The Divine Warrior in the Exodus Narrative*. GorBibSt 58. Piscataway, NJ: Gorgias, 2014.

Utzschneider, Helmut, and Wolfgang Oswald. *Exodus 1–15*. Translated by Philip Sumpter. IECOT. Stuttgart: Kohlhammer, 2015.

Van Brugge, David. "Mentoring for the Kingdom's Sake: A Sermon Based on Exodus 18." *PRJ* 5.2 (2013) 5–14.

Van Seters, John. *The Life of Moses: The Yahwist as Historian in Exodus-Numbers*. Edited by Tj. Baarda, A. van der Kooij, and A. S. van der Woude. CBET 10. Kampen: Kok Pharos, 1994.

Van Wijk-Bos, Johanna W. H. *Making Wise the Simple: The Torah in Christian Faith and Practice*. Grand Rapids: Eerdmans, 2005.

VanGemeren, Willem A., ed. *The New International Dictionary of Old Testament Theology and Exegesis*. 5 vols. Grand Rapids: Zondervan, 1997.

Vanhoozer, Kevin J., ed. *Theological Interpretation of the Old Testament: A Book-by-Book Survey*. Grand Rapids: Baker Academic, 2008.

Voelz, James W. *What Does This Mean? Principles of Biblical Interpretation in the Post-Modern World*. 2nd ed. St. Louis: Concordia, 2013.

Vogt, Peter T. *Interpreting the Pentateuch: An Exegetical Handbook*. Edited by David M. Howard, Jr. HOTE. Grand Rapids: Kregel, 2009.

Vriezen, Th. C. *An Outline of Old Testament Theology*. 2nd, rev., and enl. ed. Oxford: Basil Blackwell, 1970.

Walsh, Jerome T. *Old Testament Narrative: A Guide to Interpretation*. Louisville: Westminster John Knox, 2009.

———. *Style and Structure in Biblical Hebrew Narrative*. Collegeville, MN: Liturgical, 2001.

Waltke, Bruce K., and M. O'Connor. *An Introduction to Biblical Hebrew Syntax*. Winona Lake, IN: Eisenbrauns, 1990.

Walton, John H., Victor H. Matthews, and Mark W. Chavalas. *The IVP Bible Background Commentary: Old Testament*. Downers Grove, IL: InterVarsity, 2000.

Watts, John D. W. "The Song of the Sea — Ex. XV." *VT* 7.4 (1957) 371–80.

Weiser, Artur. *The Old Testament: Its Formation and Development*. Translated by Dorothea M. Barton. New York: Association, 1961.

Wells, Jo Bailey. "The Book of Exodus." In *A Theological Introduction to the Pentateuch: Interpreting the Torah as Christian Scripture*, edited by Richard S. Briggs and Joel N. Lohr, 51–82. Grand Rapids: Baker Academic, 2012.

———. *God's Holy People: A Theme in Biblical Theology*. Edited by David J. A. Clines and Philip R. Davies. JSOTSup 305. Sheffield: Sheffield Academic, 2000.

Wendland, Ernst H. *Exodus*. PB. Milwaukee: Northwestern, 1984.

White, Douglas M. *Holy Ground: Expositions from Exodus*. Grand Rapids: Baker, 1962.

White, Thomas Joseph. *Exodus*. BTCB. Grand Rapids: Brazos, 2016.
Wicke, Donald W. "The Literary Structure of Exodus 1:2–2:10." *JSOT* 7.24 (1982) 99–107.
Widmer, Michael. *Moses, God, and the Dynamics of Intercessory Prayer: A Study of Exodus 32–34 and Numbers 13–14*. Edited by Bernd Janowski, Mark S. Smith, and Hermann Spieckermann. FAT 2.8. Tübingen: Mohr Siebeck, 2004.
Williams, Ronald J. *Williams' Hebrew Syntax*. Rev. and exp. by John C. Beckman. 3rd ed. Toronto: University of Toronto Press, 2007.
Willis, John T. *Yahweh and Moses in Conflict: The Role of Exodus 4:24–26 in the Book of Exodus*. Published by Joseph Alobaidi. BH 8. Bern: Peter Lang, 2010.
Wilson, William. *Old Testament Word Studies*. Grand Rapids: Kregel, 1978.
Woudstra, Marten H. "Calvin Interprets What 'Moses Reports': Observations on Calvin's Commentary on Exodus 1–19." *CTJ* 21.2 (1986) 151–74.
Wright, David P. *Inventing God's Law: How the Covenant Code of the Bible Used and Revised the Laws of Hammurabi*. Oxford: Oxford University Press, 2009.
Würthwein, Ernst. *The Text of the Old Testament: An Introduction to the Biblia Hebraica*. Rev. and exp. by Alexander Achilles Fischer. Translated by Erroll F. Rhodes. 3rd ed. Grand Rapids: Eerdmans, 2014.
Young, Edward J. *An Introduction to the Old Testament*. Rev. ed. Grand Rapids: Eerdmans, 1964.
Zucker, David J. *The Torah: An Introduction for Christians and Jews*. New York: Paulist, 2005.
Zweck, Dean. *Freed to Follow: A Commentary on Exodus*. CRC. Australia: Lutheran, 1993.

www.ingramcontent.com/pod-product-compliance
Lightning Source LLC
Chambersburg PA
CBHW052340230426
43664CB00041B/2501